Postcolonial Politics, the Internet, and Everyday Life

Contemporary Information and Communications Technologies (ICTs) are now an inescapable part of everyday life as well as an integral element to large scale political-economic change. In this close-up study of pioneering and longstanding Internet discussion forums, M. I. Franklin explores the practice of everyday life online. The author traces the online practices and discussion content produced by postcolonial and diasporic communities as they (re)articulate gendered, political, ethnic and cultural dimensions to life for postcolonial societies on-the-ground. In a neoliberal global era, however, possibilities for intercultural and intracultural empowerment evident in the postcolonial politics of representation of these communities have to contend with new and entrenched political-economic and sociocultural pressures from all sides. Franklin argues that these Pacific traversals in public, open cyberspace trace another possible future for the Internet; more hospitable and equitable than the one currently being put in place by large corporations.

This book will be of interest to students of international relations/ international political economy, anthropology, cultural studies, science and technology studies.

Marianne Franklin is Assistant Professor of Social and Political Theory at the University for Humanist Studies Utrecht, The Netherlands. She also lectures in the International Relations and Social Sciences Masters programmes at the International School for Humanities and Social Sciences (ISHSS) of the University of Amsterdam.

Routledge advances in international relations and global politics

Postcolonial Politics, the Internet, and Everyday Life

Pacific traversals online

M. I. Franklin

LONDON AND NEW YORK

First published 2004
by Routledge
2 Park Square, Milton Park, Abingdon, Oxon, OX14 4RN

Simultaneously published in the USA and Canada
by Routledge
270 Madison Ave, New York NY 10016

Routledge is an imprint of the Taylor & Francis Group

Transferred to Digital Printing 2007

© 2004 Marianne Franklin

Typeset in Baskerville by Wearset Ltd, Boldon, Tyne and Wear

British Library Cataloguing in Publication Data
A catalogue record for this book is available from the British Library

Library of Congress Cataloging in Publication Data
A catalog record for this book has been requested

ISBN 0-415-33940-5

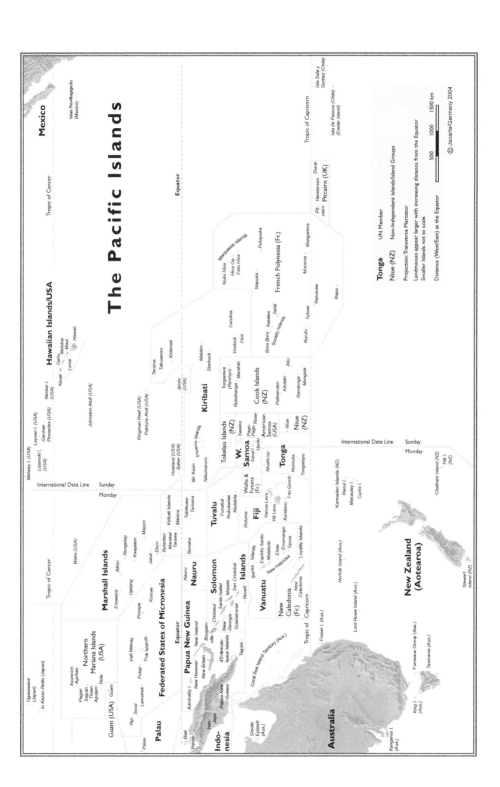

The Pacific Islands

for Tifa and Mulu

Contents

Illustrations

Acknowledgments

There are many people who contributed directly to the research, writing, and endless revising phases that are bound up in this book. People who supported and guided me during all that life-related stuff along the way. People who were there for me anyway. It's great to have finished this book, but these working relationships, friendships, love, and acceptance are worth a whole lot more.

For their insight, practical help, ongoing support, expert knowledge, time taken to answer my questions, and hospitality – online and on the ground – I'd like to thank Al Aiono, Futa Helu, Tapuaki Ha'unga, 'Alopi Latukefu, Taholo Kami, Helen Morton Lee, Teresia Teaiwa, Okusi Māhina, and Max Rimoldi. And to all the patrons of the Kava Bowl and Kamehameha Roundtable a great big "Thank you" shout. Without you all, this book would not have come to be.

A whole lot of people have contributed to my intellectual growth and emotional health of late. Much appreciation goes out to Susan Banducci, Robin Brown, Terrell Carver, Matt Davies, Gavan Duffy, Cynthia Enloe, Judie Hammond, Jeff Harrod, Jeff Karp, René Konings, Katie Krall, Becky Lentz, Lily Ling, Aileen Lonie Raes, Marcel Mausson, Chris May, Henk Overbeek, Nalini Persram, Spike Peterson, Jindy Pettman, Jayne Rodgers, Anne Sisson Runyan, JP Singh, Inês de Sousa, Susan Stocker, Richard van der Wurff, and Sally Wyatt for the mentoring; philosophical, political and crotchety debates; gins; music; boat trips; hot tips; opportunities; career coaching; life coaching; meals; gigs; "sessions"; Leffe Blondes; slumber parties; inspiring telephone conversations that go beyond the immediate moment; neat ideas; supportive, kooky, and timely emails; invitations; collegiality; role models; laughter; wine, food, and song; places to stay in amazing cities; lunches; editing and role-play; fun places to hang out in during conferences; job references; faith in me; friendship; goodwill; good advice; and great company. A very, very special thanks to the Routledge Politics editorial team – Heidi Bagtazo, Craig Fowlie, Grace McInnes and Harriet Brinton – also; for your professionalism, friendship, and support way beyond the call of duty, sound guidance and firm hand, patience, the music, and the cocktails.

The following publishers have kindly granted me permission to reproduce previously published material. Parts of Chapters 2, 4, and 6 appeared as: "InsideOut: Postcolonial Subjectivities and Everyday Life Online," *International Feminist Journal of Politics*, vol. 3, no. 3, Nov. 2001; "Sewing up the Globe: Information and Communication Technologies and Re/Materialized Gender-Power Relations," in *Changing Genders in Intercultural Perspective*, edited by Barbara Saunders and Marie-Claire Foblets, Studia Anthropologica Series, Vol. 5, 2002, Belgium: Leuven University Press; " 'I Define My Own Identity': Pacific Articulations of 'Race' and 'Culture' on the Internet," *Ethnicities*, vol. 3, no. 4, Dec. 2003, pp. 465–490.

To my lifelong friends Marjolijn Adriaansche, Lesley Astier, Richard Dale, Pierre Florac, Taka Hosoda, Danielle Kraaijvanger, Giles Scott-Smith, Inbal Telem. I hope you all realize just how much your tireless support and shared memories over the years mean to me. My love also goes out to my *whanau*: Margaret, John, Diana, Dave, Elizabeth, Feto'ai Ailepata, Christopher, Sarah, Jonathan, Nicola, William, Jessica, Axel, David Britten, Paul Roper, Tracey Hendy, Ingmar Andersson, Pam Egan. Thanks for being family and taking care of me. Love also to Marion Coleman and David and Angela Reynolds, who still watch over me even though I'm (supposed to be) grown up now. Love also to Mulu and Tifa for the Fa'a Samoa they gave me as young child in Apia and Wellington. I dedicate this book to you.

And all my love to Jochen Jacoby; you made all the difference.

Marianne Franklin
Amsterdam, June 2004

1 Introduction

[Our] economy, society, culture, and indeed our very existence, are not fenced in by our national boundaries. We are inextricably part of larger entities: the Pacific region and more importantly, the world economy. . . . Conversely, our very existence as small isolated groups of people occupying a vast surface of the earth, like human groups occupying the scattered oases of the Sahara, is our unbolted back door. The result is that our Pacific region is the favourite ground for weapons testing by all major powers of the world, toxic waste disposal, and rapacious ocean resources exploitation.

(Hau'ofa 1987: 164–165)

A considerable percentage of the world's Pacific Islanders live overseas . . . New Zealand, Australia, Japan, the US, Great Britain, Germany; the list seems endless. . . . Noteworthy, of course, is the fact that the KB [Kava Bowl] is being accessed more than 600,000 times per month, making it the most popular Poly [Polynesian] site on the 'Net. Even more interesting, though, is the fact that 'hits' are coming from more than 60 countries around the world. Polys are everywhere.

(KBAdmin, KB, 11/16/98)

This is the tale of two Internets. Two visions of the future, in effect. The first tale is, by now, received wisdom in those societies that are the hub of the current world economy (Hau'ofa 1987). This is an Internet of a global market-cum-democracy-cum-progress paradigm that is beholden to large-scale and microscopic layers of commercialized and privatized information and communications networks. The other tale, on the other hand, is being written by ordinary users every day as they commute and commune in the cyberspaces of a noncommercial, openly accessible Internet (KBAdmin, KB, 11/16/98).

Some of those who figure in this second tale are from the South Pacific Islands or are members of Pacific Island communities in the hi-tech heartlands of the United States, Australia, and New Zealand for the most part. Since the early days of the Internet/World Wide Web,[1] before the "dotcom boom" of the late 1990s, they have been creating rich online archives of everyday life in postcolonial and diasporic settings. Their texts are inscribed with personal and group experiences, contested meanings of culture and politics, shifting power hierarchies of race/ethnicity, sex/gender, and class/status. The lives of Pacific island peoples in and beyond the Pacific islands are being (re)articulated[2] in these cyberspatial traversals, which bespeak political and economic power differentials between the various island groups of the Pacific Ocean and their erstwhile (and ongoing) colonial rulers – differentials that also resonate in the lives of many twentieth-century postcolonial diasporic groups in their new homelands and vis-à-vis their societies of origin. As they come and go, the online textual production and the personal, sociocultural, political, and economic geographies they (re)articulate have been tracing a nascent *postcolonial politics of representation.*

But how can this be a tale of *two* Internets? Is there not only one World Wide Web? One global information infrastructure? One key actor in the history of "the" Internet, the US industrial-military establishment? Is not the Internet simply a digitalized, supranational version of a shopping mall or mail-order catalogue? And even if one can book holidays, buy books, or find a date online, is this latest communications array more of a negative influence on "real-life" social relations, political participation, reading and writing skills than a positive one? Whatever the preferred answer to these queries may be, they all presuppose that "the Internet" arrived one day (not so long ago) ready-made. As I shall argue, from a critical constructivist understanding of technological change, this belies the complex sociocultural, political, and economic contours of any technology's historical trajectory – and more so for those technologies seen as harbingers of significant and widespread "structural" shifts in the modern era: the printing press, railways, air travel, the telephone and telegraph, the Internet. Hindsight, in this respect, is not necessarily beneficial.[3]

Back to the two tales in question. The first, that of computer-mediated *haute finance* (Polanyi 1944: 13–14), is a world of gargantuan electronic financial movements twenty-four hours a day, of incessant corporate splits, mergers, and takeovers, of economic booms and busts. It is a world that privileges the technoeconomic intermingling of corporate investment and government geostrategic agendas. This is the Internet of rising share prices and profit margins, of increasing organizational and tactical intricacy coupled with massive storage capabilities and increasing security threats. With this future come not only huge investments in research and development (R&D) but also a political and sociocultural commitment to a particular vision of digitally integrated communications that rest on proprietary computer codes and other jealously guarded keys to a whole set of "global solutions" – solutions that are being sold not only to non-Internetted societies and their "knowledge workers," but also to publics much closer to home.

The second tale is that of noncommercial interpersonal communication through and on the Internet/World Wide Web – an Internet that relies upon easy, affordable access to computers and telephone lines, relatively "low-tech" hardware and software configurations, and viable transmission pathways for different technoeconomic political and geographical situations. This Internet's cyberspaces are where people talk-write about their everyday lives, confront political and social issues of the day, muse on their (mutual) hopes and fears in what are spontaneous, negotiated sorts of intercultural and intracultural exchange. *Inter*cultural in that the World Wide Web and email enable (like the telephone, radio, and television in their own ways) new sorts of nonembodied linking between different social groups and cultural traditions. *Intra*cultural in the sense that dispersed populations from respective societies come into contact with each other, in the qualitatively different communicative spaces and circumstances that are unique to the hyperlinked, textual environment of the World Wide Web.

But neither is this Internet self-explanatory. Its spaces and places have to be put in place as well, websites organized and moderated, appropriate software and hardware configurations set up and maintained, server space and participation flows accommodated and paid for, sociotechnical standards worked out *en route*. In order to illustrate how nonelite uses of Internet technologies are not necessarily beholden to, let alone accounted for in, the first tale, this study reconstructs some key themes and moments from the online archives of everyday life of two long-standing, interrelated, and vibrant Internet communities: more specifically, the main discussion forums of websites set up for people descended from the inhabitants of, or living in, Tonga, Western Samoa, and American Samoa. The argument is that not only are these sorts of *everyday* online practices integral to an equitable Internet future, but they are also substantive, albeit underacknowledged, elements of "the" Internet to date. These visible emotional and symbolic interactions have been traced and hermeneutically reconstructed here through a critical content analysis[4] of the millions of texts that embody these practices of everyday life online.

The *problématique*

This study is located in the broader context of how neoliberal macroeconomic orthodoxies and investment strategies have come to predominate the discourse and R&D trajectories of information and communications technologies (ICTs) in general and Internet technologies especially.[5] Since the 1990s (depending on where the point of reference is), email and World Wide Web interactions have become integral to business, educational, and everyday interpersonal communications in many societies. Cause and effect arguments notwithstanding, this degree of everyday "onlineness" and its emergence in such a short time span (ten to fifteen years for the World Wide Web) reveal the *inter/subjective* dynamics[6] that, as critical international relations/international political economy (IR/IPE) scholars argue, constitute world politics. As Internet technologies become more deeply embedded in sociocultural, political, and economic relations, the need to research and theorize these dynamics more adequately remains. The emergent experiential, cognitive, and conceptual domain delimited by ICTs is still undertheorized in IR/IPE. Even after over two decades of neoliberal economic restructuring, processes of "neoliberal globalization," the discipline still tends to treat ICTs as exogenous, causal agents of macro-level structural changes from which broad changes in material *gender power relations* are then seen to follow.[7] Perspectives from a "worm's eye view" are not considered. Hardly surprising, perhaps, given that this discipline's analytical and empirical lenses are still trained on the epic stories of big-power politics, big business, big science, war, and peace.

A bottom-up view of this nascent domain for action and analysis is cognizant of ways in which ICTs in general and Internet technologies in particular are carriers of, and sites for, the "circulation of meanings" that many critical IR/IPE scholars argue are integral to the above epic stories (Murphy and Rojas de Ferro 1995; Jensen 1995). If that is the case, and given the broader socioeconomic context in which the widening gap between the world's "information rich" and "information poor" corresponds to that between (and within) "developed" and "underdeveloped" worlds and their privileged and underprivileged groups respectively, everyday uses of the Internet need to be addressed by any critique of the contemporary world order.[8] The approach opted for here is to delve more deeply into what is actually being said, produced, and enacted on and through the Internet/World Wide Web and then juxtapose these multiplying moments to their respective online *and* broader "offline" contexts. This is pertinent for critical IR/IPE scholarship simply by virtue of how the physical topographies of ICTs alone cannot adequately account for the substance and import of Internet-based practices. The geographically dispersed and nonembodied constitution of cyberspatial practices of everyday life can be a productive entry point for critical theory and research into the microcosm of the "new world order," if for no other reason than the fact that these practices, and archives, are writ large in the ostensibly global cyberspaces of the World Wide Web.

That said, a number of questions arise when this scenario is related to the online presence and activities of Internet practitioners who hail from (post)colonial, non-Western societies. With respect to the various (diasporic) populations of the South Pacific Islands who regularly use the Internet, are there any repercussions for immediate or wider relationships with others in the immediate community on the ground, "back home" in the islands, strangers and authorities online and "offline"? From the vantage point of the Samoas and Tonga in particular, pressured by the exigencies of "global market forces" and structural adjustment-cum-good governance criteria, how do expatriates' online practices reflect on

Tongan and/or Samoan society and "culture"? How do expats and at-home practitioners, or those from different Pacific island societies, inter-act when they encounter one another in the South Pacific Internet forums? What commonalities are there? Misunderstandings or moments of mutual recognition? For scholars interested in where circulations of meanings, ICTs as empowering *and* overpowering media and sites for action, intersect with the intricacies of sex/gender, race/ethnicity, and status/class, what do such practices of everyday life suggest about the surrounding political-economic and sociocultural order?

The South Pacific Islands online

The Internet forums studied here emerged from the pioneering Pacific Forum (http://pacificforum.com) and its Kava Club/Kava Bowl Discus-sion Forums. The Pacific Forum was set up by Taholo Kami in 1995 during his study in the United States as an online meeting point for "lonely" Tongans living overseas, although there were Tongan-based participants from the outset (Kami 2001: interview). The Kava Bowl (KB), as it came to be known, quickly established itself through a core of "faith-ful regulars" and a fluid number of others; up to 600 on Kami's mailing list (ibid.). The KB (Figure 1.1) steadily developed into a serious, and at times highly politicized, debating forum that attracted both popular and academic attention (Morton 1999, 1998a/2001; Ogden 1999; Wired 1998a, 1998b).

An early spin-off from the Pacific Forum was the Polynesian Cafe (http://polycafe.com), run by Al and Sue Aiono out of their home in Long Beach, Los Angeles (many American Samoan and Western Samoan groups are based in the West-Coast United States). The Kamehameha

Figure 1.1 Kava Bowl banner, 2001.

Roundtable (KR) Discussion Forum (http://polycafe.com/kamehameha/kamehameha.htm) was set up as a speciality website for Samoan particip-ants. The Polycafe's websites, while populated largely by American-based Samoans, sees itself as a generically "Polynesian" meeting place on the World Wide Web (Figures 1.2 and 1.3).

Tongan, Samoan, and other Pacific Islanders regularly crossed between these websites, and others, from the beginning, inclusiveness being an important characteristic of these places. Other closely related sites for this study were the discussion forum of the Tongan History Association (THA), and that of the South Pacific Information Network (SPIN) founded by the Australian-based Tongan, 'Alopi Latukefu. Both of these had close offline personal and professional links with each other, as well as with Taholo Kami and his team of voluntary moderators, the KB Administration (KBAdmin).

The Kava Bowl went offline in 2001 (the result of a personal decision by Kami), although the Pacific Forum portal remains as a clearing house for Pacific Island-related websites. In 2004, former Kava Bowl regulars still participate on the Kamehameha Roundtable (see Chapter 7). Since the mid-1990s, the Pacific Forum and the Polynesian Cafe Internet portals have been the backbone of the "South Pacific Islands online," their website design and software having been adopted by many other Pacific Island websites that sprang up in their wake (Taholo Kami being adviser to and/or designer of many of these). These are asynchronous Internet forums, not real-time live chat sites, using software that allows participants to "post" topics for discussion in a communal hyperlinked visual space. The responses (*follow-ups*) form into *discussion threads* of varying length, levels, and relevance to the original message (*initial post*). People sign off in various ways, with various email addresses that may or may not be oper-

Figure 1.2 Polynesian Cafe banner, 1997.

Figure 1.3 Polycafe banner, 2001.

able.[9] Participants (get to) know each other in these forums, whether they use their "real" names or nicknames ("handles" or "nics"). *Posters* can also move from these online forums to the relative privacy of email interactions. For cyberspace life spans, these websites are striking for their longevity (between six and ten years on going to press), vitality, and wealth of textual production alone.

While Tonga, Western Samoa, and American Samoa are the geographical and cultural focal points, participants come from all over the South Pacific region. As I have said, the majority of participants live in the United States,[10] although many others are based in Australia and New Zealand; some others in Europe and elsewhere. By *diaspora* I am referring to geographically dispersed populations that left the Pacific Islands in the 1960s and 1970s (as is the case with my own parents' two Samoan employees) and settled in Australia, New Zealand, Hawaii, and the mainland United States. The population drain continues today as younger people leave in search of education, employment, and "overseas experience." These movements have seen concentrations of Tongan, Samoan, and other Pacific Islands groups in urban centers of these Pacific Rim countries (Clifford 1997; King and Connell 1999; Ward 1999; Lee 2003; Fitzgerald 1998). Their relationship to their homes, immediate and extended family, and social obligations "back home" is complex. It involves the movement of financial and in-kind remittances between countries and within dispersed family and social networks; conflicting sociocultural expectations for second and third generations growing up in the

West, albeit often as disadvantaged groups therein; urbanized versions of "ancient rivalries" (ethnically designated gangs, for instance); and political contestation or support of sociopolitical establishments "back home."[11] There are more than a few regulars who participate from Tonga and Samoa, as Internet access and ICT infrastructures make uneven inroads into South Pacific Island societies. As is the case everywhere in the world, the infrastructure hubs and access points are urban: Apia in Samoa, Nuku'alofa in Tonga, Suva and Nadi in Fiji (the ICT and intergovernmental institutional hub for the region). As for home use versus institutional access, many participants take part from high schools and universities or the occasional Internet café or other public access point. For example, in the Tongan capital of Nuku'alofa, a key public access point is the Royal School of Science. Those participating from the islands do so from their places of work (by their own admission) or from home (until the first telephone bill arrives, apparently – (Kami 2001: interview). Everyone is welcome in the KB and KR; they can participate in the discussions whatever their gender, ethnicity, or creed, and according to the explicit and implicit ground rules developed over the years. And many do.

These "serious" discussion forums are not posited here as necessarily more significant than their popular live chat counterparts.[12] Nor have they been studied as if the views articulated here are fully representative of the various distinct Pacific Island communities in the United States, New Zealand, or Australia (Macpherson 1997; Macpherson *et al.* 2001; Lee 2003). Besides, not everyone is "interested in politics" (Justin Kaitapu 1999: interview). Al Aiono and Taholo Kami are aware of how these interconnected forums quickly established themselves as "pretty serious [places where] the intelligent patrons go" (Aiono 1999: interview). Over the years, they have also been tracing ongoing and shifting on-the-ground affiliations and concerns of Pacific Island communities, immediate and extended families, church and community networks in cities, places of work and study, and political and social issues in the Pacific and beyond. Internet technologies lend themselves well to Pacific Island communicative cultures, which are characterized by multivocality, oral narratives, and oratory styles (Friedman 1998; Wendt 1999). The "Polynesian diaspora" online bears out other studies that show how Internet-based communications serve "intensely diasporic relations . . . [that have] meant integrating over distances through any means of communications" (Miller and Slater 2000: 2/18).

Situating the study

Historical and sociocultural contexts

A premise for this study is that Internet technologies have become part of many people's everyday lives and indispensable for all manner of political and economic activities. They are embroiled in any number of broad sociocultural and political economic changes denoted by the "buzzword" of globalization. The "global shift" often attributed to technology – with a capital "T" – is as much a sea change in political and economic thinking, policy making, and rhetoric as it is a material, macro-level set of changes in trade, production, finance, and labor relations.[13] There is little consensus about whether the world is a better place by virtue of having access to email, zillions of websites, and live coverage of the latest mayhem on one's computer or TV screen by virtue of (relatively) new ICTs. In any case, the corporations that now own and control the lion's share of these techno-economic undertakings are among the largest capitalist enterprises to date, IT–telecom–media conglomerates such as the Microsoft, Time Warner, those of Bertelsmann, and Murdoch being cases in point. Moreover, the physical configurations, politics of content, and access to the World Wide Web alone are implicated in the latest security dilemmas of the post-Cold War period, both as microscopic software viruses and as indiscriminate forms of organized "cyber-terrorism." While seemingly far removed from the more prosaic rituals that make up everyday life online, these more grandiose dreams and schemes are inscribed in the (postcolonial) politics of representation in play here. They straddle both a myriad of everyday practices on the one hand, and those bound up in the ownership and control strategies of commercial enterprise on the other. In reverse proportion to their land mass, population size, and GDP/GNP indicators, the Pacific Islands and their respective diasporic communities are relatively proactive in terms of their online presence, activities, and uptake of Internet technologies (UNDP 1999; Ogden 1999; UNESCO 2002). As they traverse and converse with each other online, these practitioners are actively appropriating and reconfiguring the places, spaces, and informal architectures of Internet communications. Both minute, mundane, and magnified by virtue of being on the Web, these practices and productions are substantive and substantial components of both these Internet tales.

Social constructivist moods and the postcolonial turn

This study is situated in the aftermath of the methodologically and politically charged theoretical "Third Debate" in IR/IPE – one that followed on the heels of the demise of the Soviet Union but effectively began in the late 1980s with a range of metatheoretical critiques of "mainstream" IR/IPE (Lapid 1989; Burchill *et al.* 2001; Der Derian 1995), debates that drew from ongoing debates in other disciplines (Cahoone 1996; Nicholson 1990; Best and Kellner 1991). The objects of criticism were, and still are, the methodological and theoretical foundations of "mainstream," "malestream," or "Eurocentric" modes of scientific inquiry. The alternatives proffered are variously referred to as postpositivist and/or

poststructuralist/postmodernist frameworks.[14] At the risk of oversimplify-
ing a vast and rich literature, *in toto* these critical moments all reflect a
mood of "social constructivism." This term also has a host of definitions
and applications (Reus-Smit 2001; Ling 2002). Social constructivist moods
variously stress

> how systematic knowledge-seeking is always just one element in any
> culture, society, or social formation in its local environment, shifting
> and transforming other elements – education systems, legal systems,
> economic relations, religious beliefs and practices, state projects (such
> as war-making), gender relations – as it, in turn, is transformed by
> them.
>
> (Harding 1998b: 4)

The theoretical framework for this study is located in the cross-currents
of how these moods have been carried over into IR/IPE debates. More
specifically, it lies at the intersection of postcolonial, critical Marxian, and
feminist IR/IPE frameworks that take issue with the reified forms of objec-
tivism and epistemological ethnocentrism of "positivist" research modes
(L. T. Smith 1999: 40–44; S. Smith 1999: 42 *passim*) – the bulwark of the
social sciences. All these critiques look to dismantle an ideological claim
that there is a one-to-one correspondence between the "objectively
observed" object of study, the facts accrued, and the explanatory-cum-
predictive models of interstate behavior.[15] Critics target the uncanny
working relationship between this philosophy of science, "objective"
empirical research principles, and the way in which world politics appears
to have functioned to date – namely, through an institutionalized
(inter)state system where political and economic cooperation is predicated on, first, a "natural" condition of anarchy and, second, the equally
"natural" urges of constituent "state actors" to maximize their geostrategic
self-interests. In short, this is the "real world" of international relations. It
should not be forgotten that IR/IPE is a discipline that not only lived
through two world wars, the Cold War, and the triumph of uncontested
capitalist modes of accumulation, but also came of age in this period. Its
core lexicon reflects this legacy: explanation and prediction of war and
peace; the security dilemma vis-à-vis changes in bipolar, multipolar or
"hegemonic" world orders; models of – and for – inter*state* relations; and
models of – and for – liberal (capitalist) economic relations. This lexicon
informs the most durable images, analytical lenses of "world politics"
(Peterson and Runyan 1999; Fry and O'Hagan 1999). Critical voices argue
that these models only appear to conform to this "reality"; the evidence of
cause and effect is purely circumstantial, in other words. The persuasive
connection between this (neo)realist *Weltanschauung* – ongoing Euro-
American political and economic power in a capitalist world – is historical,
not an ontological given, the argument goes. Other critics in this mode

also point to the way in which neoliberal versions of this sociohistorical power grid are designed to benefit the already privileged power brokers in the world, leaving the rest either to join the neoliberal "global economy" or to be damned. The small island states of the Pacific and Caribbean Oceans, and sub-Saharan African countries, are all subjected to this direct and indirect political and economic pressure and the historical circumstances whence it came.[16]

The whys and wherefores of this historical interpretation can only be alluded to here. What is more pertinent right now is another historical and intellectual mood: the "postcolonial turn." The postcolonial turn is both a historical period marking decolonization and its aftermath, and a variegated set of theoretical critiques of Eurocentric knowledge production and political economic self-interest that have roots in the history of the Enlightenment (Harding 1998b; Moore-Gilbert, Stanton and Maley 1997). I will return to this term in due course. Suffice it to say that the participants of the Pacific Forum and Polycafe forums originate from societies that were once (some still are in varying degrees) British, German, and French colonies. The Pacific Ocean was a region of strategic significance in the later history of the British and French colonial empires, the theater for the "Pacific War" between Allied troops and imperial Japan during World War II and an ongoing site for French and US military-industrial interests. It is also where (neo)colonial rule and indigenous sovereignty political movements have been in direct confrontation with one another. It is in this complex political economic and sociocultural history that participants on the KB and KR interact with each other, from the Pacific Islands themselves or from the (presumably) better-off situations of urban centers in Pacific Rim societies.[17]

Conceptual parameters

Some key terms need initial delineation, namely, *the practice of everyday life* as formulated by Michel de Certeau, *feminist research methods* and *Internet research ethics*, and the term *politics of representation*.

The practice of everyday life

Michel de Certeau's conceptualization of "the practice of everyday life" lends itself very well to researching and tracing the (cyber)spatial practices of nonelite groups. De Certeau emphasizes the inventiveness, the creative resistances of ordinary people in their daily practices of reading/writing, work, shopping, cooking, and so on. He argues that the spontaneous practices comprising the daily habits, social relations, and cultural reproduction of ordinary people (nonelites) are deeply relevant to understanding how capitalist societies function, control their populations, and maintain their power bases. These ground-level forms of everydayness, and their political implications, are part of the "public" record even when hidden from view (Highmore 2002: 145–173). De Certeau's emphasis on the political potential lying in how ordinary people "make do" (*faire avec*) within structural and institutional restrictions to action and choice, and the overlooked creativity contained in their "practical arts" (*arts de faire*), places these "subaltern" practices squarely center stage.

Echoing the practice theories of Michel Foucault and Pierre Bourdieu, although differing from Henri Lefebvre in his conceptualization of everyday life as indelibly alienated social relations (Davies and Niemann 2000), de Certeau's conceptualization of an empowering "everyday" still critiques the controlling apparatus of technoeconomic and political power and concomitant dynamics of capitalist accumulation and commodification.[18] Following de Certeau, I argue that online discussions also operate as vibrant practices and cyber-traces of the everyday in their own right, which makes them not immediately reducible to the insidious processes of commodification now evident in the current R&D trajectories of ICTs. These websites' leaderships and their populations "poach" (de Certeau 1980a: 10) from (pre)existing ICT configurations by making do for as long as is feasible or desirable.[19] In cyberspace, the physically proximate practices and strictures of urban-based everyday life (Giard and Mayol 1980: 18–22) are transmuted into nonproximate ones with a "global" scope for interaction. Like people moving through, and thereby recreating, cityscapes' intimate and public spaces, these practitioners leave palpable, electronic, and textual traces of their comings and goings in cyberspace.

Feminist and ethical nodes

A methodological premise to the gathering and reconstruction of these online texts is informed by both feminist-inspired theories and research methods, and particular ethical issues that arise when one is doing Internet research. As de Certeau puts it, ethics

> defines a distance between what is and what ought to be. This distance designates a space where we have something to do. On the other hand, dogmatism is authorized by a reality that it claims to represent and in the name of this reality, it imposes laws.
>
> (1986: 199)

Feminist scholarship, whatever the various political-ontological standpoints may be (Nicholson 1990, 1997: 1–5; Jaggar 1983), addresses sex/gendered, ethnic/racial, and class/status "silencings" in theory and research in various ways (Gal 1991; Fildes 1983: 66–68; Ortner 1996: 32–33, 53–55, 153–155). A "feminist stress on the personal" that privileges "issues of experience and subjectivity" (Fildes 1983: 62; Butler 1990:

324–325) in the subject material chosen, subjects investigated, and knowledge produced is an important practical and empirical element to feminist-inspired method. In addition, analytical categories such as *gender* and *ethnicity* have replaced empiricist and essentialist notions of "sex" and "race," and have also critiqued the gender-blindness of Marxist theories of "class." Postcolonial, Third World, and black feminists have added their voices to these debates by focusing on another set of erasures handed down from the colonial era (Narayan 1997; Collins 1997; Teaiwa 1999; Ling 2002; Chowdhry and Nair 2002; L. T. Smith 1999; hooks 1990). From the disciplinary halls of anthropology, critical and feminist ethnographic method has also looked to improve upon the way in which societies and cultures have been treated by the way in which Western and colonial ethnographic method mystifies its own research practices (Fabian 1983; Stacey 1997; di Leonardo 1991). All these streams confront Western and/or objectivist research modes by pointing out that no knowledge exists separately from its broader sociocultural or political economic context and concomitant power relations between he (*sic*) who knows and that which is "known." Precisely because traditions of knowing and the credit accruing to those who "know" are so culturally embedded, the onus is on the researcher to account for – articulate – these dynamics *in the findings* too. New empirical research topics, styles, and combinations, along with an ongoing "deconstruction" of the aforementioned mainstreams (Devetak 2001b; Borradori 2003), have ensued.

By whatever research mode it may be conducted, Internet research into active online communities/discussion groups presupposes some measure of participant observation. Unlike live chat, where entry and exits are made visible by "avatars," both researcher and participant can remain nonvisible whilst observing. As in live chat scenarios, though, participants can multiply their presence through different appellations or avatars (par for the course for asynchronous website users). The ethical-practical decisions that ensue from this sort of "onlineness" need to be addressed by a researcher sooner or later. Furthermore, there are the ethical issues around ascertaining and/or protecting the "identity" of participants when citing them in the research findings. As scholarly conventions require transparent and accessible sources, the fluidity and impermanency of online sources create citation and legitimacy headaches of their own.

One other point is specific to Internet research sites. The "manifest content" of these discussions is cumulative: the visible, electronically shaped products of people posting messages to each other. All of these become part of accessible, online records as they go. In openly accessible research fields such as these, a researcher's (relatively exclusive) access to the "data" is both tempered and enhanced.

In the beginning, my own presence in these forums was essentially "'lurking' . . . reading messages without contributing any of my own" (Sharf 1999: 249). But I soon decided to make my presence known.[20] That being said, this decision has an ethical twist of its own when re-presenting these "patterns of naturally occurring discourse" (ibid.: 248) in an explicitly critical feminist analytical framework.[21] Feminist and/or postcolonial insights do not proffer any easy answers to all these conundrums, least of all in new research terrains such as the Internet. Rather, they look to consistently articulate the conditions under which the "data" were gathered and then handled, as opposed to extricating all research "bias," "subjectivity," or "normative" conclusions from the findings. Second, the ethical issues around (in)appropriate use of online utterances by the researcher persist whether or not "real" names or pseudonyms are used, whether or not these have been posted in an openly accessible website (these interactions take place in a "public space," ergo are "public record"). For the same reasons, the researcher's co-participation and complicity are underscored by this relative publicness. Be that as it may, in both on-the-ground and online participation–observation scenarios, Observer and Observed are operating in a mutually enacted environment – unevenly, however, for the voice that predominates after the fact is that of the Observer.[22]

My analytical and organizational interventions will be made explicit at different points in this study. The danger of overstating one's role and influence in the events and utterances that unfold is countered by the inadequacy of simply stating one's feminist credentials at the outset and then proceeding without another word. In these forums, many of the more politically and culturally charged debates also pivot on who has the right to say what, on which "true" story or interpretation is at stake, as we will see.

Politics of representation: whose and for whom?

> We all now use the word representation, but, as we know, it is an extremely slippery customer. It can be used, on the one hand, simply as another way of talking about how one images a reality that exists 'outside' the means by which things are represented: a conception grounded in a mimetic theory of representation. On the other hand the term can also stand for a very radical displacement of that unproblematic notion of the concept of representation.
>
> (Hall 1996a: 443)

Stuart Hall's distinction between mimetic and constitutive notions of "representation" is not an easy one to digest. Nor is it a familiar one to IR/IPE discourses. In this study, the term *politics of representation* acknowledges both these elements. To put it simply for now, it connotes the power (relations) of depicting (in any way) lived lives (articulations and perceptions of social worlds). The *politics* entailed here is the "gap between representations and those they are supposed to represent; the gap between orthodox symbolic languages and their utilisation" (Ahearne 1995: 158).

In IR/IPE, "representation" mostly refers to various sorts of (representative) democratic systems in the first instance and its mimetic function in theoretical-empirical terms in the second. Neither of these applications is adequate for the aforementioned constructivist moods or the sociocultural dimensions of life in late capitalist societies. Critical scholars have, nonetheless, started to address the latter vis-à-vis the impact of ICTs upon politics, economics, and society, albeit from a materialist, structuralist understanding of the aforementioned "slippery customer." David Harvey epitomizes both an explicit mimetic theory of representation and its implicit "radical displacement" when arguing that any

> system of representation, in fact, is a spatialization of sorts which automatically freezes the flow of experience, and in so doing distorts what it strives to represent.... But here arises the paradox. We learn our ways of thinking and conceptualizing from active grappling with the spatializations of the written word, the study and production of maps, graphs, diagrams, photographs, models, paintings, mathematical symbols, and the like. How adequate are such modes of thought and such conceptions in the face of the flow of human experience and strong processes of social change?
>
> (Harvey 1990: 206)

In contradistinction to Hall, Harvey's compelling account of technosocial change (as hi-tech capitalism writ large) posits representations of "social reality" as ontologically separable from the "flow of human experience and strong processes of social change." In Harvey's account, representation is effectively "mimetic." But a recognition of "material" realities (of socioeconomic and political power relations) need not deny a constitutive role for "symbolic" versions or "radical displacements" thereof. The myriad of pictorial, textual, oral ways in which any known world is articulated, perceived, or experienced by participating subjects coalesce along various axes of gender, ethnicity, and class-power relations. And the knowledge gleaned also emanates from an "extraordinary diversity of subjective positions, social experiences and cultural identities" (Hall 1996a: 443). There is a subtle but crucial political and analytical distinction between the quest for recovering social relations from alienated modes of production and the recognition of this "double articulation" of material and non-material realities and inter/subjective locations. For

> events, relations, structures do have conditions of existence and real effects, outside the sphere of the discursive; but that is only within the discursive, and subject to its specific conditions, limits and modalities, do they have or can they be constructed within meaning. Thus, while not wanting to expand the discursive infinitely, how things are represented and the 'machineries' and regimes of representation in a

culture do play a *constitutive*, and not merely a reflexive, after-the-event role. This gives questions of culture and ideology, and the scenarios of representation – subjectivity, identity, politics – a formative and not merely an expressive, place in the constitution of social and political life.

(ibid.: 443; original emphasis)

What is still needed in critical analyses of shifts in the ownership and control of ICTs in general, and Internet technologies particularly, is more grounded theoretical nuance to these "scenarios of representation," their formative *and* expressive dimensions.

Chapter outline

The book is divided into nine chapters, centered on four chapters that focus on some substantial discussion themes from the Kava Bowl and Kamehameha Roundtable Forums. Chapters 2 and 3 provide the historical background and theoretical and methodological rationale underpinning these reconstructions. The last two chapters return to the historical and theoretical issues raised in these early chapters in light of these Pacific traversals online.

Chapter 2 is a brief overview of the recent technical and political economic history of IT and telecommunications. The Internet/World Wide Web of today both predates, and emerges during the "global restructuring" of, telecommunications and public utilities sectors, broadcasting, and the emergent multimedia sectors and organization of production and distribution in traditional manufacturing sectors. These processes were indebted to the rise of neoliberal orthodoxy in industrialized hi-tech societies and its execution at a transnational level by bodies such as the International Monetary Fund, the World Bank, and the World Trade Organization. This chapter looks specifically at how the idea of "global" change and neoliberal macroeconomic imperatives were actively constructed and projected through the image-making power of "corporate communications." The argument is that "'machineries' and regimes of representation" played both a formative and a powerful expressive role in the liberalization–privatization drive of telecommunications and ICT-related undertakings in the 1990s. The absorption of the Internet's historical and technical particularities therein is neither incidental to nor a function of these projections.

Chapter 3 introduces the practice theory of Michel de Certeau and argues why this is pertinent to studying both postcolonial practices of everyday life and how these unfold in cyberspace – online. Investigating *la vie quotidienne* uncovers heretofore overlooked words, actions, and communicative practices, and allows silenced voices to inflect the standard accounts. As these practices are "natural occurrences" in a cyberspatial scenario, they bring with them textual conventions, moral economies, and communicative hierarchies respective to these practitioners. I deal in two ways with the methodological implications of this sort of qualitative content analysis and the way the discussions have been reconstructed. The first draws this chapter to a close by covering the immediate empirical components of the research. Together, this theoretical discussion and the selection and interpretative interventions made in order to gather, collate, and reconstruct years of online textual production comprise the *hermeneutic schematic* for the four chapters that follow. The schematic is unpacked and discussed more fully in Chapter 8 in light of these reconstructions. Chapters 4–7 contain four clusters of recurring and interlocking (yet self-contained) discussion themes. Sex–gender roles are examined in a post-colonial and/or diasporic context from the "inside out" (in Chapter 4). The contested meanings of democracy in the postcolonial Pacific islands and online (re)articulations thereof are the subject of Chapter 5. Chapter 6 looks at (re)articulations of postcolonial self/group identity formation along race/ethnic/cultural lines. Chapter 7 examines these groups' moderation styles and behavior as emergent "moral economies" that inform all discussions in these forums.

In these discussions, other histories and ways of seeing the new (global) world order make themselves heard. The difficult aftermath of decolonization and neocolonial economic relations in the South Pacific intermingle with the gendered/ethnic/class contours of life as a disadvantaged "ethnic minority" living "overseas" or local politics in Tonga and Samoa, as formalized debates, casual conversations, streams of consciousness, satire, and autobiographical accounts. In the same debates, participants also broach a number of ongoing themes in the social sciences and humanities: the public–private dichotomy, democratization and development, the "politics of identity," and the (in)applicability of modern models of nation-state and citizenship criteria for non-Western societies. Everyday experiences and philosophical issues are interwoven and counter one another all the way along. So do all manner of written idioms, stylistic conventions, and colloquialisms. Sometimes these do not mesh with academic idioms. More often than not, these online interventions are more eloquent, more circumspect renditions of theoretical debates. The distinction between my chosen analytical terms and those of the people I cite have been made visible, rather than explained away. The verbatim citations from the discussion threads – with all their vagaries of spelling, syntax, punctuation, and formatting – also underscore this other "gap between representations and those they are supposed to represent" (Ahearne 1995: 158). The same goes for the complexity and open-ended style of the debates themselves vis-à-vis my hermeneutic interventions.

In the penultimate chapter, I return to the feminist and postcolonial premises of the research itself. Chapter 8 looks at the "empirical material" of the central chapters; its collection, collation, and interpretations. A third tale of the Internet in effect where my own "learning curve," and that of Internet research *per se*, intersect with feminist sensibilities, namely, research which "to be consistent with feminist politics and principles, demands that researchers write themselves into their accounts of the research process" (Henwood *et al.* 2001: 11). In Chapter 9, I suggest some directions for critical IR/IPE by arguing that ICTs need to be taken seriously, as constitutive of the contemporary world order and new conceptual domains – and likewise for their race/ethnicity, class, and gender permutations. I do this by opening a number of black boxes that are still hurdles, I argue, to critiques that still rely upon varying degrees of structuralist and/or technological determinism. These reflections do not discount the immense power of vested commercial, military, and political interests looking to appropriate Internet technologies for exclusive proprietary ends – pressures that are already impinging upon everyday and noncommercial designs and uses of the Internet/World Wide Web. But such trajectories are neither preordained nor uncontested, and neither are the various political and economic elites that stand to gain by them. In the final summation of the analytical contributions that a worm's-eye view study of everyday life online can make to critical theory and research, I return to the postcolonial politics of representation being traced by the online practices of the KR and KB participants. These are but one example of a myriad of alternative uses and applications of Internet technologies that are not premised on the for-profit ethos.

A final word of caution. The point of juxtaposing these two tales is not to compile an exhaustive compendium of "common or garden" everyday life online that is then presented as some sort of idealized cyber-reality. The point is that "virtual" (online) worlds and on the ground realities are "co-constituted" (Harding 1998a, 1998b). The political, technoeconomic, and sociocultural contours of this co-constitution also includes the fraught relationship between (former) colonizers and colonized peoples. Their lives and arenas of action are also at stake in these contending visions of the future.

2 Marketing the neoliberal dream

Introduction

In May 2000, a job vacancy for telecommunications–information technology specialists was placed in a Dutch newspaper, *de Volkskrant*. Its lead caption (in English), "you can't predict the future in telecoms unless you create it," does two things simultaneously: it repackages an adage about self-fulfilling prophecies while acknowledging the volatility of returns on investments in "new" ICTs. As Internet technologies are appropriated by commercial interests with access to huge financial resources, technical know-how, and market access, popular imaginaries have been put to work in selling this commercial vision of communications futures. Twentieth-century industries of persuasion known as public relations and marketing look to control consumption patterns before and after a product goes on the market. The technohistory of any new artifact, (un)predictable consumer behavior, and investment patterns meet, and diverge, somewhere along paths carved out by advertising campaigns.

In the aforementioned ad, the addressee (*you*) is pictured as a man standing alone on a beach, his back turned to the viewer as he gazes into the far horizon. In the foreground, footprints in the sand take the eye to this distant figure. This *you* is male and European (judging by his garb), and the future is his to have. Once he has created it, that is. The text (now in Dutch) underneath the image goes on to assert that the point of *creating* this "future in telecoms" is to be "always one step ahead." Logical in the world of business. Pause for a little while longer, though. In this entrepreneurial vision of first come, first served, socially equitable and accessible "telecoms futures" are irrelevant. By association, so are four-fifths of the world's populace still without basic telecommunications services. This ad epitomizes how, in a period in which public telecommunications were redefined as profit-maximizing, transnational, and privatized corporate enterprises, the future is framed in terms of the communication needs of a (mainly) white, male corporate client. This Internet is the provenance and progeny of capitalist accumulation. Equitable ICT trajectories are seen to follow accordingly. However, a burgeoning literature on the history of noncommercial software developments and on increasing socioeconomic gaps in ICT access and application suggests otherwise (Warschauer 2000; Manièe de voir 1996a, b; Loader 1998; McChesney *et al.* 1998; Schiller 1999). Allright, the reader may say; this is only an advertisement, after all. Exactly. The point is the pervasiveness of advertising in consumer societies and the way in which the "advertising work" (Williamson 1978) mediates, informs, and reconstitutes popular imaginaries and political economic undertakings. Hence advertising's imagings and meaning-makings are not incidental to a

> global political economy [which] advances on contradictory terrains, sometimes reinforcing, sometimes obliterating cultural, regional, and religious differences, gendered and ethnic divisions. Flows of immigrants, media, technology, and commodities have similarly uneven effects.
>
> (Clifford 1997: 9)

This chapter looks more closely at some examples of this particular "circulation of meanings" (Murphy and Rojas de Ferro 1995) in the intersecting histories of telecommunications, information technology, and the media. It does so through a selection of corporate advertisements that date from the mid to late 1990s – years in which corporate restructuring processes across the board, the popularity of the World Wide Web, and the privatization of public telecommunications intersected. There are three main sections. The first section is an alternative narrative to the accepted wisdoms that uncritically couple the causes of so-called globalization processes with the interactive and "translocal" characteristics of Internet technologies *per se.* Where – and why – "developing" economies, such as those of the South Pacific Islands, are excluded from this particular narrative is also a moot point. With this set of historical contingencies in mind, the second section argues why a closer reading of the cultural artifacts produced by advertising and marketing (ads) can unsettle the supposed inevitability of technoeconomic "global shifts." To illustrate this, a cluster of ads from erstwhile public, national telecommunications operators using ads to re-present themselves as for-profit and global corporations are "deconstructed."[1] The dynamics of these ads' production, distribution, and reception (by their "target audiences") are different entry points for analyzing both their manifest content and their latent "meanings" (see van Zoonen 1994; Rayner *et al.* 2001: 63–71; McQuail 1987: 29 *passim*). These ads work hard to re-present the deregulation, liberalization, and then privatization of public utilities as a *fait accompli,* based on a technological imperative rather than high-level political economic decisions. In their repackaging of political and economic decision making as global technomarket imperatives, they make full use of various connotations of sex and gender and the multiple ways that these can be received by respective ("target") audiences.[2] A range of Western-based historical-cultural references and a degree of ambivalence to some of the social implications of these large-scale reorganizations are also at work at the subtextual, subliminal level. Some use sexualized visual images quite blatantly. Others are more oblique. The last examples make full and ironic use of sex–gender as "performativity": phallocentric prowess and arch femininity respectively (Butler 1990; Saunders and Foblets 2002: 18 *passim*; Carver 1998b).

The third section discusses three theoretical implications of this sort of analysis for the hermeneutic schematic of this study. The first is a conceptualization of *technology* as both an analytical category and an object of research that treats technologies (large and small) as historically and socially constructed, thereby imbricated in respective gender power relations. This links the materiality of technologies as things, processes or systems to accompanying "*machineries*" of representation. A more complete conceptualization of these two rather static categories in IR/IPE allows for an examination of the *inter/subjective* and, thereby, political dimensions to seemingly inchoate large-scale technoeconomic shifts.

1 Historical rewind

Telecommunications' restructuring and the Internet

The most recent reorganizations of the international/national communications landscape date back to the 1980s at least, in both technical and regulatory terms (see Dicken 1992; Lühje 1997; Sassen 1991). This period of neoliberal globalization and the concomitant explosion in global financial markets also heralded the arrival of megacorporate conglomerates as key players in the interweaving of IT, telecom and the media. These twenty-odd years saw the integration of pre-Internet telecommunications (the telephone, television, and radio) with information technology and then traditional print and broadcasting "mass" media sectors. The 1990s Internet "boom" in popularity occurred at *roughly* the same time.

The political and economic significance of the World Wide Web and electronic mail (email) technologies were not immediately acknowledged by politicians or regulatory bodies. It is with the oft-cited statement from the Vice President of the United States at the time, Al Gore, on the *Global Information Infrastructure–Global Information Society*, the GII-GIS in his keynote address to the First World Telecommunications Development Conference held in Buenos Aires in 1994 (Lühje 1997), that is seen as marking a change in attitude. This announcement coincided with a comparable declaration of intent by the Microsoft Corporation in which it aimed its sights on Internet technologies – browser software for the World Wide Web especially (Franklin 2003a). Both these moves overlapped with pronouncements by the World Trade Organization, the International

Telecommunications Union, and the OECD *inter alia* that linked the furthering of free-market principles to R&D in the "new media" (OECD 1998b; Grassmuch 2002: 196–197; European Commission 1997; World Bank 1998; *The Economist* 1995).

In the go-get-'em mood of corporate and public sector "restructuring" along neoliberal lines, capital-intensive "natural monopolies" such as telecommunications, energy, water, and public transportation systems were also targeted for revamping through cost-cutting measures and privatization (which created immediate revenue and dispensed with long-term government expenditure). They were no longer deemed the responsibility of governments to keep afloat (Trebing 1994; Bauer 1994); they must become for-profit enterprises with transnational as opposed to national market reach, and focused on commercial as opposed to everyday communication needs. Developments in information technology – digitalization and miniaturization in particular – provided the technological imperative said to be "driving" these regulatory and organizational changes. National telecommunications operators, flag-bearers for first colonial might and then the modern nation-state (Torrè 1995, 1996; Mattelart 1994), were transformed into privatized corporations. Good business practices, monopolistic tendencies, size and scope of eventual mergers, and acquisitions within this integrating multimedia private sector were to be watched over by international and national-based quangos (quasi nongovernmental organizations).

This account needs elucidating in three respects. First, let us consider the organizational and institutional decisions taken based on (private) portfolio investment priorities, a plethora of "change management" theories and drastic cutbacks in public expenditure by governments across the board. *In toto*, these decisions meant the substitution of vertically integrated corporate structures for horizontal, "flat" company structures. This accompanied a drastic reduction in workforce (both at the managerial level and on the factory floor). The 1990s saw a wave of corporate buyouts, takeovers and "strategic alliances" in telecommunications equipment manufacturing, transmission, and services. The IT and traditional manufacturing sectors also incurred similar changes in a period that saw the so-called shift from a "Fordist" to a "post-Fordist" organization of production (Bernard 1994). The irony is that despite the downsizings and disinvestments, by the turn of the century the aforementioned dinosaurs (natural monopolies) of the telecommunications (and traditional "mass media") sectors had regrouped to form even larger corporate conglomerates. Apart from the dominance of the Microsoft Corporation in all things computer related, take for example the merger between Time Warner and CNN, and then AOL (until 2003 at least), a merger of print media, satellite television, and Internet services. Or take Rupert Murdoch's News Corporation, which dominates satellite television in the Asia-Pacific region and owns major highbrow and tabloid newspapers there as well as in the

United Kingdom and United States, and the Fox Entertainment Group (which includes Twentieth Century Fox) in film and television. Or take the media concerns and political networks of Bertelsmann in Germany, Berlusconi in Italy, and Dassault and Lagardèe in France. By 2000, the host of smaller IT service and software development companies that sprang up in this same period either had been swallowed up in a swathe of corporate splits, mergers, acquisitions, and bankruptcies, or had come into their own (Microsoft again, Oracle, Netscape, Napster, to name but a few). The privatization of "natural monopolies," epitomized by new Telecommunications Acts in the United States and the European Union in the mid-1990s, have actually meant more market concentration and diminished accountability.

One thing did stay relatively constant during these years: the close working relationship between military-related and corporate-led techno-logy R&D. The rapidly achieved popularity of the World Wide Web and email in particular pushed this ongoing link out of the analytical limelight for a time, until the events of September 11, 2001 and since, arguably. In historical terms, this sort of technological "success" cannot be put down to the US military's role in developing the Internet infrastructure of distrib-uted servers in the 1980s alone. Another historical contingency also bears noting at this point: the way in which "new" ICT transmission networks overlay older ones put in place by the British Empire a hundred years ago and then developed by post-World War II military-based satellite commu-nications. The ensuing skewing in "global" coverage continues today, as telecommunications maps will show (Mansell and Wehn 1998; Fuchs and Koch 1996; TeleGeography Inc. 2000).

Second, this period saw some more micro-level developments in Inter-net-related technologies, not all of which were the preserve of corporate R&D (Grassmuck 2002; Rogers 2000).[3] Here, key moments include the invention of "browser" software in the early 1990s, which heralded the arrival of the World Wide Web as "we" know it; the tensions between pro-prietary and nonproprietary software for open or commercial computing; and the increasing distinction between "good" and "bad" computer pro-grams (viruses) and programmers (hackers). By the mid-1990s, the dotcom gold rush was in full swing, with the establishment of a powerful global financial market for technology stocks and shares (the NASDAQ) and the now familiar stories of boom and bust around companies such as Amazon.com, America Online (AOL), Worldcom, Napster, and others. As using the World Wide Web and/or emailing became part of everyday life – of the working day in hi-tech societies at least – Internet technologies became big business.

Finally, there are all the psychoemotional dimensions to these political and technoeconomic events and the habit-forming practices they set in motion. In capitalist, consumer societies, image making and breaking are fully integrated aspects to strategic changes in both the corporate and the public sector (Champlin and Olson 1994; Kleinsteuber 1996; Mattelart 1995). The 1990s saw expensive marketing campaigns launched by privatizing telecommunications operators/service providers to sell themselves and their "product": communication. Initially these marketing campaigns looked to sell new ICTs – the Internet – as new commodities in themselves (or, rather, related services and access). As the decade rolled on, PR and marketing shifted to the World Wide Web. The Internet *tout court* thereby became both a medium for communication and information products, and then a commodity in itself. The increasingly commercialized visuals of the Web, spam-filled email inboxes and advertising-as-keyword search bear witness to these commodification processes.

The precise relationship between Internet technologies and neoliberal globalization processes is a debate in itself. The uneven distribution in the costs and/or benefits of those societies and groups that get to benefit is all too apparent (Golding 1998; Holderness 1998; OECD 2000, 2001). There is a tension, moreover, in the distribution of responsibility for these processes and their outcomes between various watchdogs, their respective political bosses, and the ever-growing conglomerates signaled in these ads. On the one hand is an ideal of an unrestricted global market in goods and services that is premised on ICTs' global "reach." On the other, governmental and regional-level watchdogs have been mounting rearguard actions to counter a number of "anticompetitive" practices by these transmuted "global" corporations. During this same period, a host of noncommercial, equitable design concepts for ICTs, alternative websites, and online interactions have been also unfurling. These question in their different ways both the historical veracity and the social fairness of the telecom futures being touted in these ads and accompanying literature, company annual reports, and development reports.

Be that as it may, advertising and marketing's brief is to package these sorts of contingencies into tidy, self-serving certainties. In the history of any technology, how it is taken up by ordinary people and "domesticated" through everyday uses is not always predictable. Representations of telecommunications restructuring in this period are more than mimetic representations of an external reality. They not only "displace" – divert – attention from what were incomplete processes but, in so doing, contribute to a certain narrative of technoeconomic historical inevitability. The gendered, race/ethnic, and class permutations of these imagings cast a different light on what were – and still are – highly uneven and contestable technoeconomic and political trajectories. In the illustrative examples that follow, the future of *globalcapital.com* is depicted as both an eroticized ("sexy") and a cozy, domesticated relationship between "consumer" and "provider."[4] But first, let's take a look at where the Pacific Islands fit into this narrative.

Neoliberal globalization, the Internet, and the South Pacific Islands

As the latest generation of technical fix-its, ICTs have been touted as a way for nonindustrialized areas to "leapfrog" their way over previous "stages of modernization" (see Singh 1999: 4–6). Various intergovernmental organizations such as the OECD (2001) and UNDP (1999) have all been reporting on the consequences of the widening gap between the "information rich" and "information poor" of the world, with ensuing statements of intent designed to narrow this "digital divide."[5] This broad tendency is visible in regions like the South Pacific and the Caribbean, whose small island countries are spread out over vast tracts of ocean and have widely dispersed and relatively small populations: tens of thousands of inhabitants as opposed to millions (Taylor 2004).[6] They comprise a wide range in GDP: countries like Western Samoa in the UN's category of "Least Developed Country" (Mansell and Wehn 1998: 27–31, 102–103), but also Australia and New Zealand, members of the "developed country" club. Excluding the latter two and Papua New Guinea, the islands of the South Pacific, with a total population of 1.9 million (see UNESCO 2002: 13), do not constitute the same sort of mass-market opportunities for investment portfolios as, say, "emerging markets" like China, with its estimated 80 million Internet users, Brazil, or, potentially, more prosperous parts of sub-Saharan Africa (Kaba 1999). Moreover, this vast area that is the Pacific Ocean (roughly a third of the planet's surface) is reliant on unevenly distributed transmission pathways, capacities, hardware availability, and access points (Table 2.1). The same goes for how Internet technologies have been taken up, accessed, and used in the various Pacific islands themselves (Wired 1998a: 162; UNESCO 2002: 12–14; Ogden 1999).

Western Samoa and Tonga are cases in point. In this same period, and in a region that is known for its championing of the neoliberal cause (Jesson 1999; Kelsey 1997), these small-island developing states[7] have been under pressure to cut public spending by privatizing what telecommunications services they already have (South Pacific Forum 1998; UNDP 1999). Development priorities as laid down by Australian, New Zealand, US, and EU aid donor agencies follow the neoliberal rationale for privatizing all public utilities as part of the structural adjustment programs and "good governance" criteria (AUSTEO 1997; Fry 1997a, b; South Pacific Forum 1998; CTIN 1996).[8] For the small, vulnerable economies of the Pacific islands, kept largely afloat by direct aid and financial remittances from families abroad (King and Connell 1999; Chapman 1985), these exigencies clash with political and economic autonomy. Closer to the bone, perhaps, they directly affect the income generated from the cash cow of telecommunications traffic for economies with few options for generating foreign exchange (Melody 1994, 2001: interview; UNESCO 2002: 24–30). The positions taken by Pacific Island leaderships to these policies have been a source of friction between them and their larger neighbors-cum-

Table 2.1 ICTs in Western & American Samoa, Tonga & Fiji vis-à-vis New Zealand, Australia & USA circa 1999 (i)

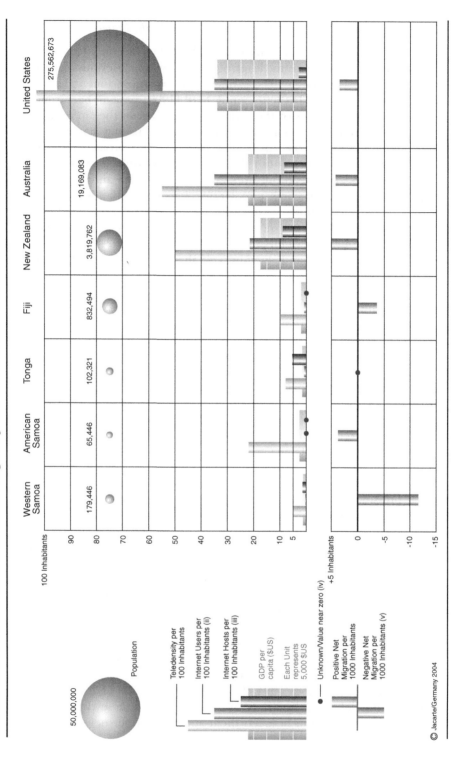

© Jacarte/Germany 2004

Notes

i   This graphic is an amalgamation of cross-referenced statistics taken from various sources for the cusp years, 1999–2001. This is a snapshot of ICT indicators (now comprising both telephony and the Internet) for the period between the Internet "boom" and the "dotcom crash." Compiling *comparable* statistics remains difficult. The huge differences between the Pacific Islands and larger economies (NZ, Australia, the United States) in population, teledensity (no. of telephones per 100 inhabitants in a region), ICT infrastructures and, now, Internet access and use (see below) are plainly visible. The larger economies' populations (based on 1999 census estimates), ICT infrastructures and Internet indicators have continued to grow vis-à-vis the much smaller, and poorer, ones. Sources: US Census Bureau (1999); *CIA World Fact Book* (2000); UNDP (1999); Siemens (2001); ITU (2000, 2001); South Pacific Forum Secretariat (1998); Millar (2000); Commonwealth Organization (2001); SIDSnet (2001); UNESCO (2002); *Wired* (1998, 1999); Samoan Sensation (2001); South Pacific Forum Secretariat (1998).

ii The term "Internet *user*" is a relative one, because "there is no standard definition of frequency (e.g. daily, weekly, monthly) or services used . . . [and while] there are several well-known sources of Internet users for different countries, they are often collected from various national surveys that are not comparable and typically ignore developing countries completely." (Minges 2000).

iii Another flexible term. The total number of computers connected to the Internet (hosts/servers) does not necessarily correlate with total *users*, one host can serve many users. Neither are hosts/servers necessarily resident in their designated country of origins Tonga being a case in point.

iv This indicates both a lack of disaggregated statistics (American Samoa); values that are either given as zero or work out, per inhabitants, as close to zero (Tonga and Fiji respectively).

v   A key aspect to the region's complex demographics is the relatively slow population growth; "not the result of low fertility but, rather, reflects massive emigration to New Zealand, Australia and the United States . . . ten of the fifteen Pacific Island countries [had] net population losses in recent years . . . up to −3.5% per year" (UNDP 1999: 3; see also Lee 2003).

benefactors. In addition, some governments have not been slow to clamp down on dissenting news coverage of local affairs closer to home, integrate income generated from telecommunications with individual business ventures, or even turn a blind eye when these and other ventures fail. Yet despite the tendency to see all this as a "doomsday scenario" (Latukefu 1999: interview) for ICTs and development priorities in the region, however defined and by whom, countries such as Trinidad, Jamaica, Tonga, and Samoa have been active on the World Wide Web since the early days (Dyrkton 1996; Miller and Slater 2000; Corcoran 1997; Morton 1999; Clark 1999; Ogden 1999). The online presence of their (expatriate) populations, some astute moves at the international level of telecommunications regulation, and variously successful business ventures put Tonga, and the even smaller islands of Niue and Tuvalu, on the Internet map in this period (Wired 1998b: 104, 162).[9]

One other historical point, namely, the political independence of many Pacific Islands in the 1960s, which saw their entry into the UN accordingly. The same period saw the first wave of significant emigration out of the islands to New Zealand, Australia, and the United States (Lee 2003: 6–13). During the full-employment boom of the 1970s, Pacific Island populations (from Samoa, Tonga, Niue, the Cook Islands, and others) comprised factory workforces or pools of low-wage labor in these countries as they worked to achieve a "better life and more opportunities."[10] In so doing, these various expat communities became distinguishable populations in the cities of Australia, North-Island New Zealand, and the West Coast of the United States, for example, with specific socioeconomic and cultural demographics (Jolly and Macintyre 1989; Macpherson *et al.* 2001). These first generations of Pacific Islanders and their descendants, born and raised overseas, constitute the postcolonial Pacific Islands. Those who hail from the Polynesian group of islands (the Samoas, Tonga, Hawaii in particular) refer to themselves as the "Polynesian diaspora" in these Internet forums.

The intricacies of sociocultural similarity and/or difference among island groups notwithstanding, grist to the mill in many of the discussions studied here, social relations in these societies "are not geographically bounded, so children become familiar with other villages, other islands, and even other countries when they travel to visit or live with kin" (Morton 1996: 27). In this sense, Internet technologies have become integrated into the "traveling cultures" of Pacific Island peoples (Clifford 1997; Lee 2003: 8–10). Both diasporic island populations and their respective governments "back home" are aware of the political economic and cultural stakes in how ICTs are developing – or not – in the region. In the meantime, thousands – if not millions – of daily online communications traffic crisscross the Pacific Ocean between communities in the United States, Australia, and New Zealand, interspersed through the even greater number passing between the financial markets of Tokyo, London, Paris, and New York on either side of the Pacific Ocean.

2 The "advertising work"

Advertising has always been about repackaging manufactured commodities *as* desire. In that sense, advertising and marketing shape, influence, and draw upon popular imaginaries (Herbert 2000). Over the twentieth century, advertising's art of persuasion became a billion-dollar industry in itself. This interplay, between material and symbolic worlds and intersubjective receptions of the same, was also evident as ICTs have become not only a key site for the "'communications' aspect of the consumption process" (Leiss *et al.* 1990: 50), but also the catalyst for the marketing of (tele)communications, and thereby social relations, as the global commodity *par excellence*. Selling power is contingent upon not only media coverage but also ICT transmissions and, more and more, the commercial spaces provided by and on the Web.

The advertisements studied here show two things. First, they show how the global political economy is also made up of the "circulation of meanings" (Murphy and Rojas de Ferro 1995). Like all well-designed advertising, the immediate brief of these ads' *Global-Speak* (circulated between 1995 and 2000) is to celebrate and normalize (domesticate) the above unfinished *business* of telecommunications restructuring. In this selection, a set of transgendered and transcultural tropes is at work as commercialized ICTs are portrayed as the "Royal Road" to social and economic well-being for "all men" and "all women" (Emmott 1999). The second aspect to these ads is their strategic locations in highbrow and popular business literature such as the *Financial Times* and *The Economist* (in the United Kingdom), *Fortune* magazine and *Business Week* (the United States), and billboards in "liminal spaces" such as airports and railway stations. Wherever it may be placed, advertising is a "privileged discourse for the circulation of messages and social cues about the interplay between persons and objects" (Leiss *et al.* 1990: 50) which excels in using "the medium as the massage" and vice versa (McLuhan and Powers 1989: 63–64). This also includes the infinite reworkings of gendered "signifiers" (Williamson 1978: 41). Corporate and, increasingly, political undertakings work on the premise that

> marketing and advertising are essential in our complex market-oriented economy.... The marketing system should be seen as a "provisioning technology." ... Its strategies are based on the premise that the consumer, as ultimate decision maker, is a rational problem solver who takes full advantage of this technology.
>
> (Leiss *et al.* 1990: 34)

Somewhere between these "provisioning" technologies, their placement, manifest content (images and words), and reception, "meaning" is "created" (Williamson 1978: 14). The power and efficacy of marketable sound bites and imaging are integral to the (un)conscious creations of meaning that preoccupy advertising, ironing out historical "leaps" backwards and forwards, smoothing over the battles over ownership and control that are being waged, as is the case in this sector at the time.[11] Moreover, advertising and marketing is not just part of (what is substantial)

> business expenditure undertaken in the hope of moving some merchandise off the store shelves, but is rather an integral part of modern culture. Its creations appropriate and transform a vast range of symbols and ideas; its unsurpassed communicative powers recycle cultural models and references back through the networks of social interactions. This venture is unified by the discourse through and about objects, which bonds together images of persons, products, and well-being.
>
> (Leiss *et al.* 1990: 5)

Corporate visions of ICTs inform, and make use of, these dynamics. How did these visions of ICTs and neoliberal restructuring imperatives come to be inseparable in both public and scholarly imaginations? In a short space of time, and thanks partly to these "discourses through and about objects," a "semantic transformation from 'international' to 'global' took place so rapidly that theorization [was] overwhelmed by professions of faith" (Mattelart 1994: 211). In the ads that follow, this new faith is invocated by the Global-Speak mantra *global, network, communicate.*

Going global

The aforementioned profession of faith maintains that the "global" denotes everybody, the whole world. A 1996 advertisement for Siemens-Nixdorff, a European-based telecom–IT conglomerate for software "solutions" that "offer everyone everything" (*Financial Times*, February 1996), encapsulates this collapsing of "the one" and "the other" into the "we" of "everyone." The "everyone" here is white and European: two women and one man. The younger woman is being offered/represents, among other things, Internet shopping (by taking a "cyberstroll through electronic megamalls"), the older woman likewise for networking ("your solutions and services partner"), and the young man fast access to information and knowledge (to get a "crucial knowledge edge").

Another cogent example of this recourse to unitary universality can be found in an advertisement for Cable & Wireless (*Financial Times*, April 1995, reproduced as Figure 2.1). Here, the question of what are "real," "true," "accurate" "global communications" rests on a *trompe-l'œil*; the "authentic" (and by implication "politically correct") map of the world used to personify the so-called C&W Federation (giving a political connotation to what is a very loose business alliance) is contrasted to maps of the "rooted," geocentric worlds of the "big four telecom companies."[12] Here, the old guard's style of selling "around the world" from "just one country" is equated with "a funny old world." The latter is underlined by the use of the respective visual distortions of world telecommunications. The "autonomously" operating Federation is represented by a map of "the world according to Cable & Wireless" and further underlined by the captions "free to pick and choose," "a world of difference"; to wit, "global communications" will be authentic (federalist and so "free") and not nationally identifiable (and so, again "free").

Figure 2.1 "The World according to Cable & Wireless."

Not only is the Cable & Wireless Federation truly democratic, but it also truly represents (transgendered and transcultural) "you." The point here is that the very map representing said "world of difference" is centered on the Pacific Ocean – a re-presentation of colonial histories, for Cable & Wireless was the British Empire's agent for laying the earliest submarine links between this "core" and its colonies at the "periphery." A "funny old world" indeed.

But the terms "global" and "worldwide" are not only contrasted as in the above examples, but also used synonymously. One of the "old guard" personified in the latter advertisement – Deutsche Telekom (now privatized and the biggest operator in Europe) – did not hesitate to call upon the "funny old world" of big power diplomacy signifiers to inaugurate its own "global alliance" (*Sunday Times*, March 1996, reproduced in Figure 2.2).[13] Here, three male hands grip each others' wrists, signifying not only where "real international understanding starts," but also the physical linking in telecommunications networks (cables, satellite links, switching equipment) – interconnectedness, no less. Here, a "truly global dimension," a "truly global basis" of business communication is synonymous with "worldwide," "international" "consortiums" and "partnerships." It is the traditional international relations representation of the world as a

Figure 2.2 "Real international understanding starts here."

state-centered, male domain that is called upon and reiterated in this quaint conflation of "global" with the European Union ("the world's single largest market place") and the "global dimension" with the United States and the "Pacific Rim."

These examples illustrate different ways in which the global appellation has become a site for an exchange of "meanings" – an exchange that is nevertheless explicitly anchored in (neo)realist representation of twenti-eth-century technocommercial developments as classical geopolitics.

But this can also be seen beyond the world of advertising in supporting, and oft-cited publications such as *The Economist*. In one of its earlier telecommunications surveys (September 30, 1995), a relationship between the telephone, the gender politics of its use, and the liberalization of the sector is made and exploited through certain well-known cultural (reli-gious and domestic) icons. In this case (Figure 2.3), William Blake's *Europe: A Prophecy* is pictured by *The Economist*'s outsourced illustrator as transmitter for the mobile phone conversation of a generic "Mr. and Mrs." standing at/on opposite ends of the globe under the heading of "The death of distance."

The cover of this issue also features a Roy Lichtenstein–inspired drawing of a woman talking on the phone with two captions: "suddenly distance no longer mattered!" and "Darling the telecoms revolution is finally happening." Within one frame, the stereotype of a gushing woman-as-chatterer, woman-as-passive-recipient becomes a reference to the pre-sumably *novel* activity of finding ways to transcend distance between oneself and loved ones.[14] Not only this, but the necessity of this "revolu-tion" to relieve the "horror" of contemporary telephonic connections for computer users is represented (again by the same artist for Figure 2.3) by a rendition of Munch's painting *The Scream* (Figure 2.4). The trick here is that the ubiquity of the telephone, its social use and role in the domestic sphere (in many women's lives particularly), and its original role as a dis-tance leveler, let alone the still-remaining lack of telephone connectivity for the majority of the globe, are conflated with and then banalized by the technical fix-it hype of latter-day transmission capacities of telecommuni-cations. Such expressions of the "global" are imbued with and given import by their gendered connotations. Moreover, the selling value, the self-confirming, persuasive power of the term and its derivatives permeates these scenarios, where there is no squeamishness in using "one of the more common, rather overused buzzwords of our times" (Gurevitch 1991: 178). Quite the reverse, in fact. As about-faces and shifts in the articula-tion of this term increase, particularly in the telecommunications and IT sectors, so does the persuasive power of (strategic) repetition. The more the term "global" and its offshoots become entrenched in the respective re/presentations of changes in world order, the greater its assumed onto-logical and epistemological status.

Figure 2.3 "The death of distance."

Network

A lot of the application and development of Global-Speak over the past few years is related to the aforementioned cross-fertilizations between the jargon of the telecommunications industry, computer technology, and popular-academic discourses on the "globalizing" functionality of new(er) ICTs. Older terms were recharged with new meaning. Networking is a case in point. Just as the meaning and infrastructure of telecommunications have been shifting onto a "virtual" plane (Jordan 1999: 1 *passim*), the idea of network is doing so too. This intersects with a grand notion of the

Figure 2.4 "We're still trying to connect you."

"global market" for which telecommunications networks are being designed, constructed – or restructured – into the/a single so-called integrated and seamless commercial network.

Some interesting juxtapositions occur here when traditional masculine and feminine metaphors are mixed to create more fashionable connotations of network(ing). NTT[15] does this in a particularly powerful way in an advertisement designed to convey the "vast system of lines, links and connections" – the NTT network – "behind the telephone that rests so comfortably in your hand" (*Financial Times*, January 16, 1996, reproduced as Figure 2.5). Mobile phones represent the heads of knitting needles from which a half-knitted garment – a map of connections – is suspended. The mixed metaphor occurs through the caption: "Building Telecommunications Systems That Help Build A Better World." Here the vocabulary of architecture and carpentry, traditional masculine domains, is mixed with the more abstract visualizations of comfort and continuity conjured up by the reference to knitting, traditionally a feminine activity.[16] In one

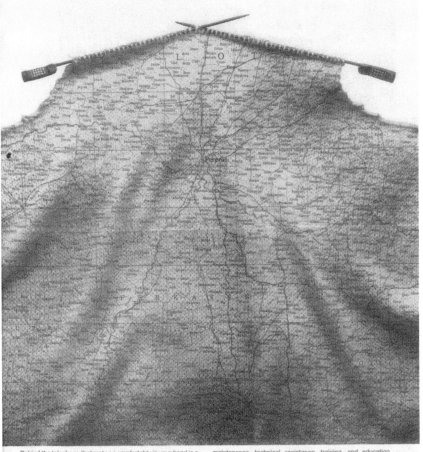

Figure 2.5 "Building telecommunications systems that help build a better world."

semantic and visual swoop, the domain of construction/action is amalgamated with the domain of domesticity to recreate "the communications infrastructure" of what is still primarily a domestic (*sic*) carrier, albeit a significant one in terms of turnover and traffic, as "the means of communication."

This domestication of communication-as-expansion – to wit, this "outing" of traditional feminine activities, usually regarded as "not purposeful" – is also present, this time on behalf of France Télécom, another domestic telecommunications operator that was privatized in this period. Here the gendered signifier of domesticity is needlework, called upon to sell the ill-fated Global One alliance with Deutsche Telekom and Sprint (a US operator) as "a single network" (Figure 2.6). Again, traditional

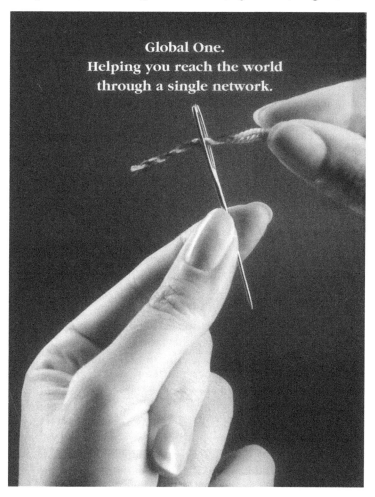

Figure 2.6 "Global One. Helping you reach the world through a single network."

masculine and feminine activities are combined: building "the world to come" is likened to threading a needle. The latter in turn represents the "single point of contact" for "seamless" services. It is a woman's manicured hands that thread the needle here, with the Global One network the eye of the needle and the three-way alliance the multicolored thread. I do not want to belabor the sexual undertones, but Global One is how "the world" is entered – "reached." However, this "world to come" is not pictured. Rather, it is evoked by the (absent) garment to be sewn. The very incompleteness of this picture is its suggestive device. Following Williamson (1978), this "present absence" creates a representational space for projection, to be filled by the viewer, through its very reliance on subconscious connections between biblical references and sex–gender archetypes.

These are just some examples of advertising's ability to mix up and exploit traditional sex–gender roles. To do so it relies on the viewer – the target audience – to make the connection; for the most part, the well-heeled male business executive or consumer. This use of mixed feminine and masculine signifiers was prevalent in this period as technical, engineering, and scientific terms for telecommunications were replaced by these cozy ones of domestic familiarity. This shift illustrates and underpins the point made earlier about network: long a functional part of telecommunications jargon, the term has become a central "meaning component" of global communications. The vagueness created by the state of flux of these very same alliances – in their coupling and uncoupling as they struggle and negotiate to maintain "global market share" and influence – is both convenient and necessary for the interchange of meanings. These imagings rely on the fact that these nascent networks are also amorphous, extremely fluid representations of space even as their material import is not.[17]

In the meantime, networks and their composite equipment can no longer be represented or regarded as engineering artifacts alone. They are now naturalized as representations of an organic, biospheric whole (Kelly 1994: 47). This cross-fertilization of communication networks can be seen in a color poster from Lucent Technologies,[18] addressed, as a welcome, to its new employees from the buyout that took place at the time of two Philips subsidiaries in France and Germany. Here references to change, procreation, and "global presence" accompany the image of planet Earth and two – white – men shaking hands in the foreground. This "rapidly changing world of communications," which sees the "rebirth" of hardware manufacturing into a world defined by software-based services, is Earth as biosphere. Satellite imaging systems, and their use in advertising, have had an impact "in quite radical ways, [on] how we represent the world to ourselves" (Harvey 1990: 240; see also McHaffie 1997). The "more than a 100 years of experience" being referred to in this ad is also a reminder of how innovations dedicated to the removal of spatial barriers in all of these respects have been of immense significance in the history of capitalism, turning that history into a very geographical affair – the railroad and the telegraph, the automobile, radio and telephone, the jet aircraft and television, and the recent telecommunications revolution are cases in point.

(Harvey 1990: 240)

Such innovations have also been a very gendered, intimate, personal affair.

Let's communicate

At the normative heart of the futurism and gadgetry is *communication*, marketed as a metaphor for inter/subjectivity and commodity. British Telecom (*Financial Times*, September 13, 1995) evokes the coziness of chatting ("Let's talk") and the urgency of the global business imperative for communications services by forefronting the image of a silver tea and coffee service. Private/domesticated communication and notions of personal freedom – "Communication is all about freedom" – are paired with the commercial arena of market-led "advanced, fully-integrated communications services on a truly global scale" and notions of choice ("introducing a new concept in communications. Choice").[19] This then allows tele/communications to be essentially the prerogative of private capital and so necessarily existing in a "competitive market" environment. Yet such a business-like wedge between the coziness of tea drinking and the ideals of consumer choice is not as transgendered as it would appear: the shadowy figures in the background are clearly male and the setting a transcendent place for jet-setting "choice, both globally and locally."

Implicit in this commercial communication is the unfinished agenda of reconciling competing and crisscrossing systems and computer languages that are not a priori compatible. Global-Speak tenderly muffles the deeply problematic issues of technical communication standards in a limitless market economy. In practice, the shifting demarcation lines of various new technologies first need to be pegged out in order for parties to "communicate." The boom in "global" alliances between operators, software houses, cable TV, the railways *et al.* is to secure beneficially compatible systems and transmission pathways – for now and the future. Hence, the "promiscuity" of global alliances notwithstanding,[20] agreements on technical protocols, software and hardware compatibility, local and international charges, and special rates are sites for technical as well as regulatory and political economic struggles.

Another, often brushed aside factor in these regimes of representation that go deep into ICT architectures is the unmitigated predominance of

English/Roman alphabet-dependent codes for ICTs and their user interfaces. Operational standards based on the English language and/or the Roman alphabet, can only purport to provide equitable access to Internet technologies for all; the large majority of the world's population do not speak English. "Developing" or "transitional" economies in the post-Cold War world are supposed to be able to "leapfrog development" by gaining mobile, digital, and intercontinental telecommunications simultaneously. Deutsche Telekom, for example, invokes the opening up of the European Community's internal borders and, while hardly identifiable as generically English speaking, mixes an image of open customs points (Figure 2.7) with the marketing of the GSM (Global System for Mobile Communications) standard in its claim to have "broken the global language barrier" (*Financial Times*, February 26, 1996). GSM is one of various proprietary mobile communications systems competing to be the "new global telecommunications language."

(Re)materialized gender power relations

All three aspects of Global-Speak's mantra, global – network – communicate, appeal to presumably shared sociocultural and political-economic imaginations. Meanwhile, extant telecommunications architectures and

Figure 2.7 "We've broken the global language barrier."

multifarious inter/cultural communicative practices are being redesigned
or decommissioned according to the imperatives of commercialized, high-
workload transmission webs that circulate and mediate this self-fulfilling
prophecy. These imagings underscore McLuhan and Power's insight into
how any new

> medium, by dilating a particular sense to fill the whole field, creates
> the necessary conditions for hypnosis in that area. The medium
> becomes an unknowable force to the user. This explains why all soci-
> eties are initially numbed by the adoption of any new technology.
> (McLuhan and Powers 1989: 94)

Despite the refrain of novelty, a "global" communications infrastructure (namely, a worldwide telephone network) is already in place (Torre
1996: 12), well embedded in its colonial past. Neither is geographical
spread or expansionist agendas exclusive to these technosocial visions;
capitalism has this logic anyway. In these representations, and the material
processes they project and rationalize, "the world's" multifarious communications "needs" are subsumed under a highly selective and ethnocentric
experience of time and space (Esteva 1992; Slater 1996). Second, the
global–network–communication mantra has gone hand in hand with
"global" reorganizations or production that have seen the increased
exploitation of men, women, and children in the "global South" and
"closer to home." Rearrangements in banking and finance further facilitate these "expanding (rather than contracting) technology gaps and economic inequalities" (Gordon 1995: 3). Advertising's long history and
"machinerie" of sexploitation has been brought to bear on this version of
events, which subsumes those who are "actually" excluded under those
who are being "virtually" embraced (Mattelart 1994: 209 *passim*).

By the time the "Infonet" ad (*Financial Times*, November 3, 1999, reproduced as Figure 2.8) for "seamless" and "snag-free" communications services that "run as smooth as silk" appeared, the material-discursive
groundwork had already been laid. Silk stockings, high heels, prone femininity are an "absolute necessity" for any self-respecting ICT service
provider. The male customer ("you") is confidently addressed by the proffered service: the femininely "integrated multi-service network."[21]

This evocation of smoothness and effortlessness belies the "multiple
contradictions" (Harvey 1990: 232) and equally impressive financial outlay
of global players in the commercial arena of ICTs, where R&D budgets
increase in inverse proportion to the certainty of the outcome. At corporate levels, "production, restructuring, and growth of spatial organisation is
a highly problematic and very expensive affair, held back by vast investments in physical infrastructures that are always slow to change" (ibid.:
232, 233). Not only is service deliberately linked to sex, but in the shape-
shifting, horizontal (prone) relationships in this representation of ICTs,

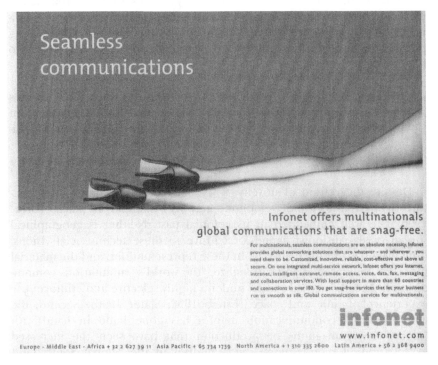

Figure 2.8 "Seamless communications."

size as a prerequisite for success is replaced by reach. A full-sized ad for another consortium encapsulates these subconscious links with its image of a naked boy toddler urinating proudly upwards into an adult-sized toilet bowl (*de Volkskrant*, November 29, 1997: 16v). A stereotype of male prowess evokes potential success, growth – and potency – in terms of reach. In the Benelux countries, such an image of a naked child might suggest supreme ignorance (coming as it did as child pornography rackets were uncovered at the time), or sublime cunning that could exploit such taboos through an ingenuous reference to similar statuettes that are common in the Netherlands and Belgium.[22]

These last two imagings epitomize the technosymbolic merging of communication with commodified information exchange as well as (re)materialized gender power relations of everyday telecommunications: ICTs. These glossy projections of the future pivot on the exploitation and recycling of sex–gender dualisms and power hierarchies, reconstituting them in the process. It is a "global communications" package that is now being exported, literally and figuratively, as a cure-all for political disenchantment, socioeconomic inequalities along race/ethnic, gender, and class lines, and national economic well-being.

3 Theoretical and research implications

> One of the major problems affecting contemporary research on com-
> munication is amnesia, the absence of a 'collective memory', the
> forgetting of the social and political stakes at issue ... the patterns of
> implantation of communications and information technologies and
> the development of their uses as social constructions. They take shape
> through adaptations, transitions, resistances, and above all through
> contradictory meanderings where collisions of different actors, ideas,
> material interests, and social projects are sure to occur.
>
> (Mattelart 1994: x)

Advertising campaigns such as these contribute to this sort of historical
and cultural amnesia; contestation and agency are repackaged as
inevitability. Everyday communication, without which social relations
would not exist, become the global commodity, an object of desire *par
excellence.* Drawing on a selection of culturally specific references to carry
their global message, the "telecoms futures" being peddled here subsume
gender, class, ethnic, and sociocultural variations to a Eurocentric and
androcentric universalism. Three theoretical points arise from this brief
study with respect to narratives, visions, and uses of these same technologies. They are also relatively undertheorized elements in post–Third
Debate IR/IPE theory and research.

Technology

Technology is understood here as more than gadgets, complex technical
networks, or communications systems. The thing-ness of technology can
be more productively examined if it is broken down into its constitutive
sociocultural practices. The "discourses associated with these practices
must be seen as expressions of more general sociocultural value systems,
sets of assumptions not only about technology, but about social reality,
and about gender relations as well" (Frissen 1992: 31). Taking this understanding of technology seriously from within IR/IPE means to study it as
more than an exogenous force, or even an endogenous empirical actor in
the international state-system (Talalay, Farrands, and Tooze 1997). ICTs,
whether they be disaggregated into their composite artifact, complex
network architectures, software and hardware components, also entail
"ways of doing things" (Castells 1996: 29–30). These ways come about
through a "set of choices" that are, in turn, imbued with and given "all
kinds of meaning and symbolism" (Street 1992: 9, 11). All technologies –
no matter how seemingly "inevitable" or "revolutionary" – can be analyzed
as historical and sociocultural relationships; as the purvey of human
agency, the site of intense struggles, even if these are not always immediately apparent. Internet technologies, whether at the point of production,

consumption, everyday uses, and/or modes of reception, need to be grasped as a "contradictory field in which we struggle to define the systems of representation through which ... we live the 'imaginary' relations between ourselves and our real conditions of existence" (Hall in Grossberg 1996b: 159). Thinking about commercializing and strategically significant technologies this way can help destabilize any predominant "narrative field" – in this case, of corporate marketing and neoliberal politics and the concomitant inequities of gender, class, and ethnicity underpinning these "logics of appropriation and domination" (Haraway 1992: 288, 289).

"Machineries" of representation

To recall, the notion of representation in IR/IPE is defined by the political history of the Westphalian nation-state and its export beyond Western Europe. As I argued earlier, this restrictive understanding needs to be loosened up in order to incorporate the multiple experiences, perceptions, and expressions delimiting and, in turn, constituting everyday uses of technologies such as the Internet (radio, the telephone, and television being other well-researched cases in point). Whether it be applied as an analytical concept or an empirical category, (political/politics of) representation operates in inherently ambiguous and ambivalent ways. Furthermore, in its narrower political science rendition, the term is insufficient – more mystifying than elucidating – when applied beyond the confines of Western, capitalist societies. As Stuart Hall warns,

> when we naturalise historical categories (think about gender and sexuality), we fix that signifier outside of history, outside of change, outside of political intervention ... it is only through the way in which we represent and imagine ourselves that we come to know how we are constituted and who we are. There is no escape from the politics of representation, and we cannot wield 'how life really is out there' as a kind of test against which the political rightness or wrongness of a particular cultural [political economic] strategy or text can be measured.
>
> (1996b: 472, 473)

This conceptualization need not preclude critical analyses of *material* political economic power relations, ownership, and control, changes in representative democratic political systems, or where ICTs operate in any of these scenarios. Changing constellations and generations of hardware and software, the environmental effects of computer chip manufacturing, the boom and bust cycles of gadgets (fax machines, laptops/palmtops, multitasking mobile phones), macro-level restructuring of telecommunications and other key sectors for hi-tech, industrialized economies – these all constitute representations of, and for, the future. The way meanings are circulated, transmitted, reinforced, countered, or absorbed every day are the link between "capitalism and its accompanying messages" (Murphy and Rojas de Ferro 1995: 63–64).

The ads discussed in this chapter illustrate some of these politics from the past decade or so. The aim of a "good" – successful – advertisement is to make complex and incomplete connections not only self-explanatory, but also desirable; to sell "air," if that is what it takes. This is what Judith Williamson has called "the advertising work" (1978: 15). The private enterprise of "global communications" is not the only telecoms future on record, however. Incorporating the meaning-making of these key players in any narrative of telecommunications restructuring underscores how the ostensibly "global" political economy is also "a cultural and identity-inducing matrix of practices and institutions" (Rosow, Inayatullah, and Rupert, 1994: 1). Admittedly designed to sell "global communications" of a certain ilk to a corporate, well-heeled, and mobile audience, their reliance on Western sociocultural and historical settings to project a "triumphalist myth of immediate, gung-ho globalization" (Mattelart 1994: 211) bespeaks broader geographies of gender power relations.[23]

Inter/subjectivity

Meaning-making is an inter/subjective process where perception, experience, and various sorts of articulation all play a role in the symbolic and physical circulations of meanings. A more fluid, micro-level treatment of inter/subjectivity in IR/IPE as the study of people as well as systems is still cognizant, nonetheless, of "structural" power. Overemphasizing the latter, though, can obscure the particularities of class, gender, race, and/or ethnicity in any systemic moment, can reify the structure beyond its active elements/active agents. The converse is also hazardous. Over-privileging and decontextualizing inter/subjectivity means that these same active elements/acting agents (even those of nonelite groups) are dissolved into "a pluralism of powers, practices, subject positions . . . a theory of necessary non-correspondence" (Grossberg 1996b: 155). This other side of the conceptual coin does not deal well with more systemic intransigencies. In order to account adequately for the contingencies of race/ethnicity, sex/gender, and status/class, theory and concomitant research methods need to be "unwilling . . . to accept the necessity of either correspondence or non-correspondence, either the simple unity or the absolute complexity of the social [political economic] formation. . . . [Correspondences] are historically produced, the site of the struggle over power (ibid.: 156). The corporate hagiography of this tale of the Internet does just this. With its imagings of "necessary correspondences," commercial visions both exclude and absorb the multiplex, informal forms of "global communication" that have always made up the larger part of Internet-based interactions. They also exclude alternative, more equitable and inclusive trajectories for "creating the future" of ICTs.

Concluding comments

This chapter has had two broad aims: to give an alternative historical account of the top-down tale of the Internet as a corporate tool and commercial enterprise first and foremost, and then to illustrate how vested interests sell this account. In contrast to what was the case in the 1980s, when the Internet was still the domain of academics and computer programmers, a causal connection has come to be *assumed* between its later popular success: "convergence" of IT and telephony and digitalization, privatization of public utilities (telecom, railways, water, and electricity), and the rise of multimedia megacorporations such as Microsoft, Time Warner, *inter alia.* Though intertwined in historical time, these shifts need to be kept analytically and historically distinct. Much of the *advertising work* of marketing and advertising is intended to blur these distinctions, and the contested versions of events that lie beneath their surface. Under the auspices of powerful vested interests that are directing sociotechnological change into certain directions (or at least looking to appropriate unexpected ones), less glamorous or "sexy" Internet practices and possibilities are silenced, written out of the official accounts. Advertising executives and corporate IT strategists know that physical placement, discursive hooks, and subliminal forms of messaging work together. If critical scholarship does not take this to heart, responses to how all the (as yet) unwired women and their menfolk will fit into these Internet futures will be down to those who are currently setting the Global-Speak rules. Hence, an understanding of meaning-making "counts.... [scholars] have a responsibility to help fashion – and interrogate – new representational spaces that are resistant to some aspects of the emerging world order" (Agnew and Corbridge 1995: 227).

Four interim conclusions can be drawn at this stage. First, the history – and so the future – of the Internet (however defined) is inconclusive and contestable, especially since it is still being written. Likewise for the way in which ICTs are being used, or not, in regions such as the South Pacific. And similarly for the everyday sociocultural dynamics of these communications. Second, as these advertisements illustrate in their own inimitable way, a "telecoms future" is indeed being put in place. The Global-Speak of the current telecom/media/IT military-industrial complex articulates but one node in an ongoing struggle over ownership and control of the future for hi-tech societies, and those that have fallen off the edge of the "global information highway."

Third, since the mid-1990s the Internet has been increasingly commercialized, coming under increasing surveillance by nervous governments and moral watchdogs; its users, informal uses, and the databases that accumulate have been mined, electronically tagged, and reregulated. Arguing whether or not this taming of the "wild west" of early cyberspace is a good or a bad thing is not the task of this study. Exploring the everyday interplay between "the experienced, the perceived, and the imagined" (Harvey 1990: 219) is, however. This relationship is not lost on corporations or governments, which are well placed to exploit the "relationship between power and representation" (Stratton and Ang 1996: 362).

For a critical constructivist understanding of these changes, as large-scale and minute processes, this is a politics of representation that entails the "double articulation of the signifier, first to a web of connotation (signification) and second, to real social practices and subject-positions (representation)" (Grossberg 1996b: 159). This double articulation involves the gender, class, and race/ethnicity dimensions of both top-down and bottom-up online practices. Even in a commercialized, digitally integrated capitalist universe, "producers are never totally in control of the ways in which their products will be used" (Silverstone and Haddon 1996: 50). Finally, a privileging of gender as part of an analytical dyad in this study focuses on how application, design, and everyday use of ICTs are interrelated with contending assumptions about masculinity and femininity. These also work for comparable assumptions about the operations of class, race, and ethnicity in online scenarios. So, despite the danger of essentializing a concept that is in itself "constructed" (Haraway 1992: 287), gender is a thread running through the conversations reconstructed here; as are race/ethnicity, class, and status-based social relations. For in lived lives, none of these analytical categories ever "exhibits itself in pure form but [rather exhibits itself] in the context of lives that are shaped by a multiplicity of influences, which cannot be neatly sorted out" (Bordo 1990: 150). The designers and paymasters (*sic*) of these particular ads, and many like them, are well aware of these dynamics even as they apply them for their own ends.[24]

3 Everyday life online

Michel de Certeau's practice theory

Introduction

> Everyday life is that which is given (or comes in part) to us each day; it is that which crowds, even oppresses, us each day, for there is an oppression of the here-and-now [*oppression du présent*]. Every morning, what we take on, as we awake, is the weight of life, the difficulty of living in such and such a situation, whatever the fatigue, whatever the desire. Everyday life *is that which intimately concerns us*, from the inside.
>
> (de Certeau in Giard and Mayol 1980: 7; my translation, original emphasis)

> [T]he job of description can be the necessary prerequisite for allowing new forms of 'political' critique to emerge. By locating the politics of gender in the everyday, feminism provoked a transformation of politics itself: who could have predicted that politics would come to include the sexual and domestic?
>
> (Highmore 2002: 28)

Twentieth-century critical (poststructuralist) French thought has been making steady inroads into IR/IPE through the uptake of the work of Foucault, Derrida, Bourdieu, and Deleuze and Guatarri for the most part. Another influential French thinker, working within the Marxian tradition, has also been gaining a foothold: Henri Lefebvre. Lefebvre's theorization of spatiality and alienated social relations vis-à-vis the "dialectics of everyday life" (Highmore 2002: 113 *passim*) has opened up new avenues for studying the concomitant material and phenomenological shifts in space, time, and structural power in hi-tech capitalist societies (Harvey 1990; Rodgers 2003; Davies and Niemann 2000). Another thinker from this generation, Michel de Certeau (1925–1986), is less well known even though his work also speaks to these concerns (de Certeau 1980a: 97 *passim*; 1986: 171 *passim*). He is more familiar to anthropology, cultural studies, science and technology studies, and media theory (Highmore 2002; Mansell and Silverstone 1996; van Zoonen 1994; Clifford 1997; Ortner 1996).

In this chapter, I argue that de Certeau's contribution to conceptualizations of the practice of everyday life for IR/IPE lies in his emphasis on how the everyday operates through the accumulation of nonelite forms of cultural (re)production. His work provides an analytical and practical research agenda that permits the study of both "agency" and "structure" and, moreover, from an intercultural and gender-sensitive perspective (de Certeau in Giard and Mayol 1980: 7; Highmore 2002) – theory and research from "below," in other words. That being said, the Michel de Certeau who is being introduced here is a more politically radical thinker than most Marxian receptions of his thought would claim. Derogatory characterizations of his oeuvre as "postmodern," "atheoretical," or "apolitical" have not helped matters either (Roberts 1999; Highmore 2002: 26 *passim*).[1]

Murmurs about de Certeau's research politics and political activism can be heard in many corners of academe, nonetheless. His work is part of the linguistic, (de)constructivist turn that characterizes poststructuralist thought (broadly defined) on the one hand and the antiessentialist stance to large-scale change and sociocultural formations taken by feminist and postcolonial critiques on the other. A central tenet of his thought is the epistemological and ontological status of the "Other," as an immanent social agent (see Ahearne 1995; Buchanan 2000; Fabian 1983). His interest in all those "absent figures" who are nonetheless at the "center of our scientific stages" (de Certeau 1984: ii/1980a: 33)[2] informs his critique of the self-perpetuating link between elitist knowledge production and the interlocking histories of imperialism/colonialism and capitalism. His work thereby resonates with theory and research that makes heard the silenced voices of nonelite, non-Western, and/or nonmale agencies (de Certeau 1984: 1–2/1980a: 33–34; 1986: 232, Peterson and Runyan 1999: 172–173). At the same time, it is an immanent critique of ethnocentric and elitist modes of inquiry from within critical thought as well (de Certeau 1984: 45 *passim*/1980a: 101 *passim*).[3] His argument that (nonelite) everyday practices indelibly mark, co-construct, and potentially contest given sociopolitical economic spaces and social orders is applicable to everyday practices in and through cyberspace.

This chapter lays out the *hermeneutic schematic* informing this study by linking Michel de Certeau's thought to postcolonial (cyber)spatial practices. The first section deals with the key tenets of his "practice theory." As always when moving a body of thought or one thinker's oeuvre to another literature base, there are contentions and intersections that need to be delineated. The second section discusses the most pertinent of these, particularly with regard to the notions of "cyberspace," "postcolonial," and "diaspora." The third section deals with some of the empirical components of the research, the methodological implications of which I discuss more fully in Chapter 8.

1 Michel de Certeau's practice theory

As I have already noted, Michel de Certeau belongs to the generation of (post-)Marxist French intellectuals who came of age during the protest movements of 1968 (see Highmore 2002: 137 *passim*). His political writing is to be found in two collections: *Culture in the Plural* (de Certeau 1997a) and *The Capture of Speech and Other Political Writings* (de Certeau 1997b).[4] This study draws on his best-known theoretical work, *L'Invention du quotidien 1: Arts de faire* (1980a), published in English as *The Practice of Everyday Life* (1984) and its companion research monograph by Luce Giard and Pierre Mayol, *L'Invention du quotidien 2: Habiter, cuisinier* (1980), not published in English until 1998.[5] In this section, I look at three critical strands in this "scandalous" thinker's work (Godzich 1986: x).[6]

The first strand is a conceptualization of everyday life (*le quotidien*) as that which is created ("invented") through the movements, words, and habits of ordinary people. In this sense, these practices and their respective spaces are where *non*elite sociopolitical agency can be located, albeit as locations that are delimited by overt and covert operations of power-holding elites and their accompanying "systems of representation." These impositions are endured, resisted, and ignored on a daily basis in the workplace, on the street, at home. For research purposes, the "everyday evidences a discernible form and conceals a knowable logic" (Buchanan 2000: 90) that is "situational" (ibid.: 88). Because everyday life is not "a laboratory experiment, therefore our means of analysing it should not turn into one" (ibid.: 88). The second strand is how power-brokers and affiliated elites, through their control of the "spaces of representation and representation of spaces," have refined multiple ways of controlling their respective populaces, at home and abroad (de Certeau 1984: xiv/1980a: 14). For de Certeau (echoing Foucault and Lefebvre), the "marriage" between instrumental rationality, modern nation-state apparatuses, and capitalism is necessarily suppressive of nonconforming sociocultural relations and expressiveness. The study of these silenced, dismissed everyday practices is at once "critical practice and . . . a form of practical criticism" (Highmore 2002: 26, 113) that emphasizes the way "representation" operates as power politics and contestations of the same.

A third strand is de Certeau's center-staging of these "ordinary" practices as *inter*subjective inter*actions*. This is not a behavioralist, Pavlov's dog notion of social relationships or identity formation as action–reaction, however. It is a psychodynamic understanding of how "subjects" interact with and counteract one another as individuals and as members of a collective – relations that operate at conscious and unconscious levels of re-cognition that coalesce within lifetimes and through succeeding generations. Following Freud's insights on the psychopathology of everyday life, de Certeau argues that articulations of the everyday are significant – not incidental – to the overt and covert functioning of a sociocultural and political economic (world) order (de Certeau 1984: xiii/1980a: 12).[7] As they emerge and submerge over time, these habits, patterns, and detours can be traced (Giard and Mayol 1980: 14 *passim*). *Doing* is the focus, in that process and practice are used as verbs, not nouns (de Certeau 1984: xviii/1980a: 20). Everyday life is where power is exerted through the "oppression of the here-and-now" but also where it is queried, "poached" from, and thereby resisted.[8] Gender power relations calcify and "wobble" at the micro level of intimate relationships as well as at the level of institutionalized forms of status, wealth, and emotional gratification (Peterson and Runyan 1999: 46–48). The researcher thereby "discovers before [her] interlocutors, who, even if they are not specialists, are themselves subject-producers of histories, and partners in a shared discourse. From the subject–object relationship, we pass to a plurality of authors and contracting parties" (de Certeau 1986: 217).

This historical-methodological point resonates with critical IR/IPE in three ways. First, if "everyday life invents itself by poaching in countless ways on the property of others" (de Certeau 1984: xii/1980a: 10), then, second, the "presence and circulation of a representation (taught by preachers, educators, and popularizers as the key to socioeconomic advancement) tells us nothing about what it is for its users. We must first analyze its manipulation by users who are not its makers" (de Certeau 1984: xiii/1980a: 12). Research politics and political action are situated in everyday life because its many " 'ways of operating' constitute the innumerable practices by means of which users *reappropriate* the space organized by the techniques of sociocultural [and political economic] production" (de Certeau 1984: xv/1980a: 14; emphasis added).

In presenting an immanent critique of how politics needs to be rethought (whether as organized forms of mobilization, democratic theories, or forms of direct action) in the light of capitalism's hegemonic power, de Certeau acknowledges the seductive rewards of "logocentric" thinking (1980a: 19; see also Godzich 1986; Nustad 2004; Borradori 2003). Both elites and nonelites live and think in the "technocratically constructed, written and functionalized" spaces of the social (and world) order (de Certeau 1984: xviii/1980a: 17). But because of the narrow margins for maneuver for those who are not privy to the advantages that accrue through power and privilege, de Certeau argues that nonelite "tactics of consumption, the ingenious ways in which the weak make use of the strong, thus lend a political dimension to everyday practices" (1984: xvii/1980a: 18–19). How so exactly? Let me unpack these three strands a bit more.

Everydayness

For de Certeau, "everydayness" comprises a "proliferation of stories and heterogeneous operations that make up the patchworks of everyday life"

(1980a: 20; my translation). Physical displacements and oral articulations are "constructed-in-process" by those who inhabit and think them. These patchworks – the domain of "popular culture," in other words – have been marginalized, virtually silenced by the powers that be (de Certeau 1984: xvi–xvii/1980a: 17–18). The multifarious *"manières de faire"* (ways of doing things) comprising the everyday become substituted by regimes of representation: ideas and systems based on how things *should* or *must* have been done (see Ahearne 1995: 132 *passim*; de Certeau 1984: 94/1980a: 175 *passim*). The power differential lies in the gap between ordinary people's lack of access to the regimes – "techniques of sociocultural production" – that constitute (covert and overt) gender power relations. This is what de Certeau means when he refers to the difference between nonelite producers – *fabricateurs* (de Certeau 1984: xii/1980a: 11 *passim*) – in the workplace on the one hand, and those who own and control the means of production and, by extrapolation, the socioeconomic "establishment" on the other. Producers in the first instance are engaged in a process of

> production, a poiēis . . . but a hidden one, because it is scattered over areas defined and occupied by systems of 'production' (television, urban development, commerce, etc.), and because the steadily increasing expansion of these systems no longer leaves 'consumers' any place in which they can indicate what they make or do with the products of these systems.
>
> (de Certeau 1984: xii/1980a: 11)

In this sense, de Certeau's concept of everyday life and the experiences, spaces, inter/subjective interactions (such as cooking, running errands, household spaces, everyday uses of local amenities) that comprise it entails actions and behaviors that "poach" from the established order (de Certeau 1984: 6 *passim*/1980a: 41 *passim*; 1986: 199 *passim*; see also Roberts 1999: 27).

Tactical and strategic operations

In any established "order of things" (Foucault 1973; de Certeau 1986: 171 *passim*), the difference between those who have power and who can exert it (re-present "normality," "common sense," "norms and values" for one and all) and those who do not can be understood as the distinction between the "strategic" and the "tactical" operations of everyday life (see Buchanan 2000: 89; Ahearne 1995: 161–164; Highmore 2002: 156–161). These are played out, articulated, and received in varying degrees as an uneasy truce between power-brokers and their subjects, or "audience" (de Certeau 1984: xvii, 38–39/1980a: 19, 88–89). For de Certeau, *strategy* is posited as the calculus of force-relationships which becomes possible when a subject of will and power (a proprietor, an enterprise, a city, a scientific institution) can be isolated from an 'environment.' A strategy assumes a place that can be circumscribed as proper (*propre*) and thus serve as the basis for generating relations with an exterior distinct from it (competitors, adversaries, 'clienteles,' 'targets,' of 'objects' of research). Political, economic, and scientific rationality has been constructed on this strategic model.

(1984: xix/1980a: 20–21)

Under these conditions, "polysemic" everyday practices from below are inherently tactical. A *tactic* is a

calculus which cannot count on a 'proper' (a spatial or institutional localization), nor thus on a borderline distinguishing the other as a visible totality. The place of a tactic belongs to the other. A tactic insinuates itself into the other's place, fragmentarily, without taking it over in its entirety, without being able to keep it at a distance. It has at its disposal no base where it can capitalize on its advantages, prepare its expansions, and secure independence with respect to circumstances.

(de Certeau 1984: xix/1980a: 21)[9]

Political agency can be – and is – exercised every day, whether or not practitioners are aware of it (Buchanan 2000: 89; Thompson 1963). This creative agency cannot be reduced to the pronouncements of either respective political vanguards or political incumbents' "spin doctors." Everyday practices are tactical *because* they are vibrant, diverse, and unpredictable in the final analysis. Practices of this sort need to be taken seriously, for they persist within, between, and in spite of power-full "*machinerie de la représentation*" – machinery of representation (de Certeau 1984: 147/1980a: 253; see also Hall 1996a).

Representation

De Certeau finds the political substance of this push and pull between tactical practices (as spoken or written recitations, physical displacements) and hegemonic, strategic ones by locating the respective techniques and systems of representation that are in play (de Certeau 1984: xiii–xiv, 147/1980a: 12, 253; Buchanan 2000: 89),[10] namely, the way in which human subjects are made into (research or political) objects, truth is frozen in time, history fixed in space, social relations and cultural "traditions" reified (de Certeau 1980: 249 *passim*; Ahearne 1995: 131). Acknowledging Foucault's insight into the psychological, corporeal, and cognitive disciplining of Western medical, educational, and political institutions, de Certeau asks rhetorically:

Is there a limit to the machinery by which a society represents itself in living beings and makes them its representations? Where does the disciplinary apparatus end that displaces and corrects, adds or removes things from these bodies, malleable under the instrumentation of so many laws?

(1984: 147/1980a: 254)

The "scriptural economies" of these representations (de Certeau 1984: 131 *passim*/1980a: 231 *passim*) record the official version of events. Assumptions about truth-value and empirical or analytical "relevance" become contained in which records – archives – are filed and then consulted over time. Scriptural economies serve strategic ends in that access to official archives, authorship, and scientific legitimacy, policy making on the ground, the physical and virtual entry and exit points of the "global information infrastructure" and concomitant knowledge industries (software), the ownership and control of cultural reproduction (media), designate literal and figurative power. All along (in)subordinate knowledge practices, like "savoir-faire," "folk wisdom," "old wives' tales," or myths and legends, persist (Giard and Mayol 1980: 149–154; de Certeau 1984: xx/1980a: 23). Everyday articulations are ignored precisely because they are amorphous, informal, and thereby difficult to pin down. Hence, projects that attempt to "re-capture" these instances and honor them entail a politics of research (see de Certeau 1984: xix/1980a: 21). As Ortner puts it, this approach focuses on

looking at and listening to real people doing real things in a given historical moment, past or present, and trying to figure out how what they are doing or have done will or will not reconfigure the world they live in.

(Ortner 1996: 2)

(Spatial) practices

De Certeau makes another set of distinctions in his conceptualization of "practice," one in which he critically draws on the practice theories of Michel Foucault and Pierre Bourdieu (de Certeau 1984: 45 *passim*/1980a: 101 *passim*). Everyday life comprises textual and spatial practices: as reading/writing and physical and cognitive traversals, whether these take place in city streets, kitchens, or in Internet discussion forums. Written, read, or oral "texts" are *spatially* drawn by those who write, speak, and move in them. If the spoken word is also a form of spatialization, then there is also a politics of representation at stake in the presence or submersion of oral histories and other nonwritten narratives (de Certeau 1984: 148/1980a: 255; and see Friedman 1998). In his application of the notion of "text," de Certeau is positing that meaning is not only contained in the semiotic structure, or even the manifest content, of written text (Hawkes 1997). Meaning and interpretation – "Content" – are at all points (albeit in different ways) social interchanges between producers and audience. As such, the "text" cannot be analyzed in isolation from the particular and broader sociohistorical context of its production and reception. In short, "any account is an account of a journey – a spatial practice" (de Certeau 1984: 115/1980a: 206); a *traversal* in all senses of the term. In not subscribing to the "high structuralism" of semiotics and linguistics, de Certeau allows for a more politically grounded approach to everyday spaces as texts; as material and virtual traversals.[11] A research politics such as this questions, on both entering and leaving the field,

> both the text's power of composing and distributing places, its ability to be a narrative of space, and the necessity for it to define its relation to what it treats, in other words, to construct a place of its own. The first aspect concerns the space of the other; the second the place of the text.
>
> (de Certeau 1986: 67–68)

This field of thought, feeling, and action that links texts (words, images) and physicality (geographies and topographies) is an understanding of space as historically constructed social relations. As Clifford notes, for

> de Certeau, 'space' is never ontologically given. It is discursively mapped and corporeally practised . . . it is not a space until it is practised by peoples' active occupation, their movements through and around it. In this perspective there is nothing given about a 'field.' It must be worked, turned into a discrete social space, by embodied practices of interactive travel.
>
> (Clifford 1997: 54)

Every day, meanings are exchanged, circulated and then relived. They are "practised by people's active occupation" (Clifford 1997: 54; and see Huyssen 1990: 259 *passim*; de Certeau 1986: 171 *passim*) and therein also contested. Online textual-spatial practices are emerging to reinforce, counter, or reconfigure extant ones, be they of the tactical or the strategic variety. Pacific Island communicative cultures – as oral recitations, bodily engravings, song, and cumulative narratives – recognize this insight as a matter of course.[12] For Western scriptural economies, this understanding of space as qualitative and relational (versus fixed and quantifiable) runs counter to how historically based truth (claims) as written knowledge have become tied to forms of direct governance within bordered geographies (Anderson 1991).

This stress on interactivity puts the deeds of the objective, dispassionate "knowledge expert" firmly into perspective. In other words, the "objects" of research are living, breathing beings with something to say that necessarily impacts on the knowledge produced, as a "shared discourse" (de Certeau 1986: 204, 217). In any case, acknowledged or not, all knowledge production is beholden to its particular sociocultural and political economic context – a seemingly obvious point in critical/constructivist claims, yet one that is not necessarily resolved methodologically (see Chapter 8). Michel de Certeau recenters the aforementioned "shadowy" players by putting the spotlight on their inter/subjectivities as opposed to those of either powerful – and dissenting – elites:

> Our sciences were born with that 'modern' historical act that depoliticized research by establishing 'disinterested' and 'neutral' fields of study supported by scientific institutions.... Having become actual seats of logistic power, scientific institutions have fitted themselves into the system they serve to rationalize, a system that links them to each other, fixes the direction of their research, and assures their integration into existing socioeconomic framework.
>
> (1986: 215)

This has implications for how researchers locate, position themselves in the field, and more so when this field is spliced with "non-Western" practices of everyday life, their practitioners, and respective tactical and strategic operations.

2 Contentions and intersections

Interdisciplinary caveats

Because of his eclecticism and his own multidisciplinary career path, let alone the way the very notion of the everyday has become appropriated by advertising and marketing (see Chapter 2), de Certeau's work does not sit easily in any one discipline (Ahearne 1995: 2–4; Godzich 1986: vii–viii; Buchanan 2000: 1 *passim*, 97).[13] That being said, some brief comments are needed with respect to the interdisciplinary nature of his approach and how it has been perceived by Marxian frameworks in particular.

First, this treatment of de Certeau supports John Roberts's general aim of excavating the original political import of the *everyday* in early twentieth-century Marxian thought. It does not concur with his final conclusions, however. In his article, Roberts revisits the political historiography of the "everyday" in order to "restore an expanded understanding of the term [albeit] ... not to diminish the postwar theorization of the everyday in France, but to problematize its history and incorporation into contemporary cultural studies" (Roberts 1999: 16). What I take issue with is his verdict on how de Certeau's contribution is "paradigmatic" of this "postmodern incorporation" (ibid.: 28) of a once critical category into a "philosophically diminished cultural studies" (ibid.: 29). There is no reason to assume that de Certeau's understanding of the "everyday as a site of complex and differentiated social agency and subjectivity" (ibid.: 28) *necessarily* separates political action from any "structural engagement with the problems of material distribution and economic justice" (ibid.: 28). That de Certeau's approach has been "poached" in turn by apolitical, empiricist audience research projects and, moreover, that "everyday life" itself has become the site *par excellence* for inculcated consumption patterns in consumerist societies is all the more reason for recalling the critical kernel of his work. Stressing the productive intersection between Lefebvre's more pessimistic view of everyday alienation and de Certeau's insistence that this need not mean losing sight of unexpected and spontaneous forms of sociopolitical resistance is more to the point.

That said, de Certeau's terms of reference, vocabulary, literary style (Buchanan 2000: 33 *passim*), and highly critical stance toward universalistic epistemological standpoints are part of the critiques of "rational man" and "his" "instrumental reason" emanating from feminist, postcolonial, poststructuralist *and* postmodern literatures (Huyssen 1990: 276, note 39). A categorical dismissal of de Certeau's political credentials because of his focus on how meaning is constituted by and through language, power through symbolic and material "circulations of meaning," is inaccurate and unjust. For de Certeau, meanings-as-practices are deeply political. They have material and figurative characteristics that are imbricated in the political economy of their respective social (world) order (de Certeau 1986: 119). At the same time, resistance by those who are often cast as silent victims of an existing order (de Certeau 1984: xiii/1980a: 12), appropriate and rework these impositions in an array of "other" spoken, written, and physical practices (see Roberts 1999: 27 *passim*).

This is a selective introduction to de Certeau's thought. The link still needs to be made to the practice of everyday life of postcolonial diasporas on the one hand and the emergence of cyberspatial practices (tactical and strategic operations thereof) on the other in the twenty years since he died. The need for updating and extension notwithstanding,[14] this thinker contributes to a strand of critical theory and research that "takes seriously the problem of combining the 'political-economic' and the 'cultural' without reducing one to the other" (Jackson 1993: 224). Hence his circumspection about political vanguards' claim to represent all downtrodden groups as well as the more relativistic tendencies of some interpretative modes of inquiry. This is why (meta)theoretical issues and their practical – empirical research – implications are treated in his work simultaneously. This "double/multiplex" (Friedman 1998: 37) approach is central to de Certeau's research politics.[15] Locating the subtleties of everyday practices and letting them remain fluid does not in itself lead to a "dissolution of collective politics into cultural politics" (Roberts 1999: 27). Nor does it mean an "inevitable" resignation to the gender power relations of a "class [based or any other] society" (ibid.: 27) where only a "politics of feints, dodges and lucid subversion" (ibid.: 27) is permissible. What de Certeau and many postcolonial/feminist critiques are getting at is the need for more modesty on the part of those claiming the right to "represent" the "other" sociopolitical reality. As we shall see, Pacific Island diasporic groups' online textual-spatial practices underscore these tactical "dodges" vis-à-vis strategic impositions continually. In these (cyber)spaces at least, people can articulate "resistance and creativity" because they are enabled to "'rewrite' the oppressive details of their surfaces" (ibid.: 27) in their "enactment[s] of fantasy and autobiographical storytelling, [cyber]walking and day-dreaming" (ibid.: 27).

A fourth point relates to where this particular tracking of de Certeau's work intersects with other disciplines, including the more recent one of Internet research.[16] Postcolonial anthropological and feminist work privilege the "everyday" (Clifford 1997: 53–54; Wilson 1999: 2–4). As I have noted, his approach is also sympathetic to various sorts of critical discourse analysis and their various ways of focusing on the constitutive role of language in meaning-making processes and inter/subjectivity (Fairclough 2003). His methodological interventions are also imbued with an ongoing critical thread that highlights differential gender power relations in academic knowledge production (Clifford 1997: 52 *passim*; de Certeau 1986: 199 *passim*). In media studies and cultural studies, de Certeau's accent on users as active, nonpassive appropriators and designers of cultural and technological artifacts (1984: xii–xiv, 29 *passim*/1980a: 11–13, 75 *passim*) has become a key point. It is also prominent in work on consumption patterns, uses and gratification research, reception analysis, technology and everyday life research (see Silverstone and Haddon 1996; Curran and Gurevitch 1991; van Zoonen 1994). Seeing as the theoretical canon of twentieth-century international relations pivots on historical analyses, de Certeau's historical work is also instructive (Ahearne 1995: 9; de Certeau 1988).

Another aspect to note is where de Certeau lines up with "Third World" or postcolonial streams in feminist theory and politics. While his work also critiques Eurocentric models and ways of "othering" subaltern groups, as Ortner notes, this mutual interest has not been as productively drawn as it could have been. Somehow, "practice theory" and feminist theory (broadly defined) have ended up on either side of a "fairly deep divide" (Ortner 1996: 3).[17] In IR/IPE debates, where lines are being drawn between (post)structuralist and/or constructivist approaches and then between their respective (non-)Marxian proponents, Lefebvre and Bourdieu have been largely incorporated by Marx's heirs while Foucault, Derrida, and Deleuze and Guattari have been taken up by those who take their distance from Marxian/structuralist ("globalist") models. This is a gross simplification of a rich and intense set of IR/IPE debates but, nonetheless, the accompanying polemic about postmodernism, as both a historical and a theoretical (per)version of social theory, may go some way in explaining why de Certeau's work has been overlooked in this literature. I would argue that this is a loss: his is a subversive political theory (see Buchanan 2000: 91) in that it refutes the peopleless and anarchic "vacuum" in which most IR/IPE models are placed (see Wendt 1999: 402; Wilson 1999: 2). As Wlad Godzich points out,

> de Certeau has clear, practical aims. There is thus something very atheoretical about his endeavor, not because of any opposition to theory as such, but because the old construction of the opposition of theory and practice is part of the speculative edifice that de Certeau no longer finds hospitable, or perhaps more accurately, affordable. It exacts too high a price [for those it professes to be helping] for the amenities that it provides. But this atheoretical stance does not make for an absence of theory in what he writes. . . . It simply makes for a different positioning of the theoretical.
>
> (1986: viii)

This repositioning of the subject–object to a subject–subject relationship in processes of knowledge production and political mobilization (de Certeau 1986: 217, 225–233) opens up productive avenues for engaging with postcolonial and diasporic practices of everyday life, online and/or on the ground.[18]

(Cyber)spatial practices and postcolonial diasporas

If ICTs are socially and historically "co-constructed" (Harding 1998a: 146; 1998b; Haraway 1990), then they do more than simply impact upon inter/national political or economic relations as external forces. In the struggles for ownership and control of acknowledged significant fields of sociotechnological change, both "tactical acts" and "hegemonic strategies" are in play (Wilson 1999: 2). All of these have gender, ethnic, and class contours to them as various vested interests and inter/subjectivities become (re)articulated by and through the material and so-called virtual features of the Internet/World Wide Web. The practice of everyday life thereby acquires both cyberspatial and postcolonial dimensions. So how does de Certeau's stance connect with those practices of South Pacific Island diasporic groups, whose *oppression du présent* straddles life in Western societies and the Pacific islands? James Clifford locates these conceptual and historical conjunctures well when he points out that contemporary

> articulations of 'diaspora' . . . [are] ways of sustaining connections with more than one place while practising non-absolutist forms of citizenship. . . . The diasporic and hybrid identities produced . . . can be

both restrictive and liberating. They stitch together languages, traditions, and places in coercive and creative ways, articulating embattled homelands, powers of memory, styles of transgression, in ambiguous relation to national and transnational structures. It is difficult to evaluate, even to perceive, the range of emerging practices.

(1997: 9, 10)

Which brings me to the multifarious "invocations" (ibid.: 244) and experiences that constitute the *postcolonial* – as concept and experience. This "elusive and contested term ... designates at one and the same time a chronological movement, a political movement, and an intellectual activity, and it is this multiple status that makes exact definition difficult" (Moore-Gilbert *et al.* 1997: 1). The postcolonial/post-colonial denotes more than a bygone era of colonial rule.[19] Western Samoa and Tonga belong to this category in the sense that they both ceased to be New Zealand and British protectorates respectively in the 1960s. It denotes more than "before" and "after" chronologies.

The 'post' in postcolonialism does not indicate the belief that colonialism is dead and buried, a matter of the past with no bearing on the present. Quite to the contrary, it is a form of periodization which aggressively signals the centrality of colonialism to the entire historical period after it. . . . The colonial encounter was also decisive in the making of the modern world.

(Seth 1999: 215)

It has also come to designate an important constellation of theorizing and research that anchors the social and historical construction of contemporary realities in the history of colonialism and its aftermath, one that involves both colonizer and colonized (Ashcroft *et al.* 1998: 186; Chowdhry and Nair 2002; Ling 2002). This intellectual enterprise

foregrounds the connection between knowledge and power, and also between knowledge and forms of human community, of ways of being in the world. What is at issue here, it is important to emphasise, is much more than the "cultural imperialism" and arrogance which were part and parcel of the colonial enterprise. . . . What postcolonialism seeks to problematise and call into question, however, are the knowledges that accompanied and characterised colonialism and its aftermath. Postcolonialism also draws attention to the fact that ... ways of constructing and construing the world are always connected to ways of being-in-the-world.

(Seth 1999: 218)

Postcolonial critiques of "the controlling power of representation in colonized societies" (Ashcroft *et al.* 1998: 187) see these connections as imprinted upon everyday practices and experiences of ethnicity and/or race, which have been represented in hegemonic accounts of the "exotic other," experiences and structures of discrimination and oppression as the "subaltern other," labeling of colonized, non-Western societies as uncivilized, undeveloped, and so on. The historical period of colonialism (now officially "over") overlaps in this respect with the ongoing "political, linguistic and cultural experience of societies that were former European colonies" (ibid.: 186). How far political independence has gone hand in hand with economic well-being is a moot point, one that is present in many of these groups' discussions online. The role of missionaries and the Church, the impact of colonial administrations and contemporary economic dependence on dominant neighbors, key historical narratives, and cultural rituals all figure in debates about how South Pacific societies have been or should be represented – all grist to the mill.

At the heart of much poststructuralist/postcolonial literature is a strong critique of Western knowledge (re)production, the ongoing existence of a center–periphery divide between West and "the rest" notwithstanding – for example, how knowledge (re)production is complicit with the colonialist political and scientific project, forms of institutionalized racism and/or cultural "bleaching" in the name of integration, white middle-class blinkers in feminist theory toward women of color, and so on. All in all, these critiques entail a rethinking of what constitutes inter/subjectivity, an insistence that there is not a unified, single, neutral "knower" standing outside the world as a "modest witness" (Haraway 1997b).

Aside from "disciplinary and interpretative contestation" (Ashcroft *et al.* 1998: 186) around the term in the South Pacific context, it is the material, cultural, and symbolic consequences of colonial "contact" that concern these societies. How these are to be judged – good, bad, un/avoidable – and how these are lived and experienced lies at the heart of the online discussions, as they do in the lives and (diasporic) communities they articulate. Dealing with the postcolonial entails more than a yearning for halcyon days of the past. Whose memories dominate is a cultural product in what Wilson calls this "mixed-up era of technoeuphoric globalisation and heightened localisation and reindigenisation" (1999: 2). Hence, postcolonial articulations involve disputes about ongoing and internalized "oppressions of the present" and their sociocultural and political economic implications.

I follow Albert Wendt's cue when he stipulates that the "*post* in postcolonial does not just mean after; it also means *around, through, out of, alongside,* and *against*" (quoted in Wilson 1999: 3; original emphasis). As Wendt astutely notes, the prefix can elide the complexity of "defiant texts or scripts of nationalism and identity. Much of the indigenous was never colonised, tamed or erased. And much that we now consider indigenous and postcolonial are colonial constructs (e.g. the church)" (Wendt 1999: 403). Many of the sharpest online discussions from the next chapters pivot on this insight. Added to the fluidity of the prefixes in "pre-" and "post-colonial" is a comparable elasticity with the aforementioned notion of *diaspora* (Clifford 1997: 9–10). Using the two terms as a collocation is not to posit them as synonymous, or inseparable. The former implies the latter as historically situated lives with both material implications and symbolic meaning-making – for instance, in terms of the personal and community-level dynamics of "being Tongan," "being a Samoan woman today." Diaspora as a term denotes the spread, the spatiality of these lived lives and the nonessentializable nature of their sociocultural and political economic contexts.

From proximate quartier to cyberspace

ICTs are no more exogenous features to "postcolonial" and/or diasporic histories and lived lives than they are to those political economies in which they were first developed. All I am noting above, arguably under-scored by the "translocal," to use Clifford's phrase, characteristics of Inter-net technologies is that *diaspora* and *postcolonial* are "traveling terms" "in changing global conditions" (Clifford 1997: 244). World Wide Web com-munications refract and "dehierarchize" the physically proximate features of urban neighborhoods and their surrounding cityscape. In an online *quartier*, spatial practices of the everyday can be discerned not only in the immediate on-screen content, symbols, and conversations, but also in the complete or partial texts left behind in caches, pointed to in "file deleted" or "server down" notices, online statistical records such as "total hits," elec-tronic tags such as "cookies," the server logs, email "mailboxes," the ubiq-uitous hyperlink itself, the appearance and disappearance of avatars in live chat scenarios, and so on. While these are digital comings and goings, they are nonetheless actual ones, part of a whole new set of polysemic "murmurs" of the everyday that overlie those on the ground ("offline"). The texts comprising these discussions have their own particularities: "onlineness," as we will see. Cyberspatial practices construct other sorts of proximity, (re)embodiment with both familiar and new tactical and/or strategic operations in play.

Another caveat is that the everyday practices of (dispersed) non-Western peoples are not reducible to those quintessentially European ones analyzed by de Certeau and his colleagues, Giard and Mayol. But this is not to say that they belong to the subordinate end of a tradition-versus-modernity spectrum. Moreover, Pacific Island diasporas are clustered in urban centers in the West, and when they are not, their Internet access mostly occurs in urban centers in the islands (Apia, Honolulu, Suva, Nuku'alofa). For second- and third-generation Pacific Islanders growing up in the United States, Australia, New Zealand, and elsewhere, these spatial practices are part and parcel of shifts – both liberating and frustrating – in personal, family, social, and cultural relationships. When meeting and conversing online, these practitioners trace their own "tactical" (re)appropriations of Internet technologies for their own personal and community needs. At the very least, these traversals underscore de Certeau's goal of retrieving the agency of "everyday life" from power-elite representations of what "culture," "politics," "the Internet" actually do, or should entail. Such vested interests are quick to categorize everyday life, online or offline, to the realm of the "banal" and the "irrelevant" (Giard and Mayol 1980: 7–9). The subaltern "others" absented from mainstream accounts have always been "there," in the center of their own worlds, their own inter/subjectivities, political economic and sociocultural institutions, and struggles.[20] These distinctions need to be borne in mind when setting out to study the everyday life of, say, a French working-class family (ibid.), an Internet community (Rheingold 1994), and that of (diverse) Pacific island diasporic groups' online traversals (also, arguably, an "Internet community").[21] On the ground, these discussion forums' constituencies are living as a "minority of a minority" (Aiono 1999: interview) in hi-tech societies and conversing with each other under different criteria online, albeit with ongoing references to those "back home in the islands." The diverse "cultural practices" (Ashcroft *et al.* 1998: 62) at stake emanate from several sources and create different pressure points at one and the same time. The World Wide Web has provided an arguably larger, more accessible, more permeable space in which to observe and/or participate in these traversals. For postcolonial diasporas, everyday life has its own set of "oppressions of the present." And the past, for that matter.

To sum up: In unison with critical constructivist moods in IR/IPE, Michel de Certeau's practice theory is one that privileges modes of inquiry that are "speaking up" as opposed to "speaking down" in its emphasis on nonelite expressions and experiences of agency (Chen 1996; Ahearne 1995: 15 *passim*; de Certeau 1984: 130, 222, note 28/1980a: 227, 362, note 28). Nonelite Internet practitioners leave behind them visible and audible traces as they enter and exit their online *quartiers*. Time needs to be taken to follow these movements and moments as constituting "space as a practised place" (de Certeau 1984: 130/1980a: 227) where "people's active occupation, their movements through and around [any space]" happen (Clifford 1997: 54). This recalls a research ethics that makes explicit how all discourses are

> mode[s] of language use ... [that] constitute forms of social interaction and practice. As such, they are not irrational, but they are subject to the pulls and pressures of the situations in which they are used as well as to the weights of their own tradition.
>
> (Godzich 1986: xx)

How does one go about studying such practices? In the next section, I deal with the empirical research component to this study.

3 Everyday life research online

While differing in temperament and emphasis from his more pessimistic contemporary Henri Lefebvre, Michel de Certeau focuses on everyday life practices *as they unfold* in space and *over time* in capitalist societies. Whereas the former sees everyday life as "an arena for the reproduction of dominant [capitalist, alienated] social relations," for de Certeau the everyday can still be "a site of resistance, revolution and transformation" despite the strictures imposed by the powers that be (Highmore 2002: 17, 28–31). Either way, as both an "object" of research and a site for research, everyday life is "characterised by ambiguities, instabilities and equivocation" (ibid.: 17). The vast amount and variety of data concerning everyday life appear to be in inverse proportion to analytical – explanatory – efficiency; nuance and fluidity overpower causal clarity. Practice theorists and "everyday life" research into everyday uses of technology – in the home or workplace – operate within a theory–research nexus that grounds detail – practices and processes – firmly in broader analytical frameworks (Mansell and Silverstone 1996; Callon and Latour 1981). As Pierre Mayol and Luce Giard show in their application of de Certeau to researching everyday "living" and "cooking," a variety of research methods can be used to examine how "*la vie quotidienne*" operates: from mapping spatial and affective interactions within a family home vis-à-vis the immediate neighborhood to recording women talking about cooking (Giard and Mayol 1980; Highmore 2002: 152–153, 158).

However, this shift in perspective, moving from the favored "macro" perspective (of IR/IPE in this case) to the more "micro" approaches of everyday life research (Highmore 2002: 24–26), does give rise to some thorny methodological issues. For a start, a privileging of the "cacophony of the everyday" (ibid.: 23) does not offer ready-made parameters for data gathering. Nor does it provide tidy taxonomies for presenting the results. In mainstream international relations/international political economy, where, by and large, "parsimonious" theoretical hypotheses are seen as synonymous with "rigorous" scientific method, linear historical narratives seen as synonymous with explanatory (predictive) veracity, and statistics seen as facts, this is inexplicable. Moreover, paying attention to the complexity of everyday lives and arguing that these are relevant to the study of the international state system, world order/s, war, and peace is not regarded as part of this discipline's brief. Incorporating participant-observation techniques or using a "mixed method" creates more consternation with respect to where the outer and inner limits of the research field lie. Ben Highmore addresses this credibility gap for "everyday life theory" and, indeed, much research done in a "social constructivist" mood very well in noting that unless it is going to simply register the cacophony of the everyday, [everyday life theory] has to find some way of ordering, of organising the everyday. Here the theoretical is precisely the problem of ordering and arranging, of making some kind of sense of the endless empiricism of the everyday. . . . So even at the level of collecting data, more fundamental problems intrude, namely the problem of making the everyday meaningful in a way that doesn't imprison it at the level of the particular, or doesn't eradicate the particularity of the particular by taking off into abstract generalities. This problem can be seen as the dilemma of negotiating between the microscopic levels (most frequently classed as everyday) and macroscopic levels of the totality (culture, society [and world politics] and so on).

(2002: 23, 24–25)

I deal with these practicalities in two ways. In the section below is a summary of the empirical parameters of this – Internet – research field: where it took place on the Web, the time span, how material (the "discussion threads") was gathered, collated, and then handled. Together with the previous section, this is the "hermeneutic schematic" for the next four chapters. As this study is informed by feminist and postcolonial critiques of "objective" knowledge production, the personal and institutional settings of these empirical elements need to be addressed. I do this by unpacking the methodological implications of the empirical component in Chapter 8. The rationale behind this two-tier approach is a rejection of "determinist approaches both to narratives of a human life and to narratives of technological change" in the first instance and an "approach to technology [that] emphasises the many issues which need to be considered when attempting to understand *both its development and use*" in the second (Henwood *et al.* 2001: 24; emphasis added). To this I would add a third ingredient: a rejection of structurally determinist accounts of how technology, society, and culture interact during periods in which a "global shift" is deemed to be occurring.

In neither account do I assume that the technical features of Internet technologies are either self-evident or *terra incognita* to the reader. Some may be way ahead of me in terms of in/formal computer programming knowledge or training, dexterity with software research tools, discussion or newsgroup moderating, website design, and so forth. Of that I have no doubt. But others may still be wondering what Internet relay chat (IRC) discussion, a live chat avatar, "posts," or HTML (hypertext markup language), IPs (Internet protocols), and suchlike actually are. Others may not even care. Internet technologies are a constellation of highly specialized and banal codes, technological artifacts, and integrated systems. They comprise various degrees of interactive and passive operability, low and high thresholds of expertise, and access to more deeply embedded codes below the "user interface" – and, above all, ever-increasing degrees of integration and interoperability, adaptational malleability, and inertia at the same time (Quintas 1996; Hawkins 1996; Franklin 2003a).

I will assume, though, that the reader has some working knowledge of electronic mail (email), World Wide Web use, and personal computing word-processing or "office" software for writing and administrative tasks. Lest I be accused of being pedantic or patronizing, the first two activities have become fully incorporated across the board in universities, schools, and government departments only since the mid-1990s (an uptake contingent upon national-regional technology policy, dispersion patterns, university budgets, and private income brackets). Nowadays, academic conferences, teacher–student, and peer-to-peer exchanges would be unimaginable without the ubiquitous email, PowerPoint presentations, and online teaching software. Writing and thinking are also increasingly framed by computer programs, a development that is greeted with various degrees of lack of interest and dismay.

Online topographies

To recall. The discussion forums and live chat sites of the Pacific Forum and Polynesian Cafe have been going strong since the early 1990s, steadily patronized by a core of regulars and people "passing through." How many exactly depends on the parameters that are set: if by email listserv lists, then the total is in the hundreds; if by the number of "hits" a website gets, then thousands to tens of thousands. The age range of participants is from 17 to 50-plus years of age (by their own admission). There are grandparents, parents of young children, university and high-school students, young professionals, and the occasional participant using public Internet access (libraries, for instance). When not high-school students (often discernible by both topic and idiom), participants tend to be in their twenties or thirties (Aiono 1999: interview; Kami 2001: interview). Many participants are practicing Christians and/or socially "conservative" (Pacific island churches are important social backbones in the islands and abroad), particularly those using the Tongan-based Kava Bowl.[22]

There is also a fairly equal spread of men and women – both by name and by explicit identification (Morton 1998a/2001), although this depends on the subject matter, as we will see. My own feminist sensibility has meant that I have privileged the women's voices and explicit "gender content" whenever possible, especially given the enabling properties offered by online (quasi)anonymity in certain instances.[23] The data pool of discussion threads studied here spans 1997–2002 mainly. Not counting a substantial set of threads on religion and sexuality, for the reconstructions in the next four chapters, the total number of five years of individual messages read, printed, collated into their respective threads, and then grouped according to recurring and/or significant themes is at least

6,500, a total of about 250 integral threads. The breakdown of this data pool is given in Table 3.1.

The average number of follow-ups per initial post (which is the beginning point for collation) is about twenty-eight, although intense debates can go up to over 100 messages, ranging from the very brief (a couple of sentences) to pages long. There is a positive correlation between a high follow-up rate and participation, despite multiple postings from individuals (Figure 3.1).

The peak years for both forums were 1977–2001, which is when their constituencies consolidated and online interpersonal and power relationships crystallized. An important thing to remember is that these are open, accessible websites. Access to the various forums (live chat excepted) is not password protected, nor is it contingent upon a mandatory registration of one's "membership" and thereby personal information data-collection. Although moderated, and "owned" by their individual founders, who also carry partial legal liability for online content, the forums are largely self-regulating.[24] The demographic and thematic composition of the Kava Bowl and Kamehameha Roundtable have differed to some extent in terms of topics raised by their respective populations (Tongan or Samoan respectively), online visuals, and moderating and writing styles. The Kava Bowl Forum was originally a Tongan meeting place – for both the diaspora and those in Tonga, albeit with regular visits from Samoan and other guests. It dealt mainly with Tongan preoccupations, though not exclusively so.[25] The Polycafe was set up later with a "Polynesian" angle and is heavily patronized by American and Western Samoans based in Los Angeles (and other parts of the United States), Australia, and New Zealand. These distinctions are not overly emphasized here because the two forums have been hyperlinked to one another, and participants have crossed back and forth all along. I have noted these overlaps, and certain distinctions and divergences, where apposite.[26] In 1999–2000, a demographic shift started to occur between and within the two forums. As the

Table 3.1 Data pool: discussion threads/chapter theme

Theme	Total initial posts	Total follow-ups	Total posts	Average follow-ups
I'm tired of slaving myself	42	957	999	22.7
A play on the royal demons	21	1,285	1,306	61.2
I define my own identity	28	685	713	24.5
Please refrain from using capitals	71	2,000	2,071	28.2
Kava Bowl weekly discussion topics	52	1,100	1,152	21.2
Total	**214**	**6,027**	**6,241**	**28.2**

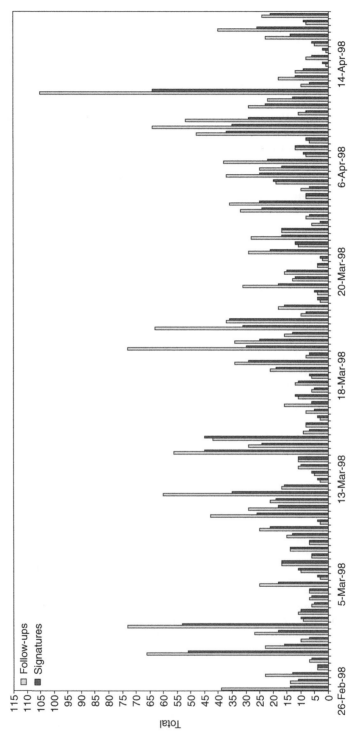

Figure 3.1 Participation rate in the Kava Bowl, February–April 1998.

Kava Bowl started to go offline at regular intervals in early 2000, KB regulars simply shifted to the Polycafe/KR, eventually merging what had always been two closely linked spaces (other Tongan-specific websites were by now on offer anyway). How this panned out online and the potential of this for offline relationships between Samoan and Tongan communities are also part of these particular online traversals. By 2001, the Kava Bowl discussion forums had gone offline.[27]

The second and third generations of the mid-twentieth-century "Polynesians overseas" produce the largest number of online texts. When these participants are interacting with those posting directly from Tonga, Samoa, Fiji, or elsewhere, there can be some sharp disagreements. Where someone is posting from becomes manifest at these moments, and also points to other sociocultural and psychoemotional subtexts in play. For instance, those hailing from beyond the Pacific Islands – often looking to get in touch with their or their children's "Poly" roots[28] – can be taken to task for their (perceived) relative lack of on-the-ground knowledge and experience. For regular or new posters of (non-)Polynesian origin, the same applies. In more intense debates, credible arguments can become linked to ethnic/cultural "credentials" of various degrees. While the KB and KR forums were set up for "serious" discussion, and things do get serious, this does not preclude the regular and sophisticated use of humor, satire, and (self-)parody. Whether participants know each other already or have traced each other through extended family connections, they interact online in a number of guises. Participants identify themselves in various ways and for different reasons, as we will see.

There are at least three places to locate self-references: the name (signature) following the title of the message; the (sometimes different) signature in the body of the message itself; and when a participant is directly addressed by their interlocutor by their "real" name or "nickname." These three indicators can occur in any combination, according to the whim of the poster, the relationships between participants (some in fact may be sitting in the same room, are friends or relatives), and as a response to direct confrontation. Online forms of anonymity are, I would contend, less of an issue than one would think, as a closer reading soon shows who the poster is "really."[29] But the use of pseudonyms is more prevalent in more sensitive topics: homo/sexuality, domestic violence, premarital sex, interracial relationships, contentious Pacific Island political issues.[30] One more observation: I would hesitate to reduce the KB and KR discussions to personal identity "crises" only. There are many other topics, spanning local current events to world politics, sport and entertainment; global finance; Pacific politics and economics (of Samoa and Tonga especially); US, New Zealand, and Australian politics; and lots on contemporary social issues. Both portals make space for special-interest subsites with names such as the "Faith Forum," the "Moana Lounge," and suchlike.

Another key input into the Kava Bowl's discussion content, or a consistent source of provocative initial posts at least, was the *Weekly Discussion Topic* (WDT); 71 in total from 1997 to 1999 of which 52 were available for this study (Table 3.1). Emanating from the "pen" of the KB Administration (KBAdmin), these threads were predominantly about Tongan cultural and political issues for contemporary times. The WDTs were popular and created some of the longest threads in this time. The initial posts that kicked off these Weekly Discussion Topics were largely the work of Sandy Macintosh, a non-Tongan (palangi) regular and mainstay of the KB Administration who is still active on the KR. The vivacity of the ensuing threads simply attests to Sandy's status as online (elder) mentor for many of the participants (some of whom are his former pupils). Sandy has often been acknowledged for his local knowledge and fluency in Tongan (he has worked in Tonga), his role in keeping the forums going, and his persistence and engagement with many discussions. Like all non-Polynesian participants (myself included), Sandy is not excluded on the basis of his race/ethnicity. For these are not culturally exclusive cyberspaces in that respect, albeit ones that do have a set of evolving "ground rules." As we will see, when "disrespectful" behavior has occurred, it has been dealt with in specific ways, ways that also trace the postcolonial politics of representation articulated by these practices.

Citing and protecting sources

I have already mentioned some of the ethical dimensions to Internet research, both in itself and from a postcolonial, feminist perspective. The first is when and how the researcher should situate herself during any participant observation scenario, and how much observation is carried out vis-à-vis direct participation (here meant as posting messages myself). Remember that asynchronous discussion software permits any observer-participant to effectively remain "invisible" if they wish, which further complicates the accountability and power differentials surrounding research into "real people" or real-life online interactions (as opposed to fantasy ones, arguably) when observing from afar. To reiterate, I made myself known (as a researcher) early into the research. The forum leaderships and regulars with whom I have posted got to know me accordingly. Apart from "offline" email communications with participants (*ad hoc* rather than formal communications), I have interviewed the forum moderators, aired concerns and earlier drafts with them, and published early version of the findings on the Polycafe's netzine, *iMana*.[31]

Another issue around informants' integrity and right to remain anonymous arises when citing the online texts themselves, especially when they constitute the empirical substance, as is the case here. For an academic research monograph, one of the more pressing issues is the convention of providing transparent, traceable sources of citation vis-à-vis protecting informants' privacy – a key tenet of anthropological research ethics, at least. Both these issues are exacerbated in Internet research scenarios. What is a "real" name? More often than not, participants use a variety of noms de plume that are every bit as "real." They also form a subtext in their own right (Morton 1998a, 2001; Jordan 1999: 59–79).

My approach has been the following: in open Internet forums such as these, participants' interventions are in a sort of public (cyber)domain. Their interventions are, thereby, available for citation. In principle, academic citation decorum intersects here with Pacific notions of "due respect" being paid to the person who is being cited (Chapter 7). In short, transparency preempts (relative) anonymity in this case. Nonetheless, this decision was based on a series of consultations over the years, through responses to a message I posted on the KR about the rights and wrongs of quoting participants, and ongoing consultation with Al Aiono and Taholo Kami (the founders of KR and KB respectively) concerning this citation style. Direct permission was asked for all (relative) offline communications such as email or face-to-face interviews. The placing of all these threads and their authors in the bibliography thereby completes these various academic and sociocultural requirements – the ultimate token of respect for this mixed genre of spoken–printed word. All excerpts in the text indicate the author of the *initial post*, abbreviated name of the discussion forum (KB, KR, THA, SPIN), and the date (month, day, year): for example (MA, THA, 02/29/00). The full bibliographical reference is based on this "signature" (which can be either a name or a whole phrase). Authors and dates of follow-ups to these initial posts are noted accordingly, with varying degrees of detail added where apposite. My argument is that these online texts and their authors demand the same level of courtesy and citation rigor as any other written source. Being Internet documents, and therefore prone to eventual deletion from the server, does not alter their literary status in this respect.[32] I will return to these practical-ethical considerations in Chapter 8.

Another thing to note, a point to which I will return, is the fluidity and amount of textual production involved here. Visible as hypertexted layers and lines of text that wend their way down and across the screen (hence *discussion threads*), these are as intensely *intertextual* as they are *intratextual*. This demands adjustments in how one reads, locates, and interacts with any posting on-screen or as a printout, as it is clicked open, read through, and then closed again. Despite the increasingly sophisticated visuals of user interfaces, Internet-based communications are still predominantly text based (see Figure 8.1, pp. 208–211). One more thing to bear in mind when proceeding to the next four chapters: In these cyberspaces, participants' language and syntax seldom mesh with those of academic lexicons. Colloquialisms, slang, and (un)conscious misspellings are a crucial visual (and phonetic) element to these threads, as is their intertextual – and intercultural – complexity. And, as always, the relationship between events,

actions, and the accompanying narratives is not transparent. People contradict themselves regularly (as they do in on-the-ground conversations), and a
person's own account may well diverge from (their own or others' perceptions of) their behavior at the time. Such contradictions are not explained
away here. Nor are these online articulations posited as more or less relevant, or authentic for that matter, to the offline events and experiences with
which they are dealing. Rather than edit out or explain away apparent
inconsistencies in the manifest content, my interpretative intervention is
designed to make allowances for the complexity of this relationship
between online debates, offline lives, the people who take part in both, and
the variety of possible interpretations of the same material by other readers.
Hence, all excerpts have been reproduced here exactly as they appeared on-
screen, with all the idiosyncratic visuals this entails for a printed format.

Conclusion: a hermeneutic schematic

'Interpretative' is a label that covers rather diverse research traditions
that all start from the way human beings experience, define, organise
and appropriate reality.

(van Zoonen 1994: 131)

How can one construct an intelligible articulation from the archive that
doesn't submerge the polyphonic beneath the editorial voice at work?

(Highmore 2002: 24)

How these conversations and relationships, embodied electronically as
spontaneous, movable texts and digital traces on the Internet, have been
gathered, sifted, organized, and then reconstructed in this study involves
the theoretical-methodological dimensions of "interpretative" research
modes and the everyday-as-archive (van Zoonen 1994; Highmore 2002). *In
toto*, this chapter is the *hermeneutic schematic* for this study of the practice of
everyday life online by postcolonial Pacific peoples living in the
contemporary neoliberal world order. By *schematic* I mean "a structured
framework" (Webster's Dictionary) for collating, organizing, and then
reconstructing these online traversals and their offline reference points.
This schematic is one "way of perceiving cognitively and responding to
[this] complex situation or set of stimuli" (ibid.). It is not being presented
as a comprehensive model for, or of, these online–offline conditions and
the everyday concerns that are brought with them. Rather, it is a conceptual, navigational device for exploring these online traversals.

Second, the term *hermeneutic*. I am not referring here to the body of
theory and research known as hermeneutics and represented by the work
of Hans-Georg Gadamer and Paul Ricoeur (Ulin 1984: 91 *passim*, 126–127;
Fabian 1983: 176–177, note 13). As an adjective, though, hermeneutic
refers to these scholars' focus on the relationship between texts, their

producers, and the broader sociocultural and political economic contexts of their production, and interpretation. As such, this schematic acknowledges that academic scholarly practices have appropriated the

> power to define [these particular] situations and identities, to frame issues and problems, to legitimise interpretations and experiences [that are] unequally distributed along lines of gender, ethnicity, class and a range of other social and discursive formations and (re)produces such inequalities at the same time.
>
> (van Zoonen 1994: 134)

Dealing with the spoken–written word of living people as they come and go online, coming to terms with the particularities of these communicative practices and relationships, is a hermeneutic enterprise. The product is thereby another part of the online–*offline* tapestry being woven, albeit one that has been completed long after these online productions were recorded. For critical IR/IPE research of this sort, the term hermeneutic

> signals a self-understanding of anthropology [and qualitative research enterprises] as interpretative (rather than naively inductive or rigorously deductive). No experience can simply be 'used' as naked data. All personal experience is produced under historical conditions; it must be used with critical awareness and with constant attention to its authoritative claims.
>
> (Fabian 1983: 89)

The constitutive role of language in the practices of inter/subjectivity contributes to the "density of social life" (Ulin 1984: xv). In terms of the politics of knowledge production, this undertaking recognizes that as

> fieldwork comes first and analysis later we begin to realize that the Other as object or content of anthropological knowledge is necessarily part of the knowing subject's past.... That the anthropologist's experienced Other is necessarily part of his [*sic*] past may therefore not be an impediment, but a condition of an interpretative approach.
>
> (Fabian 1983: 88, 89)

Feminist sensibilities concur with Fabian's point here. As Liesbeth van Zoonen argues, what "feminist research has to add to interpretative [hermeneutic] research strategies is a notion of power, and acknowledgment of the structural inequalities involved in and coming out of the process of meaning-making" (van Zoonen 1994: 134; see also Henwood *et al.* 2001: 24–26). Critical theory and research with new domains (such as the Internet) and/or non-Western cultures (most of the world) elucidates the "reflexive character of all interpretative processes in that knowledge of the radical other, whether human interactions, informants, or texts, discloses the uniqueness or historical particularity of the interpreter's cultural tradition" (Ulin 1984: 126–127). As any scientific knowledge entails interpretative operations of some sort or another, IR/IPE is no exception, whether or not this is hidden from view in rational-choice, positivist modes of inquiry (Ling 2002: 15–17).

To sum up: This method can be categorized as a "mixed" qualitative research. As Internet-based and informed by conventional sorts of data gathering (email correspondence, face-to-face and telephone interviews, research visits to the South Pacific Islands, the United States, Australia, and New Zealand, and the usual secondary sources), it is also a "multi-sited" one (Hine 2000; Miller and Slater 2000). The online texts and the interpersonal relationships and substantive themes they articulate have been treated as practices of everyday life in their own right. The manifest content and the conditions under which they have been written bespeak offline and on-the-ground dimensions, experiences, and interventions. The Internet technologies that are used and adapted along the way (email, IRC software packages, moderating and administrative tools, server and transmission services, PC or Internet access and functionalities) are co-constructed by these textual-spatial comings and goings. Even as a myriad of separate texts (*posts*) are accessed, thousands of theme clusters they belong to (*threads*) collated and cross-referenced over the years, and the particularities of their "onlineness" noted, these Pacific traversals have been occurring within broader online and offline technoeconomic and sociopolitical contexts.

4 "I'm tired of slaving myself"

Sex–gender roles revisited

Introduction

> [Philosophical] constructions ... depend on seemingly clear-cut oppositions and irreducible conceptual pairs: spiritual and material, universal and particular, eternal and temporal, male and female.... These pairs raise two problems: on the one hand, as a result of their extreme rigidity, all that does not fit neatly within their oppositional relations tends to be marginalized or even suppressed; on the other hand, these oppositions impose a hierarchical order. For example, in the Platonic framework later appropriated by Christian thought, truth and goodness coincide with the spiritual, universal, eternal, and male side of the opposition at the expense of the material, particular, temporal, and female side.
>
> (Borradori 2003: 138)

> The dichotomy between a public sphere of the economic, and a private personal realm, assigned "naturally" to women, in fact places women in a double bind.... [A] solution ... would imply not only changing the definition of success but also introducing into public life patterns of behaviour and emotionality previously confined to the domain of typically female activities; the importance of relationships for life -fulfilment, the value of work done well for its own sake, helpfulness to others and the like.
>
> (Benhabib and Cornell 1987: 9)

Since the 1970s, the analytical, descriptive, and prescriptive efficacy of dichotomous "conceptual pairs" have been both debunked and underscored in academe. While the interactive multilateral dimensions of Internet-based communications have contributed to critiques of dichotomous rigidities in Western thought, they have also given rise to a few new ones: online or offline, real or virtual, digital or analog, zero or one. Dichotomous thinking and argumentation in modernist scholarly knowledge production is quite tenacious. The opposition made between public and private spheres, and its broader corollaries (state–society, state–market), is central to both political science and IR/IPE discourses. It has certainly been an axis for debate about the effects of ICTs on the "public sphere" in liberal democratic societies (Toulouse and Luke 1998; Loader 1998; Wilhelm 2000). In one way or another, Internet technologies have been splicing through the carefully groomed legal and regulatory distinctions between publicness (civil society/public sphere) and the private as personal (intimate lives/domestic sphere).

This particular dichotomy also absorbed "second-wave" feminism of the 1960s and 1970s. Feminist IR/IPE has also persistently pointed out where and how the past twenty years of aggressive global restructuring processes have been anything but gender neutral in their ramifications in the home and in the workplace, and how these two "spheres" are mutually constituted and contingent upon gender power differentials. As I argue in Chapter 2, neoliberal "imaginaries" have also come to dominate ideas about the sociocultural implications and political or economic role for ICTs of late. In these overlapping discourses, the ongoing ontological split between "public" and "private" is in operation. Many online practices, non-Western social formations, and then the gender, class, and race/ethnic contours to all these are all too easily subsumed by debates founded on this "irreducible" pair. All the more reason for beginning, then, with a set of discussion threads that show how and where private lives, personal dreams, and social and "public" obligations are enmeshed in everyday life anyway. This is an interconnection that is further underscored by being articulated in an online public–private space, namely, in exchanges about how "traditional" and "modern" sex–gender roles[1] affect the women participants of the Kava Bowl and Kamehameha Roundtable, as individuals and community members.

The discussion threads reconstructed in this chapter are from both women living in Samoa and Tonga and those living elsewhere. They discuss changing attitudes and expectations about sex–gender roles, femininity and masculinity, sexuality, and selective moralities from their local, personal, and diasporic standpoints. They talk openly about the stresses and strains of intimate and familial relationships as an array of historical-cultural obligations and personal choices, none of which is self-evident or easy to live with. This is the *manifest content* of these particular threads. While there are many other discussions that tackle related issues (homosexuality, changing sexual mores for Pacific island societies and their communities living abroad, religious issues, or church–community relationships), this chapter focuses on threads that explicitly deal with "being a woman today" (and, by implication, "being a man") in a postcolonial diasporic context.

These conversations underscore how the public–private distinction remains an incorrigible *problématique* in Western discourse – incorrigible because even as critical scholarship uncovers the ethnocentric and androcentric precepts behind such dichotomies, the intellectual and literary lexicon at our disposal is permeated with them. The emergence of practices of everyday life that have online – cyber – dimensions has brought the *problématique* more sharply into relief. When nonelite, non-Western Internet practitioners are involved, the aforementioned "double bind" (Benhabib and Cornell 1987) is both figurative and literal. These reconstructions underscore how not even critical analytical categories, collocations, or typographies can provide "unproblematically a uniform, set of meanings which are common to all" (Fildes 1983: 68). Just as everyday life is characterized by both its fluidity and deeper currents of habit and ennui, the threads covered here trace just how intimately connected the "material realities and … ideological tropes" (di Leonardo 1991: 25) of (postcolonial) gender power relations can be. Second-wave feminism's catch-cry "the personal is political" (meaning that "there is no private domain of a person's life that is not political and there is no political issue that is not personal" (Charlotte Bunch quoted in Sargent 1981: xix)) perforates everyday cyberspace too. Likewise for Cynthia Enloe's oft-quoted extension of this insight: the personal is international (Enloe 1989).

Chapter outline

The chapter is organized in three sections. The first looks briefly at how feminist theory has critiqued the public–private distinction for its inherent androcentric and ethnocentric bias. Critics point to how these biases confine "women" and the "feminine" to house arrest, as it were; the private sphere is conflated with domesticity and "feminine" activity and subjectivity accordingly (Nicholson 1997: 1–10; Sargent 1981: xi–xxiii). The point of this discussion, with feminist skepticism about women-as-private-subjects and men-as-active-agents as a guide, is that intimate or personal exchanges in public cyberspaces are just as pertinent to understanding online practices as are "public" political debates. Whether these happen in the relative intimacy of a particular Internet forum, they are writ large in the cyberspaces of the World Wide Web. This age-old distinction and its critics get rearticulated, recalibrated, and electronically recorded accordingly. The second section is a walk-through of the more substantial discussions on sex–gender roles for Samoan and/or Tongan women primarily, although not exclusively. The women met here are regulars on these forums and active in all other major discussions. In these threads, they express personal concerns and respond to those of others about multiplex expectations and experiences in and outside their islands of origin. Some women have Pacific Island partners. Men are present as well but these particular discussions are dominated and mainly initiated by women.

The third section discusses some empirical and analytical particularities to these online texts. The dynamic at stake here, and for the three chapters following, is that of online *and* offline as a dynamic relationship constituted by qualitatively distinct, albeit intersecting, domains of action, experience, and interaction. The term *onlineness* denotes these operations of inter/subjectivity, while the term *textual surfaces* (following Carver 1998a) denotes the spatial–visual qualities of the content, the way this is co-produced and multilaterally read. Two examples, subthreads of those examined previously, will serve to illustrate these dynamics. The first is an interaction in which I took part and the second is one in which participants pause to discuss where Pacific Island societies and their diasporic populations are situated within "globalization." As the other chapters will show, these broader debates and events are never far away, no matter how intimate, personal, and culturally specific the discussions may get.

1 Feminist theoretical and practical nodes

> You wrote "it is good to see that you can get along with the way women are viewed by men" – this is definitely NOT the case – it's just that I refuse to be limited by that type of narrow thinking, I refuse to let it hinder me, my life and the pursuit of my goals.... I find this most interesting – especially being both women (correct me if I'm wrong) yet having totally different views on the role of Tongan women within our society.
>
> (Legacy_NZ, KB, 05/24/99 in Lausii, 05/18/99)

While the above statement lends itself well to standard feminist takes on how femininity, masculinity, sex–gender roles are made, not given, with its "staunch" position on gender stereotyping, this participant is also pointing to some strong disagreement between her and other participants. Comparable debates and political programs in feminism are also fraught, and more so when it comes to the public–private nexus. At the heart of debates in the 1960s and 1970s and since then are very different views on human nature, political economy, and the very definition of "gender" (Jaggar 1983; McDowell and Sharp 1997: 263–268).

Second-wave Marxist and socialist feminist theory and activism engaged with Marx and Engels's linking of the institutionalization of private property, and the capitalist mode of production, to the sexual division of labor (Carver 1998a: 221–228; Nicholson 1997: 1–5; Fildes 1983; Hartmann 1981). To wit: men go to work to produce surplus value under alienated conditions of labor, and women stay at home to reproduce more workers to produce surplus value. Feminists have pondered over how this hierarchical separation between "public" power (and alienation) – for men only – and all sorts of "private" domesticity (and exclusion) – for women – relates to "patriarchy" (Lerner 1986: 212–229, 238–240). The latter denotes either a distinct or a universal social system through which women are a priori "oppressed," "domesticated," or excluded from "public" political life (Rubin [1975] 1997: 30, 32). These "materialist" feminist approaches posit the capitalist mode of (re)production and the aforementioned social and sexual power hierarchies as a historical stage of patriarchal relations. All in all, and collapsing a rich feminist historiography, "public/private" denotes and critiques symbolic and material gender power relations that are reproduced or justified along distinct, albeit interacting, boundaries (Hennessy 1993). Fierce disagreements notwithstanding, a feminist critique *tout court* posits that such dualisms serve to perpetuate a pernicious set of "sexualised, racialised, and class-based" (Chang and Ling 2000: 27) meanings, institutions, hierarchies, power relations, and ideologies (Fildes 1983: 66–69) that subordinate an "array of embodied beings culturally positioned as women" (Butler 1990: 325).

To "fast-forward" from these interventions to *c.*2004, the increasing ubiquity of the Internet since the mid-1990s is impacting upon daily lives, politics, economics, and social theory, broadly defined. The gendered–ethnic–class connotations of these new activities effectively form their own "seams" (*coutures*) in cyberspace (Giard and Mayol 1980: 24–25). What emerges is an electronically mediated challenge to the beaten path worn between either "a public" or "a private." Not only does this corseted dichotomy constantly need to be unlaced, but other supporting grammars beg inclusion (see Ortner 1996: 153–154). As Chandra Mohanty points out, the lexicon at our disposal needs to articulate and allow research into

> a temporality of *struggle*, which disrupts and challenges the logic of linearity, development and progress which are the hallmarks of European modernity … suggests an insistent, simultaneous, non-synchronous process characterised by multiple locations, rather than a search for origins and endings.
>
> (1997: 93; original emphasis)

If we are allowed to cut loose from these linear moorings, what emerges is how (postcolonial) inter/subjectivities are embedded in multilayered experiences, sociocultural interactions, and assumptions, new and old. These strain against respective "public–private" institutions and conventions that have become frozen-in-time (de Certeau 1986: 119–233); they intersect with how a "subject," alone and/or in community, is constituted at various instances by her intimate and social duties, roles, relationships, separately and together. How she sees herself, what she says and to whom, how others react, what social and historical expectations are brought to bear form the stuff of communicative practices (see Williams 1977: 23). The respective gender power relations that get played out move in, skip around, bump against all manner of institutions, psychological structures, and daily *conventions* (Giard and Mayol 1980: 14–17). And in non-Western, postcolonial scenarios, as Ling points out, subjectivity (personal experiences and situations) refers to the internally absorbed, personally-felt, mixed selves that derive from contending ways of thinking, doing, and being.... The very condition of postcoloniality means an intimate mixing of subjectivities, not one distinct identity labelled 'southern', 'minority', or 'Other' tagged on to a more familiar ones like 'northern', 'majority', 'Self' in order to achieve a more representative 'objectivity'.

(Ling 2002: 21, 236)

Taking a close look at how everyday life unfolds, manifests itself, online can temper the subsuming of multiplex experiences and communicative practices under an updated version of an "unwitting duplication of the Eurocentric, bourgeois bias inherent in the notion of a separation of spheres" (Fildes 1983: 68; Giard and Mayol 1980: 14). Nevertheless, feminist critiques still speak to postcolonial arguments about the dialogical elements of the "colonial encounter." "Non-Western" societies have always been engaging with generically Western technologies and political systems (Narayan 1997), building upon extant social and cultural networks but also renegotiating these, their own place in them, and themselves along the way. These threads are read from a position that regards "the subject" as non-essentializable in the first, not the last, instance. In this sense, the subject,

rather than being a fixed entity which enter[s] into social relations with its gender (and class and race) fixed in place, [is] always fluid, in the process of becoming, anxious to create and hold onto an identity which is constructed through discourse and everyday actions.

(McDowell and Sharp 1997: 6)

Given the "power dynamics of naming 'others'" (di Leonardo 1991: 15), there is also a methodological rationale for beginning the viewing and "reading" of these online discussions from a feminist-inspired, bottom-up angle (Harding 1998a). First, theory and research into non-Western corners of the Internet and, moreover, women's place and roles therein, are relatively recent (see Harcourt 1999; Kolko *et al.* 2000). Focusing on the (arguably outdated) connection between the personal and the political revisits how "personal statements remain a source of suggestive illumination of the texture of life" (Fildes 1983: 63). For everyday online scenarios and articulations, let alone for those that are not generically "Western," this accent can thereby circumvent any tendency to head for the safety of categorical definitiveness too hastily. As this and subsequent chapters will show, such tidy ends are not so easily achieved when living between – and in – two or more cultures and their expectations. The public–private–personal (re)articulations examined here depend on who is talking, to whom and for whom (ibid.: 68). These discussions between diasporic generations of South Pacific Island women communicating with friends, strangers, extended family, elders, and community leaders on and through the Internet point to the "varying ways in which women themselves perceive their situations" (di Leonardo 1991: 17). The personal-political import thereof is made quite manifest in the interlocutors' own words.

A useful heuristic device for grasping the bottom-up dynamics and vocalizations at stake in these threads is that of *insideout*. Rather than as a spatial – bordered – dichotomy, though, insideout conjures up the image of a garment being turned inside out so that the inner textures to the fabric, and its seams and imperfections, are visible. An inside-out garment can still be worn even though it looks different, does not appear as it was "designed" to be worn, and so on. In addition, this is also a recurring trope in postcolonial theory and research and related feminist strands. As Pacific communities articulate their lives and experiences, well aware of distinctions to be made between their online interventions, life in the islands and overseas, the online archives forming as they write-speak records the complexity of everyday life in diaspora, living as "a minority of a minority" or in the islands. Insideout, in this spelling and understanding, is not intended to posit yet another dichotomy. Rather, the accent is being put on how

> 'inside out' is to be impure, working at the borders, risking mixture, outreach, and invention; for to be inside out means to be creatively perplexed, upside down, out of whack, reversible, expressing the inside wholeness of self and community in outside masks and distant mirrors, in signs that baffle and menace as much as they reveal.
>
> (Wilson 1999: 2)

From this self-awareness and communal cyberspace flow conversations about wo/manhood, sexual and family politics, sex–gender hierarchies, and sexual and social mores in themselves and how they relate to "traditional" and/or "modern" sex–gender roles and values. The women in these threads are querying, thinking out loud, stating a claim or position against or for how they envisage their own lives. The starting point for many is the unspoken assumptions and expectations from family, community, or society as a whole. For instance:

> [I]t appears a large portion of the Tongan culture is based on age-old rules which contradict the very doctrines with which we set our standards by today. It amazes me how much we accept our culture without question.
>
> (Coral, THA, 07/17/98 in Jatu, 05/26/98)

Responses constitute the long, fluid, open-ended, and interwoven online textual and physical movements[2] examined in these four chapters.

Individual postings can be lengthy, eloquent, short and sharp, funny, angry; can contain literary, idiomatic, satirical, and autobiographical prose, asides and interpolations of varying moods. In terms of issues around the politics of representation in and for postcolonial settings, loaded terms such as "tradition" and "culture" are treated here as contestable. In other words, these reconstructions and my reading of them are not intended as fuel for anthropological debates on the "invention" of tradition, "tradition" or "culture" *per se* (Wassmann 1998; Helu 1999d, e; Ortner 1996: 59 *passim*; di Leonardo 1991: 1 *passim*). I leave it to the reader to decide where "traditional" notions of sex–gender roles end and "modern" ones begin. Participants make it very clear what their own opinions are, where the tensions, contradictions, and personal dilemmas lie.

The sampling technique and presentation of the online texts from here on is premised on their being stand-alone statements as well as forming part of long-standing discussion themes from these forums, and interventions in this study. They can also challenge the standpoint taken here. This does not mean to say that in either of these locations they are vehicles for any one interpretation. They are parts of multilateral *conversations-as-written-texts*. Neither have selections been chosen on the basis of whether they are "good" examples of external literary or stylistic standards, academic argumentation, ideological purity, or English syntactic exemplification. While it would be inaccurate to claim that I have selected and edited without being aware of my own preferences (those passages I find amusing or eloquent, and so on), I have tried not to get too wrapped up in editorial asides. Readers will find in these reconstructions (partial and selective) some superb pieces of traditional written prose, ground-breaking creative prose too, off-the-cuff rants, intimate autobiographical moments, streams of consciousness, extreme forms of colloquialism, internally contradictory passages, strong and "lame" interventions. All of these are part of the multiple voices of (online) practices of everyday life: production, content, and various receptions at the same time.

While I take responsibility for both these selections and their placement, this editorial privilege need not preclude me giving ample space in which participants' words can be savored, whether as substantial selections, larger samples of ongoing threads over the years, or cited fragments. The ensuing high level of citation also underscores that these are re-presentations of often long, interlocking discussions that span months and even years at times; the relationships being built up and played out over time, and their dialogic and iterative qualities and intertextuality, are part of these online "patchworks" of hyperlinked textual layers on-screen. The threads themselves also have some formal qualities (a point I deal with in Chapter 8). As Internet-based textual surfaces they need lateral, inside-out, "reversible," *and* linear reading (Wilson 1999: 2). Not only the manifest content, but these properties of "onlineness" underscore how, in this case, the "domestic/public dichotomy ... may exist in multiple forms with multiple meanings ... [including] the varying ways in which women themselves perceive their situations" (di Leonardo 1991: 24, 25). While for some, the topics broached and the opinions expressed in this chapter may appear to be "clementary," for these interlocutors they are neither straightforward nor self-explanatory. Everyday online archives such as these, and their creators, are very much alive.

2 Online confidential

The oral and debating traditions of the peoples of the South Pacific find themselves well suited to the interactive, conversational, and oratorical qualities of online discussions, to its imagery, and to its embedding in Western forms of textuality (de Certeau 1980a: 231 *passim*).[3] This next section walks through a set of threads by women that are explicitly speaking from the *insideout*. As they do, participants both confirm the power (positive and negative) of plural extant sociocultural networks and expectations and renegotiate them; the individual's place in them and implications for respective family structures and communities are touched on along the way.

Postcolonial (re)articulations of wo/manhood

In a discussion about "women's right," the following declaration/criticism/entreaty was posted:

> [W]e (Tongan) as a nation [are] coping with significant social change ... is the increasing number of educated Tongan women who [are] opting for the single life a sign of an active feminist revolution? The simple answer is NO. In fact, it is a dismal picture of the current state of affairs in Tonga ... despite the grounds for optimism, the traditional role for women in Tongan society has not [been] transformed. Even today, the ideal of good wife and wise mother is not an anachronism, the weight of tradition continues to bear heavily upon Tongan society. ... Even though, Tongan women are changing their attitudes about their social roles, men. it seems are not necessarily going along with that change, You only need to read KB [Kava Bowl forums] to justify this. ... Women are still viewed by most Tongan men [as] responsible for most domestic chores and are the primary carers of children. There is a good reason to question whether the Tongan women [should] strive for the same kind of equality so resolutely fought for in the developed countries; [should] the Tongan women respond positively to the bra-burning antics that accompanied feminist campaigns in the developed countries?
>
> (Lausii, KB, 05/18/99)

What is being addressed here is how new conventions are being taken up, or considered vis-à-vis established social conventions and sex–gender roles (and perceptions of Western-style feminism!) both "at home" and "overseas." But then, it depends on how one looks at such things. The view above was countered, in the spirit and tone of a semi-formal debate, by the following:

> Thank you so much for your comments on the state of affairs for Women in our Kingdom. I must seriously disagree with you however on some points. . . .[4] I was much disturbed when reading your posting because you made Tonga out to be some sort of cesspool for gender discrimination, when in fact, there are more women working in the civil service in the Kingdom than here in New Zealand, also out in the villages, a lot of women provide the backbone for much of the families – and I can assure you their roles . . . are not those of a docile domestic worker, but rather of a strong nurturing and dignified female figure, some of which simultaneously hold jobs!. . . Tradition is not a hindrance – but rather something I very highly esteem. Our 'fahu' system[5] is unique and esteems the woman as the most important member of the family – not even the glorious western world has such a provision. And merely because individualism is highly prized in the rest of the world, does not mean that we should automatically adopt it – please do not be resigned to making Tonga into another semi-Western clone!
>
> (Legacy_NZ, KB, 05/20/99 in reply to above)

Threads dealing with the maintenance of cultural integrity vis-à-vis the dominant political economies of the Pacific region and changing sex–gender roles crisscross and merge into perceptions of femininity and masculinity for the specific Tongan or Samoan (Polynesian) context, questioning these in themselves or the effect of negotiating them in other sociocultural conditions. They are a subsection of more general "politics of identity" debates on these forums (see Chapter 6). But in these cases the genderedness of postcolonial identity formation and obligations take center stage. The following crosssection of a longer thread in the Kava Bowl, entitled *I'm Tired of Slaving Myself – The Role of the Woman* (Lafemme Nikita, KB, 05/19/99), shows several entry points into this problematic for women living in contemporary (non-)Pacific Island settings. The effects of becoming aware of the downside of any one set of "cultural values" are all too clear, albeit a source for some irony:

> [T]he thing I have observed and found much dismay is the understanding . . . in [Samoan culture] that the women feel . . . it is their responsibility to feel that they should assist in the kitchen to help serve while our men sits.
>
> (Lafemme Nikita, KB/Polycafe, 05/19/99)

[A]men sistah ... when's our next beauty salon appointment?... Just curious, are you Samoan? If you are, then you must be one hella of a samoan female, taking no s**t from any male. Are you a Women's Lib activist? I don't think our Samoan women can stand up for themselves because they are afraid.

(ROTFLMAO, KB, 05/19/99 in Lafemme Nikita, 05/19/99)

Our men are exhibiting a "learned behaviour" that has been passed down for many, many generations.... Unfortunately, when they come over from the islands, this "learned behaviour" comes right along with them. It's the first thing they take out of their suitcase.... It's up to the younger generation to break that cycle.

(CrazeeLuv, Polycafe, 05/19/99 in Lafemme Nikita, 05/19/99)

With a Samoan mother and Tongan father, my upbringing was certainly an experience especially with the 2 different cultures.... Unfortunately being an only girl, my father wouldn't let me touch the lawn mower!!! Or do anything strenuous as females are 'delicate' in his eyes.

(Afa Samoan, KB, 05/19/99 in Lafemme Nikita, 05/19/99)

The predominance, humor, and eloquence of women's voices in such threads also show how open Internet forums permit them a space to express themselves. They press on and loosen gendered conventions and hierarchies of the right to speak[6] by making use of the more permissive features of online debate: (quasi) anonymity, informal syntax, and the immediacy – and safety – of posting a message, for instance.[7] For women who are no longer prepared to "be seen and not heard," Internet forums permit them to "'push against oppressive boundaries' to 'invent spaces of radical openness' within which to challenge dominant power, taking it on from the margins" (hooks in McDowell and Sharp 1997: 3). The thread wends on:

I just want to say that not all our men are this way.... So let's start by understanding that we are a new generation, don't take away all that we've learned as a culture but bring in to light all the new things we can teach.

(Found me A Strong Samoan Man, KB, 05/20/99 in Lafemme Nikita, 05/19/99)

Don't get caught up in the westernized role.... Our culture dictates much of how we raise our families, it is the core of our being and we choose to do with it is ours to use.

(Hamo, KB, 05/20/99 in Lafemme Nikita, 05/19/99)

I'm a young woman and growing up in a new generation. . . . I find my peers (the 30 something crowd and up) have it a lot easier than did our mothers before us. It is our mothers who truly were under-represented, barely vocal and hardly seen. . . . I have not heard any-thing in my upbringing COMMANDING[8] that relationships be dichotomised. . . . Woman and Samoan . . . and quite capable of carry-ing both.

(KC, 05/20/99 in Lafemme Nikita, 05/19/99)

I think the Samoan couples (first generation) here in the States are developing new attitudes towards one another. . . . I still cater to my husband (whether at home or in public) by putting him first because I was raised that way, the Samoan culture expects that of me and IT'S OKAY WITH ME!!!

(Am there now. . . , KB, 05/20/99 in Lafemme Nikita, 05/19/99)

Revisiting obligations

The debates are liberally sprinkled with attitudes that stem from the strict Christian mores of many of the posters – an important and at times con-tentious part of contemporary life in the Pacific islands. Nevertheless, for societies in which non-Western understandings of aristocratic (female) rank and status are also contemporary political and social markers (Tcherkézoff 1998), being a woman entails any number of crosscutting obligations. In an intensely debated thread from the Kamehameha Roundtable entitled *Where are the Caring Women?*, the (male) instigator of the initial post, after carefully outlining the various positions of his grand-mother, mother, and sisters vis-à-vis motherhood, concluded (after more than a page):

My mother does not envy the conflict of values, emotional strain, and sheer physical fatigue as many young working [women] suffer. . . . I wonder if my sister with her liberated views of women's roles thinks that she falls short in one area where my MOTHER excelled. My mother and Grandmother knew where they stood. They knew what it meant to be a mother, wife. They knew what to expect of a man (and their expectations were generally lower, or more tightly focused than my sisters). I think with the world changing so rapidly the distinctions between the roles and responsibilities of men and women are blurring. The women of this generation do not know what they WANT or care very little about mother-hood and honouring (not obeying) their husbands. Perhaps their self esteem as caring women is low as stress and the break down of relationships continues to rise rapidly.

(KZ7, KR, 03/28/00)[9]

This declaration of alarm – and insight into family politics – does not go unchallenged as the protests fly in from annoyed, amused, and unrepentant (non)feminists, working mothers. The ensuing to-and-fro between KZ7 and various women covers the whole gamut of sexual politics.[10] As political statement:

> In many societies including Polynesians, an IDEOLOGY of motherhood pervades all levels of society, claiming the adherence of women from all walks of life and socio-economic backgrounds. I believe that the ideologies of motherhood and femininity are closely enmeshed so that a woman's sense of femininity is entwined with the potential or actuality of motherhood.
>
> (Venus, The Aphrodite, KR, 03/28/00 in KZ7, 03/28/00)

> What a load of crap. . . . As far as I'm concerned, and I proudly speak as a feminist, not enough has happened. The women's movement has moved backwards with young women being lulled into the belief that they have achieved everything. . . . Go through what women have asked for in the women's movement, and you'll see that very little has been achieved. And if you aren't a male, then it really does prove that women have been duped.
>
> (NINJA, KR, 03/28/00 in KZ7, 03/28/00)

Despite many postings that would disclaim any "feminist" tag, they still show all too familiar gender power issues albeit with a particular postcolonial tint. Personal testimony (this thread carries some lengthy autobiographical accounts) expresses these tensions and triumphs very effectively. The following two women had this to say to KZ7's nostalgia for "traditional" (Samoan) sex–gender roles:

> Libby women versus LAZY deadbeat men? Is that how we now dichotomize the issue? . . . Had you caught me several years ago, I would have definitely sliced you down to bite-size and fed you to the sharks. Nowadays, there is nothing that any man can tell me that will break my stride because odds are, they will never be able to do as I have. Never juggle career, college and bear a child as I have . . . and all of it, without running home to Mom or sitting on the dough [the dole] to get through the harder end of the reality of being me.
>
> (P., KR, 03/28/00 in KZ7, 03/28/00)

> Do you mean to imply that women who are not full-time homemakers are less caring? If so, then I take exception to that very strongly. Yes, I work – full time. And yes, I have to put my son in the hands of strangers while I work. But I can assure you, that makes me no less devoted to my son than any stay-at-home mom.
>
> (Teuila, KR, 03/28/00 in KZ7, 03/28/00)

That said, the posters/women disagree with each other as well, depending upon their religious convictions, generation, or geographical position. On the whole, though, there is an acknowledgment of being-in-debate and an attempt to clarify a range of conflicting duties and experiences.

Queries and affirmations

KZ7's position statement is not just a rehash of "masculinism" (Peterson and Runyan 1999) or "neotraditionalism" online, although he is put firmly in his place by his interlocutors. Women participants are also exploring what are/are not appropriate, tolerable femininities/masculinities. Here, intracultural exchanges can become intercultural in an Internet and diasporic scenario. Expressions of discomfort and a search for authentic signposts are part of this process.[11] They weave in and out of confessional and declamatory interventions on familial networks and obligations, work and school relationships.

The next section is a sort of "edited highlights" from another intensely personal thread entitled *The ROLE of a SAMOAN WOMAN in Today's Society????* that encapsulates all these – and more – crosscutting currents and standpoints. The initial poster is interested to hear from others about a complex sociocultural and historical issue:

> Being a Samoan woman myself, I am curious as to the views my fellow Samoans may have in regards to what they think my role in today's society may be.
>
> (Gorgeousss, KR, 02/10/99)[12]

Her interest stems from her perception of the increasing assertiveness of Samoan women in the home and in leadership roles vis-à-vis how

> what I understand [is that in] the Samoan culture, a woman's place is in the home listening and obeying her husband.
>
> (ibid.)

The latter is posited against her observation that

> this is no longer the case. Samoan women are some of the strongest people I know and I see many of them in strong leadership positions. Many of them are very aggressive, practical, and WISE LOLOLOL[13] ... myself not excluded LOLOLOL (just kidding) but seriously, Samoan women are a force to be reckoned with. So in comparison with our past and culture versus what society holds in store for us today, what is the ROLE of a SAMOAN WOMAN?
>
> (ibid.)

Most of the responses are affirmations for her view:

> We are no longer seen as yet another group of submissive Polynesian women. Nope, we are actually seen as respectable and formidable women.
>
> > (Jade, KR, 02/10/99 in Gorgeousss, 02/10/99)

Change and choice are key interacting factors here for Jade, who also identifies himself as a US resident:

> I'm glad to know that my little girl will be able to know that the only limits as a Samoan and an American female in today's society is only herself.
>
> > (ibid.)

So on the one hand, for her,

> the role of the Samoan woman ... is one that is very expanded and growing. We are everywhere and truly are a force to be reckoned with. It is no longer just the voice or faces of the Samoan male that is being felt in today's society. Nope, it is their sisters. mothers, daughters, and nieces.
>
> > (ibid.)

But on the other, it is also down to personal endeavor:

> I would want other Samoan females to know that wherever you begin in life ... don't take it as the only dimension in your life ... be open to new and different facets of life, but be cautious as well. . . . We owe it all to each other and to the mothers, aunts, and grandmothers that have paved the way for us.
>
> > (ibid.)

Some personal testimonials in this thread underline the female role models provided by their older, though not necessarily more conservative, relatives:

> My grandmother has always been the dominating force in my family, and I mean that in a good way. . . . She is the glue that holds all of us together. My Grandfather usually defers to her judgement. . . . Outside the family, she is a shrewd business woman/entrepreneur and has earned and received the respect of those who know her. . . . I had always thought that the women were the reigning force in the family hierarchy. I was surprised to read that ... my family is the exception, not the rule.
>
> > (Ally, KR, 02/10/99 in Gorgeousss, 02/10/99)

They also muse about

> a mix of the new role for up and coming Samoan women and then I
> see the more traditional role for Samoan women. I guess it all varies
> in age and where you are.
>
> (Mysterious Girl, KR, 02/10/99 in Gorgeousss, 02/10/99)[14]

Another poster presents her mother as leading

> the pack in exemplifying the ENDURANCE of a woman under the
> pressures of society, family and her partner in life. Coming from such
> a line of women who have also experienced the age-old canon of men
> placing their women in check, has left an indelible imprint to rede-
> fine my role as a Samoan woman.
>
> (A., KR, 02/10/99 in Gorgeousss, 02/10/99)

She then goes on, echoing others in this string, identifying with her
"female ancestry," but also the different circumstances of her own life. For

> I am not my mother but an extension of her. Without need for expla-
> nation, I have found value in being me and being the neoclassic
> Samoan woman.
>
> (ibid.)

This participant has even more to say on the balancing act between equity
in intimate relationships vis-à-vis the sociocultural assumptions tied to
these in broader contexts:

> I know well enough of the Fa'a Samoa [the 'Samoan Way'] to interact
> independent of him [her husband] among his people for I am not
> only his woman, but my mother's ambassador.
>
> (ibid.)

She wants to affirm both without compromising either "in both mainland
[the United States for American Samoa] and traditional places" (ibid.).
But not everyone is so self-assured. Mafine notes, for instance, that on

> this woman of today topic … I can only say I'm still stuck in the past
> but slow ungluing myself and emerging into the present.
>
> (mafine, KR, 02/10/99 in Gorgeousss, 02/10/99)

Others concur that

> the 'traditional' role for the Samoan woman has been and still is (to a
> certain extent) secondary to her male counterpart.
>
> (Bitchyspice, KR, 02/10/99 in Gorgeousss, 02/10/99)

But not everyone agrees with this opposition between "traditional" roles and modern changes in the first place. Bevo contends that

> the traditional Samoan view of women is [not] as submissive as you suggest. . . . Samoan women have played a big, and important role in Samoan society. I believe that women are the movers and the shakers in Samoan communities . . . women have always held influence. Even in Samoan history, some of the most powerful and important people are women. . . . Samoan women are beginning to immerse themselves in the American culture and therefore are swept up with the women's movement here in the West. But I believe that women have always been power brokers in Samoa.
>
> (Bevo, KR, 02/10/99 in Gorgeousss, 02/10/99)[15]

Queries about "which society – Samoan or American?" (KL, KR, 02/10/99 in Gorgeousss, 02/10/99) concern posters as well, for it is important to know in assessing a situation. First, locate the "where" and "then I'll comment" (Bevo, KR, 02/10/99 in reply to above). For others, however, location is a red herring, given the

> big spread (geographical) that we are now in . . . [and how] as our people move out of Samoa and more into the Western culture, our views, lifestyles etc are subject to change [and so] I feel that the role of the Samoan woman today cannot be zoomed down to one 'list' of attributes.
>
> (Bitchyspice, KR, 02/10/99 in Gorgeousss, 02/10/99)

Because both female and male posters are comparing and contesting assumptions, prejudices, and experiences in these threads, affecting these in their lives or simply taking a stand these interactions should not be seen as transparent, unproblematic statements. They are ideas-in-progress as much as they are credos. Bitchyspice, who heads her message with an ironic title, *to cook, clean and look after the kids . . . lol*, suggests that it might be an idea to

> take a broader look at the issue and ask "What is the role for ALL WOMEN today?", and then apply it to our own cultures and situations (American, New Zealander, Samoan, Tongan etc), then we might get a better sense of what our roles may be.
>
> (ibid.)

(En)countering others

While these women want to celebrate their cultural/ethnic/gendered uniqueness, they certainly do not see "traditional" roles and attitudes as unassailable:

In our culture, men are free to explore the world in whatever way they like before marriage, but NOT us girls. Western education informs us about equality of both sexes, our culture teaches us differently. They sometimes clash and be confusing at times, but the latter will always take precedence for some of us. University education sometimes enlightens one's mind to perceive/discern the inequalities inherent in our society, whereas our culture expects us girls to accept things as it is. . . . Maybe my perception is not applicable to all Tongan girls out there, but this is my own contemplation of our Tongan culture based on my own world.

(Ice Maiden, KB, 05/18/99 in E. Tigris, 05/13/99)

As to equality, I understand you, yet it does pain me to see double standards used not as a personification of age old traditions (when both parties had duties and obligations) but as a means of suppression.

(Ryah, KB, 05/18/99 in reply to above)

Yes and No. . . . It all depends. . . . I think it all depends on the extent & the objective of a woman's pursuit for equality within a relationship. If she's attempting to take over the family, thus leaving the husband as the "hiku" [lower], and herself as the "ulu" [head], then that's TOO BAD!! A woman like that is nothing but a TROUBLE-MAKER to the family!!. . . sometimes Tongan men can . . . be so ignorant as to claim that since Tongan women are educated, education plagued their minds with all sorts of formidable feminism ideas which are "out of place" in our culture and way of life. Maybe it can be justified but that's not the case in every situations. Sometimes, what some of our educated Tongan women prefer is a "life-partnership" kind of relationship rather than a "dominant-submission" one in which the woman has NO voice at all in the family. . . . We're living beings with minds of our own!! Don't forget that!

(Ice Maiden, KB, 05/18/99 in E. Tigris, 05/13/99)

This thread turned into an intense debate about the rights and wrongs of premarital sex – for Tongan women in this case – and how this relates to practical realities.[16] Claims and counterclaims, personal testimonies wended their way through the issue of changing sexual mores in Tongan gender power relations, colonial missionaries' impact on Pacific island societies, double standards held by men vis-à-vis female virginity, ideals of masculinity and femininity, and respective domestic roles.[17] Fe/male posters who insist on the maintenance of (biblically referenced) virginity were given short shrift by many women (Ortner 1996: 43 *passim*, 53 *passim*). In a follow-up to another thread (KZ7, KR, 03/28/00) a participant notes that there is something absurd in the fact that your post could have been written on March 28, 2000 . . . I have no respect for these "traditional" institutions that are so biased and oppressive against women. It is SOCIETAL, not NATURAL. To be the vehicle for new life is woman's privilege. To bear sole responsibility for the emotional and spiritual well-being of the children – this is a demand I, and many other women, reject. . . . There has been this bizarre dichotomy between what is masculine and what is feminine, what is essential (MAN) and what is inessential (WOMAN). Woman is, like man, a human being.

(Princess, KR, 03/29/00, in reply to KZ7, 03/28/00)

Such online confidences operate differently from games or fantasies played out by fictitious characters experimenting with new sorts of "virtual reality" (Shields 1996; Ludlow 1996; Kolko, Nakamura, and Rodman 2000; Jordan 1999), even though they can be playful. They are the traces and expressions of the daily practices of real people and their online personae. These conversations-as-written-texts have both authors and addressees who are related in some way, or, if not, have become known to each other in the process of articulating what it means to belong, be connected in some way to a set of cultural and historical heritages. Whether by the burgeoning techniques of hyperlinked conversations, use of inference, symbols, references to offline relationships, or online variants of Polynesian social controls when a "lack of respect" is shown, the process of discussion and how it interfaces – and collides – with lived lives and relationships is central. This is the other angle of being inside out. For an

'inside-out' Pacific of global/local interweaving . . . implies that the inside is already outside and vice versa: the boundary does not hold, impurity and difference exists as everyday fate, and the categories mix and bleed into one another in unstable new ways.

(Wilson 1999: 6–7)

In the process, intimate lives are "outed" and engaged with, online.[18] The issues and lives at stake intersect with the personal choices, the upper limits of Western-style individualism, and the exigencies of other obligations. Christian belief systems and church affiliations also bring with them their own gender–power baggage – for example, in an initial post entitled *Why is it that when a Tongan woman marries a man, it is expected of her to drop her religion for his??*:

I have never quite been able to comprehend why in our Tongan culture it is simply expected of a woman to follow her husband's religion. But most of all I can't seem to understand how anyone could expect an individual to conform and believe in something that is foreign to them.

(kode, THA, 03/30/99)

I don't know about the culture, but I am a woman, that when I got married me and my husband went to my religion, we agree to go there before we were married.... I don't think that is a culture thing, it just depend from you and your husband.

(a friend, THA, 03/31/99 in reply to above)

From the Tongan Culture's perspective, it is perfectly normal. Not an iota wrong with it. However, if you are trying to answer from a Western Culture's perspective, then there are millions ways that could be wrong. Therefore, if you are not in Tonga at the moment, the chances are you should do whatever you want to do. But if you are back in Tonga, your life will be much easier that way. Trust me. Which one is right and which is wrong? To be truthful, they are both right. It all depends where you are. On top of all that, you make your choice and live with the consequences of your choices. That's all. We simply cannot apply our Western assumption on marriage to something that may look the same but it is not. Now, do you want to know if you should follow him? It's all up to you. Remember, when you are married to a Tongan person, you become part of that extended family. It is expected of you to be part of that family, whether you like it or not. Confused? I don't blame you. Good Luck.

(counsellor, THA, 04/01/99 in kode, 03/30/99)

Such tricky intimate, familial, and social negotiations are the fabric of post-colonial and diasporic lives, all of which unfolds under certain culturally (en)coded conditions and "moral economies" on/offline (see Chapter 7). Despite the fact that the inherent fluidity of this seems fixed as these discussion threads become temporal cultural artifacts, these interactions and their cultural permutations and reiterations still remain personal – intimate – even as they are "for the public record." They are also powerful correctives to some feminist-inspired counterdichotomies. Posters have an eye, and an ear, for a broader audience as well. An initial post by a male regular led to a lively exchange when he entitled his message *Does Searching for Equality by a woman destroy the harmony in a Tongan family!* (LUT, KB, 05/18/99).[19] His female interlocutors had a range of responses:

Women should continue respecting the husband [no] matter what background, colour, limitation he has and moreover know their place in the family circle.

(bset, KB, 05/18/99 in reply to above)

Face it 'men' time is changing and so are women ... I know that this is relatively new in Tongan family life (giving women equality in a marriage) but hey, try it cause you might like it. (I know we do).

(wonderwoman, KB, 05/19/99 in LUT, 05/18/99)

I am not a feminist but I strongly believe that we, as women, will no longer allow ourselves to be 'doormats'. I am not suggesting that we abolish our role as traditional Tongan women. . . . Far from it! I am only saying that we deserve better.

(funnygirl, KB, 05/20/99 in LUT, 05/18/99)

Contemporary thought is great in contemporary homes and society ie. US, UK, Europe, Aust and NZ. However this many [*sic*] not prove to be the case back in the islands. . . . It is crucial to hang on to tradition and culture. So much so that the part women play is vital to the survival of these traditions. . . . The only downfall perhaps is that island men rarely exercise the grey matter long enough to digest island women issues and how they fit into modern Westernized society. But we are learning.

(CaptKJustice, KB, 05/19/99 in LUT, 05/18/99)

And amid high levels of earnestness, self-satire and gentle – although not always – teasing have a place as well:

Look, to keep things simple and back to tradition. Women: Get back in the kitchen and just make babies, that's your job. Men: I'll see you in pub after work.

(Traditionalist Hunter Warrior Knight Crusader Terminator, KB, 05/18/99 in LUT, 05/18/99)

The following loud outburst (in capital letters, thus shouting) is a good example of tongue-in-check reprobation/exasperation. But it also highlights the way postcolonial masculinities (in this case) too have to contend with conflicting expectations in new contexts and pressures:

THE DIFFERENCES BETWEEN A TONGAN MAN IN TONGA AND A TONGAN MAN IN THE STATES. The major difference is this . . . RESPECT!!! the real men from the islands are gentlemen . . . not "gangstas", "players", "ballers". they are MEN that know how to treat a lady! hey ladies am i right? or am i right? much love to all the MEN that these BOYS in the States consider to be "F.O.B's"[20] . . . we consider you to be the real MEN!!"

(a girl's point of view, KB, 01/28/98)

To sum up: These online records lie in the online–offline shorelines of meaning-making. The participants are well skilled at navigating these lands, celebrating or subverting their outer and inner limits in discussions. Interactions between author and reader/s – with the two roles rolled into one – create interwoven threads. Although compacted into a computer screen at the time of reading/writing/accessing, residing in servers and caches, and only activated by scrolling, clicks, and hyperlinks, they are also writ large on the World Wide Web and lived daily in offline scenarios. These stretch out behind and reach back onto the screen. Everyday online practices of talking–writing–linking perform (self)representative tasks that are open to multiple cross-readings, fraught with mutual (mis)understandings, subject to eventual censure – from within and without. Postcolonial gendered intersubjectivities are never far from other ones and their meta-narratives either. The sociocultural and historical dynamics of these online conversations and altercations attest to how movement "between cultures, languages and complex configurations of meaning and power have always been the territory of the colonised" (Mohanty 1997: 94).

3 Offline-and-online parameters

> Everyday life [*la vie quotidienne*] . . . is related to the public space in which it unfolds . . . we are no longer working on disconnected things in the social realm but, rather, on the relationships between them; more precisely, on the seam [*couture*] that joins the one to the other, the private space to the public space.
>
> (Giard and Mayol 1980: 14; my translation)

Michel de Certeau and his colleagues Luce Giard and Pierre Mayol emphasize the interconnection between nominally distinct spheres of visible inter/action (in public) and personal intimacy (the private/domestic sphere). In various ways, the stress is on the mutual constitution of "ordinary" practices and extraordinary, structural power relations – not only from a data-gathering, analytical, or interpretative point of view, but also as a primary tenet of thinking about what constitutes politics. But as the material unfolds in an *online* setting, with the techno-formal particularities of digitalized surfaces, there are both theoretical and empirical implications: handling Internet-based textual surfaces and being online.

Textual surfaces

By textual surfaces I am referring to what is up on-screen on entering any Internet discussion forum, but these ones in particular (see Chapter 8): words, hyperlinks, graphics, and so forth along with the actual content. But more than that needs to be said about the "textual surfaces" (Carver 1998a: 7–9) of these interactions – as form, content, and meanings. In this chapter, reinterpretations of "traditional"–"modern" sex–gender systems and the open querying of gender stereotypes provide the stuff of intellectual debates and permeate more autobiographical accounts. Another aspect to the textual surfaces is the effects of how participants indicate themselves in the form of Internet-style identifications, where a signature is not necessarily one's name or handwriting, but a series of fixed or fluid noms de plume, nicknames ("nics"), or other "handles." Another "exchange of meanings" and set of relationships are being indicated as a poster identifies and situates herself by any combination of categorizations, giving her actual name notwithstanding. For example: man/woman, gay/straight, non/religious, old/young, married/single, sister/brother.[21] There are also signatures that indicate other sorts of inter/subjective positionings. For example: ignorant/expert, supporter/critic. And then there are those cultural or ethnic identifications or admissions such as: of mixed/pure blood, Polynesian/palagi.[22] A poster can be quizzed or admonished accordingly. These signatures, often subtexts in themselves, zigzag through the threads. They have a bearing on the shape and flow of a thread and the amount of textual layers available for (opening and) reading. How these personal choices, online personae, relationships are brought to bear on the way a thread or group of threads develop is also related to frequency of participation and degree of familiarity between participants (see Morton 1998a/2001). There is a lot of humor, satire, and irony as well, in the tradition of both social gatherings and (Tongan) Kava Clubs on the ground.[23] The main conceptual-analytical point here is how these postcolonial traversals, online, underscore the ways in which the "various ways of speaking, introducing oneself, being present in the social world by a 'public' subject are, in short, nothing other than the indefinite jousting [*assaut indéfini*] for position among their own kind" (Giard and Mayol 1980: 34; my translation).

Back to the unrepentant push-and-pull of dichotomized thinking when moving to an Internet setting and online scenario, particularly for the social sciences, where on-the-ground scenarios are still given ontological privilege. Communicative practices enabled by Internet technologies entail a more recent, electronically mediated challenge to the well-worn path between yet another much-cosseted dichotomy: the separation between the "local" (national-state) level and the "global" (that is, the international/transnational) levels of analysis and action. This becomes more acute when one is witnessing how exchanges of personal experience are continually overlapped with references to specific and broader geopolitical and economic contexts. Here, the intimate exchanges of the previous section are visibly meshed with historical and political commentary. While any reconstruction is selective, and the ones quoted in this chapter focus on "personal" and intimate lives, more than a passing reference to these additional layers of discussion is required here. References to broader events and issues are integral to the more intimate textual surfaces of these peregrinations. Two examples will suffice to highlight this point and serve as an aide-mémoire for subsequent chapters.

First, an intercultural elision that became apparent through the responses to an initial post of my own on the "public–private distinction" (*sic*). My question was taken up in a different way than I had expected by my interlocutors. I headed the initial post thus: *The "public–private distinction" – is there one??!* (MA, THA, 02/29/00).[24]

> Unfortunately, the answer is NO. Polynesian culture is rooted in a communal relationship. . . . Privatisation is merely a foreign concept and does not thrive in Polynesia.
>
> (True Polynesian, THA, 02/29/00 in reply to above)

> [S]urely this is difficult to maintain these days, even in the islands.
>
> (MA, THA, 03/01/00 in reply to above)

> As said, Privatisation is not what being a Polynesian is all about. Once one start to set boundaries around him/herself and claim total possession over his/her belonging he is not a true Polynesian anymore, he becomes a breed of selfish being and a foreigner and hence we say "fie palangi" (wanting to be a white man (non Polynesian)). However I agree with you, being a Polynesian is hard [to] maintain these days both inside and outside Polynesia.
>
> (True Polynesian, THA, 03/02/00 in reply to above)

I had begun with the notion of public–private as an issue of inter/subjectivity. My interlocutors responded according to another, overlapping, issue, namely, public versus private issues of ownership and control and how these pertain to the Pacific Island societies in general and the Tongan sociopolitical landscape in particular (see Chapter 5). That the two treatments are not that far apart, in both theoretical and political practice and private lives, was all too clear in how this discussion developed and eventually stalled. My main interlocutor, True Polynesian, while taking a stand on "authentic" Polynesian (Tongan) values vis-à-vis public and private ownership, did not see the personal vis-à-vis the public as a problematic or politically relevant issue, beyond those marked by individual choice. That is:

> [W]hat would you say to the notion of the 'personal' in your model of Polynesia as open and sharing? Are not some of the 'tougher' discussion threads also about what is allowed or not? Where the line is between 'personal-private' and 'public'?
>
> (MA, THA, 03/03/00 in reply to above)

> [W]hat don't you understand in the word "personal"? The word speaks for itself and only the person concerned can speak for him/herself.
>
> (True Polynesian, THA, 03/03/00 in reply to above)

This double articulation of the public–private distinction is always present anyway, blurry when dealing with the sociocultural or political implications of Internet technologies, and even trickier when taking both of these into an ostensibly intercultural scenario. When online and involving postcolonial politics and diasporic populations, these include new(er) permutations of some specific mechanics and politics of inter/subjectivity that blur these conceptually and politically troubled parameters even further. What is striking about these gender-focused discussions is how they operate both as personal testimonies and as public statements, acknowledging the distinctions but without balking at the paradoxes they are confronting.

A second example relates to the historical background to any of these discussions and how they unfold. Protagonists are well sensitized to how the personal and the political – the private and public person and their respective communities – are mutually constitutive. These sensibilities are expressed in various ways, as interpolations or major "subthreads" in their own right. In a thread about intimate (extended) familial relationships in Pacific island societies, entitled *brother/sister* (Jatu, 05/26/98), this subthread emerged:

> As a note to this discussion, I would warn participants against 'romanticising' the traditional culture of Tonga or any of the Pacific. . . . At the same time however, we must not be revisionist in our interpretation of the Pacific, and re-invent 'Pacific islanders' to historically reflect who we are now, from a traditional perspective. The influences are far more complex and involve the interaction between Pacific and European/Western culture and religion.
>
> ('Alopi Latukefu, THA, 05/31/98 in jatu, 05/26/98)

> I agree . . . but after 30+ years of being indoctrinated to particular lexicon, values and experiences, it's difficult (impossible?) for me not to process, speculate, and learn information without a tainted view . . . I believe I'm not exclusive to this type of ethnocentrism . . . [such] posts are a bit stifling you know . . . [they] stop speculation before it has had its run.
>
> (Jatu, THA, 06/01/98 in reply to above)[25]

> Stifling your thesis development was certainly not my intention.
>
> ('Alopi Latukefu, THA, 06/01/98 in reply to above)

> What I am trying to illustrate is that as a palangi [non-Polynesian], quite ignorant in Tongan history, anthropology and academia, I may take a different approach in this forum than what may be deemed the correct, or objective one.
>
> (Jatu, THA, 06/03/98 in reply to above)[26]

In the next chapter these issues are brought sharply into relief in discussions about Tongan politics and the future of Tonga in a "global"

world. Here, they operate more as murmurs, counterpoints to the manifest content, or divert into subthreads. The hyperlinking functionality of
World Wide Web software permits such visible – legible – asides in the
midst of larger discussion threads. In so doing they provide an overlapping sonority rather than indicate a diversion as such. This is at once part
of the manifest content's textual surface (evidenced by laterally snaking
subthreads) and the *onlineness* of conversing in written form in asynchronous online communicative spaces (see Chapter 8).

Onlineness

The empirical research of the second volume of *The Practice of Everyday Life*
(de Certeau 1980a) carried out by Pierre Mayol and Luce Giard (1980)
takes the aforementioned treatment of micro- and macro-level data as
corollaries and puts it to work in their urban ethnographies of a working-
class household and women talking about cooking, respectively. There, as
well as here, the aim was to show the aforementioned seam – *couture* – in
operation, as spatial and conversational articulations of the everyday that
include the supposedly "banal" and "domestic" sphere. The same awareness can be applied to observing how everyday (cyber)spaces are constituted, where and for whom Internet portals, websites and other entry
points are designed and run, and who does the talking and what about. As
some of the gendered–ethnic–class contours become more possible to
trace empirically, it is apparent that the content being produced is not
irrelevant, hermetically sealed from offline influences, or foreclosed from
theory and politics. At the same time, the practices unfolding there have
formal properties and ongoing relationships that are specific to being on
the Internet; this is the characteristic of *onlineness*, to put it simply.

Positing a specific characteristic of onlineness is not to lurch into airy-
fairy celebrations of "cyberculture" over and above the nuts and bolts, as it
were, that make any of these electronic interactions possible or the power
struggles going on behind the screens, so to speak. Internet technologies
comprise physical-digital architectures as well as experiential spaces and
places, visible comings and goings, audiovisual but predominantly written
textual practices. These all contribute to the material and symbolic operations of various online "exchanges of meanings" and their offline nodes
where pertinent. The practices of everyday life online are at once self-
contained and porous to offline practices. They articulate corporeal and
noncorporeal displacements and returns that (re)constitute particular
and broader gender power relations. For non-Western and/or diasporic
communities on the Internet, these have inter/intracultural permutations
and tensions. Personal lives, public personae, and the "intimate other" are
interrelated affairs (Chang and Ling 2000; Ling 2002: 20–23; Agathangelou 2003). Online, these affairs are articulated and read in both recognizable and new ways. New, because Internet technologies permit

different communicative spaces and openings for relating. For oral communicative cultures that silence or dismiss women's voices and/or subaltern ones, or written traditions that require rigorous editing and gatekeeping operations before one's words are given due attention, the increasing facility with Internet communications through long-term use at regular intervals has had an empowering effect. Everyday life, as both oppressive routines and familiar conventions, as inextricably affected by capitalist social relations (Lefebvre in Highmore 2002: 113 *passim*), and as a site for *perruquer* in the face of powerful machineries of power also operates in Internet forums. And by the middle of the first decade of the twenty-first century, with the increased familiarity of Internet technologies for scholarly and everyday – banal – interactions, there can be a tendency to forget

> too quickly this long process of familiarization [*accoutumance*], one risks losing sight of the true power, however obscured, with which [Internet] users . . . get a grasp of their own surroundings and the discrete, albeit tenacious, way in which they insinuate themselves into a public space in order to appropriate it.
>
> (Giard and Mayol 1980: 24–25; my translation)

The personal is international in cyberspace, too

As Internet research establishes some sort of foothold in academe or even as the World Wide Web is used as a vast resource base, data access point or document-retrieval clearinghouse, it is still tempting to "domesticate" informal, organic online interactions such as these. Relegating their textual surfaces and onlineness to lower registers of the political, the social, the relevant, perpetuates a monolithic, monocultural, and commodified representation of the Internet – cyberspace. This sort of visualizing is at the heart of corporate R&D trajectories for the future. A closer examination of non-Western diasporas' online presence and articulations further underlines how such a conceptualization carries along with it a somewhat ethnocentric, gender-blind assumption about who actually uses, benefits, and so should contribute to the long-term development of equitable and accessible ICTs. In cyberspace as well, power works in less than mysterious ways for the (cyber)spaces made available and

> in which social practices occur affect the nature of those practices, who is 'in place', who is 'out of place' and even who is allowed to be there at all. But the spaces themselves in turn are constructed and given meaning through the social practices that define women and men as different and unequal.
>
> (McDowell and Sharp 1997: 3)

So, in the midst of discussions about sex–gender roles come other ones that raise these sorts of questions about how globalization processes are impinging upon the public and/or private fabrics of Pacific island societies and communities abroad. Moving even further out than the exchange mentioned earlier on "romanticising" Pacific island social mores, the same women participate in overlying threads such as one entitled *Views on Globalization?*

> I'm a computer novice and this is the first time I've entered a new discussion thread. . . . I am very interested in people's views and opinions on Globalisation as a whole or from any perspective i.e. in relation to Samoa etc.
>
> (Leilani, KR, 08/05/98)

> [T]he worry that I have about Globalisation is the effect it will have (or is having) on smaller entities within society. . . . This is where I see it affecting Samoa. As we move closer to this thing called 'globalisation' and 'universalisation', then the more our needs, wants etc etc will be generalised by the larger corporations. This is where the minority lucks out and has to make do with whatever is available on the market . . . at the same time as this phenomena is the expanding influence of America on the world . . . have you realised how sitting close to 'globalisation' is the idea of 'Americanization'?
>
> (Bitchyspice, KR, 08/05/98 in reply to above)

> One of the main ideas of the 'new world order' is the notion that the balance of power would be determined more so on the economic battlefields. . . . If so we would have to admit that it is much less gruesome. However, whether it's less devastating is still open for discussion.
>
> (JR, KR, 08/06/98 in Leilani, 08/05/98)

> Will the little people be totally powerless (as if we aren't already!) as their companies shut down because they have been bought by Rupert Murdoch or whatever? . . . I think globalisation has a lot of benefits, but its consequential backlash is equally scary . . . hmmmmm . . . reminds me of colonisation a bit don't you think?
>
> (Bitchyspice, KR, 08/06/98 in Leilani, 08/05/98)

> [G]lobalisation is enhanced by communication, finance, environment and consciousness. . . . People are thinking of this planet as a single place or one community. . . . How will this phenomenon impact on the Samoan Islands? Not much. If worse comes to the worse, we can always plant more taros, fa'is and go back fishing . . . or live out of the land to survive any catastrophic events from the crash o the global economy!!! LOL.
>
> (New Kid, KR, 08/06/98 in Leilani, 08/05/98)

Globalisation is the reality of our times ... I think we will continue to see the expansion of corporations.... Whether this will be seen as a benefit from the perspective of the citizens ... is still not clear. I think that depends in large part on the type of leadership in place in those countries.

(JR, KR, 08/06/98 in Leilani, 08/05/98)

These musings (re)articulate questions about who cyberspace (a "global" space/place by definition, arguably) belongs to; whether or not it is for all-comers or to be developed for commercial exploitation. This cannot be addressed in either/or terms, least of all with respect to nonelite and/or non-Western approaches to this (relatively) new cognitive and experiential domain. In spite of the strategic forces reducing the Internet to yet another marketable commodity, modernization/development "must," or governmental tool for lucrative avenues to foreign exchange, the Internet is also more of a space and place for cultural production and everyday socializing than has been experienced heretofore. This "everyday" Internet recalibrates standard renditions and critiques of the personal–political/public–private. The content being produced through online discussions comprises a lot more than just a bunch of disembodied, off-the-cuff streams of consciousness and nonsensical and whimsical jottings of the fictitious "posters," even if they also exist in their own literary right. They are the traces and expressions of real people and/or their online personae. These conversations-as-written-texts have both authors and addressees who are related in some way, or, if not, have become known to each other in the process of articulating what it means to belong – be related – to a certain cultural heritage and/or cultural group. Participants appropriate (poach from) and develop off-the-shelf software for their own needs. In the process of crosscutting conversations, inner lives are "outed." At the same time, the broader political economic and sociocultural contexts are captured in the same frame. These Internet practitioners are well skilled at negotiating these online–offline *coutures*.

The cyber(spatial) traces that are the digital comings and goings that one sees snaking downwards, on and off the computer screen, compact complex interrelationships into the same visual frame. The topics broached and ensuing arguments are then writ large in open cyberspace. What these people talk-write about thereby performs a representational task that is open-ended, fraught with misunderstandings, open to multiple cross-readings, and subject to eventual censure – from both within and outside the immediate communities and societies involved. This representational function, even obligation, has become more marked over the years (see Chapter 7). For critical IR/IPE into Internet-mediated practices, this is a politics of representation in the making, deeply relevant to everyday lives and global politics as participants communicate about things that matter to them. The cumulated online archives record the complex diasporic and postcolonial contexts in which these women and men are living. Participants are well aware of the interconnections and contradictions between their online interventions, the postcolonial politics of life in the South Pacific Islands, and the complexities of these for Polynesians living and growing up abroad.

Concluding comments

Bearing in mind that these samples are a small part of the online tapestry of the Pacific Islands on the Internet, some concluding comments can be made. First, the thread entitled *I'm Tired of Slaving Myself* (Lafemme Nikita, KB/Polycafe, 05/19/99) began by arguing that while dichotomies such as public–private are limited and limiting, they nonetheless constitute the way social sciences construct the social world-as-object in the first instance and then operate as gendered and socioculturally lived tropes for assigning "difference" or delineating belonging. This first set of reconstructions show online practices of everyday life (and conversely) challenge this sort of foundational thinking. Not necessarily as the product of Internet technologies *per se* (as this would simply posit another sort of technological determinism), but as diasporic and postcolonial practices that appropriate current ICTs. With their own textual surfaces and onlineness, yes, but also with close ties to on-the-ground lives.

Second, this chapter has introduced the ways in which practices of everyday life online operate in tangibly gendered ways for these communities and Internet forum constituencies. The floor was given to (re)articulations of how the "personal is political, is international" vis-à-vis changing or contested sex–gender roles for (Pacific Island) women. What becomes apparent, and together with the reconstructions that follow, is a far more multiplex delineation of publicness, personal politics, intimacies – and the "interstices" between – than classic public–private dichotomies would allow. The same follows for those looking to understand these conversations as either "virtual" (as opposed to "real") or "traditional" versus "modern" interpretations of gender power relations. The women here underscore the workings of this institutionalized "double bind" (Benhabib and Cornell 1987: 9) and double standard for many women still, let alone for "non-Western" women living in the West.

Third, the intimate details and politicized interventions are nonetheless embedded in the qualities of onlineness, the way these forums are run (see Chapter 7). As content and form they need to be comprehended politically and socioculturally (Giard and Mayol 1980: 24–25). Far from showing a passive consumption of a predetermined technology (de Certeau 1980a: 11–14), or "just" providing mutual support networks,[27] these threads trace (postcolonial) gender power relations as they are (re)iterated and (re)contested everyday (McDowell and Sharp 1997: 266–267). Their constitutive communities and online traversals form an integral and vital part of the symbolic and material substance of the World Wide Web, its constituent places and spaces.

To set the scene for the next (more recognizably political) discussions of the next chapter, another observation bears reiterating. These online traversals and everyday practices need to be grasped as part of the (post)colonial historical context of the South Pacific Islands themselves, one that is openly recognized, for better or worse, as a "global" context. They trace numerous interactions between this ocean's peoples and their diasporas, former colonizers, and global exigencies in their contemporary "globally restructured" everyday lives, both on- and offline. These bespeak centuries of "precontact" migratory movements, political economic relations and histories, and (post)colonial rule that have impacted on how the ostensibly "empty" South Pacific ocean has been represented and is seen in light of neoliberal restructuring imperatives.[28] As for those issues that concern the women of the KB and the KR, these representations impact upon everyday gender power relations, love relationships, family obligations, and the desire to be "my own woman" on "my own terms." The eloquence and forthrightness of these women is not confined to questions of the "domestic" sphere and "women's issues," however. They are just as vocal, albeit for different reasons and with differing allegiances, in debates that belong to the "public/male domain" of politics, as the next chapter shows.

5 "A play on the royal demons"
Tongan political dissent online

Introduction

Since the World Wide Web/email and "dotcom" booms took off in the 1990s, political establishments and theorists have turned their attention to the Internet as both an enabler for (new) and a threat to (established) political conventions. Questions posed include: How do – and should – Internet technologies provide added value to the "public sphere" of democratic societies? Or are they detrimental to the latter, leading to "inauthentic" sorts of citizen participation or excesses? Are Internet technologies cause or effect of neoliberal globalization imperatives? Are they harbingers of "democratization" or exacerbating an entrenched socioeconomic and geographical "divide" between the (ICT) haves and have-nots? To date, political establishments' responses to these questions seldom make allowances for multifarious noncommercial alternative media or activist groups' perceptions and uses of Internet technologies. Instrumentalist and PR-related applications tend to predominate in political parties' and individual politicians' approaches to the Internet.[1] Autocratic, authoritarian, and various forms of "single-party" democracies have their own set of responses, which overlap situations of (the lack of) press freedom and forms of direct government intervention into citizens' Internet activities respectively (Dai 2000). How the government of the Kingdom of Tonga has been responding to these technopolitical developments is both typical and exceptional, given the small size and the lo-tech and "undeveloped" status of this country (see Chapter 2). ICTs have figured in the political economy of the "Friendly Islands," as both mediators for sociopolitical discontent and new ways of accumulating foreign exchange, all along – in the first instance, as (relatively new) media for ongoing agitation on the ground by political dissidents who have been mobilizing for constitutional change; in the second, as strategic opportunities for the Tongan government and royal family to create foreign exchange and "corner" the ICT market in the local-regional free-market context.

With the above debates and events as the backdrop, this chapter reconstructs a set of intense political discussions that mainly took place on the Kava Bowl between participants from the "Tongan diaspora" and those living in the Kingdom.[2] These threads encapsulate years of debates about the pros and cons of "democracy" – as an abstract concept, as a set of values for the South Pacific Islands generally, and as a key theme for organized political dissent in Tonga in particular. While specific to this country, these online altercations highlight an oft-overlooked aspect to everyday democratic politics, namely, that any form of democracy is historically and socially produced, constituted by practices in the making and by interlocking discursive terrains, gender power relations and respective subject positions, and many an unspoken assumption (see Williams 1977: 29 *passim*). The argument of this chapter is that psychoemotional, intercultural, and intracultural nuances are rarely addressed in analyses of the fraught relationship between ICTs and (theories of) democracy. What tends to be overlooked is how democracy "is a multivalent concept with not only political, but also cultural, ideological, moral and even emotional connotations. In consequence, democracy may have different meanings in different cultural contexts" (van Meijl 1998: 391).

These reconstructions have been read as part of (indeed they speak directly to) a particular technohistorical and discursive conjuncture. The conflation of essentialist understandings of "democracy" with geostrategic and commercial trajectories for the Internet has been absorbed into neoliberal versions of modernization–development discourses (Nustad 2004; Rist 1997). Democracy, ICTs, market forces, economic growth, human rights, and development have become inseparable (US Department of State 1999b; AUSTEO 1997; OECD 2001). Neither an economic alternative nor a fully fledged debate is thinkable, it seems. These latest modernization discourses are "transferred," along with various technological paraphernalia and structural adjustment policies, to the "global South" without further discussion. In this broader historical and policy-making context, what happens when social and political discontent and dissent are able to be expressed in moderated Internet forums for non-Western constituencies? With respect to South Pacific Island political cultures, that of Tonga especially, how do appeals to "traditional" and/or "modern" democratic values, and defences of national-cultural integrity in the face of internal and external pressures for change, operate in online debates about the whys and wherefores of political change in Tonga? How are these positions inflected with different historical narratives with respect to certain online–offline subject positions? While these debates articulate the particular sociocultural and emotional contours of Tongan politics and society, what do they reveal about the various meanings that constitute "democracy," as principle, ideal, and practice?

Chapter outline

There are three main sections to this chapter. The first briefly outlines the Tongan political situation on the ground, to which these threads manifestly speak. This is a backdrop of increasing agitation for significant electoral reforms as well as (online and offline) political campaigning around the respective general elections in Tonga. There are at least three layers of interpretation at stake here. The first part is to locate these *Tongan* discussions within a broader historical interplay: the legacies of colonial rule and neocolonial (by the United States and Australia for the most part) interests in the South Pacific region; various stages, experiences, and perceptions of neoliberal globalization since the mid-1980s vis-à-vis ICTs; and the impact of various indigenous peoples' political movements in the region, which encompass a set of local responses to these geostrategic and historical factors. These are imbricated in both human rights and indigenous rights discourses (UN 2000; L. T. Smith 1999). Various political movements in the Pacific region for indigenous autonomy, sovereignty, or land rights (see Helu 1999c: 32 *passim*; Wood 1997) operate between the lines of these threads' focus on "pro-democracy" and "human rights" activism in Tonga.

The second section reconstructs the main discussion threads, which are among the longest and most dense on either the KB or KR.[3] The issues being broached are not only politically sensitive, but personally and socially so as well. Hence the widespread recourse to anonymity in these discussions. In terms of how the threads emerged over the years, there are four discernible "*coutures*" in their thematic fabric vis-à-vis Tongan-specific and general theories or ideals of democracy. There are two accents to this fabric that pertain to where participants' subject positions crisscross with each other online and offline: "situated experience" and inter/subjectivity.

The third main section looks more closely at these online–offline nuances. Where participants are living and their (self-)designations and/or socioeconomic positionings in Tongan terms are inflected in the way lengthier discussions unfurl in that they can be food for debate as well.[4] Contradictions and non sequiturs are integral elements of these cumulative and overlapping threads, which are, to recall, ongoing multilateral conversations.

These discussions are accessible to readers who are not *au fait* with South Pacific societies and political cultures. For these conversations are all about "ambivalent attitudes towards democracy" (Tarte 2000: 5). That being said, three interpretational hazards need to be mentioned with respect to the complex political situation in many Pacific Island societies. First, one must beware of dehistoricizing and thereby romanticizing South Pacific sociopolitical systems before "contact."[5] Second, one should avoid assuming that the aforementioned conflation of development, democracy, and human rights discourses with neoliberal mantras is either unproblematic or challengeable from one historical-political standpoint only. Third, it is necessary to be aware that even liberal – "model" – democratic systems (those of the United States, Britain, Australia, France) differ in how they apply, understand, and question their respective democratic precepts, electoral systems, and political institutions.

Reconstructing these debates has another set of complexities. The competing historical narratives and their respective sociocultural and political economic dimensions constitute a distinct set of threads in these forums, but they are also part of a host of other conversations. In terms of their online particularities, the debating style of these texts both draws upon and diverges from how public political forums operate, in Tonga as well as in Samoa. Online, they are more informal, less gender-exclusive and hierarchical in permitting participants the right to speak. On the ground (tourist versions thereof notwithstanding), formal kava ceremonies, informal kava clubs (*faikava*), and public political forums are largely male and/or aristocratic preserves. In this Kava Bowl, women are active and prominent participants in this online rendition of an "informal kava party [for] commoner classes ... which includes no chiefs.... [The] whole aim here is to freely and openly discuss topical issues and any subject under the sun that may catch the interest of those participating" (Helu 1999d: 5). The KB permits the outing of political dissidence or dissatisfaction for many, a chance to air their political views without fear of reprobation.

1 Tongan politics: offline and online delineations

Delineations on the ground

> Our small Pacific Island nations are forever struggling to stay afloat financially. We lack the magnitude of natural resources, industry, skills and infrastructure of the larger Western countries. Our weak economies increasingly cause an inexorable drain on human resources when many see emigration as the only route to personal survival and advancement. Our homelands rely disproportionately on foreign aid, and increasingly on the remittances from Islanders working, or living overseas.
>
> (KBAdmin, KB, 06/17/99)

The initial post quoted above succinctly sums up the complex political economic and historical geographies of the twenty-first-century South Pacific in general, and Tonga and Samoa in particular. The problems facing small island countries looking for economic stability as well as political and sociocultural autonomy since full independence in their immediate region (dominated by Australia, the United States, and New Zealand) and vis-à-vis neoliberal political economic exigencies are major ones.[6] Viable solutions to endemic economic vulnerability are compounded by environmental and historical factors that include the effects of global warming, fisheries depletion, cyclones. The picture is further complicated by the way in which (nuclear) geostrategic and economic interests of larger powers (French, US, Japanese, and Australian) intervene in the region to the present day. Like many small island countries, Tonga and the two Samoas are dependent on direct foreign aid – from Australia, New Zealand, the European Union, and China (since 1999). The aid is provided with varying degrees of conditionality. As I noted in Chapter 2, Pacific island countries have been subjected to the stringency rules of IMF–World Bank structural adjustment programs. Regional and "global" intergovernmental agencies and individual governments all keep a close watch on any local political or economic events in these countries. All these internal and external pressures are at play in the discussions.

The political histories of the "three remaining truly aristocratic societies of the South Pacific" (Hau'ofa 1992: 3/5), namely Tonga, Samoa, and Fiji, are particularly pertinent. That of the Kingdom of Tonga is the grist to this discussion mill, a society with a political core that is, according to some commentators, an "absolutist," "feudal" monarchy (van Meijl 1998: 389). After at least a decade of conflict in the mid-nineteenth century, the constitution of 1875 finally cemented the rule of King George Tupou I over rival chiefs, codified and limited (from a hundred to thirty) male and chiefly rights to land tenure, and installed a Bill of Rights and legislative and judicial procedures. Executive power still resides with the king (*Tu'i Tonga*), who appoints his Ministers of the Crown (*Ma'u Mafai*) from the remaining nobility (*Hou'eiki*). This constitutional setup has remained largely unchanged ever since, an institutional socioeconomic division that has been underscored in language uses, educational opportunity and socioeconomic obligations (Helu 1999b; 1999c: 132–136; 1999e: 195–196).[7]

Contemporary Tongan political conventions are encoded in a written Constitution. It is a constitution that adheres to principles of representational democracy models, albeit tempered by rights and obligations based on chiefly privilege. It is the founding document of "modern" Tonga under the reign of this royal dynasty. It has been robustly criticized, nonetheless, by an increasingly vocal and economically influential sector from the majority of commoners (Hau'ofa 1992: 3/5). The king and cabinet (twelve nobles appointed by the monarch) preside over a Legislative Assembly, which is divided between nine noble representatives selected from (and by) Tonga's thirty-three aristocratic families, and nine People's Representatives who are elected by the country's designated commoners – over 90 percent of the population. In short, the royal family and nobility effectively own and control political economic life through this direct control of the legislature (by twenty-one to nine), cabinet, and judiciary.

The direct descendant of King George Tupou I, King Taufa'ahua Tupou IV, has been in power since 1945, making him one of the world's longest-reigning monarchs. He has close ties with European aristocratic circles and a historical connection to the British monarchy through his mother, the late Queen Salote. His oldest son and heir apparent is Crown Prince Tupouto'a. His younger son, Prince Lavaka 'Ulukalala Ata, has been prime minister since 2000. The king's oldest daughter, Princess Pilolevu, resides in Tonga. She is Patron not only of the Tongan History Association (THA), whose Internet forum and membership was closely affiliated to the KB, but also of a nascent royalist party, *Kotoa*, that emerged in the lead-up to the 2002 general election.

Not unlike many other ruling dynasties, the Tongan royal family has accumulated a personal fortune in overseas bank accounts. How much exactly is in itself the source of constant speculation and public criticism (James 2003; Pacific Magazine 2002). In any case, significant parts of Tonga's telecommunications, IT sectors (which are significant by Pacific Island standards, based on geostationary satellite rights, telephony, and Internet services), television, and print media are government owned, or controlled by the two oldest children of the king. The crown prince owns and controls Internet services and access (through the Royal School of Science), (mobile/wireless) telephony, and electricity. Princess Pilolevu heads the satellite business, Tongasat. Several public scandals surrounding the business dealings of the royals, perennial charges of nepotism and corruption in the public sector (Pacific Media Watch 2003), and the emergence of an organized political opposition to this status quo (see below) fuel the immediate content of these online discussions. The more prominent of these affairs include the government sale of Tongan passports in the 1980s to immigrants, mainly Chinese; the Tongasat satellite business deal that went sour; the whereabouts of overseas earnings from the sale of the ".to" Internet domain at the height of the dotcom boom; and in 2001 the controversy about the whereabouts of public monies in the aftermath of "dubious investment manoeuvres" by executives heading the Tonga Trust Fund (James 2003: 175).

The second delineation to political debate and agitation on the ground is the emergence of a vocal, organized, and relatively successful opposition since 1992 that has been advocating electoral reform in order to grant "commoners" more direct say in governing the country. In addition, it has been calling for more accountability from the ruling elite. Calls for constitutional change have been an ongoing theme in Tongan elections since the 1970s at least, and are a main tenet of the Tonga Human Rights and Democracy Movement (THRDM). In these threads, it is referred to by an earlier name, the Tongan Pro-Democracy Movement. It counts among its membership prominent intellectuals such as Futa Helu and Epeli Hau'ofa, under the leaderships of 'Akilisi Pohiva and with the support of prominent journalists such as Kalafi Moala, owner-editor of the beleagured *Taimi 'o Tonga* newspaper (Pacific Media Watch 2003; Pacific Islands Report 2002). By urging for constitutional change, activists have been at the forefront of moves to significantly curb the ruling elite's grip on political office by amending the 1875 constitution. Steady electoral success has been booked in the past decade or so for candidates on the pro-democracy ticket: a majority of commoners' seats in 1996, five of the nine seats in 1999, and seven of the nine in 2002. Given the ambiguous institutional political party status of the THRDM (ostensibly a movement rather than a political party as such), low voter turnout in the 2002 elections, and the variation between the results in Tongatapu (the seat of government) and those in outlying islands, the jury is still out as to whether the movement could claim a clear mandate in 2002 (James 2003: 174).[8] Be that as it may, calls for constitutional change remains a major part of the political landscape, and the electoral successes of the THRDM have been steady since its inception in 1992.

As critics of government's political performance, prominent activists have been subjected to various forms of pressure, including imprisonment and public relations battles fought through the local media. Government moves to restrict foreign media ownership in 2003 have been seen as a ploy to banish the critical journal *Taimi 'o Tonga* (Pacific Media Watch 2003). Pohiva and two prominent Tongan journalists have been jailed or detained on more than one occasion, in 1996, 1997, and 2001.[9] In the threads looked at here, the lead-up to and aftermath of the 1999 general election are a core theme as the political opposition gained ground in electoral terms and, arguably, increased its "grassroots" support base in Tonga. A third element that is a background murmur to these discussions is the various indigenous peoples' and sovereignty political movements throughout the Pacific, New Zealand Maori, Hawaiian, and Fijian indigenous sovereignty movements being cases in point. A key tension here is between the rights of indigenous peoples based on principles of self-determination (UN 2000) and those based on the UN Declaration of Universal Human Rights.[10]

Delineations online

It is in this context that these online interactions, between Tongan-based and expat Tongan nationals for the most part, need to be read. The very notion of what it is to be "Tongan," how Tonga is ultimately to be defined (Helu 1999d: 8), is as much a historical, a political issue as it is a "cultural code" (see Chapter 6). The samples below, taken from three different albeit overlapping threads, encapsulate the above complexities. The first is by a fervent supporter of the "democracy movement," the second from a non-Tongan (palangi) regular and another who calls herself/himself OneTongan.

> IF, and the emphasis is on the world [*sic*] IF – we give the power to the people (true democracy). The system will correct itself with its

checks and balances. The present form of government lacks that unfortunately.... The people who support the democratic movement ... love the country and the people just as much as those opposing the movement ... you're assuming that we'll replace our Custom and our Culture with Democratic rights. That assumption is wrong, of course, because ... these rights are weaved into the fabric of our society, it identifies who we are as human beings, and true democracy will only bring out the best in it ... the rights of the people, that is at the center of the Democratic Movement.

(Tokoni Mai, KB, 05/16/99 in NINJA, 05/12/99)

[Y]ou can not assert that the status quo represents some sort of authentic Tongan tradition passed down from when the first canoes arrived millenia [*sic*] ago. Change has occurred throughout Tongan history.... It may well be that further changes are needed now.

(George Candler, KB, 03/09/99 in Ghost, 03/05/99)

Where did you get your culture from? First the king and "nobles" taught the commoners to BOW to them. When the palangis with Christianity came to your shore, you added biblical teachings to your culture. I guess you don't know that.

(OneTongan, KB, 06/08/99 in Ikani, 06/08/99)

What may appear as a Ping-Pong match between two political camps (pro-democracy/change versus pro-monarchy/status quo) is more complex than that. For many of the diasporic participants, what is "Tonga," what makes it unique in their eyes, cannot be separated from the country's political history since "contact," even if the incumbent political elite is found to be wanting. A US-based regular articulates this position as follows:

I agree ... most Tongans may want some form of democracy. However, I am certain that most Tongans, especially those in Tonga, also want to maintain the power of the Royal family. Is that an oxymoron? No. Simply a call for greater popular representation in the Government but NOT at the expense of our royal institution that makes our Kingdom so unique.

(Phil Tukia, KB, 09/18/98 in KBAdmin, 09/07/98)

In the postcolonial South Pacific, human/indigenous rights, desire for self-determination, and the downward pressures of structural adjustment, climactic change, and environmental degradation are woven through both studiously argued and fiery polemic. For instance:

The big green-machine of capitalism and imperialism bred by

democracy makes the call. The rest of us are just paying rent. It's
called assimilation – and the world has come to know it all too well.

(Makavili, KB, 08/09/98 in KBAdmin, 02/08/98)

What many people don't realise is that democracy is ... a deadly
weapon against a people of strong indigenous backgrounds ... I
understand that many of those running the government are corrupt
and it saddens me that Tonga has lost its glory days, but it could be
much worse. Had not Tupou 1 (a royal) did what he did, you can bet
your bottom dollar that ... the Tongan people would be like other
Polynesian people who would be homeless in their own land.

(Manu Lobendahn, KB, 05/13/99 in NINJA, 05/12/99)

2 The threads

Four seams, *coutures*, are traceable through this particular patchwork of
discussions.

Seam 1

The first concerns the integrity, and by implication the representative legitimacy, of the incumbent political rulers. In the Kava Bowl discussions, critics
debate heatedly with supporters, whether they are posting from overseas or
Tonga itself. In the midst of calls for greater participation in the legislature
by nonnobles and, by implication, in decision-making functions in the civil
service as well, those loyal to the status quo reject the normative claims of
Western-style representative democracy or Western socioeconomic models as
inherently or self-evidently superior. By the same token, critics point to the
structural vulnerability of both the Tongan economy and the low standard of
living of the majority of Tongans as the consequence of either incompetence
or profiteering on the part of the political elite. Historical legacy and
present-day expectations are implicit in both positions. For example:

Who do you think you are? What have you done for Tonga? The King
and the nobles did a lot for Tonga. than you and I put together. So
leave Tonga's legislative assembly as it is.

(Vai ko Hiva, KB, 08/28/99 in KBAdmin, 02/08/98)

Do you believe in democracy and if so, how do you define this democracy?. Do you believe in equality and do you separate social equality
from political equality?. Justify the contrast in living standards
between the common people and the Nobility in Tonga?. These are
just some of the questions you as a Tongan need to ask yourself.
Proud to be Tongan!

(Ghost, KB, 03/03/99)

Fervent pro-royalists are clear in what they will not countenance in calls for constitutional change:

> Dream on. Your pro-Western wishes need a wash in the nearest laun-dramat. Tonga is a Constitutional Monarchy, if you don't already know. The King does not own anyone; HM is empowered by the Con-stitution to be head-of-state ... the people are protected and given rights, too, by the Constitution.
>
> (Sione Ake Mokofisi, KB, 03/08/99 in Ghost, 03/05/99)

By this reckoning, any change is tantamount to courting instability, a threat to a "traditional way of life." The latter are inseparable in that the royalty–nobles–commons social hierarchy *are* "Tonga and being Tongan is a way of life and a strong cultural way of thinking not a government system" (Mapatongiamanu, 05/15/99 in NINJA 05/12/99).[11] Once again, both sides often refer to Tonga as inherently different from its neighbors (Fiji and Hawaii in particular). In both instances, the response has to be a local one:

> I disagree with you on your assumption that we'll lose our historical CUSTOM or CULTURE if we become more democratic. . . . Our situ-ation is DIFFERENT. This is a discussion between Tongans. It is more like an In-House sharings between members of the same family who have opposing views. The good thing about this is that they share the same values, cultures, customs. . . . This love of the country doesn't necessarily means that you have to accept what the Government is doing especially if it is not right. Love of the country can also be taken to mean changing the way the Government is operating.
>
> (Tokoni Mai, 05/16/99 in NINJA, 05/12/99)[12]

This *couture* runs along the issue of whether Tonga's political leaders are a benign autocracy, with arguably one or two bad apples whose "right to succession" should be reviewed accordingly, or the main beneficiaries of an inefficient and nepotistic system. Despite appeals to the Westmin-ster-style Tongan constitution and "traditional" political-economic obliga-tions as the bedrock of *Tongan*-style democracy, critics (echoing comparable debates about structural socioeconomic inequities in many other nominally democratic societies) argue that in practice these amount to there being "2 set of rules in Tonga. One for the King and his 'nobles' and one for the people of Tonga" (OneTongan, KB, 06/08/99 in Ikani, 06/08/99).

Whether this status quo can continue to provide relative political stability in a region characterized by "ethnic violence" and/or "neotradi-tionalist" forms of indigenous rule gained by recourse to arms is a moot point, online and on the ground. Here the legal principles of universal human rights and/or indigenous peoples' rights are neither self-explanatory nor sufficient in themselves. As Futa Helu notes, although

> in terms of the Constitution the common people have been emancipated from the arbitrary authority of chiefs, the great legal chiefs of modern Tonga ... still exercise almost unlimited power over commoners by virtue of the culture which requires the latter to defer on all matters to their chiefly masters who are never to be questioned or criticised on any issue whatsoever ... the way people in power relentlessly hunt down, in libel suits, the most vociferous critics of the present system and tradition-based privileges suggests that political persecution and subtle (therefore more pernicious) forms of human rights abuses are already in place.
>
> (Helu 1999c: 35–36)

Seam 2

The second *couture* traces specific calls for reform on the one hand and their long-term implications for Tongan society at large on the other. Calls for constitutional change, whereby all MPs and ministers are elected by commoners and nobles alike, go to the heart of centuries of "adherence to chiefly and royal successions" (KBAdmin, KB, 02/08/98)[13] that have shaped the Tongan political landscape, both before, during, and since "contact." A former People's Representative, William Afeaki, posting from Utah in the United States, put it this way in the aftermath of the 1999 general election, where

> the people of Tonga came together and spoke their will by electing 9 representatives to the House. So did the 33 hereditary nobles! Their process of election is absolutely ludicrous and it must change ... nobles in the Legislative Assembly will still be accountable to His Majesty who appoints and grants them their hereditary titles and estates. On the other hand, in the Legislative Assembly, they shall also be accountable to the people who voted them into the House.
>
> (William Afeaki, KB, 08/28/99)

These first two seams do not denote mutually exclusive positions between pro-royalty or pro-democracy but rather between those for change – of some sort – and those for the status quo. Whether for or against major reform, it is the issue of what constitutes equitable *and* effective political representation, the skill and accountability of the incumbent elites, the everyday working relationship between noble and "people's" representatives and their effectiveness in public office that is most prominent. Declared royalists are also part of the Pro-Democracy Movement and prominent activists take their chance to make this more subtle point in the relative political immunity of the Kava Bowl. For "being pro-democracy does not constitute being anti-monarchy. And being pro-monarch should not mean anti-democracy" (Kalafi Moala, KB, 09/12/98 in KBAdmin, 09/07/98). THRDM activism online is as socially and politically charged as it is on the ground. The respective pro-change or pro-status quo online geographies are arguably more tangible than they are offline, however. These positionings come to light when pro-royalists living away from Tonga are pitted against pro-change supporters. Take this interaction, for instance, in a thread entitled *NO DEMOCRACY MOVE-MENT IN TONGA, I HOPE NOT!* (NINJA, KB, 05/12/99):

> Tonga has survived being swallowed up by big countries because it was run by tradition and custom not by politics which is exactly what democracy is all about.
>
> (Manu, KB, 05/13/99 in reply to above)

> Your post deal only with the negative side of democracy. Can you now share with us the positive side. I mean, democracy cannot be that all bad, can it? OR Are you saying that it is good for everybody else including you and all the Tongans overseas (NZ, USA, Australia, Europe etc.) and it is bad for the Tongans in Tonga? Is that what you are saying?
>
> (Tokoni Mai, KB, 05/14/99 in NINJA, 05/12/99)

> Okay so u don't [like] the idea of a democracy in Tonga.... What about the multiple injustices across the country?... Every man to his opinion, mine is strong with conviction that the King needs to take heed to the predominant current forces. Monarchies only exists nowadays largely due to them acting as figureheads.... I can't say that the King has ever given reason for a political violent outburst but he has ignored the people's cry for more equality in Parliament. He must help the people in this way and not fear the inevitable. Because he holds the reins on every segment in the country.... I can't stand the present system and that's why I am thinking of leaving this country. I cannot work under these rules and corrupt departments.... Out and over.
>
> (Makafitu, KB, 05/19/99 in NINJA, 05/12/99)

Socioeconomic lines of obligation and identification intersect with these contending ideals. For instance, in a subthread that developed out of the discussion mentioned earlier, on "chiefly and royal successions," a member of the KB leadership interacts with a regular – a woman – about basic definitions:

> I am a little puzzled that the primary focus in the responses so far has been on "democracy" per se ... as though this is a topic which pits

"royalists" against "pro-democrats", and I do not see it that way. Rather, I see the question's emphasis (and maybe I am alone in this) on the process of "succession" which does not preclude maintaining the current system of monarchy, chiefs and nobles ... only revising the process by which those positions are filled.

(Sandy Macintosh, KB, 02/12/98 in KBAdmin, 02/08/98)[14]

To put it bluntly my dear Sandy, I for one don't want the Crown Prince Tupouto'a nor any of the Royal household to succeed into Political Leadership. I would very much like A Constitutional Monarchy as per the British system thank you very much. We find it hard to differentiate between the Royal Family and Politics because they are so much part, if not the core, of our current political system that you ask questions about Royal successions, it is the same thing as political succession.... I am not a fan of the Royal family, only because of the discrepancies in regards to their personal dealings in what should be Public Assets. I think that with regards to a pure Royal Succession for the Crown Prince, I have no problem, and I will hail Long Live the King, as loud as the next Royalist. I just don't want him to have the power to Veto Parliament decisions. I say it is high time, the people be allowed to take a real and effective part in deciding their future, not have the future taken away by the actions of a very few and select elite.

(Tiana, KB, 02/13/98 in reply to above)

Intersections with the more intimate conversations about traditional–modern sex–gender roles, in Tongan society at least, are not far away from these threads' manifest context. Despite the higher rank of first-born women in Tongan family structures,[15] political roles and discourse on the ground, in Samoa and Tonga at least, are dominated by men of titled rank. In this respect, the online Kava Bowl, with its numerous and vocal female – and nonnoble – voices are not representative of formal kava ceremonies, or of the Tongan Parliament for that matter. The above thread continues as follows:

You contradict, then confirm (should I say, "Just like a woman"? Naw ... I'd better not! Hehehe) and I must say that you and I are on the same page politically. You see, I am VERY much a Royalist (vis-à-vis Tonga), myself, but, like you, am concerned about the quality of the next monarch should traditional succession take place.... This whole discussion regarding the on-going democracy-versus-monarchy debate is a whole 'nother issue.

(Sandy, KB, 02/13/98 in reply to above)

Now look who's being contradictory my friend?... you're 'concerned about the quality of the next monarch should traditional succession take place' yet you still feel the Royal Family has a better candidate to offer. . . . Royal succession in Tonga unlike anywhere else in the world is not a political or public matter, it is a personal matter in the Royal household and as it has always been, traditional 'First Born' succession. I don't care about this succession as such because it is a foregone conclusion. It is the stagnant political situation with which I have the problem. Nevertheless, you're quite welcome to join me on rank in 'womanhood' anytime my friend hehehehe.

(Tiana, 02/13/98, in reply to above)

Seam 3

The third *couture* is one in which pro-royals and pro-change advocates agree with each other to a certain extent. This is the issue of poor performances in office by cabinet ministers (who are appointed from the nobility) and whether they are adequately in touch with their constituencies, especially those outside the main city of Nuku'alofa. For those who advocate more radical change, the current rulers are simply not doing a good enough job but are not under any pressure to do so and so are evidence of the need for new political blood:

> Ministers of the Crown, once they are appointed can hold that office until they are too old to serve anymore and in some cases, until they die. What happened if they do not do their job or they CONTINUE TO ABUSE THEIR POWER? The answer: Its anybody's guess.
>
> (Tokoni Mai, KB, 05/15/99 in NINJA, 05/12/99)

A large part of the THRDM's popularity, whether tacit or active at election time over recent years, has been down to the various corruption scandals, and endemic nepotism in key civil service appointments coupled with poor performance in office. Changes to the Tongan political economy over the last half of the twentieth century also eroded the incumbent socioeconomic hierarchies' presumption of educational and economic superiority over the "*me'avale*" – the common people – still further (Hau'ofa 1992). The government's abrupt treatment of political opponents (Amnesty International 1997; Coggan 1997; Dixon 1996) by arrests and imprisonment over the past decade or so has provided more grist to the reformers' mill. The following post sums up this widespread, albeit difficult to gauge in electoral terms, discontent very well. It also makes clear where change should occur:

> There are so many things that need to be changed in the kingdom starting from the very bottom. The heavy equipment operators run their own operation within the government time and pocket the money. The government operated fishmarket employees take home

meat whenever they wish without showing on the record. Habour personnels remove (form [*sic*] the premise) properties that they are not authorized to. The authorities misuse thier [*sic*] power when it comes to government properties and vehicles. The police officers are scams. The immigration/police officers at checkpoint at the Fua'amotu airport will let anything through with some bribery money. The legislative assembly members (people and noble reps.) misuse their benefits. The royal family control the tv network, space right, the internet right, the oversea land right, the cabinet seat right, the head of the military right, the right to be in Tonga, the right to modify the constitution, etc., etc., The problem is that the resources are not divided evenly and every that everyone is a scam straight from the very top to the laborers. Now how are we going to either weed them out or change the system to a more even an honest system? I think we should correct the top because when the person at the top is an honest one, he/she won't allow any dishonesty or twisting the system.

(Fonua 'a e kakai 'a e fonua, KB, 02/16/98 in KBAdmin, 02/08/98)

But it is not only the aristocratic political representatives who come under the spotlight. Prominent pro-democracy activists themselves, who are members of a loose coalition at the best of times, get thrown into the fray, either under their own volition by mixing it with the participants online (Moala and Afeaki) or as public figures in their own right. If these politicians and intellectuals are not being taken to task for being abroad, their performance itself is questioned directly – and defended. For instance:

I was a Representative of the People in the Tongan Assembly for two consecutive terms. I know what I am talking about. This is my business. I am a Tongan citizen and subject, therefore, I have vested interest in the future of Tonga and its government. Under the Tongan constitution, there are two offices that are given the powers to make laws in the land i.e. the King and the Legislative Assembly. The latter must be given full rights to do that. Right now, Cabinet and the Privy Council introduced all the Bills to the House.

(wpafeaki, KB, 08/29/99 in William Afeaki, 08/28/99)

Let us focus in the real issue here, what are we, the people of Tonga, going to achieve from this? Or, should I say benefit from this? If the members of parliament are serious about this issue what can't they halve their salary and donate the other half for charity?... Of the nobels, I'd rather keep the devil I know than the devil I don't know.

(vai ko hiva, KB, 09/01/99 in reply to above)

As for the Devil that you know and the one that you don't know, perhaps it is time for you to find out more about the latter and get to know him better. We need constitutional reforms in Tonga and not a revolution!

(wpafeaki, KB, 09/01/99, in reply to above)

The leadership of the THRDM are not spared from criticism, either. In one of the longest threads, entitled *Pohiva's credentials?* (Manu 05/18/99), a pro-royalist is taken to task for casting aspersions on Pohiva's educational credentials vis-à-vis those of the royal family.[16] The social implications of THRDM claims are regarded in a dim light by pro-royalists, who see social and political decline if the incumbent system were to be radically altered. These sentiments are strongly felt and emphatically and regularly expressed. For others, Pohiva is the quintessential "VOICE OF CHANGE in Tonga ... fighting for the right of the people to choose and elect their own leaders" (Tokoni Mai, KB, 05/14/99 in NINJA, 05/12/99). Somewhere in between are politicians like Afeaki:

I feel 'Akilisi's proposals are extreme and would disrupt a lot of values that we currently cherish and enjoy. I truly think that the Pro-Democracy Movement is losing momentum and credibility. There is an urgent need therefore, that we come up with alternatives that would being a more accountable government without disrupting and sacrificing the other niceties of Tongan living!

(wpafeaki, KB, 09/03/99 in William Afeaki, 08/28/99)

Be that as it may, for others the issue is not personality politics but rather an antiquated and contradictory political system:

There is no point in discussing the merits of mere people ... because then we lose sight of the bigger picture, and this can also be labelled as useless and ridiculous personal slander. It is the System that's crooked, enabling even more crooked decisions and people to prosper.

(Tiana, KB, 02/13/98 in KBAdmin, 02/08/98)

Seam 4

The fourth *couture* runs through the cultural backdrop and historical legacy of colonial rule in the whole region. It traces the relationship between various indigenous peoples' understandings of democracy for postcolonial and global times vis-à-vis Modern Age experiences of national identity formation (Anderson 1991), a process in which Tonga carved its own niche in the mid-nineteenth century under Tupou I. What is called "traditionalism" – it appeals to precontact practices and institutions as a reaction to Western ones – is highly contested in Pacific intellectual and academic circles. South Pacific indigenous, postcolonial politics often runs aground on what Hau'ofa categorizes as a form of

> romantic neo-traditionalism ... championed by those who are reaping the juiciest fruits that the world capitalist economy gives. These champions tend to wail by the banks of the River of Babylon and proclaim undying devotion to what they have abandoned.
>
> (Hau'ofa 1987: 165)[17]

On the other hand, rejection of the sociocultural and political economic implications of nineteenth- and twentieth-century colonial administrations, and more recently of "globalization," are also part of a conscious counter-politics and postcolonial intellectual movement, the Hawaiian and New Zealand Maori sovereignty movements being two of the more high-profile examples of these. Four inflections are evident in this seam. The first is that of how the very "traditions" and the history making that underpin them are disputable in themselves. Are not the traditions that are being so "fiercely" defended simply "palangi implants" anyway and, more to the point, where do the colonial missionaries and the Christian churches they set up figure in Tongan "tradition"?[18]

> Who cares what the palangis [non-Tongans/Westerners] want? Why not let the Tongan people decide what sort of government they want? Again, in the absence of change they are deciding what sort of system they want, and are leaving Tonga in droves. The country is literally bleeding to death yet some Tongans remain wedded to this outmoded, archaic century old system. The current Tongan monarchy is, after all, a palangi implant. Look at an official portrait of HM. It is very instructive, and provides a powerful metaphor concerning the nature of this system that many are so keen to preserve. What you see is a Polynesian dressed in a lot of European trappings. And so is the current system of government in Tonga.
>
> (George Candler, KB, 09/09/98 in KBAdmin, 09/07/98)

Second, not only are the historical and cultural "facts" contestable at any point in time, but also contemporary Tonga's socioeconomic hierarchy is a key target for pro-change advocates. For instance, along with parliamentary access, land tenure is based on noble – and male – privilege. Despite the *fahu* system in which oldest sisters have a high socioeconomic rank within the extended family (*kainga*), women are not represented in Parliament (see the next section). These differences and their interrelationship with complex familial and cultural networks of economic obligation (*kavenga*) constitute the third inflection: the purported universal applicability of (neo)liberal macroeconomic models and representational democratic systems across the board.

It would be convenient to link pro-royalists' recourse to notions of Tongan "tradition" when objecting to universal suffrage as merely a rhetorical device in these discussions. This is too simplistic an interpretation in light of the range of arguments and the intensity and longevity of overtly political debates in the KB and the KR. Likewise, when attributing the pro-royalty stance of many "offshore" discussants to forms of "long-distance nationalism" on the one hand or "neotraditionalism" on the other (where an Internet forum is regarded as the latest stage on which to rehearse these sentiments). A closer look at the ebb and flow of these threads shows that the knife cuts both ways. Support for either the THRDM platform or its opponents can come from participants who live in the liberal democracies of the United States, Australia, and New Zealand especially. The realities of socioeconomic disadvantage, everyday discrimination, and "underperformance" in education, employment, and health in these officially egalitarian meritocracies are also used as evidence that life – and media freedoms – in "democratic" societies are not all that they are cracked up to be. This is the main point being made by many an opponent to the more "pro-Western" dimensions of political activism on the ground in Tonga. So, for those women and men, at home and abroad, who equate sweeping constitutional change with yet more Western impositions on the sociocultural and historical legacy of Tonga *per se*, the status quo/the royal family and self-determination go hand in hand. There are subtle shades to any of these positions. For example:

> First you're assuming that you [THRDM advocates] have a monopoly on the idea of "change." As I stated, all Tongans have all kinds of ideas of how changes are to be made. For instance, I favor a change to return the Monarchy to the old Polynesian system. That's when everything was decided by a more democratic Council of Chiefs. Changing the present system to a more Palangi-like democracy is just too Palangi for me.
>
> (Sione Ake Mokofisi, KB, 09/17/98 in KBAdmin, 09/07/98)

But once again, the tables get turned on this appeal to precontact forms of political organization in a region where Christianity has been fashioned into various "South Pacific" religious organizations: "so it isn't democracy you object to, its" palangi-like ideas. And Christianity, is this not palangi-like? (George Candler, 09/17/98, in reply to the above).[19]

This inflection emerges further on in the above thread as culturally specific issues of accountability and applicability:

> Democracy is not a bad political system. Monarchy is also not a bad political system. They should be looked at as "tools" to be used to "operate" a society compatible with its cultures, beliefs and other necessary environments. We must, therefore, define the "ideal" society for Tonga. For example, an independent island, preserve its traditions and cultural activities, maintain its strong belief in Christianity, inheritance of land, respecting of elders and females and so on. . . . We then

ask, what system that can deliver this "ideal" society??? Democracy? or Monarchy? I think we can find the answer.

(S Pusiaki, KB, 09/21/98 in KBAdmin, 09/07/98)

And further on:

I understand the "reality" of Tonga perfectly, no doubt about it, but my concern is with the "ideal" society you depicted above . . . and true also, that we don't have to "copy." but how can Tonga bring to life the "ideal" society, without doing the kopi kat thing . . . it is hard to imagine either.

(tootsy, 09/24/98, in reply to above)

What many of the participants in this forum are articulating, to judge by an analysis of over a thousand separate postings, is that, yes, Tonga's leadership needs to change, but how and to what extent is a particularly "Tongan" problem. This is to my mind the gist of the arguments between two seemingly diametrically opposing camps:

I have watched this debate absorb our little nation of Tonga for the past 12 years and I have come to my own conclusions. . . . Do we need Democracy? In a country like the USA, yes. In Tonga . . . No – but a system with more accountability is necessary. The Ministers should be elected from the people and the Nobles could form a separate House for approval and debate of issues brought through the elected house of parliament. Cabinet would be formed from the Parliament. The King is STILL the head of state. MY OBSERVATION: it is NOT the kind of system that decides on a successful Government . . . it is the integrity and vision of leadership that is more important.

(vatu, KB, 02/12/98 in KBAdmin, 02/08/98)

Before we look at the particular offline and offline accents of these *coutures*, let me briefly recapitulate. In Tonga, criticizing "the government" is tantamount to criticizing the monarch and his ministers.[20] Hence in the more polarized debates "pro-democracy" views can be accused of being "anti-royal" – "anti-Tongan." In this view, calls for radical constitutional change cast aspersions on the very essence of "Tongan-ness." Conversely, not all those who profess to being "pro-royal" reject the need for change as such. Made explicit only at times, these discussions are another way of hammering out what culture, identity, politics entails for a postcolonial society that is economically beholden not only to its diasporic populations (through remittances), but also to direct injections of funds from aid donors. The appeals to maintaining Tongan politicocultural "tradition" vie with astute commentaries on the everyday vagaries of class/status, race/ethnicity, and gender inequities in any nominally democratic society.

Sometimes the two tendencies are present in the same intervention or in various postings from the same participant. The following post encapsulates these countervailing tendencies. It is a passionate and wry account of life overseas for many of those making up the Pacific islands diaspora, thought to be living in the lap of luxury. Class and status position and relative privileges accruing shift accordingly, and affect political perspectives in turn, as this intervention indicates:

> Excuse me, I take offence at this comment that we Tongans do not know any better . . . that we are brainwashed . . . that I am used to having it so bad . . . that I have a dictator ruling over me. Are you talking about Tongans or Cubans? Do you know what a dictator is?? Do we hear any boat loads of refugees coming ashore in Australia from Tonga, or do we hear Qantas special flights bringing refugees from Tonga to live in Tasmania??? Have things changed so badly in Tonga that I, in Sydney, am not aware of? What's this rubbish about electing my leader, pay him and expect him to do a good job?? I live in Sydney, I elect people to lead me who do not do a good job as far I am concerned – not good for me anyway, good for them and their business friends and political allies, but not good for poor old Altius, commoner, work 9–5, get minimum wage, pay lots of taxes, struggle on public transport to get to work while the people I elect get transported around in air cond. limousines doing deals left, right and centre, pocket a lot of extra money, fly first class, kids at top exclusive private schools, ski at the Swiss Alps, eat at first class restaurants, fly to Paris for shopping and stop over in Monaco for a bit of casino ALL ON ALTIUS' TAX!!!! I was born in Tonga, very friendly place, friendly leaders, no police coming around at midnight and scare us to death or throw us out of our little Tongan house (dictators do that!), my father gets a piece of land which lies unused in the islands, we have come to Sydney to get a better life. I struggled, I worked, I studied, got my degree and am enjoying a Government job. I love Tonga and our political system. If I had the money I would go back today. I am not being brainwashed, never had it so bad as Cubans or some Indians in India or struggling Africans. I have no inferior complex to being a commoner. I am just another commoner in Sydney. . . . I do not count. But I am happy. Hope you are.
>
> (Altius, KB, 06/08/99 in Ikani, 06/08/99)[21]

The way this political declaration is linked to personal geographies points to some important online–offline dimensions of these "plays on the royal demons." (Falani Maka, KB, 03/06/99)

3 Online–offline nuances

These are, in shorthand, standpoints that are derived from *situated experience* and *inter/subjectivity* – or, to put it another way, the class/status and race/ethnicity permutations of the insideout dynamic explored in the previous chapter and those of "everyday embodiments" in the following one. Generational, class, and other demographic geographies create their own twists and turns within and between various threads. These may be becoming evident to some readers by now, so the following observations will serve as highlighters. Because no one line of division can be strictly drawn between pro-royalists/pro-status quo, and pro-change advocates, these do crystallize in terms of posters' (stated) situation (at home or abroad) as well as their stated/assumed social (self-)demarcation (commoner or nobility, pro- or anti-change.) The thread as a visual image onscreen, its textual surface, explicit lines of identification and affiliation, styles, and argumentation all vary accordingly. Their articulations also overlap, counteract, and (try to) trip each other up over the course of a prolonged thread or period. "Situated" also denotes not only where a participant is physically posting from – the Pacific Islands/Tonga or the West – but also where they are living and/or whether they admit to being of "noble blood" or not.[22] This particular line of division operates on all sides of the debate. For pro-royals this means having to respond to accusations of either double standards (see above) or ignorance of "how things really are in Tonga." For example:

> To answer your "question:" I do go back to Tonga when I feel like it, and it's a free country where everyone is allowed to travel freely, speak his/her mind, but most importantly, to choose to remain as much Tongan as he/she likes. Living in another country does not negate my love for my home island.
> (Sione Ake Mokofisi, KB, 02/13/99 in George Candler, 02/09/99)

Where one is – or isn't – also matters to pro-change activists, moderates and interested bystanders. The following selections show at least three different angles on these personal, "ideological," and diasporic geographies in operation. First, reasons for leaving Tonga in the first place:

> I am a pro-democracy believer, this was due to my experiences growing up as a child and also as a young adult in Tonga.... As we have observed for decades, Tongans grow up in Tonga and due to the lack of opportunities locally look overseas and emigrate not only for a better life outside, but also to help the rest of the family still living in Tonga.
> (Tiana, KB, 03/09/99 in Ghost, 03/05/99)

Second is the need for dealing with the "oppression of the present" (de Certeau 1980b: 7), whether or not structural political change in Tongan or Samoan politics is achieved and, if it is, is achieved without violence (James 2000: 275; Tcherkézoff 1998):

> My parents are from Tonga and I was born and raised in the United States. The only "thing" that I follow is the upbringing of my family and our heavenly father.... Tongans are so hung up on this caste system that they can't seem to see straight.... I just wish that the people that ALWAYS have something negative to say about Tonga and it's government, would DO something instead of showing off their fancy education and expansive vocabulary. I can sit back with my Master's or PhD and criticize a systems that's been intact for thousands of years OR I can sit and do something positive for myself and the immediate community around me. I know there are TONS of Tongans out there who are helping themselves and others in their community and they're not doing it by whining and complaining on an Internet forum.
>
> (Observer-MT, KB, 03/08/99 in Ghost, 03/05/99)

Third is the claim that Tongan problems require "Tongan" solutions:

> I know you were born and raised up here in the States and has been fua kavenga [beholden] to the "Palangi" people. We the Tongans that were born and raised in Tonga has been fua kavenga to the Tongans especially our King and his family and . . . our Nopele [nobles].
>
> (Pure-Tongan, KB, 12/17/99, in reply to above)

This last intervention also shows where personal geographies become a fracture line as opposed to a seam – *couture*. Dismissing diasporic opinions (whether pro-change or otherwise) out of hand is part and parcel of both content and political rhetoric. How "relevant" the points of view of those growing up in Utah or Los Angeles are to the political situation in Tonga is grist to the mill in debates where diasporic Pacific Islanders have the cogency of their views contested regularly by participants living in Tonga. For instance:

> ARE YOU TONGAN AND WHERE HAVE YOU BEEN LIVING? cause you don't sound like one Tongan at all, and I think I have the feeling that you never lived in Tonga for a little period of time to know whats going on around in our land.
>
> (Finemui, KB, 02/13/98 in KBAdmin, 02/08/98)

The Kingdom of Tonga does not permit its citizens dual passports; one is either a Tongan citizen (passport holder) or not, regardless of residence.

So, when challenged directly, diasporic Tongans need to position themselves in particular ways. Here is but one example:

> I am NOT a U.S. citizen. I still proudly hold my Tongan passport and will continue to do so. While I am a staunch liberal Democrat here in the States, I also understand that Tonga is a completely different setting, with historical circumstances contrasting to the United States. Thus, whatever liberal views I may have here, may not be so right in the Kingdom. As for any so-called motivation to preserve my own sanctity in Tonga, I'm afraid that is simply not so because I do NOT live in Tonga despite my citizenship. Hence, I cannot BENEFIT from whatever I am espousing about the Kingdom.
>
> (Meilakepa, KB, 02/12/99 in George Candler, 02/09/99)[23]

In terms of those diasporic posters (the majority) who object to the pro-democracy arguments on principle, the perception of relative privilege vis-à-vis their interlocutors posting from the islands leaves them open to accusations of "armchair nationalism" as well:

> Royal ideology is popular and does take up a lot of space on the KB forum. If one feels so strong on an issue, what does one do with it? In Tonga if you jump up in protest against the governing bodies, you'll most probably be shunned and told to keep quiet. So, since a number of us are not in Tonga, what can we do?
>
> (Ikani, KB, 06/09/99 in Ikani, 06/08/99)

References to specific offline affiliations, including autobiographical details, are scattered throughout these threads.

> You are right up to a point in that to proceed to a level as you are mentioning is quite frightening, but I must say that from my observation as a Tongan living in Australia for most of my life, most of the Nobles/Ministers are incapable of taking Tonga into the next Millenium. With all the royalty in key positions, Tonga is like their "family business". . . . For Tonga to move up in the world, we must take into account ideas from people who have researched and observed first hand such a change. We cannot afford to be narrow minded in such a changing world, otherwise Tonga will be left behind. I believe that once the King is gone, the Island's future is very bleak (the King has such respect from his people, including myself, but who is of the same calibre that would be capable of taking over?). What Akilisi [the THRDM] is trying to do is, in itself, a way of helping Tonga stand up and look at its current position, and make informed decisions on certain issues, eg are you happy that the King lives in luxury whilst his people are contemplating where their next meal is coming from?

Before we eliminate such opinions (as that of Akilisi's), let us first of all study indepth such ideas/opinions, and make informed decisions.
(Fakapale Lot'aniu, KB, 02/14/98 in KBAdmin, 02/08/98)

These details trace the socioeconomic hierarchies, within and beyond the islands, that are at stake, including implicit allegiances to the Tongan nobility and the personal experiences of political harassment to be discussed in what follows. Other standpoints are informed by benefits and obligations that come from birthright privileges – for certain women and those with "royal blood" as well as the structural exclusions from being a woman and/or commoner. These interventions need to be read therefore with an awareness of how diasporic and local experiences are spliced with extended family, gender–class–status loyalties and how these in turn provide a subtext to the manifest declarations for either sociopolitical change or "preservation." For instance:

I grew up in Tonga and I love the place. I often wonder about this debate so I'd like to throw in a few thoughts, perhaps fish for a few more responses.... Tonga is such a beautiful place with beautiful people. As the 'friendly islands', wouldn't it be fitting for it to be a place of totally equal opportunity, where all individuals were equally respected just for being people, no special conditions attached? Alas that may only be in Utopia. I agree ... that if there is a need for change in Tonga, then a variation of democracy that is suitable to Tongan society should be worked out. But how much will a 'more democratic' system with a 'less powerful etc' monarchy, take away from Tongans what it means to be Tongan?
(Jamie, KB, 09/12/98 in KBAdmin, 09/07/98)

Diasporic Tongan communities have fractions that are as fiercely loyal to the Tongan monarchy as those who urge constitutional change. Prominent intellectuals, journalists, and working-class Tongans – and non-Tongans – are present at any point. In this respect, being an "expat" can become a key element of the argument in itself, as the following observation shows:

There is a humorous side to the discussion re democracy in Tonga. I have been labelled as a liberal by Mr. Mokofisi [pro-royalist]. I'm emailing his post to all my liberal friends who for years have accused and labelled me a conservative for my beliefs in the basic principles of democracy (justice, human rights, and moral decency) and for my biased endorsement of Christian principles (as opposed to endorsement of Islamic or other religious beliefs). Anyway, thanks Mr. Mokofisi for your comments. Your point is taken. I trust you have taken my point. It is not an attempt to persuade you, rather a statement of what I believe IS!! Criticisms – welcomed indeed! One last correction before I'm over and out. I am not a part of a political party in Tonga or elsewhere (as you've stated), even though I endorse the principles of democracy. (Most of my colleagues around the world do!). And am not currently living in Tonga. In fact I'm a Tongan born American who lived in Tonga but is now banned in Tonga ... for my writings.

(Kalafi Moala, KB, 09/15/98 in KBAdmin, 09/07/98)

The operations of ethnicity/gender/class lines embedded in the offline–online dimensions of these debates also bear mentioning, as they are more implicit than is the case with other themes. The first relates to gender power relations from the point of view of women in politics, namely, women's presence in political leadership in societies dominated by male voices. Discussions about modern/traditional sex–gender roles or postcolonial self/group identity formation unpack accepted wisdoms about being a "woman" or a "man" in Polynesian/Western context. However, in the threads analyzed here, participants do not foreground "gender" or "race" in the way they do elsewhere (see Chapters 4 and 6). Nonetheless, the participation and voices of women in these *online* political discussions do make themselves felt.[24]

This brings me to another online–offline nuance: the role and input of prominent non-Tongan (palangi) regulars and moderators, which cut across the altercations between diasporic and nondiasporic participants. Two of the more regular and engaged participants in these debates are not Tongan, although they have both lived and worked in Tonga. Despite some quizzing, both have supporters who urge them on. How non-Tongans' contributions are validated is clear by others' responses to their positions. Their interventions are incorporated as part of these online traversals:

I ... have been following these posts with a great deal of interest and though I side more with George's and Tania's arguments. I am very impressed with Sandy's enthusiasm and eloquence. What a pity should these posts be lost in the Archives. A few points could be better documented and then this exchange would be the best this forum or others like it has had to offer. Thank you very much for your serious contributions.

(Pila, KB, 03/09/99 in Ghost, 03/05/99)

Thus far, I have been emphasizing the relatively inclusive online setting for these discussions, especially in light of tight social and media controls on the ground in Tonga. Nonetheless, forms of exclusion – or silencing – do occur in what are after all highly politicized discussions. There is one sharp example of this. One participant, identifying her- or himself as "homeless," was shouted down when criticizing the expenses involved in renovating the king's mansion in San Francisco. Other participants doubted the participant's legitimacy because she or he accessed the forums from a public library as opposed to school, university, work, or home-based access point. The intensity of reactions to Homeless (who states that he or she is using public library Internet access) illustrates the complex assumptions at work between Tongan populations in the islands and those overseas. Despite the approbation, Homeless persists, and loudly (hence the use of capitals):

> I CAME HERE TO THE US ON AN IMMIGRANT VISA BY MYSELF TRYING TO MAKE IT HERE.... LIFE IN TONGA IS NOT ALL COCONUT TREES AND BEAUTIFUL BEACHES.... WHY AM I A HOMELESS TONGAN? ITS BECAUSE I LIVE FROM ONE PLACE TO ANOTHER TRYING TO FIND A BETTER JOB.... I AM NOT OPPOSED TO THE KING ... ALL IM TRYING TO SAY IS ... HOW ABOUT THE POOR PEOPLE OF TONGA? WHERE DOES ALL THIS MONEY COME FROM?... CANT IT BE USED IN OTHER THINGS? (IF ONLY YOU WERE IN MY SANDALS YOU WOULD KNOW).
>
> (KB, 03/09/99 in HOMELESS TONGAN, 03/09/99)

The sharp reactions to the homelessness of this participant intersect with not only the assumption that living overseas is synonymous with upward mobility, but also gender power relations in Tongan society. As Futa Helu points out, any debate about political change is occurring in a contest where

> birth and wealth all feature in the social calculus that determines one's status in the community.... Although in terms of the constitution the common people have been emancipated from the arbitrary authority of chiefs, the great legal chiefs of modern Tonga ... still exercise almost unlimited power over commoners by virtue of the culture which requires the latter to defer on all matters to their chiefly masters who are never to be questioned or criticised on any issue whatsoever.
>
> (Helu 1999c: 34)

By way of drawing what is an unfinished debate to a close for the time being and before making some concluding observations, the next sample will serve as both coda to this chapter and a segue into the next one. In a lengthy intervention, the participant ponders the possibility for institutional change in Tonga in the light of structural inertias in both Tongan society and the regional/global political economy at large. This intervention, like many others, does not abstract political or technoeconomic issues from the sociocultural and historical complexity of a postcolonial society confronting its royal – and historical – "demons." In this sense, more pessimistic analyses of the latest electoral successes of the THRDM and whether the pro-democracy debates can leverage radical change under the current monarch tend to overlook the fact that the historical record of political change elsewhere – for model democracies as well – is a protracted, if not bloody, one. As Jamie notes, looking backwards to some halcyon precontact past is not a solution, but neither is armed rebellion (violent revolution in some scenarios) the aim of pro-change activists either:

> What does it mean to be a true/full Tongan? Would Tonga be 'Tonga' in the heart of it's people with a system other than the one that is currently in place? Did the system which is in place now destroy the original 'Tonga' that existed before then? Is being Tongan a variable or evolutionary condition? Does all this matter? Tongans in Tonga today still live by many of the freedoms and restrictions imposed on them by culture for centuries.... Palangi ideals may have been adopted, but the system that was created in the 1800s equally allowed the Tongan way of life and it's values to persist.... If a political system (monarchy, democracy, constitutional monarchy etc) can be viewed as a means to achieve a desired end, then the important question for Tonga is 'who has the right to decide what is best for Tonga', and having established that 'what do they want to achieve'. A system that is good for 'traditional Tongans' is a different thing from a system that is good for anyone else in the world, whatever their high ideals might be.... As for us overseas, when are we constructively helping, and when are we not? I personally believe that all humans are equal whatever their circumstance. In the past I have often found it difficult living in Tonga because at face value anyway, the classification of Tongan society makes equality not always apparent. But that doesn't give me much more than the right to simply express myself and respect another persons right to likewise do as they will. At the end of the day whatever system Tongans in Tonga choose for themselves, I hope it continues to preserve the high level of tranquillity and contentment that has always been a part of Tongan living, even before the palangi came, and much moreso than for most other societies in this world, whether democratic or not. I hope that is something that is obvious to everyone concerned.
>
> (Jamie, KB, 09/12/98 in KBAdmin, 09/07/98)[25]

Concluding comments

These threads indicate that ongoing electoral successes by pro-democracy politicians and/or support for the status quo cannot be reduced to the operations of an "older-style fashion of personalised politics, rather than as an ideological battle over ideas that remain poorly understood by the mass of people" (Edwards and Tuisoso quoted in James 2003: 174; see also James 2000: 275). And when these online interactions are juxtaposed with political debates at any election time in the United States, Australia, and New Zealand or calls for constitutional changes in the latter two constitutional monarchies, the following wry observation by Prince Tupouto'a is also pertinent:

> Democracy is a delicate principle which by nature is simultaneously desirable, unstable and vulnerable.... Living up to the basic demands of a democratic system, the public have the final say as to which crowd of hooligans shall control the government until the next elections. But economic and political stability has been assured because the same people [global business] have paid for both sides. Thus, regardless of which hooligans and bounders rule the country, the same interests shall continue to be both protected both at home and promoted abroad.
>
> (HRH Prince Tupouto'a, personal email, 06/07/99)[26]

In these threads, "democracy" operates as a trope for the inner and outer limits of sociopolitical change – what this means in principle and in practice in the postcolonial South Pacific. Whether Tongan society is to be defined as "democratic" *per se* is as much of an issue as whether the way it is currently operating is or not – a fine line perhaps for onlookers, but an important one nonetheless for participants. The length and tenacity of these discussion threads, the passion, eloquence, and reiterations of "ideological principles" indicate a high degree of emotional and intellectual commitment to one premise of democratic ideals: the articulation of "separate and even opposing interests" (James 2000: 275). On the ground, Tongan society is characterized by a reticence in expressing (spontaneous) criticism of the government. The outspokenness online is in stark contrast, as is the unedited nature of the interventions. The extensive use of optional anonymity brings with it both protection and opportunities for participants who are aware that, on the ground, there are

> social and political inducements to staying silent in public about this matter, i see no problem with people voicing their concerns here, there, in any matter ... it isn't the speaker who is important, it is the truth they are trying to discover ... only those fearing the truth, need to stop the speaker.
>
> (voiceless, KB, 06/08/99 in Ikani, 06/08/99)[27]

Some tentative inferences can be made from these textual surfaces and their offline sociopolitical context. First, as in all debates about the rights and wrongs of (constitutional) monarchies and incumbent political elites, positions become quickly polarized. Loyalties are not always clearly split along class–status lines, and historical interpretation plays an important role in arguments for and against any change to the power, role, and indeed existence of a royal house. This also holds true for the discussions on the Kava Bowl. Given the close social networks at home and abroad (churches, extended families, networks of socioeconomic obligation) and the historical significance of the royal family for contemporary Tonga, protest comes with a heavy historical payload. It would be easy for this reason to simply see these debates as a slanging match between "conservative" defenders of the status quo and "modernizing" advocates for change. Both sides are active in any one thread, get hot under the collar, are prone to rhetoric, non sequiturs, and personal attacks, and are quick to resort to historical "fact" to back up their arguments.

That being said, and not forgetting that such behaviors are part and parcel of any intense political debate, regarding these threads as expressions of a simple dichotomy between traditionalists and modernizers would belie the complexity of these online and offline debates, and the complex political economic situation in the Pacific Islands as a whole. As many participants insist at all points in the spectrum reconstructed here, Tonga is already a democracy of a particular sort. Not only are Tongan history – various versions thereof included – and that of the Pacific Islands in general since "contact" at stake (Helu 1999a: interview; Hau'ofa 1992), but so also are the legitimacy and integrity of the current political system and its ruling elite. The upshot is a dilemma about "cultural survival" (Helu 1999b). On the one hand, political and social protest and agitation for change have to be thwarted if these mean a loss of uniqueness, and loss of economic control to the Western powers that be. On the other hand, grinding financial scandals have been taxing a political elite whose accountability is seriously questioned by a substantial part of its constituency. It is a tricky balancing act between change, preservation, and self-determination for small political economies in an ostensibly globalizing world. The answers for many are to be found close to home. In the words of one pro-change supporter, the "democracy we want is very Tongan. It uses the culture as it is. We want the King to be the king, like now, but we want the people below him to be more representative of the people" (Fifita 2000a, 2000b).

Throughout the contemporary South Pacific, political movements for indigenous sovereignty and land rights (Aotearoa/New Zealand, Hawaii, Fiji), or universal suffrage and democratic reform (Samoa and Tonga), whatever their modus operandi, are indelibly inscribed in articulations of postcolonial identity formation. This are in turn informed by the discourses of universal human rights, indigenous peoples' land rights, and nationalist movements. All of these are now occurring within a predominantly neoliberal atmosphere. These wrangles over the rights and wrongs of the incumbent political regime in the Kingdom of Tonga are reminders of the multivalent meanings, historical particularities, and psychoemotional investments of *any* democratic society's self-image. Such discussions, their cultural and geographical specificity notwithstanding, thereby allow for insight into historical and sociocultural experiences of how some members of a non-Western, officially democratic society perceive internal and external pressures for change. Because they have been unfolding in cyberspace, where incumbent power elites and social conventions can be bypassed to a certain extent, their "translocal" nature as public *online* deliberations connects the local nuances to broader debates about democracy, governance, accountability in a post-Cold War era. I would also argue that they also confront those of us from quintessential democratic societies with our own ingrained myths about the voracity and effectiveness of our respective systems of democratic representation, consultation, and deliberation with their concomitant dynamics of public consent (making) and (in)direct political pressure.

Back to the "South Pacific online." When the disparate, albeit related, Pacific Island communities come together in these open (cyber)spaces and places, their everyday lives, experiences of discrimination and/or empowerment from inside and outside their immediate surroundings, and their ideals for the future start to mix and mingle in new ways. In toto, these conversations point to understandings of democracy as far more than those "restricted to an analysis of its operation in the ... parliamentary sector of political dimensions" (van Meijl 1998: 391). Where these specific debates speak to the emergent politics of representation of postcolonial and/or diasporic Pacific Island/Polynesian generations is a more pertinent question for these online traversals where intersubjective understandings of "identity," "culture" and nationhood are inflected with the geographies of diaspora, gender, race, and class.

6 "I define my own identity"

Rearticulating "race," "ethnicity," and "culture"

Introduction

> The concept of race itself [is] inextricably woven out of the history of the conjunction of knowledge and power in European and Euro-American expansion and economic and sexual exploitation of "marked" or "coloured" peoples.
>
> (Haraway 1992: 153)

> [A] boundary is as much about identification as it is about exclusion. Sometimes the implications of this double function are trivial; sometimes they are not.... In its search for ultimate truth and infallible knowledge, the Western philosophical tradition denies the potential instability intrinsic to any contingent boundary. The suppression of the contingency of boundaries and of the structural ambiguity that pertains to their double function carries with it a substantial political import.... [Reflecting] critically on the nature of limits and boundaries transforms our well-established way of thinking about identity as a homogeneous and self-enclosed totality.
>
> (Borradori 2003: 145, 147)

"Ethnic cleansing," "ethnic violence," "fundamentalism," "rogue states," "clash of civilizations" – these recent epithets for contemporary "politics of identity" (Castells 1998) encapsulate the racialized historical legacy and "structural ambiguity" of the one nation–one identity matrix in Western thought (Haraway 1992; Borradori 2003). With neoliberal globalization and/or nationalist movements dating from the post-Cold War period as focal points, the broad consensus in the social science literature (Scholte 2000: 226 *passim*; Waters 2001: 160 *passim*; Inda and Rosaldo 2002; Everard 2000) is that the

> world is undergoing considerable change. There is a clear tendency in certain quarters to an intensifying feeling of fragmentation, that the world is no longer coherent, that we are all discovering our hybrid nature at the same time as, in other quarters, people who have lived in

a state of fragmentation under the weight of social marginalisation are getting their acts together. Now this double process ... [is] of course more multiplex than simply double.

(Friedman 1998: 37)

Kava Bowl and Kamehameha Roundtable discussions have also been addressing these issues. The threads reconstructed in this chapter, probably comprising the bulk of discussions, are preoccupied with "race," "ethnicity," and "culture" as exclusive and inclusive conventions, psycho-emotional states, physical embodiments, and sociopolitical ideals for people who have been "marked" as "colored" (Haraway 1992).[1] Participants talk about living as US, Australian, or New Zealand citizens and yet finding themselves "caught between identities" (Kami 2001: interview). Experiences of discrimination (on the ground, but also in these forums) are shared along with ideas about how to transcend – or confront – everyday prejudice and isolation based on being racially/ethnically "marked." Whether messages are posted from Nuku'alofa in Tonga, Apia in Samoa, Los Angeles or Salt Lake City in the United States, south Auckland suburbs in New Zealand, or Sydney in Australia, these discussions underscore the elasticity and thereby the limits of *identity* as a catchall term for the multiplex dimensions of inter/subjectivity. At the heart of these threads, and woven through many others, are the outer and inner limits of an "identity" that can enable rather than limit action for individuals and communities who are living within and between multiple ethnic–cultural locales. From the point of view of how IR/IPE approaches handle such questions, these conversations speak directly to the veracity of modernist nation-state models and their citizenship practices as an a priori gender-neutral and raceless "container" for identification and "belonging" (Carver 1998b; Walker 1995; Persaud 2002).

Like the previous chapters' discussions about shifting sex–gender roles for diasporic circumstances and the quality of democracy in postcolonial societies, these threads are also *intra*cultural and *inter*cultural. Texts are as polemical as they are reflective, as carefully argued as they are emotionally charged. The interlocutors are of "full" Pacific Island descent, have married into Tongan or Samoan communities, or are the children of "mixed marriages." Physical characteristics are compared and portrayed quite explicitly, along with the personal experiences of racial discrimination or prejudice both from society at large and from within (diasporic) Pacific communities. The various cultural practices and rituals at stake are *Fa'a Samoa* (the "Samoan way") and *anga fakatonga* (the "Tongan way") – what actually constitutes these as specific practices, whether they are under threat and, if so, how to "preserve" them (Morton 1996: 257–265; Lee 2003). Moreover, what do *Fa'a Samoa* and *anga fakatonga* entail for those who can claim several cultural – "racial" – heritages? Debates can also begin with arguments about the "essential" (learned or genetically inherited) features of being Tongan or Samoan; whether that which is shared between these societies outweighs perceived differences. Crosscutting these reflections are claims about the need to concentrate on the mutual interests and ties that bind various Polynesian/Pacific Island ("Poly" or PI respectively) communities, many of which live as disadvantaged minorities in urban conglomerations around the Pacific seaboard. Gang violence and restricted employment and educational opportunities are recurring indicators in these communities of socioeconomic and ethnically labeled forms of marginalization when living "overseas."

While these are earnest and serious conversations, this need not preclude a sense of humor. For example, on the issue of intercultural/interracial dating, a regular notes that "I prefer banana or strawberry Polys myself. I once had a watermelon Poly but she had too many seeds. ha ha ha ... Meilakepa. Coconut Poly (Hard on the outside, soft on the inside – and sometimes flaky)" (Meilakepa, KR, 09/29/00). The flip side to this is assertions that certain "racial" morphologies are biological (and so cultural) "destiny" based on the relative privilege of racial/cultural "purity" vis-à-vis those of "mixed blood."[2] Everyday experiences of discrimination and structural exclusion based on (various degrees of) skin color are the immediate subject of many threads, as are accounts of stigmatization that occur within Pacific Island communities, from participants' own "peeps" (people).

Chapter outline

Before the reconstructions of what are among the most polyphonic and diffuse threads crisscrossing these cyberspaces, the first section of this chapter lays out some "offline renditions" of the key terms at stake: "race," "ethnicity," and "culture." Rather than attempt definitional closure, though, this section makes explicit how I conceptualize the terms vis-à-vis IR/IPE discourses. There is a distinction between academic articulations of the "problem" and its terms of reference in these fluid, open-ended discussions. After the reconstruction, in the second section, the third section reconsiders the "one nation, one identity" matrix of both mainstream and critical IR/IPE in light of these rearticulations. I argue that feminist and postcolonial approaches provide important insights into how the material (political-economic) and psychoemotional (symbolic) dynamics of inter/subjectivity are constituted by multifarious race/ethnicity, class, and gendered dimensions. In contrast to the fixity of many, even critical, analyses of contemporary "politics of identity," feminist/postcolonial frameworks place the latter firmly within – as endogenous to – specific and generalized processes of technosocial change. Identity, however it may be construed, imposed, or experienced, is sociohistorically embedded, not beyond time and/or space (however defined). Although they avail themselves of different terms at times, this more dynamic understanding is underscored by these practitioners; "identity" operates as a trope for "becoming," and doing so on one's own terms. In terms of political economic and sociocultural changes occurring in – or due to – everyday practices online, these subaltern utterances also problematize the technological and social determinism of both conventional and critical analyses of the relationship between the Internet and society.

A word of caution at this point. When one reads discussions about being "Polynesian" and/or in diaspora in the United States particularly, the views and experiences of these participants (the majority in the KR at least) are not automatically transferable to those of Tongans and Samoans living in Australia or New Zealand, let alone by those participating from the Pacific Islands themselves.[3] There are demographic and psychoemotional distinctions between the various Pacific Island communities in the United States, New Zealand, and Australia (see Macpherson 1997; Macpherson *et al.* 2001; Lee 2003). What is most striking here, nonetheless, is that these very same distinctions (and tensions) between being a Californian-based, Utah-based, or Auckland-based Samoan or Tongan are part and parcel of the debates' textual surfaces as well as of the issues they address. Interpreting these discussions means being aware of the geographic and historical specifics of various Pacific island migrations since the 1960s to Pacific Rim industrialized economies, including those younger generations who have been furthering their schooling overseas since then. Pacific island countries such as Tonga and Niue have substantial numbers of their populations residing elsewhere: the West Coast of the United States, Hawaii, Auckland, New Zealand, and Sydney, Australia, in particular. Internet access in the islands is uneven and concentrated in urban centers; Suva, Nuku'alofa, Apia, and Pago Pago, for instance. These demographics constitute their own nuances all through the debates – for instance, between US-based Tongans and those living in Tonga; between American and Western Samoans; and also between these and New Zealand-based communities, which outweigh (roughly 250,000 in 2001) those living elsewhere (90,000) (Lee 2003: 261 *passim*; Marrow 2003: 436; McNicholas *et al.* 2003).

1 Offline renditions of "race," "ethnicity," and "culture"

These textual surfaces remind the reader of how people are

> more complicated beings than ... unitary labels would suggest and our experiences of being gendered ... vary along dimensions of race, class, nationality, ethnicity, sexuality and so on. All these identities with which we are labelled ... are social constructs that are created,

given meaning, and reproduced by the differing, yet interlocking, systems of power in which we are embedded.

(Peterson and Runyan 1999: 175)

That being said, "the social and psychological interpretations of physical differences among people – interpretations that are used to organize people hierarchically all over the world" (ibid.: 175) have quite tangible manifestations and effects for differently located women and men, as individuals, (extended) family groups or specific sorts of communities. In terms of how "race" operates in these rearticulations, these threads constantly show how "the central issues of race always appear historically in articulation, in a formation, with other categories and divisions that are constantly crossed and re-crossed by the categories of class, of gender and ethnicity" (Hall 1996a: 444; see also Kolko *et al.* 2000: 4; Collins 1997; Ashcroft *et al.* 1998: 45–51, 198–206).

While "race" is the prevalent term in these online traversals, "ethnicity" is preferred in critical and postcolonial literatures. As with the distinction between sex and gender, "the term ethnicity acknowledges the place of history, language and culture in the construction of subjectivity and identity, as well as the fact that all discourse is placed, positioned, situated, and all knowledge is contextual" (Hall 1996a: 446). Concomitant processes of ethnic, sexual, and, by implication, cultural identification are thereby "deeply ambivalent" (ibid.: 445). Taking this point seriously also has implications for how "culture" as an analytical category can be better conceptualized in IR/IPE (see Weber 2001: 3–4). I follow Chen's formulation, with its murmurs of Michel de Certeau (1997a, b), here. According to Chen, however it may be delineated, culture "is pervasively politicized on every front and every ground . . . culture is neither the 'authentic' practice of the 'people' nor simply a means of 'manipulation' by capitalism, but the site of active local struggle, everyday and anywhere" (1996: 312).

2 Online rearticulations

Before I unpack and reconstruct some major discussion threads, several more general observations need to be made. First, in the threads reconstructed thus far, discussions around race, ethnicity, and/or culture have operated as subtexts rather than main themes in themselves. This set of threads begin (in the initial post) with race–ethnicity and/or culture as the main theme. As the threads unfurl, the terms get thoroughly recalibrated as participants share the various everyday tactics for dealing with ingrained and institutionalized ("strategic") forms of exclusion. They deal with the stresses and strains as well as celebratory moments in these encounters. These threads are noticeable for the way in which participants describe themselves, their siblings, and their children by skin, eye, and hair color, said culture and lineage/ancestry, and dual or singular nationalities. In these renditions, "race" is both incidental and a tangible dividing line within Tongan and Samoan communities as well as vis-à-vis society at large. As an intersubjective mode of understanding, the term's troubled political and empirical credentials are *re*articulated as discussions unfold. Participants confront head-on these ambiguities, the essentialisms, and the parochialisms they throw up as they contest them "on the ground" and online. The semantic and material connections made between "race/culture/ethnicity" (Lillian, KB, 09/17/98 in KBAdmin, 09/14/98) are treated as highly *mobile* nodes for individual and group–community (re)location. At the same time, incipient and institutionalized forms of discrimination and exclusion are laid bare as people wonder out loud about when, where, and why race, ethnicity, and/or culture end up operating as essentializing tropes for Identity with a capital "I." These threads point to how "defining my own identity" need not be "based on where you come from, on your roots, but on where you are heading, your routes" (Paul Gilroy in Golyardi and Hilhorst 2001: 5R). Race/ethnicity/culture are construed here as both contestable and retrievable for diasporic locations where "difference" can lead to both structural exclusion and personal (community) opportunities for advancement.[4] Policies of positive discrimination are particularly poignant focal points for this "double function" of boundaries (Borradori 2003: 145). For instance:

> The point is we shouldn't demand representation based on skin color. That is racist because inherent in that thinking is that ALL people of a particular race have the same needs and the same way of thinking on issues. It is not true. You can't bundle us up according to skin color. We spent two hundred and some years getting away from that mindset.
> (Bevo, KR, 03/14/01 in eb, 03/12/01)

> America is far from being color blind, and only those who live in [U]topia thinks that there's a level playing field, it is evident in the socio-economic difference in our society. I wish I did live in a color blind society, but I do not. People still hire people that look like them.
> (Sinafea, KR, 03/14/01 in reply to above)

Second, specific personal conundrums for participants with mixed parentage pivot around questions like What am I/Who are we? What is (are) my/our heritage(s)? What is (my/our) culture and where do I fit into it? How many cultures do I/we honor? Where do environment and upbringing diverge or converge with "natural" traits such as skin/eye/hair color, physique, "blood"? How dynamic are Tongan or Samoan cultural practices anyway, let alone among Tongans and Samoans living elsewhere, or being married to and having children with someone from the Pacific Islands? What does, or should, the generic term "Polynesian" mean anyway?[5] Not only are diasporic generations partaking of Western forms of questions of "who am I?" but these questions are laden with racial/ethnic overtones in situations of discrimination. Tongan onlookers consider this the impact of living in the West and being confronted for the first time with power differentials and exclusion based on how one is identified – stereotyped – by dominant society (Kami 2001: interview; Helu 1999a: interview). Whatever the personal conundrum outlined in the initial post may be, the majority of debates end up affirming that living with more than one culture is a positive rather than a negative thing, despite the emotional and material difficulties that may arise, and do for many. This brings me to a third general point: what happens when one does not fit a respective set of physical stereotypes, or cannot or will not conform to behavioral or linguistic norms of the respective Pacific Island (diasporic) communities? These queries are addressed with painstaking tenderness at times and less tolerantly at others. As always, these conversations trace (public/private) personal, political, and international – "global" – permutations of everyday life as multiplex rather than unitary – in this case, as various *bodily, cultural,* and *categorical* (cyber)spatial practices of identity formation.

Another general characteristic, apart from the wealth of social and personal detail, is the celebratory nature of these conversations. Being-one-of-many is seen as a strength, as fun, and if not, then it should be fought for, allowed to be so. Solidarity and support are key activities and motivations for many participants. Whether it is down to youthful idealism or not, these threads put to task the doomsday prophets who would see "race" or "ethnic" identity politics as *necessarily* divisive even when disagreement and social exclusion are intense and all too evident.[6] At the same time, "traditional" stereotypes from within (diasporic) Polynesian communities are challenged, as younger participants claim the right *not* to be automatically assigned any one ethnic/cultural group vis-à-vis their own sense of individuality or relationships with those from other communities. The overall tone is one of exploration and inquisitiveness about what is seen as a life-long process:

> Being Tongan means a unique starting point on a long journey to be a better human being – having learnt that there are admirable qualities in other humans on this planet which can be embraced. . . . Being Tongan is to accept that life is chaos to be enjoyed.
> (Sefita Auckland New Zealand, 03/12/98 in KBAdmin, 03/09/98)

The first subsection looks at the way "race" is articulated as *everyday embodiments.* By "embodiments," I am referring to how physical looks can matter despite protestations to the contrary. In other words, being physically distinguishable through mixed parentage as a person "of color" more or less, or having been brought up in a "strictly" Samoan or Tongan environment, creates its own personal opportunities and conflicting expectations for people from within and beyond their immediate (Tongan and Samoan) communities. The second section brings in the issue of *multiple cultural codes*; what these embodiments mean, or should mean, is permeated with how "culture" is understood and practiced (or not) in the Pacific islands and overseas. From there emerges an interest in *proudly countering categories* that consciously *look to the future*. This last section looks at how a colonial designation, Polynesian, for societies that span from Hawaii through to Tonga, Samoa (American and Western), and Aotearoa/New Zealand operates as a trope for solidarity among these, and other, Pacific peoples.

"Race" as an everyday embodiment

However they may be officially designated (as one or part of an ethnic minority) in other countries, labeled as "gangstas" and "dole-bludgers" or "overstayers," or subject to (in)direct forms of structural discrimination in the United States, New Zealand, and/or Australia, the Pacific Island communities interacting online are very concerned with resisting such negative stereotypes. They are also concerned about how these relate to the effects of social and economic exclusion for second and third generations, for they consider themselves to be as much Americans, New Zealanders, Australians as they are Tongans and/or Samoans. For instance:

> In my whole entire experience as a Tongan citizen, the thought that i am a so-called Tongan-American, never crossed my mind. Simply, i identify myselfas Tongan with no American hyphenated from the back. This is something natural to me, and to have that American attached to being a Tongan, have somekind of nagative connatation.[7] ... However, there is nothing personal against this country, 'coz I benefit a whole lot from here *America* ... compared to a life back in the isle had I grown up in there. But as long as I know in my heart, soul and mind that I am a Tongan-*American*, or what not, life is just the same.
>
> (Hakautapu, 03/09/98, KB in KBAdmin, 03/09/98)

Participants are deeply concerned about the sociopsychological effect of negative stereotypes (and how online communities can both counter or reproduce these). Well aware of how the "socially constructed nature of race" (Kolko, Nakamura, and Rodman 2000: 2) has quite concrete manifestations, participants resist being designated as either "non"-Western or "Westernized," black or white. Nonetheless, skin color – appearance – cannot be written off too lightly.

Color codes

In a provocative reply to an initial post entitled *I dislike the term Polynesian* (~ALOJAH~, 11/25/00, KR) in the Kamehameha Roundtable, a palangi/palagi (Tongan/Samoan for foreigner) stalwart of the Kava Bowl says:

> I'm not even close to white. Depending on the season, I can be any-where from a light, reddish beige to a deep, golden brown . . . but never white.
>
> (Sandy Macintosh, 11/25/00, KR in reply to above)

To which Teuila, recently widowed with a young son who is half-Samoan (on his father's side), says:

> I can't change how society or the world as a whole will identify me or my son so I just let it roll off my back. In the big picture, whether we are White, Brown, Black or any shade in between and how we identify ourselves means so very little. I will insist that my son know and appre-ciate both sides of his family tree. . . . But rather than have him con-centrate on what man-given name has been assigned him based on his genealogical background, I would have him focus more on leaving his mark on this planet as a kind, compassionate, loving human being.
>
> (Teuila, 11/26/00, KR in ~ALOHJA~, 11/25/00)

Two from the many responses to her story illustrate some of the multiple "color codes" at work. First: "We do not see the world as it is, we see the world as we are" (Tongan man, 11/26/00, KR in reply to above). And second: "I dunno about you Teuila, but I don't want a COLOR blind world. . . . This may come as a shock to many but if we all were color blind then we wouldn't see the beauty in all colors and races" (gp, KR, 11/26/00 in reply to Teuila above). And Teuila's counter, on behalf of her son and his father, is as follows:

> Of course I don't want a color BLIND world, silly! You know me better than that! Pull up them antennae dude – I want Dumpling to grow up in a world of color – recognizing and appreciating the beauty of all. What I won't accept from him is making a judgement based on color.
>
> (Teuila, KR, 11/26/00 in reply to above)

At first glance, references to skin color vis-à-vis having "pure" or mixed blood may read as rehearsals of biological essentialism. However, I would argue for a more open-ended reading of how race operates as a trope in these conversations and the lives from which, and to which, they speak – "race" both as a shorthand for physical, attitudinal, and cultural commonality on the one hand and as a call for pride, self-awareness, and the right to be distinct on the other. In both respects, it is an axis around which much intense disagreement also turns. While it is used in essentialist ways (see what follows), it is more often an elastic term for a human condition that is to be examined rather than denied or reified. Many of the more intense debates are sparked off when essentialist views are aired. One of the best examples of these dynamics is a thread that started with an initial post entitled *Fake Polynesians* (100%, 02/02/01, KR). Nearly sixty follow-ups flew in within a few days. 100% maintains that looking white is equivalent to being white in that it gets the person "off the hook" if they so choose:

> I wonder why people who do NOT look Polynesian go around telling people they are? A white woman came up to me today and asked if I was Samoan. She than tells me she is 1/4 Samoan. Big deal. She looked white to me. I can tell she was bragging as to suggest that she is one of us but thankfully did not look like one of us. I guess my point is, if you don't look Polynesian than it doesn't matter. The truth is when you go out in the real world, I'm sure you will not bring that up with your white peers.

> (ibid.)

Their argument is that as looks do ultimately govern how one is treated in society at large, then those who can "get away" with looking white, or rather, who do not look "Polynesian," are at an advantage in a racist society. Amid a lot of fiery disagreement in principle with this view, 100% stands his or her ground, reminding others that, nonetheless, in

> the real world, society judges our heritage based on our physical appearance. . . . The white woman I spoke of can shout about her Polynesian heritage until she turns brown in the face. Yet, society will still see her as nothing more than a white woman claiming heritage to a race in which she was genetically deprived. So you see, there really is no point in identifying yourself with a race that you do not resemble. It serves no purpose. Finally, It has been my observation that many of the White afakasi [half-caste] Polynesians acknowledge our heritage with a sense of relief that they were not cursed with our dark Polynesian features. They want to have their cake and eat it too.

> (100%, 02/03/01, KR in 100%, 02/02/01)

This observation is acknowledged, albeit cautiously, in terms of how overt racial discrimination is based on visual cues. As a long-serving regular shares,

> I can understand your bitterness because there is still racism in our

society. But don't you see? You are perpetuating the ignorance. . . . I'll tell you that I have the "traditional" features of an island man. My skin is dark, my hair is black, my eyes are brown, and my nose is flat (as well as runny during sad movies . . . hehehe). Throughout my life, I have been subject to racism, implied and explicit. My response has been to ignore the ignorance and treat people like I would like to be treated. . . . I'm sorry you feel less of yourself because you are darker. But too much pigment never stopped me. I never let that stop me. And I certainly don't blame my fellow islanders for my skin color. Sorry you feel that way.

(Meilakepa, 02/03/01, KR in 100%, 02/02/01)

For many other respondents, 100%'s claims about certain looks and *ipso facto* "racial purity" is discriminatory towards "half-caste Polys" (miss thang, 05/28/99, KR). Responses are varied. First are those who express various degrees of interest or lack of interest in nature and implication of skin color vis-à-vis cultural (dis)affiliation. For instance:

So what if the lady looked white with poly blood?. It's really sad because we suffer so much racism in this country already – due to the fact that we are minorities and yet, we as Polynesians tend to be discriminating against ourselves.

(SeiOrana, 02/03/01, KR in 100%, 02/02/01)

[I]t's a free country, and let her do whatever she wants and if she never discloses that fact in front of her white peers. But I understand what you mean when people like that lady just say that when it's convenient like when it comes to scholarships, college admissions, Polynesian club memberships etc. but still it's not hurting you or me, so don't sweat the hype.

(tOnGaInMaIdEn, 02/02/01, KR in 100%, 02/02/01)

Others, mainly of mixed parentage, disapprove outright with 100%'s stance:

I myself have been told by many polynesians heck even from the ones that are from my island tell me that I don't look polynesian. Even the polys that I kick it with always thought I was mix until they seen my sister and brothers. . . . Point is what exactly is a polynesian person suppose to look like? . . . as long as we know our culture and know where we come from and carry it with pride then what is wrong with that? . . . We can't let peoples stereotypes of certain cultures judge one another on appearance. My mother and I are light skin and have light hazel eyes. My mother has red hair and I have jet black hair but with red highlights in them. My father, sister, and brothers are brown skin, have jet black hair, and dark brown eyes. Does that make them more of a Tonga than my mother and I? Hell NO.

(Tonga Lady, 02/03/01, KR in 100%, 02/02/01)

I CAN'T BELIEVE IN THIS TIME AND AGE THERE ARE STILL INDIVIDUALS LIKE YOURSELF RUNNING AROUND. YOU MAY HAVE ISSUES WITH SELF ESTEEM AND YOUR IDENTITY. I THINK ITS GREAT WHEN AFATASIS CLAIM THEIR SAMOAN HERITAGE. I AM MIXED WITH CHINESE, GERMAN, AND SAMOAN.... WHEN SOMEONE ASKS ME WHAT I AM, I SAY "SAMOAN"! WHO ARE YOU TO JUDGE OTHERS AND SAY WHO SHOULD BE CONSIDERED SAMOAN. 100%, YOU ARE STRAIGHT TRIPPIN!

(lalelei, 02/03/01, KR in 100%, 02/02/01)[8]

Others set out to disprove the empirical and cultural validity of 100%'s purist claims in a variety of ways:

I have cousins running around Samoa with blue/green eyes and blondie locks with more than 50% Samoan blood pumping through their veins. I myself swear I look Samoan ... hehe ... but everyone else thinks not ... hmmm ... but I am more than half and I am soo proud of my Samoan heritage.... Please don't judge a book by its cover.... I was still Samoan when being Samoan wasn't cool.

(Breezy, 02/03/01, KR in 100%, 02/02/01)

I know some samoans who are afa kasi and have straight up chinese or palagi names and claim their samoan side more than some %100 pure blooded ones. I see Samoans who are 1/4 born and raised in the islands knowing more about their culture than %100 pure blooded ones here in California! The thing you fail to realize is some of them were raised "FA'A SAMOA" by their grandparents, geez my husband is Hawaiian/Tahitian but claims his Hawaiian side, and he has a Tahitian last name. I am half Tongan and Samoan, but I claim my Samoan side. Is that wrong? You relate to the way you were raised! You're hating for all the wrong reasons! In all actuality we did not have a choice in being AFA KASI or 1/4 or whatever the blood amount. Guess what my children claim to be? HAWAIIAN! but they also don't deny the fact that they have other polynesian blood flowing through their veins. Remember we're all family, all Polynesian, regardless of blood amount. And I don't know about you, but I am PROUD to be SAMOAN, and I am happy that woman who is 1/4 went out of her way to let you know she was 1/4 SAMOAN! Talk bout pride! you need a trip back home!

(Teine Afa Tasi, 02/05/01, KR in 100%, 02/02/01)

Conflicting expectations about the implications of a "traditional" upbringing in and out of the islands get mixed up with the gender–power hierarchies of Pacific Island societies on the one hand and tensions between those living "back home" and those being brought up in the West (all of whom can be seen interacting in these forums) on the other. This subtext to the thread does not escape the notice of one Australian-based participant, whose intervention will serve as a final illustration of how personal and cultural geographies are intertwined at any one time:

> I was raised outside of Samoa, but raised in the 'Samoan Way".... I have met quite a few people who are 1/4 Samoan and 1/4 chinese and whatever, my point is, many people talk the talk but don't walk the walk, if you can get the drift. I resent people ... talking about us as 'stateside polys' raised away from the islands. I was not raised away from the island because of choice, it was because my parents wanted a better future for their children.... I really need to point out that those on the island appear to have it all. You try being raised in a country that has conflicting cultures with your own and then talk to me about 'hate on the rest of us on the islands'. Over here, it is a great feat for a Samoan child to speak their native tongue fluently, so I take it to great offence when people like to flaunt their ties with Samoa, however, have not struggled to find acceptance from both the Australian and Samoan communities, due to their skin colour and obvious palagi appearances. If they are proud to be 1/4 Samoan just for name's sake, then to me, they are not a 'true Samoan'.
>
> (L.T., 02/08/01, KR in 100%, 02/02/01)

Support and respect

What is striking, nonetheless, about all these tough arguments is the amount of practical suggestions, advice, sympathetic accounts offered along the way. These articulate a solid repertoire of everyday tactics, of "making do." In one poignant thread, kavahine complains about how a friend's "rediscovery" of her Samoan ancestry "was one of the factors that got her into the school" even though "as kids, she hung out with the palangi girls who gave me hell, b/c I wasn't like the rest, b/c I wasn't palangi" (kavahine 09/30/00, KR). In the course of this discussion on the rights and wrongs of positive discrimination policies, Sweet Siren responds:

> I support K's friend because I believe that it's her own life and she makes her own decision. It's not our place to judge her. What she did was wrong but what goes around will surely comes around and bite her in the nose.... I, on the other hand, make use my palangi

heritage for my own advantage. When I'm being forced to collide with a harsh world that is spurned with sexists and racists, I instinctively digging into my comfort zones and solemnly declare that I'm white. That's typical human too!!!!!! Due to the existence of prejudice, people of colour often find that the environment is unsupportive and the air is polluted with racial prejudice/discrimination through benign neglect or overt hostility ... the more perfect reason for Siren to "switch on" to her palangi heritage ... makes things easy for me, you know. But when I return home, I instinctly "switch off" from my "palanginess" and "switch on" to my "Tonganness".... It's something beyond my control. I think I somehow portray the experience of many half caste peeps in my situation.... I want to be treated equally not differently.

(Sweet Siren, 10/02/00, KR in kavahine, 09/30/00)

Not everyone agrees, however. Another Kava Bowl and Kamehameha Roundtable regular puts it this way:

Your own personal examples show how you protect yourself through your dual identities as a Palangi and Tongan. So tell me, would you ever use your Palangi background at the expense of a fellow Tongan? That is what Kavahine's friend did. The friend was not being persecuted or undergoing hardship. The friend simply took advantage of an opportunity that was meant for people who really needed it. So in that sense I RESPECTFULLY take offense with your open support for this "friend."

(Meilakepa, KR, 10/02/00 in kavahine, 09/30/00)

Introspective discussions such as these also need to be read from the broader perspective of the gender power relations of postcolonial everyday life in and beyond the Pacific Islands in a contemporary "global" context. This internal/external dynamic is never far away from the personal issues at stake in these discussions, first because

through colonization, westernization, modernization and growth we take on the socialization and values of the dominant culture that has the grasp of our economy and our future. We then associate the incoming culture as better and some of us want to be like them because we perceive them as better or want to be accepted by them, or achieve the things they achieve. Yes, many of us will talk their talk and walk their walk.

(Blossom Iwalani Fonoimoana, KR, 07/18/00 in MARY, 03/01/01)

And second, because the roads to (re)empowerment are two-way. As another participant notes:

[F]irst, we minorities were frustrated that white people didn't give us any advances in anything including education ... then we hated our half-poly for being part white because some of us felt that they didn't recognize their culture ... now, that when a sister ... whom is mainly palangi still holds to the little part of her polynesian culture ... you're still not satisfied ... there ain't nothing wrong with what she is doing ... i say rock on withca bad self girl and claim your culture.

(ana, KR, 10/18/00 in kavahine, 09/30/00)

Multiple cultural codes

Closely allied with debates about race as everyday embodiments are the copious threads on an equally elastic term: culture. Everyday life in the inner city or suburbs does not always jell with cultural practices (brought over) from the islands. What are at stake in some quite specific discussions are which elements of said culture need to be passed on in order to ensure ease with and knowledge of the (grand)parents' way of doing things, including linguistic competency. For feeling marginalized cuts both ways when one is of mixed heritage. The threads focused on in this section articulate any number of informal and formal practices that are seen to comprise a respective "cultural identity." Threads dealing explicitly with culture as a practical and political problem acknowledge, at least in principle, the idea that culture (or "tradition") is malleable, flexible, and so contestable. Parents who grew up in the islands or abroad, children who are parents in turn, and partners and children of mixed marriages discuss which aspects of Samoan and/or Tongan culture are being lost, changed, or should be preserved. Economic patterns of familial and social obligation, the nature and appropriateness of "gifts," the role of formal ceremonies overseas, and so on are all discussed.[9] One of the Kava Bowl's regulars rereads assumptions about urbanized cultural communities' (lack of) awareness of "traditional" culture in an interesting way. Many notions do not, in this participant's view, always come from outsiders. A number of archetypical "Tongan" and/or "black/urban youth" cultural attributes are taken to task in this excerpt:

Definitions of what a Tongan is will reflect whatever experience and knowledge each individual brings to the table ... no definition is either right or wrong. However, it seems like there is always someone who is trying to make his voice heard above everyone else's, proclaiming that his definition is by far the most right, and from that definition should every Tongan standard be predicated. I have little experience with all the ballyhoo that goes on with the majority of the Tongan celebrations. I lived in Tonga for three years when I was a little kid. I can't speak Tongan, I am a terrible tao'lunga dancer, in fact I probably spelled it wrong, I can hardly eat pork, in fact I don't even really like meat that much. Reggae is not my favorite music, neither is rap ... I've never to'aed for a fai kava and never will and to top it all off, I am light-skinned and have thin hair. So now that I have failed the 'You are a Tongan if you are...' test, can I still call myself a Tongan?

(Tupou Fifita, 10/28/98 in KBAdmin, 10/18/98)

These discussions are complex, filled with arguments about the specificity as well as the commonality of Tongan and Samoan cultural practices. Given the colonial history that frames the online and offline traversals of the South Pacific, let alone arguments about "precontact" ones (Morton 1996: 21–22), there are strong emotional and political undertones in these discussions about the negative consequences of "preservation" or "adaptation." For instance:

We're not so much as losing our culture, we're adapting to todays world. Think about it, do you think our aiga [extended family] in The Samoa's could live life the way we did for thousands of years and thousands more with the way the world is advancing? No, Samoa as with the rest of Polynesia is slowly adapting to the modern day world out of necessity!

(me, 02/10/01, KR in Student, 02/09/01)

As one participant points out, these sorts of decisions are an essential part of having to "make do as we go" when living overseas or being married to someone from another culture (Soakai, KB, 09/09/97 in KBAdmin, 09/08/97). Also, maintaining a sense of perspective – and humor – is also a recurrent theme:

It is like this I know because I married a Tongan. you give all the family your money, you name all your kids after the family members. You make sure you go to church even if you can't understand the language ... always feed your in-laws or else. And deal with them speaking their language even if you can't understand what they are saying and yes they are probably talking about you.... Don't get me wrong I love my Tongan man but is not easy sometimes. But its worth it!!!!!!!

(Lahuablossom, KB, 05/23/99 in John Michel, 04/28/99)

There is also a lot of discussion about the downside of living as a member of an "ethnic minority" somewhere else and how this may be impacting on younger generations' behavior and/or ability to achieve in the host culture. An initial post, entitled *identity-crisis*, articulates the gendered and ethnicity dimensions entailed here in another way:

Okay, I'm a New Zealand born full samoan. Yet throughout my life I have continuously felt out of place amongst my culture. I was too bright or too fia palagi [like Westerners]. A lot of the time I would purposely disassociate myself from my culture. I refused to speak the language and so I can't speak it at all, I don't believe in most traditional customs regarding the female role in Samoan society and I find it really hard relating to people of my own race anyway unless they've had the same childhood or interests as me. I mean, I am quick to defend my people if they are being unfairly discriminated and yet in the same breath I would put them down and point out a lot of negative aspects of the culture. I am 21 now and trying to assimilate myself into the culture but I find it really difficult and frustrating.

(tekken, KR, 03/01/01)

Or, as Jazzy Belle says in an early discussion, echoing others who come before and after her, the pressures at any one time are economic, socio-cultural and psychological:

I am one of those Polynesians who was born in America and has assimilated with many 'American' ways that are not 'Poly' ways. . . . [M]y parents, especially my dad, has emphasized how important it is . . . to be successful. . . . It isn't a pleasant picture when the 'Whites' stereotype many polys as dumb and no-good gang-bangers. . . . [It's] hard enough being away from family, taking classes that seem like they'll never end, fighting our own battles without our own people degrading us by calling us 'oreos' or 'coconuts'.

(Jazzy Belle, KB, 05/12/98 in KBAdmin, 05/11/98)

Participants also consider culture in political terms and the implications of doing so for working together in order to "stand up for each other" (lillian, KB, 08/17/98, in John Michel, 08/14/98) in the face of adversity and prejudice. Interwoven with discussions about racial stereotypes are those that take a more proactive stance to "being Polynesian." The aim here is to bring the

Polynesian heritage to a status where it is acceptable and not over-looked in many countries . . . [to] be in a better position to help [the] Polynesian community or better educate them on some decisions they may have to make. Many polys are taken advantage of. Some may say it's because we're too nice, but I believe it's because some of us just don't know how to handle some situations.

(Jazzy Belle, KB, 05/12/98 in KBAdmin, 05/11/98)

Threads focusing more on "culture" *per se* treat it in similar ways to those looking at "race": as a mobile meaning. They (re)articulate not only how

Tongan/Samoan/Polynesian cultural practices are being lived, but also how they are being assumed, contested, and molded in all manner of everyday situations.

"I define my own identity"

In toto, when it comes to figuring out which "identity" is at stake, many participants are determined to decide for themselves no matter what the geographical or generational space may be:

> Do I think Samoans are assimilating more & more of the Western World? No for those that actually live in Samoa and Yes for those who have moved on to different countries, USA, AUS, NZ etc. . . . of course we are becoming more western, why? because we have to try and fit into the customs of the country that we have now made our new homes. . . . I love my culture and I am 100% Samoan, and I will try and teach my children what my parents have taught me, but I can not say that my children will do the same for theres and that's what scares me. I think it is in the individual whether our culture is passed on to the next generation. Hope my post has not offended anyone, but just wanted to share my true feelings about my culture and where I see it in the years to come. My Samoan brothers/sisters it is up to us whether or not we choose to forget our culture or remember our roots.
>
> (Dream Girl, KR, 02/11/01, in Student, 02/09/01)

Growing up in purposely individualist meritocracies, such as the United States, Australia, and New Zealand, creates different sorts of allegiances to nominally communal Pacific Island societies for many of the younger participants. As these exchanges of meaning – and experiences – are worked through "out loud" online, race/ethnicity, gender, and class permutations are all present. Despite improvements in recent years, many Pacific island communities are overrepresented in low-wage jobs and/or "underachieving" populations in the United States, Australia, and New Zealand:

> My parents migrated from Tonga to the United States in the early 60's. Here they worked adamantly to provide food, education, shelter, clothing and all the necessities of life for their own children and others' who came from the Island with no family or means of support here. I being one of the younger of their children did not get to see the full impact of the LONG SUFFERING they had to endure. My parents worked avidly to ensure they could give their children a better future. My father worked full time being paid close to $2. per hour and then had a side job of Gardening/Landscaping ('iate), while my

mother was a Housemaid. My parents instilled in us, their children the values of hard work, respect, culture, and dignity. We live in the very home they purchase some 32 years ago. My parents are both retired and live comfortably. This is not to say that we are well off.... Because I was born and raised here in America ... I can say that I have had the best of both worlds! While Tongan was the first language in the home, I learned English from my older siblings and then in Elementary School. I read, write, and speak FLUENTLY the Tongan and English language. My life is enriched because I have both cultures. While my parents struggled with the American Ways that seem so TABU to our TONGAN CULTURE and TRADITIONS, they learned quickly that they had to integrate the two.... I don't make this all out to sound like we haven't faced one bit of agony, trouble or strife ... there were plenty of those along with the traditional tongan upbringing.

(I've got the best of both worlds!, KB, 08/17/98, in KBAdmin,
08/16/98)

It is the differences in standpoint and experience that propel the threads. In so doing, they also indicate the pragmatic and political dimensions to defining one's "own" identity, whether as an individual, a member of an "ethnic minority" overseas, or in the Pacific islands themselves. The meaning of bloodlines (see the "100%" thread earlier) cuts both ways in effect:

Perhaps some of you may scoff at me for having pride in such a 'diluted' bloodline, however does being a half Tongan make me any less Tongan than a full Tongan? What does it mean to be a Tongan anyway? Do I have to have tapas [cloths] on my walls and attend every single wedding, funeral, birthday party, and pay homage to the touring royalty in order to prove that I am Tongan? Does the amount of blood that runs through my veins constitute how Tongan I am or not? I think not. (Tupou Fifita, KB, 10/28/98, in KBAdmin, 19/18/98)

Proudly countering categories

There is a third cluster of threads to examine here, formed around colonial categories for Pacific cultures, Polynesia, Melanesia, Micronesia. The terms are part of the Modern Age cartographies that circumscribe the multifarious islands of the Pacific today. They have delimited the way the Pacific Islands have been studied and charted ever since the seventeenth century. Postcolonial critiques have focused on the permeability of the geographies, the complexity of cultural practices that such terms elide, their reification in much research, and their empirical validity in the first place. In the Kava Bowl and the Kamehameha Roundtable, the term "Polynesian" has established a politicized currency all of its own:

> It's interesting how you can creatively use language for yourself, make new connections and symbolisms.... Although you may have trouble with the history behind the word "polynesian," other polynesians do not because they have redefined it for themselves.
> (Brown Sugar, KR, 11/26/00, in ~ALOJAH~, 11/25/00)

> The word Polynesian is better than being called savages as we have been.
> (Proud Polynesian, KR, 12/01/00, in ~ALOJAH~, 11/25/00)

The proactive use of the term "Polynesian" in these forums needs addressing for yet another reason: the oft-acknowledged "historical rivalry" between Tonga and Samoa (a reference to Tonga once ruling Samoa and Fiji). Nowadays, some of this "ancient rivalry" has been transmuted into competing gangs, awkward counterprejudices and, arguably, sporting contests. Such tensions do come through in other discussion themes, but, be that as it may, a self-conscious Polynesian identity in-the-making has been discernible all along (Kami 2001: interview). Being Polynesian, then, means creating solidarity in the face of common experiences of discrimination, in South Auckland, New Zealand, or in Salt Lake City and Los Angeles in the United States. In this respect, this designation is becoming a trope for future ideals. This is not a preordained conclusion, however. As always, a number of positions are played out. First, there are those who object outright to the term's colonialist undertones:

> And why call ourselves Polynesian, that's a mouthful and the word Polynesian comes from butchers who killed us with their weapons and hazardous diseases. I, myself am Tongan, no more, no less, and I think people should just state whether they're Hawaiian, Hamo, Maori, Fijian, Tahitian, etc. Enough of this Polynesian bs.
> (Don't you all agree, KR, 12/30/00)

> Today we have the word, which thus describes us ~ Polynesian.... I resent being called that by my fellow brethren as well as outsiders, and allowing them to be called and call themselves that. How can we adopt the name given to us by this butcher? If anyone can contrive a better name, I give them my highest regards.
> (~ALOJAH~, KR, 11/25/00)

And then there are those who would dismiss such concerns as irrelevant and, moreover, self-defeating:

[C]ategory schmategory!... by the time applications or any kind of questionnaire gets caught up in how to differ us all racially, people will be bitching about dividing us by hair color.

(afatasi_girl, KR, 07/05/00, in don't you all agree, 06/30/00)

While acknowledging the colonial origins of these nomenclatures, most others opt to simply get on with things:

YOU GOTTA UNDERSTAND SON, THE 'WHITE MAN' COMES UP WITH WAYS TO MAKE LIFE LESS COMPLICATING ... SAD BUT TRUE.... BY THE WAY I'M, HALF SAMOAN AND HALF TONGAN *hehehehehehehe*

(BrAnD-NuBiAn ... get a LIFE!!!, KR, 07/03/00, in don't you all agree, 06/30/00)

[R]elish in the thought that we have an identity, and a legacy that is unrivaled. You are dwelling on the negative ... there is more to life ... be happy!

(Fataai, KR, 11/26/00, in ibid.)

Others go further than this, though, as they look to create new, more empowering meanings and thereby identifications. These conscious recalibrations of erstwhile racialized designations are evident right from the early years of the forums. The following excerpts, posted on the Polynesian Cafe in 1998, trace some of these ideals:

When I meet a Polynesian, and it doesn't necessarily mean 'of one specific islander', I am always proud to greet them and talk with them. When my kids see an Islander, they always say 'Mommy, is that our cousin?' and I think that is so special that they recognise their own kind. I am a proud Tongan, female, mother of 4 beautiful Boys, and I have a Great Tongan husband who loves his culture.

(Polycafe/Ika Vailea, in POLYCAFE, 05/08/98)

As we take on our new identities, in New Zealand, Australia, or where ever we may be, remember our roots, our family trees.... A Polynesian ... thank you God for making me.

(Polycafe/Richard Wolfgramm, in POLYCAFE, 05/08/98)

Polynesian is in this sense as much a synonym for Tongan and/or Samoan as it is a

feeling [that] gives a whole new meaning to our many different

cultures which all polynesia islands, whether we are from Fiji, Tonga, Samoa, Micronesia, Tahiti, New Zealand and many others.
(Polycafe/Margaret Vailoa Tavai Taugavaau, in POLYCAFE, 05/08/98)

It is about the power of mutuality when living in

a world that is defined by change, our ability to assimilate the best of new cultures while holding onto traditional values is a source of strength for the Polynesian community. We are survivors.
(Polycafe/Sau Tagaloa Jr, in POLYCAFE, 05/08/98)

What is happening as these facets of everyday lives get written out, challenged, and reiterated online is a resistance to all forms of essentialism, whether from within Tongan and Samoan communities or beyond. After all, younger generations of many a diaspora do not necessarily identify with the cultural conventions and identifications of their parents' generation. So, despite countless reiterations of "traditional" notions of respect and "pride" combined with Christian moral values and/or Tongan/Samoan forms of obligation, all these are regarded as malleable to some extent. This is a fine balancing act at the best of times. It is in discussions on the meaning of Samoan/Tongan/Polynesian identity formation for the future that this consciousness is most palpable.

Looking to the future

[It] depends which perspective you take (inside looking on inside, diaspora looking from outside in, diaspora looking from outside at the outside, inside looking at the diaspora, outsider looking at the diaspora from the outside, outsider looking at the effect of the diaspora on the inside etc..). As you can see a very complex question.
('Alopi Latukefu, KB, 05/02/99, in John Michel, 04/21/99; also 1999: interview)

It bears repeating that Tongan, Samoan, and other Pacific island participants have always been interacting with one another in both the KB and the KR, and now mainly on the KR since the Kava Bowl went offline. This interaction is not insignificant simply because it is happening on the World Wide Web. And the nature of cyberspatial relationships does not cause everyday embodiments of sex/gender, race/ethnicity, or socio-economic hierarchies based on both class relations and/or status to evaporate. As Helen Morton notes about the Kava Bowl, this sort of

"virtual ethnic community" can express its "alterity" despite the non-physicality of the medium. Any Internet user group is only accessed by those interested; that is the nature of this form of communication.

However, the fact there is a recognisable Tongan site on the Internet vastly increases the opportunities for interactions between Tongans and between Tongans and non-Tongans. It also enables [participants] to represent themselves, in all their diversity, challenging stereotypes and resisting the typically limited representations of them, for example in their "traditional" dancing at multicultural festivals.

(Morton 1998a/2001: 77–78)

In the midst of the "oppression of the present" for diasporic Pacific island communities and individuals, there is an awareness that grappling with the forces of discrimination and exclusion means that "you have to represent where you are coming from" (Polycafe/Ta'alolo Mann, in Polycafe, 03/08/98), especially since "there is no text book solution to our journey" (Soakai, KB, 09/09/97 in KBAdmin, 09/08/97). In another set of discussions, articulations of identity move into futurist tropes for multiplex meanings and practices of race/ethnicity/culture. In this respect, some may hold onto clear lines of distinctiveness in the face of discrimination and/or isolation; others seek to traverse these as a way to resolve tension. Three ideals for the future constitute this fourth set of interpersonal offline–online "strayings."

First is the notion of solidarity, to be achieved by practicing "love and respect." Second is the right to be different(iated) rather than absorbed. Third is a conscious working with the symbolic power of counterrepresentations for communities and groups that suffer ingrained stereotypes in their new homelands. Solidarity can be a political response to inequality of opportunity and low self-esteem. As this New Zealand Maori participant says, Polynesian can be recoded as

our own name for ourselves ... [it] simply means human being as does many other indigenous self labels. We as Polynesian Tangata Whenua, people of the land need to achieve some sort of political, spiritual unity to be able to claim back polynesia as our own from the overstayer nations like France and America etc. I believe the names that we call our selves only serve to divide us and are the oppressors tools. We should celebrate our differences as well as our similarities. . . . Its alright to get on with it when yours is the dominant culture whose democratic systems will ensure that you stay in power. Its easy enough to get on with it when you own all the stolen land. Its easy to get on with it when your cultural ideals are the only ones that are valued in society.

(supa*maori*fulla, KR, 10/07/00, in haka, 09/28/00)

As the above sample indicates, the power of a dominant culture and/or history does not mean that similarity and difference are mutually exclusive. In this sort of "strategic essentialism," the notion of "race" can, arguably, be reclaimed from its biologically essentialist overtones, albeit with difficulty. For instance, in the following response to the post entitled *identity-crisis* (tekken, KB, 03/01/01), Bevo says:

> [L]et me take a stab. You're having trouble merging your two identities together. And make no mistake about it, you have two identities. One is your race, and the other is your nationality. You're Samoan by race, but New Zealander by nationality. Your skin is brown, but your mind set is that of a westerner. Your roots are Polynesian, but your values are probably European in nature. This is a struggle that many young poly's struggle with. How to reconcile the differences in the two cultures. It's fine when living back in the islands. But when we have to exist in western society, we must find a way of bringing the two cultures together, where one is not suppressing the other.
>
> (Bevo, KR, 03/01/01 in reply to above)

Third is the countering of cultural/racial stereotypes as a conscious countertactic:

> [M]uch respect and love to each one of you tongans, samoans, fijians, hawaiians, etc., etc., from san fran, inglewood, oakland, glendale, provo, slc,euless – what-ever-point-of-the-map-you're-located-on-because-you're-still-a-poly-in-my-eyes.
>
> (lillian, KB, 09/17/98, in KBAdmin, 09/14/98)

> Even though – or precisely because – these interpersonal and intercultural traversals are happening in public cyberspaces it is not insignificant that participants are "prepared to 'share' the [KR] forum ... [especially] considering gangs of Tongans and Samoans are literally killing each other in real life."
>
> (Helen Morton, personal email, 06/22/01)

An initial post on the Kamehameha Roundtable in 2001 underscores the way online forums such as these can provide spaces where sensitive issues can be handled in relative frankness and safety. All the rules of respect and careful moderating of "unacceptable behavior" that have contributed to the mainly inclusive character of these particular forums notwithstanding, TonganRasta asks:

> I wanted to know something. Many Tongans and Samoans (not all of course) have a hard time seeing eye to eye. I see both races duking it out all the time in the different msg [message] boards.... I see it when we walk down the aisle of a mall and one of my cousins mad dog a group of samoans walking the opposite direction. My question is why? Yeah, I know that it dates back in the old days when Tonga and

Samoa were at war, but what really happened? . . . I realize that Tonga and Samoa are both different countries, similar in many aspects can cause a rivalry, but why is that tension still there? What's the point of fighting your own brothers or your own sisters? I've seen over and over again the hatred many of my fellow Tongans have for Samoans. In fact I was one of them at one point. All that changed when I fell in love with a Samoan. I had the chance to see the Samoan culture and how beautiful it is. . . . We are all Polynesians.

(TonganRasta, KR, 06/06/01)

Without ignoring the tensions and disagreements between and within these groups on the ground, these online traversals show people defining their "own identity" together as they share the particularities, contradictions, and symmetries of everyday life in different locales. In doing so, they underscore Sankaran Krishna's insight that identity

is a constantly dynamic and performative practice . . . something based in part on a historical inventory that memorializes past encounters but also something that changes with dazzling speed within a single moment. Nuances and inflections on that inventory surface on different occasions and under different provocations. In other words . . . identity [is] a performative practice that connects and individual to a continuously changing social setting. It is moreover incompletely under the control of the so-called protagonist.

(Krishna 2002: 171)

Recapitulation

Amid all the various attitudes and experiences, two concerns work in tandem. One is how *looks matter*. For instance, one respondent in a thread entitled *WHY DO THEY DISCRIMINATE US!!!* (a blonde girl who's samoan, KR, 01/25/00) noted that "you should know very well that there are a lot of haters out there. And they judge you by the way you look" (u must be one of the haters!!!, KR, 01/26/00 in a blonde girl who's samoan, 01/25/00). This is closely linked to how a respective "culture" is *practiced*, or not as the case may be. Looks and one's cultural affiliation matter both vis-à-vis one's peer group/s and immediate community, and in terms of how one is treated, discriminated against (or not) by society at large. This is how everyday practices and politics of identity formation – of *identification*, as an individual and as a member of one or several communities – work here as verbs – doing words. As such, they are countering tendencies to use "race," "ethnicity," and "culture" as static or purist terms of reference.

Beyond the specific discussions on skin color and "blood," those dealing with "culture" bespeak particular and ever-widening multiple circles of relationships and sociocultural conventions in both their empowering and their demoralizing manifestations. These discussions (re)articulate how personal and group identifications operate, become fixed as well as stretched when living under the rules and assumptions of another, more dominant culture. The protagonists talk about "making do," and debate the (in)appropriateness of various behaviors, loyalties and cultural affiliations, and the implications of all of these on what constitutes contemporary Polynesian–Tongan–Samoan inter/subjectivity. How and what people identify *as*, with *whom*, and to what degree any said "identity" may or should be a multiple of one are posited both as ideal types and as tropes for future generations. They are also posted as antidotes to racial and cultural stereotyping from within and outside the communities. Moreover, they challenge the efficacy of accepted physical and behavioral markers of belonging to an "ethnic/racial/cultural" minority, which also include stories of ancestral lineages and origins (both as histories and categories), respective language acuity, and knowledge of everyday cultural practices. The postcolonial politics of representation being articulated in these particular discussions are about the whys and wherefores of multiple identifications, multiplex rather than singular understandings of being/belonging/doing that are framed and experienced quite viscerally as everyday corporeal, symbolic, and cultural meanings, both in online (cyber)spatial practices and in offline lived lives.

This set of threads show discussants unpacking and stretching received and assumed meanings of culture/race/ethnicity in multiple spaces and interactions that operate through and between discussions online over time as well as between participants offline. The manifest content is constituted by but also informs the sociocultural, political-economic, and *emotional* spaces of everyday life in and beyond the Pacific Islands. Up for discussion are home life, school, work, family politics, and friendship and love relationships in and between communities, class, and other social hierarchies. Added to this are the effects and meaning of social exclusion and emotional isolation for those who feel they do not fit any one sociocultural code, and the ambiguous politics and opportunities of "positive discrimination" and living in societies that privilege individual agency.

3 Reflections for theory and research

In these conversations, "identity" operates in its present continuous voice rather than as an "anthropological present" (Fabian 1983; di Leonardo 1991). Its demographically understood corollaries, namely, race/ethnicity/gender, and even class, operate as *verbs* (*doing* words) rather than nouns (designations, fixed categories) to circumscribe the daily choices and obligations that constitute inter/subjectivity as both palpable and fluid sets of meaning, being, and doing. However, positing any of these as socially constructed

doesn't mean that our understanding of race and racial categories isn't somehow real or that it doesn't have real effects: quite the contrary, those categories *do* exist and that have tangible (and all too often deadly) effects on the ways that people are able to live their lives. What it *does* mean, however, is that the systems of racial categorisation that permeate our world are derived from culture, not nature.
(Kolko, Nakamura, and Rodman 2000: 2; original emphasis)

In this respect, online renditions of these permeations are not by virtue of their digital/hypertextual qualities any less tangible; gender power relations (and their class/ethnic permutations) are quite concrete in cyberspace too, as the next chapter will show. Before we proceed, though, some reflections on how the manifest content of these threads casts a stone into the smooth pool of theory and research that causally links "globalization," ICTs (however defined), and a crisis in "identity" to one another. Without wanting to grossly oversimplify the socioculturally and politically complex set of scholarly literature from which such interventions take their cue, I would still argue that even critical IR/IPE tends to frame the above equation and how it relates to questions around inter/subjectivity in negative, crisis-ridden, and irretrievable terms – as a zero-sum game. In short, "identity" issues are those concerning a particular subject/subjectivity that is in disarray, either under the strictures of neoliberal political and economic strategies, post-Cold War or post-colonial era forms of "state collapse," or as the result of hi-tech forms of "time–space compression" and the way the "mass culture industry" has cornered the market, so to say. All of which are seen as a threat to the modern(ist) nation-state–identity matrix that is at the heart of Western political, economic, and historical experience and narratives. Neoliberalism, social "fragmentation" and ICTs are conflated in mainstream and critical (Marxian) treatments of what are analytically distinct technoeconomic and sociohistorical conjunctures. The communicative spaces and practices of nonelite Internet practices and the plethora of non-Western and non-European experiences and histories are subsumed accordingly. ICTs, the (god)child of modernity's industrialization–capitalization processes, turn on the (god)parent and, ironically and unpredictably, permit all manner of "others" to emerge in noncorporeal and nonsurveyed spaces. What ensues is tantamount to an intellectual "identity crisis" of its own.

So what – who – exactly is in crisis? Is it a sovereign Subject faced with the loss of its subjected "Other" since the decline of empire during decolonization processes in the 1960s? Or is it the loss of the Cold War certainties that separated Us from Them? Who exactly is this Individual Subject (the "Self") and its "Other" anyway? Not, I would contend, the "self" who is co-constructed and then speaks for the "absent other" (Ahearne 1995; de Certeau 1997a). Nor is it the male figure whose feminized "other" is marginalized if not erased from official histories and scholarly knowledge production. And it is certainly not the "self" of non-Western "others" whose inter/subjectivities are subsumed under scientific accounts in which they are put in their place and then "known." Critics of the self-absorbed geographies of Western (critical) thought underline these over-sights in theoretical terms (Moore-Gilbert *et al.* 1997; Ling 2002; Hall 1996b; Seth 1999; Mohanty 1997). In addition, the gender neutrality of this abstract Individual Subject has been extensively debunked by femi-nist theory and research (Nicholson 1990; Benhabib and Cornell 1987; Carver and Mottier 1998). Both streams point to how it is a certain elite He-Subject who is the implicit victim of the aforementioned processes of change in much of the literature. This is *his* identity crisis. From this exis-tentialist angst, any number of geoculturally specific shifts get projected quite literally onto the rest of the world; as "global" ones. The West-phalian state system's identity crisis is exported to all peoples, all soci-eties. The upshot is that both the "problem" and its "solution" are seen as the prerogative of subjects of hi-tech capitalist societies in the West and, more to the point, their critics from the "old" and "new" left (see Castells 1997; Dufour 2001; Harvey 1990). This reiteration of a transcendent he-subject under threat from ICTs *tout court* continues to erase the class, ethnic, and gendered undertones of the expansionist history and univer-salizing subjectivity that is purportedly in crisis. In so doing, others' pasts and visions of the future are misappropriated and counterevidence ignored. This ethnocentric and Euro-centered rendition of "identity" through which the "fate" or "crisis" of the modern nation-state is meas-ured is seen as happening everywhere and in equal measure. Other regions, societies, and populations have to bear this identity crisis on highly uneven terms.

This projection has implications for critical IR/IPE theory and research that claims an emancipatory project anyway (see Leonard 1990; Devetak 2001a; Chowdhry and Nair 2002; Franklin 2003b). The tendency toward technological and sociocultural determinism that permeates many analyses is particularly limited for dealing with how non-Western, post-colonial societies experience, perceive, and appropriate contemporary constellations of ICTs. It is more limited again, I would argue, when exam-ining nonelite and/or everyday uses of Internet technologies, in the West and/or by non-Western practitioners (this dichotomy being used here for the sake of argument only). Precisely because the exact relationship between ICTs, neoliberal orthodoxies and the political ramifications of the collapse of the USSR, and ideological shifts in (nominally) communist China are so difficult to pinpoint, analyses based on this assumed – sup-posedly observable – causal link are conceptually and empirically unten-able. Granted, strategic applications and tactical uses of new(er) ICTs have social and cultural implications; the history of radio and television and other communications technologies bears this out. However, the problematic existence of the modernist nation-state as the "imagined community" *par excellence*, which includes challenges to its identity matrix from within and without official boundaries, predates the Internet/World Wide Web. Moreover, what these conjunctions mean, and how they actually operate or emerge in both diasporic, postcolonial, and online settings, require closer examination, grounded theorizing.

Back to how the KR and KB discussion forums cast light on these conjunctures through their treatment of the racial/ethnic and gendered complexities of everyday life, as lived in and through several spaces. For a generation gap appears to be emerging in how "identity" issues are conceptualized or experienced. There is a discernible difference emerging between "traditional" understandings of inter/subjectivity and "modern" ones (borrowing from these terms' already troubled pedigree) as younger diasporic generations look to distinguish their own sense of self and community vis-à-vis their elders, family members living elsewhere on the one hand and how they get stigmatized as immigrants, asylum seekers, welfare beneficiaries, gangsters, and suchlike on the other. One regular on the KR puts it this way:

> Have we all become minions of the mainstream, shackled and riddled by shame of where we come from? We proclaim empathy for [those suffering] the racism of the mainlands, but can't understand why there are racial conflicts among our own? We probably know more American/European histories than we can of our own ... histories smattered with intolerance from riots to lynching to governmental politics, racial and societal, and we accept that as a natural due course of 'progress'. Yet. we can't even spare a moment's reprieve to see our native cultures and look at it from INSIDE out.
> (05/20/99 in Lafemme Nikita, 05/19/99)[10]

Rather than explain away the contradictions and loose ends that come with living with a mixed "bag of values" (Teni, KB, 03/09/98 in KBAdmin, 03/09/98), they are aired openly. In so doing, these texts encapsulate some "new ethnicities" (Hall 1996a) as well as some "old" and "new essentialisms" (Hau'ofa 1987). Resolution, identity formation as a zero-sum game based on being "100 percent" something or other, is not considered the ultimate goal by many. For example:

> I was raised an American (born and raised). I as well, get picked on around by other samoans because I don't know the language, and because I don't act "samoan." *Whatever that means*, I think you should be comfortable with who you are, and you don't need to please anybody else, and you're better off that way. Yeah, there will always be those samoans insulting you, but hey ... I look at it, because they see something their not use to, they decide to get really negative, and not accept people for who they are instead. The way I deal with it, is that I

just practically ignore them, because if they can't accept me for who I
am, or what I believe in, than they'll just have to live with it.

(feel the same way, KR, 03/01/01 in tekken, 03/01/01; emphasis
added)

As these threads "literally" trace everyday inter/subjectivity, they also form
(hyper)textual surfaces which, in their meaning-making, traverse the
material-symbolic terrain of self- and group identity formation that straddles the space lying between different diasporic and postcolonial generations. They do so whether they be of "full" or mixed heritage, living in
urban/rural settings in the West or in Pacific islands, moving through
cyberspaces as they write and commute, or on the ground as, and where,
they access the Internet. Michel de Certeau would regard this spatiality,
and fluidity of movement, not so much as an identity "problem" or "crisis"
in itself (de Certeau 1986: 225 *passim*), but rather the effect of different
"realities" not being *permitted* to coexist.

> I shall make a distinction between space (*espace*) and place (*lieu*) that
> delimits a field. A *place* (*lieu*) is the order (of whatever kind) in
> accordance with which the elements are distributed in relationships of
> coexistence. It thus excludes the possibility of two things being in the
> same location (place). . . . It implies an indication of stability. A space
> exists when one takes into consideration vectors of direction, veloci-
> ties, and time variables. Thus space is composed of intersections of
> mobile elements . . . space is like the word when it is spoken, that is,
> when it is caught in the ambiguity of the actualization, transformed
> into a term dependent upon many different conventions, situated as
> the act of a present (or of a time), and modified by the transforma-
> tions caused by successive contexts. . . . In short, *space is a practised
> place.*
>
> (de Certeau 1984: 117/1980a: 208; original emphasis)

What de Certeau is getting at is the difference between the fixity of "a"
place (to wit, "a" culture, "an" identity) and the fluidity of the physical and
communicative spaces delimited by the multifarious practices of everyday
life. These are created and negotiated – traversed – by people as they
interact with each other. Interactions that deal *explicitly* with "identity
formation" as a "racialized"–ethnic–cultural issue for postcolonial
diasporas and those living "back in the islands" show this "fluid tension"
between fixed places (and assumptions) and "mobile intersections" very
much in operation. This political-analytical distinction between place and
space cuts both ways in cyberspace as well. Whether an urban cityscape or
an Internet website, such spaces cannot come to life, have no substance,
until they are traversed, by pedestrians, participants in online forums. At
the same time, even as online community is formed – fixed – by virtue of

its website becoming a frequented and recognizable "place" on the Web, the Internet's physical and digital architectures also circumscribe these movements. Therein lies the political contestability – not the technological inevitability – of ICT futures (see Chapter 2). Likewise in the more specific sense of structural power relations and tacit forms of social control that operate in everyday (cyber)spaces such as these.

Concluding comments

The discussion threads that traverse these parts of the World Wide Web are weaving their own online tapestry of the everyday. As they go, they have been evolving into not only spaces for personal expression and mutual support, but also challenges to old and new sociocultural and political pressures emanating from both their "original" and their diasporic cultural contexts. They reveal complex crosscutting everyday practices of peoples hailing from small island states in a "globalizing" and "digital" age in that they also operate as a node for linking the online community with everyday lives offline. As they unfurl, the discussion threads bespeak personal choice and circumstance, group pressures and group solidarity, broader dynamics of exclusion and isolation, success and achievement. They show people "engaged in representing themselves, both for themselves and the general public" (Friedman 1998: 39). This goes beyond simple rhetoric (and interpretations that would see the manifest content of these online texts as such) by virtue of the time span, the variety, and the intensity of debate throughout the years – debates that recur and evolve as new participants confront "old" problems and "old" participants get involved again (Kami 2001: interview). The goal – ideal – of unity and community that is expressed in the vast majority of these threads by people, many of whom have offline community/family connections but who have also got to know each other online as well, is no small task either. It has to be worked at. And one way to counter inter/intracultural prejudices is to talk them through. Participants in these discussions have been tackling what are often sensitive issues head-on and using the open (cyber)spaces offered by their dedicated forum moderators to do so. People keep coming back (and attest to this) because these are places in which they can deal with issues that matter for them, in their everyday life, whether they live in the islands or "overseas." The Kava Bowl and the Kamehameha Roundtable are frequented by living, writing, reading inhabitants (whatever their noms de plume) who co-create and recreate everyday life off/online, with its own inner dynamics and external pressures. The longevity of these forums is due to this effort on the part of the moderators to ensure – and take action where necessary – that these spaces remain open and inclusive.

The next chapter looks at how these formal properties work vis-à-vis the manifest content of the discussions (the focus of these last three chapters). As I have said, like cityscapes, a website, forum, live chat line has to be inhabited for it to be alive. Again, as in inner-city areas after working hours, there are plenty of "dead," lifeless places on the World Wide Web. In the case of these online discussions and the spaces created by them, fluidity, mobility of thought and expression are not shunned. Quite the opposite. Access to these "public" forums has largely remained open, despite technical, organizational, and political pressures. Staying there and participating, being seen as a "member," does involve certain stipulations and obligations, and relates to specific online "moral economies" that develop over time, as we will see in the next chapter.

7 "Please refrain from using capitals"

Online power relations

Introduction

> [T]he virtual reality that is cyberspace has often been construed as something that exists in binary opposition to the 'real world' but when it comes to questions of power, politics, and structural relations, cyberspace is as real as it gets.
>
> (Kolko *et al.* 2000: 4)

> In an already overgeneralized sense, both too much and too little is expected of [Internet technologies]; too much fabricates another 'cyber' world that is independent, indeed the opposite of our own; too little neglects the effect of reciprocity.... In making 'cyberspace' synonymous with other-worldliness, we underestimate the effects of commutations between our world and the world of enhanced presence (namely transported, transformed, intensified across distance in a way that is distinct from physical proximity).
>
> (Weissberg 1998: 4; my translation)

The reader may have noticed by now various forms of power and influence at work during the course of these discussions – for example: challenges to a participant's grasp of the requisite historical-cultural knowledge; queries about a person's background on the basis of age, gender, and class/status; deference paid to forum leaderships or authoritative "regulars"; compliments paid to, or criticism or insults leveled at, another's argument. These operations ensue from the "ground rules" or "posting policy" of the website administrators (moderators); participants' attitudes on how to behave in any, let alone an online, environment; and the ways in which conflict online is handled. They impinge upon threads' trajectories as well as the interpersonal relations unfolding through them.

Even though these forums are characterized by their open, spontaneous, lively, and often hectic nature, their very success – the sheer volume of traffic between 1998 and 2001 especially – has required some sort of "management." While the resultant actions appear to boil down to "netiquette" (see below) or legal disclaimers, a closer look shows that technical-legal concerns are spliced with behavioral, ethical, and "cultural codes" particular to offline reference points for these forums: Pacific Island communities in urban centers or "back in the islands." From an analytical point of view, these can be traced at moments of conflict or when the leaderships intervene directly and/or exercise their authority during discussions. This chapter unpacks the technopractical, political, and sociocultural dimensions to these actions and reactions as played out in a specific category of threads. Over time, these formal online power relations have come to constitute online *moral economies.*

Moral economies

Moral economies refers to "beliefs, practices and disciplinary regimes [that] shape subject/identity formation, emotional allegiance, and motivational dynamics" (Peterson 1998: 11) for a community, however delineated. The *economies* examined here have emerged through the day-to-day "management of household or private affairs [namely] the arrangement or mode of operation" (Webster's Dictionary) of countless hypertextual-personal comings and goings. The term "economy" is used inclusively, then, in order to denote the equally important "social imaginary and symbolic ordering" (Peterson 1998: 7–8; 2003) entailed in these "modes of operation." They are *moral* economies because they are not about just technopractical issues. Their "symbolic ordering" includes the (re)negotiation of behavioral codes and linguistic modes vis-à-vis Pacific island "cultural codes" (see Chapter 6). Contentions about these rules and norms, or how the moral economies become evident during conflict, revolve to a large degree "around questions of ethics" (Kolko, Nakamura, and Rodman 2000: 2). The ethical imperative referred to in these moments is the "KEYWORD HERE: RESPECT – For self, for others, and for the general spirit of this forum" (Anni, KR, 11/23/99 in Daily Planet, 11/22/99).

The legal codicils, explicit "ground rules" and more implicit norms have been worked out over time as the forums have grown in size, participation has mutated, and the initial *raison d'être* of either the KB or the KR has been evaluated or challenged. Even though what is allowed to be posted in these "serious discussion forums" is ostensibly the decision of site owners and/or those with the technical means and mandate to enforce these rules,[1] this role of "host"–moderator is not uncontested. For example:

> sheezzz making strict laws uh huh? . . . But ya know havin an erased post means you are hiding the truth . . . ya dun want anybody to talk about it or know about it. . . . Where is the freedom of speech?
>
> (sOuLjAz, Polycafe, 05/05/99 in POLYCAFE, 05/04/99)

Nor is it exclusive. Participants also assume the moderator role themselves, and do so during more intransigent disputes:

> As one of my fellow KR patrons put it, RESPECT one's host and treat
> his place like that of your own home ... people [should] come with
> the attitude that they are ambassadors of their home, parents, society
> ... be more CONSCIENTIOUS of our host, in that we put our best
> foot forward rather then [*sic*] infringing on the space of others with
> the obscene.
>
> (Teine o le Spring, Polycafe, 04/25/99 in enough is ENOUGH,
> 04/24/99)

In this chapter the moral economies of the KB and Polycafe/KR are
analyzed by looking at when "housekeeping" issues are themes in themselves. Turning on four basic axes, these economies align, first, the views
of older (literally and in the sense of long-standing) participants with
those of newer (often younger) ones.[2] Sometimes these relationships have
to be inferred, but other times, they are made clear. For instance:

> You could've introduced yourself and enlightened the rest of the
> regular and passing patrons about your own sways, persuasions and
> politics. Some self-disclosure would have given us a clear idea that we
> have new blood among us. Others just blend in and post as they wish,
> making themselves at home.
>
> (Anni, Polycafe, 11/23/99 in Daily Planet, 11/22/99)

Second, they align gender power relations; relations of conferred status
and/or seniority based on criteria such as acknowledged factual or local
knowledge of Samoan and/or Tongan societies, persuasiveness – written
oratorical skills, and wit. Women and men are fairly equally present in
these areas and certainly in terms of online outspokenness. Third, in
sharper disagreements they indicate the support mustered, or opposition
encountered, and impact on how disputes are settled (or not). These
activities and proclivities are the visual, semantic, and symbolic ebb and
flow of these economies as they structure threads' form, content, and
interrelational substance. As such, they also contribute to interlocking and
"ongoing processes of definition, performance, enactment and identity
creation" (Kolko *et al.* 2000: 10), evident in the latent content of all the
key discussions in these forums.[3]

Background note

Any kind of navel-gazing can only occur when an online community – and
here I shall use the term for argument's sake (see Rheingold 1994) – has
been going long enough to develop a collective memory in its own right,

as it becomes more closely linked to other Internet sites and as offline relationships intervene. There comes a moment when looking back is possible and, indeed, deemed necessary. A particularly intense discussion thread in the Kava Bowl epitomizes these dynamics; one that was an online "event" in itself. In March 2000, a prominent participant and co-moderator expressed his regret about a "deterioration" in the content, quality, and style of recent discussions (the KR also underwent substantial auto-critiques in this period). After a short historical reconstruction of the "good old days" of 1997 and 1998 when the Kava Bowl was "the most popular Pacific Island site on the entire internet with more than 500,000 hits a month," Sandy then went on to make his dissatisfaction with the current tenor of the discussions abundantly clear:

> In late 1999, technical difficulties caused the site to be inactive for several months. When the KB finally came back online, many of the regular contributors had moved on to other venues [the KR included] and the dedicated band of volunteer editors were no longer vigilant in monitoring the content. . . . Now, when the world comes to KB, it learns that Tongans are little more than gang bangers, gossip mongers and, in short, insolent and disrespectful children . . . and it simply isn't interested, so it leaves never to return . . . but the memory is planted and the stereotype grows and is reinforced each day as more and more nastiness is posted here to be read by one-time visitors from around the world. Think about it folks. Is that the image of Tongans you wish to perpetuate? If so, you spit on the graves of your ancestors.
>
> (Sandy Macintosh, KB, 03/27/00)

The eighty-nine follow-up posts that constitute this thread came in thick and fast within the space of two days.[4] Reactions varied: nostalgia jostled with disdain or wit as consternation vied with various levels of support or defense for Sandy's stance – and his right to post it. Respectively:

> Sandy . . . palagi [non-Tongan] or not, I totally agree with you, wholeheartedly. . . . This was my home, here I found company, here I sang my songs, quoted my poetry, shared my innermost thoughts without any fear of contradictions or ridicule . . . it made my loneliness easier to bear, talking, listening, laughing, crying with my people, the Tongans, that I love and admire so deeply . . . as it is, alas, it is no more.
>
> (QUEENEMA, KB, 03/28/00 in reply to above)

> Hey doctor with no patients, you should be in the movies or TV. . . . One is entitled to ones opinion no matter how faecesitious [*sic*] it smells.
>
> (Buzz Lightyears Behind, KB, 03/29/00 in Sandy Macintosh, 03/27/00)

I had encouraged my children to visit KB website but no anymore . . . foul languages, heaps of gossips and disrespects among the chatters. I don't want my children to see Tonga as it is in the kb website.

(Worried Mum, KB, 03/27/00 in Sandy Macintosh, 03/27/00)

I just think that the true beauty of the Kava Bowl isn't being exposed anymore, and that KB is moving away, rather [than] opening up again and influencing others for good.

(FELLOW KBER, KB, 03/27/00 in Sandy Macintosh, 03/27/00)

This thread emerged as four to five years of steady discussion were combined with a massive increase in volume of traffic and changes in participation (Kami 2001: interview). These pressures impinged upon the costs of server space, software capabilities, time needed to administer the interrelated websites of the Pacific Forum portal, and ongoing concerns, in both the Kava Bowl and the Polynesian Cafe, about the emergence of an incipient "lack of respect" between participants. Concerns about the relationship between online forms of belligerence or "bad behavior" (the issue of what constitutes propriety anyway being a moot point) are filtered through references to comparable issues for on-the-ground communities. For the online guardians of the peace, the ethical and sociocultural implications of "antics" deemed undesirable reach out from behind the computer screen into the everyday life on the streets for younger "Polys" in urban settings – a life that is too often marked by socioeconomic exclusion, violence, lower educational performance, and limited career opportunities (see Chapter 6). Sandy makes this link very clear as he goes on to say that

> just because other "civilized" places are commonly defaced by graffiti is no reason that KB should stoop to the same level. The Kava Bowl was intended as a venue of higher principles and objectives, not the least was to celebrate the dignity of Polynesian cultures . . . something that has been completely lost of late . . . it is [not] only Tongans who abuse this place, but it is Tongans who will reap the bad rap as a result since this is a Tongan site, just as PC and KR are Samoan sites frequented by those from other cultures. so, it behooves us all, Tongan and non-Tongan alike, to set an example in our posts. . . . This attitude of it's a public forum and I can post what I want is pure garbage.
>
> (Sandy Macintosh, KB, 03/27/00 in Sandy Macintosh, 03/27/00)

The *Re: Kava Bowl* thread epitomizes these immanent moral economies as they crystallized in the thread itself as well as a moment in the life span of the forums. Their operations and formal qualities still need to be unpacked, however.

Chapter outline

The pool of threads looked at here has been sorted along four axial sets that pertain to the theme of the *initial* posts. These "axes" (in their interpretative and organizational sense) are one way of lending coherence to what are spasmodic conversations about the nature of online practices in themselves; metadiscussions, in a sense. The first axis is for those threads in which leaderships declare their intentions to delete a post and/or reiterate the rules. This often merges into the second axis: when leaderships and their rule making are directly challenged – or queried – by their constituencies. The third is constituted by "personal attacks" or "flames." While the latter are present along all the axes and endemic to Internet-mediated communications anyway, these "flame wars" have their own inter/intracultural tropes here. The last axis is an amalgam of more self-conscious posts about representation/image making in light of all three of the above, sometimes instigated by the leadership and sometimes by concerned participants.

These axes link up four implicit, albeit contested, criteria for all these discussions: free speech, ground rules, respect, legitimacy. The heated debates that have occurred when moderators opt to delete posts include both declarations of outrage and various degrees of support for whichever "fundamental principle" is deemed to be at stake. First is the oft-asserted assumption, especially by participants who have grown up in the United States, that the *sine qua non* of any Internet discussion forum is uncensored self-expression – free speech. As with wrangles about this offline, this criterion runs head-on into the technical power moderators have to insist on their rules of online conduct and limits to others' willingness to accept unmitigated self-expression; let alone the legal responsibility website owners now have to avoid liability for "spamming," defamation litigation, and suchlike. The actions taken and ensuing arguments work to the ground rules criterion. As we will see, these first two criteria are interlaced with the aforementioned notion of *respect*.[5]

These three criteria are interwoven with practices of "power over" and "covert power" (Gill and Law 1988: 73), as revealed in an online scenario. The first is the ability to delete, scold, and silence through direct – technical and authoritative – intervention. The second is more diffuse and cumulative as both leaderships and participants curb and admonish those who do not conform to the behavioral "norm," discursive styles, or linguistic conventions in ways that eventually shape what gets said and who gets to say it and for how long (and here the most persistent of dissenters is usually coaxed into cooperation). It is when a moderator's authority and/or a participant's legitimacy is at stake that the legitimacy criterion – the what/who are *you* question – comes to the fore. How the person targeted by this kind of confrontation (seen as antagonistic by Pacific island if not many other social standards of propriety) reacts can range from posting a retort to withdrawing altogether. From an analytical point of view, beyond explicit apologies or about-faces, the effect(iveness) of these more confrontational postings cannot be easily gauged; for leaving an online forum is not as obvious as the physical act of turning one's back and walking out of a room. Nonetheless, this criterion is traceable because two other subcriteria are in operation: what constitutes "profanity" and/or "slang," and the limits of anonymity as part of forums' posting policies.

Moral economies in operation

Axis 1: the ground rules

As I noted, these moral economies in the making overlap with "netiquette" for Internet text-based interactions.[6] Apart from standard legal liability disclaimers, references to "South Pacific traditions" of "decency and respect" in the ground rules of the KB and KR are clearly evident in the regularly posted reminders of the "posting policy" by the leaderships (Aiono 1999: interview).

Some practical priorities still make themselves felt on a daily or weekly level. One of these for any website moderator is the readability of the posted message vis-à-vis the server space available (as hits start to mount up in a busy website). In heavily patronized forums, the use of capital letters affects both readability and server space. While capitals can be selectively used for emphasis or as an "emoticon," when used at length or in anger, capitals not only make the messages difficult to read, but also take up room on-screen and in server logs/accessible archives. All moderators of these sites have regularly requested participants to "refrain from using capitals," for all "posts using capitals will simply be deleted, thus removing your hard work. Simply put, simply done" (KBAdmin, KB, 03/21/00). Capitals are also tantamount to shouting in an online textual scenario and have similar escalatory effects; "PLEASE don't use caps! IT is 'shouting' in the cyber community and extremely polite [*sic*]" (Sandy, KB, 03/27/00 in Sandy Macintosh, 03/27/00).

The second concern is the length of the *message heading* (the title line that appears on-screen before the actual body of the message is opened), the subject line, or the poster's signature (see Figure 8.1). In online textual environments, these hyperlinked headings can become longer and longer as they allow a participant to intervene quickly in a discussion without either editing or needing to type their reply/message in the next level. Short or long, these "top levels" (what is seen on-screen at first glance) often operate as a subthread in their own right, as a new direction in the debate, or reiterations of the initial post's message heading or interpersonal identification codes (Morton 2001). Not only do the iterative qualities of asynchronous Internet communications software compound these characteristics in the case of long and complex threads, but when coupled with capitals these can create posts that suggest more substance than there actually is, as lengthy headings also take up server space and hinder legibility as they sprawl across the screen. Thus, "long name lines" or "subject headings longer than 1 line" (POLYCAFE, KR, 05/04/99; KBAdmin, KB, 01/20/98) are grounds for deletion. In earlier versions of the KB posting policy, there were also limits set on the message length, but these have only been enforced when the body of the message was deemed to be "irrelevant,"[7] a rule that proved too time-consuming to enforce under the weight of weekly traffic.

What are explicitly forbidden, and enforced, are the following: "profanity" (POLYCAFE, 05/04/99); "outright attacks of a personal nature that could be construed as slander, or libel" (KBAdmin, KB, 01/20/98); and "attacks on anyone's ideas, politics, or religion without . . . citing reasons, examples, or other sorts of evidence" (ibid.). "Gossip" has been more recently brought under the latter category (KBAdmin, KB, 03/27/00 in Dot, 03/27/00), as has "slang" (a relative term that is examined later). In this case, language use – idioms and colloquialisms in either Tongan, Samoan, or English – becomes a bone of contention. These deletions are seen by administrators as their prerogative: "We reserve the right to delete what we feel is a violation of our ground rules" (POLYCAFE, KR, 05/04/99); "We were forced to remove a posting regarding KB services due to the negative tone in the replies. We have read the message so thanks for the comment" (KBAdmin, KB, 09/04/98). And the bottom line in the case of the KB is deletion due to "total disregard for the conservative sensitivities held by the largest portion of the 'population' in KB" (KBAdmin, KB, 01/20/98).

Deletions on these grounds are further backed up by referring to the aforementioned criterion of *respect*. Even so, an eventual deletion – or lack thereof – has often been the trigger for many of the threads examined here when this prerogative is confronted with the free speech criterion. In this respect, the predominantly "conservative" and "Christian" Kava Bowl (with a constituency posting from Tonga and Mormon centers in the United States) has been more proactive in this regard than the KR (with its largely West Coast US-based and Australasian constituency) when opting for deletion. Deletion is often strategically accompanied by reiterating its mission to provide an online

> forum that will provide a service to our Pacific Island community and while we promote freedom of speech, we also recognise the need to provide guidelines to ensure the KAVABOWL remains a fresh source of useful information. We retain the right to delete postings that we determine are not in the spirit of the KAVABOWL.
>
> (KBAdmin, KB, 01/20/98)

Even in the KB, this strict stance has not gone undisputed. Nonetheless, administrators have remained staunch in this regard and continued to moderate the traffic accordingly:

> NOTE: Free speech prevails, but with limitations imposed from respect for Polynesian culture and tradition. Those who cannot live by this code should consider either an 'attitude adjustment' or another venue for their expression.
>
> (KBAdmin, KB, 03/21/00)

The ensuing stresses and strains also relate to differences in how power is exercised at any given instance, over time, or any thread's own life span. It also intersects with the extent to which leadership styles combine with other lines of (offline community) influence and with the various responses of the online constituencies. These considerations will become clearer in due course.

Axis 2: challenging the ground rules

The impact of these direct interventions is often brought sharply to moderators' attention by participants taking umbrage at either nonenforcement *or* deletion. In dealing with these challenges, gender power relations become articulate(d) as leaderships become protagonists themselves in the ensuing debates. This is a delicate balancing act at times, especially since the forum moderators are all "volunteers and nobody is paid to do this" (Taholo Kami, KB, 02/04/00 in Taeoli, 02/04/00). This is made all the more delicate at times given the precariously swift combination of thinking–writing–sending peculiar to email/online communications, let alone misunderstandings that can arise for those for whom the online lingua franca (English) is not their mother tongue. Participants often note this in passing:

> Frankly, being an islander, and with English as one of my second languages, I take everything I read with caution. If this was a uni[versity] web site, then I would be pedantic about details. Given it is not; I try and use my coconut [head] to deduce and interpret the question congruent with the author's intended meaning i.e. with how the writer intended the post to be read in the first instance.
>
> (Principal Skinner, KB, 02/05/00 in Taeoli, 02/04/00)[8]

This axis, dialogue about the rights and wrongs of enforcement as initiated by participants, traces how moral economies have been evolving as both rules *and* ethical concerns. As clienteles and relationships between regulars ("patrons") have waxed and waned over the years, the ground rules have become integrated into the online practices of everyday life; as digitally constituted spatial – tactical and strategic – practices. Ground rules are being constantly (re)negotiated vis-à-vis "traditional" Pacific Island forms of social control and notions of free speech,[9] one especial to US society. On the whole, the ground rules are adhered to and their execution encouraged by constituencies. While there is evidence of participants opting to leave altogether on being deleted/admonished, others acquiesce and/or contribute to the debates by registering their dissent. Others continue to get enraged and post accordingly. Here there are differences between how posters in the islands see these things and how those living abroad see "appropriate" language or behavior. We see later exactly how these differences get articulated as they come to a head in a discussion.

There is also much room for maneuver in actual enforcement. For instance, most long subject headings and/or capitals are not deleted out of hand, a large degree of vernacular styles of English are left alone, and the more politically or socially sensitive nature of some discussions is allowed to run its course (see Chapter 5). In addition, the leaderships take care to give assurances about inclusiveness when positions become severely polarized or misunderstandings occur. This principle of openness and hospitality is central to the ethos of both the KB and KR, so both leaderships and constituencies are conscious of the fine line between moderation and overzealousness: "There is no sign over the [KR] door that EXCLUDES anyone based on gender, religion, creed or national origin. There is none stating that this is an exclusive site for SAMOANS only" (Pua, KR, 01/13/00 in Concerned, 01/06/00). Hospitality has its limits, though. In both forums, these are drawn by regular or "older" participants, or by those who as parents, grandparents, or community leaders offline look to set an example, and those advocating formal literary standards of writing and spelling in written-conversations. Education is valued highly in itself and as a road to betterment in the islands (of Tonga particularly) and among their diasporic populations. A widely held feeling is of being "so tired of seeing these 'fools' post messages that make no sense, have poor spelling, grammatical errors everywhere and all this 'gangsta' crap. Its embarrassing! Wake up people!!!" (Well said Sam Owens!, Polycafe, 05/20/99 in Sam Owens, 05/20/99).

The devoutly Christian group of regulars (on the KB especially), who are vocal and numerous, have lower tolerance levels for any "offensive terms." They also have influence through Pacific Island churches and (urban) community centers and/or from Tonga and the Samoas themselves. When used in Tongan or Samoan, swearwords have been swiftly dealt with by either manual deletion or software filters. That said, playful phonetic manipulations in English words deemed borderline at least are scattered throughout all the discussion threads (@$$ or a**, for instance). These can be quite inventive, given that the Polycafe software filters would read an innocent syllable in English as an unacceptable word in Samoan, rendering it un*tterable (for example).

On the issue of linguistic standards, long-standing or prominent participants clash at times with newcomers (who are either unaware of or unperturbed by these attitudes). While most agree that "everyone is for the right to free speech; the controversy is what the boundaries are and how we should enforce them" (Lafemme Nikita, KR, 04/23/99), from at least the KBAdmin's point of view these boundaries are clear:

> [I]n this forum, the classic "American" definition [of free speech] does not apply here. On the contrary, the code asked for here is tempered to meet traditional Polynesian, and particularly, Tongan ethics of reverence and respect. There is no swearing tolerated here.
>
> (sandy, KB, 04/23/99 in reply to above)

The second gradation is objections to "gossip": personalized posts about someone or their (extended) families. The posts in question here form an axis in their own right (axis 3, p. 188). Suffice it to say that they illustrate the to and fro between participants and moderators about the limits to deletion as the ultimate enforcement of overt power online.

Profanity or slang?

Another query from participants is about the coupling of this "no profanities" clause with a later one, the "no slang" clause, and these are complaints when the vernacular – slang or "gangsta" talk – is used by (mostly teenage) participants. There are three gradations. One is outright approval of moderators' decisions across the board: "Thank you Polycafe for doing away with posts with slang and profanity!!!" (Sam Owens, Polycafe, 05/20/99). The next gradation is outright objection to the very same or overzealous enforcement on the basis that the right to free speech overrides other considerations. All these interjections buck the rules in their use of capitals, "bad" spelling, "slang" and mild "profanity." For instance:

> I post an innocent question and statement about the crap that is in here, and you go and erase MY post?! what the hell is that?
>
> (Tom, Polycafe, 05/14/99)

> KB-ADMIN CAN YOU EXPLAIN WHY DO YOU HAVE TO DELETE AN ENTIRE POST. . . . WHY CAN'T YOU DELETE THE OFFENSIVE POSTING AND NOT BE TOO DAMN LAZY AND DELETE THE ENTIRE POSTING.
>
> (taeoli, KB, 02/04/00)

The slippage between profanity and slang being made here is because many are concerned about how a "world online audience" (New Kid, KR, 01/30/99) may judge these texts and their producers. Allusions to norms about propriety on the ground – at home, in church – are common in objections to "informal" language of any kind:

> I am sure no one cares to have obscenities scribbled over the living room of their homes. WHY THEN DO IT HERE?
> (Teine o le Spring, Polycafe, 04/25/99 in enough is ENOUGH, 04/24/99)

> Do you swear at a minister during church? Do you swear at your family's funeral? Do you swear at a matai? [Samoan chiefly title].... There are places where language should be used appropriately.... If no set standards were placed on this place, then we may as call this place a hang out sleazy bar. Respect is not too much to ask for.
> (Reader, Polycafe, 05/05/99 in POLYCAFE, 05/04/99)

More purist versions of this stance that regard swearwords, slang, and/or colloquial spelling as one and the same do not go undisputed. Dissenting voices underscore the heterogeneity and shifts within constituencies, tone, and stylistic features as texts accumulate and proliferate. And here silent participants and less frequent posters count also, as does the conscious use of satire and irony in responses. In the next sample, this tactic is put to good use in a thread where reiterated objections to swearing and slang jostled with laments about breaches of the freedom of speech criterion:

> I personally love using profanities. The language of the sewer delights me. The first stream of daily profanities erupts from my lips at 6.30 am when, at the screech of the alarm clock, I tumble unceremoniously onto the icy cement floor.... The second stream of profanities ignites when I can't 'do my job' easily on the bathroom throne. The third ricochets around the tiny bathroom when the razor cuts my chin during shaving.... BUT upon exiting my cockroach-friendly apartment, I forget all about freedom of speech, and behave with relative decorum and respect for the sensitivity of others.... I thank you for the enlightenment, Madam, and wish you a good day.... Most respectfully yours-in-the-faith-in-freedom-of-speech.
> (Ki'i Sulu, KB, 04/26/99 in Lafemme Nikita, 04/23/99)

Where profanity ends and slang begins for these groups is not just an issue of literary standards *per se*. It is also about the politics of language use for postcolonial populations interacting with each other in open, public cyberspaces on the one hand and as socioeconomically disadvantaged "ethnic minorities" "living overseas" on the other hand (see Chapter 6). This concern is well illustrated in a thread entitled *Thank you Polycafe for doing away with posts with slang and profanity!!!* (Sam Owens, KR, 05/20/99) – one that also encapsulates the moral economies at the time:

A few months ago, I posted a discussion thread about being tired of hearing Polynesians talk slang and what type of image or impression it gave to others. . . . I am very happy to see that the Polycafe has raised their standards. . . . This is only going to help in destroying the stereotypes that have been bestowed upon our people. I would like to see that our people are known more for just being big people who can kick ass. . . . If I want to read or listen to slang or profanity, I can go down to the parks and look at the graffiti for that garbage. Thank you for ridding this website of all the riffraff and all the gangsters.

(Sam Owens, Polycafe, 05/20/99)

BRAVO!! . . . WE ISLANDERS NEED TO RISE TO A HIGHER STANDARD RATHER THAN SINK LOWER INTO HOODLUM. ITS SAD TO SEE ISLANDERS COME TO THE STATES FOR A BETTER EDUCATION AND LIFE AND THEN END UP LIVING AND TALKING LIKE GANGSTERS. IF YOU DON'T PULL YOURSELF UP, NOBODY ELSE WILL.

(Better quality of life please, Polycafe, 05/20/99 in reply to above)

On the other hand, though, idiom is not tantamount to profanity, nor are colloquialisms necessarily "bad." A regular, Lisa, reflects on her own discursive style when posting in different parts of the South Pacific islands online:

Sam . . . doing away with profanity was a great move. But I have to say that I ride the fence on the slangs being cut as well. I don't see anything wrong with [it] . . . on days when I feel like relaxing a bit with my words and corresponding in this public forum with friends and family, opting to use some slang, or even made up words of our own, mostly just for fun . . . maybe I see things differently . . . I don't care for the whole misspelled words, tough guy attitude, "Slang" crap either, but the posts which are by far the more offensive ones are . . . the ones that are posted to purposely be hurtful. . . . Much gratitude to the Café's administration for cracking down. I am a Polynesian woman who is versed very well, in both verbal and written concourse, but you will catch me on days where I am sending shout outs, what's up etc.. to friends and families. I feel they are harmless forms of communication and hold ho [sic] hurtful meanings such as profanity does.

(Lisa, Polycafe, 05/21/99, in Sam Owens, 05/20/99)

In the islands – overseas

The thread just discussed articulates the demographic – class, generational, gendered – complexity of these groups after roughly five years of "being online," as access became gradually (although patchily) available in the Pacific Islands and as their popularity spread.[10] In the same month as this last thread, a subthread of a discussion on the ground rules shows another angle to these representational issues. It went like this:

> Most of the reason people come in this cafe is to read the drama. Its entertainment, and whether you like it or not, it brings people in here.... One question I have is about your thoughts on slang. I don't see anything wrong with it. A lot of our people grew up like that, why would you wanna bann something like that. But like u said, it's your house and your rules.
>
> (Keepin it real, Polycafe, 05/04/99 in POLYCAFE, 05/04/99)

This observation points to how a *couture* becomes a latent fracture line between regulars (whatever the differences between them) posting from the mainland United States, New Zealand, and Australia, those from Western and American Samoa, Tonga, and Hawaii, and newcomers who challenge the established order of discussions (see Axis 3, p. 182). In a sharp retort to the above point, the poster who calls her/himself "concerned" writes:

> Speak for yourself. People like you grew up uneducated and slang as your 2nd or 3rd language but most Samoans and Poly people I know are respectable and have pride in the way they communicate ... shiz man go back to Samoa or Tonga or wherever you from. But let our people in America and other countries have a fair chance to make something decent and respectable of their lives.
>
> (concerned, Polycafe, 05/04/99 in POLYCAFE, 05/04/99)

The responses to this challenge underscore how language uses become indicative of generational differences, socioeconomic – status and class – differentiations, and intracultural subcultures or "social problems" (gangs, for instance), as much as an issue of personal taste. Using a different name-line (which is also part of the retort), this participant asks:

> [F]irst of all, who the hell you think you're talking too, talking about uneducated and using slang as your first language. Have you ever been to Samoa?... Don't act like a kid and talk down to people like your better than them. I for one grew up in a minority community, that's why I talk the way I do. My family started off poor, and I'm proud of it. You wanna talk about getting things in America, let's play a little ghetto game called Big Bank take Little Bank. I'm sorry you feel like that about your own ppls [people].
>
> (Please! concerned my @$$, don't talk about slappin somebody, Polycafe, 05/06/99 in POLYCAFE, 05/04/99)

Living as part of an ethnic minority, in the United States in this case, becomes a focus for articulating the underbelly of being-from-somewhere-else. In these forums, these circumstances are confronted by everyday life in the islands (Chapter 6). As another intervention notes:

> [S]ome people come out here to America and forget where they are from. They try to fit into the life style of the Americans, but they can forget it. No matter what, you will always be a Samoan.
> (Putting it to the point, Polycafe, 05/06/99 in POLYCAFE, 05/04/99)

This ties in with others in the thread who admonish "concerned" for calling someone names and casting aspersions on where they are/are not from:

> [W]hat do you mean 'go back to Samoa or Tonga' ... Where are you from? just because you are living in 'America' doesn't mean that's where you're from.
> (ConcernedForYou, Polycafe, 05/04/99 in POLYCAFE, 05/04/99)

When prompted a bit later, this participant goes on to elaborate how

> [y]ou Samoans in 'Welcome to America' seem to put down ['the people in Savaii'] all the time. Just keep in mind, all Samoans, no matter where you've set up welfare at, have roots leading all the way to Western Samoa! So stop being so proud of being in 'America' because you might get your fobby[11] butt deported to where you're legally from!
> (ConcernedForYou Too, Polycafe, 05/05/99 in POLYCAFE, 05/04/99)

It takes a poster from Samoa to defuse the situation:

> Sitting here in Samoa and reading some of these comments is really amusing. Don't bother slapping anyone back to Savaii because they certainly do not belong here.
> (Samoan in Savaii, Polycafe, 05/13/99 in POLYCAFE, 05/04/99)

Finally, someone, echoing those threads dealing with Polynesian identity formation from the previous chapters, puts things into perspective:

> The Cafe is here to help us explore our Poly Roots and build unity as a people. Samoan, Tongan ... We need to build each other up, not dogg each other. ... Al, keep cleaning up the graffiti in the Café, this way all the patrons will enjoy the cafe. Alofa.
>
> (Fatu, Polycafe, 05/04/99 in POLYCAFE, 05/04/99)

Highlighting these geographical, class (and status) distinctions in the gender power relations of the ground rules, the above threads also trace different attitudes and expectation based on educational background, socioeconomic positions, or relative skill and ease with written forms of spoken oratory. They lead on to the third axis: "flames," or personalized comments. Here the ground rule on "[no] outright attacks of a personal nature" (KBAdmin, KB, 03/27/00 in Dot, 03/27/00) comes to the fore for both moderators and participants:

> Any personal comments or personal attacks should be deleted!... I think that KB Administration should delete right away any [slanderous] comments.
>
> (safata, KB, 01/29/99)

> I second that motion.... I read those derogatory remarks and I am suprised [*sic*] that nothing is being done about it.... Personal attacks should not be T-O-L-E-R-A-T-E-D on this forum period.
>
> (Polyway, KR, 01/29/99 in reply to above)

And with the above are other questions about what are/are not generically Polynesian (Tongan and/or Samoan) public communicative norms, and whose interests the forums are/should be actually serving. Whether this is an indication of these forums being "victims of their own success" or the permissive qualities of online communications *per se*, or not, the few still extant threads of this ilk and the calls for decorum that follow from them do show that how these economies unfurl is down not only to the leaderships but also to their constituencies.

Axis 3: who are you?

> [Online, a] "who are you?" response to a real name [not a nickname] is a confrontational device that one would never do on the ground.
>
> (Teresia Teaiwa 1999: interview)

> I also find that when one does post such opposing views to the norm, personal attacks are made. Whilst personal attacks do not bother me, you get to the point where you lose interest and feel you are banging your head against a brick wall.
>
> (Lucy Tuaifaiva, 05/20/99, personal email)

These observations are examples of potential/former participants who have opted out of participating. They both made it clear they were not condemning the spirit of these forums, as their decisions were taken for several reasons. Nonetheless, their experiences relate to those (sub)threads that carry demarcations about belonging and participation – the legitimacy criterion. In an asynchronous Internet discussion, participation is only made visible by the act of posting a message (as opposed to avatars in the case of live chat). At the same time, the standards and mores constituting both manifest *and* latent content are brought in from offline as well as created from within (online in conversation). In these spaces, silence (or recourse to facial or physical expressions) is not an option, as in face-to-face encounters. In order to counter, to affect how the thread looks and how the content actually unfurls, people have to register their reactions in a literal sense:

> Don't be content on being a mere spectator. If you don't get into the foray, you get benched on the sidelines, plagued by obscurity. The KR is. after all, a CONTACT forum.
>
> (concerned, KR, 01/13/00)

All well and good, but it takes a thick skin and the confidence afforded by long-standing online presence/participation to proceed in cases where one is directly greeted with "what/who are *you?*" in a follow-up post. Whether these are part and parcel of oratorical rhetoric or to be taken seriously, more than one newcomer has received this sort of challenge. So have palangi/palagi regulars in the KB whose knowledge of Pacific islands history or customs is assumed to be found wanting. Online prominence in this context can be both a curse and a blessing, especially since a number of these challenges are addressed to such regulars.[12] These can range from the gentle inquiry:

> TIM SAMSON [Sansom] WHAT RACE ARE YOU? if your not Samoan then how did you find out about this site? don't get mad now i was just wondering . . . thank you for your time and god bless!!!
>
> (just wondering, KR, 10/11/99)

to a sort of public challenge (in this case it turned out to be somewhat tongue in cheek):

> Safata or Satana or who ever you are: I have been flicking through the board on a daily basis and I find this character (safata) to be a bag of nothing. Safata raises issues that are sometimes interesting, but he or she cannot provide any logical or factual, let alone any coherent proposition(s) to reach a valid . . . conclusion.
>
> (Maui, KB, 02/09/99)

and to the ostensibly more malevolent. This thread eventually turned on the initial poster, who duly retreated:

NEW KID – WHO ARE YOU – WHERE DID YOU COME FROM – WHAT DO YOU WANT – WHERE DO YOU HOPE TO GO????? You need to take up another hobby or vocation. Your comments are tired and you need to take a rest – or give the rest of us some serious recess from your peanut gallery style!!

(Daily Planet, KR, 11/22/99)[13]

This sort of "slapping" can indeed be disconcerting, and those who respond by retreating altogether are difficult to trace. The targets mentioned here waded into the thick of it and responded accordingly, backed up by overwhelming numbers supporting their presence and berating the initial posters. Persistence is not always a prerequisite for the latter, however.[14] The argument also gets personalized quite quickly when offense is taken, positions are polarized in a delicate topic, or if an opinion about others' contributions is couched in slang like "buffoons," "riffraff," or "gangsters." As one regular states, "I am far from any of these 3 descriptions" (Lisa, Polycafe, 05/21/99 in Sam Owens, 05/20/99). Those who react quickly or "petulantly" are usually advised to "calm down.... Be slow to anger and quick to listen" (langimalie, KB, 03/27/00 in Sandy Macintosh, 03/27/00). These transgressions of both explicit online rules and implicit sociocultural norms reveal the *couture* between online practices and offline parameters of social control and decorum; "the Cafe is much like a family owned store back home in the islands" (Teine o le Spring, KR, 04/25/99 in enough is ENOUGH, 04/24/99). Demographic changes in this respect have had an impact on how these moral economies have evolved. For many of the "old guard," it

> really is a shame that people come in here and destroy this website by posting ignorant and derogatory comments (especially towards fellow polys). I wonder if these youths would post those things if they knew that their parents would read it. I very much doubt it.
>
> (Disappointed, Polycafe, 04/24/99 in enough is ENOUGH, 04/24/99)

Anonymity

More needs to be said about how these interventions take advantage of online (quasi-)anonymity. The software used by the KB and the KR permits people to post under various "names" and/or email addresses; a message can be posted without an active – or coherent – email address/addresses. This has several aspects to it. In the tightly knit communicative and socioeconomic hierarchies of many Pacific Island societies, the ability to be anonymous online permits the loosening up of gendered and social hierarchies (as seen in Chapters 4 and 5). The products – nicknames and other "handles" – are another articulation of the various aspects of postcolonial *and* online practices of identity formation.[15] In this way, anonymity "loosens tongues" in empowering ways: women find new expressive spaces, and participants can voice their opinions and objections to events (at home in the islands, and here, online) with relative impunity.

This side to online debates has not gone unnoticed in either Samoa or Tonga. On the one hand, the interactive aspects of Internet communications allow such online traversal to get away from "traditional hangovers" by allowing "people to find themselves as individuals" in what are nominally communal societies (Helu 1999a: interview). On the other hand, local leaderships in Tonga or Samoa and those of communities living abroad have been known to exert direct pressure on website owners when the discussions are seen as cutting too close to the bone. Other commentators are more circumspect about these empowering potentials, given the current political economy of Internet technologies, where there is "no free lunch" with regard to the "psychosocial satisfaction" of ICTs given the global (and local) political economic interests that "control it ultimately" (Okusi Māhina 1999: interview).

Another aspect is how these practices of hypertextualized anonymity underscore Morton's research showing how "naming on the KB [and KR] is primarily relational and responsive" ([1998a: 19] 2001). Thus, seeing the same person "using a variety of names, according to the content of the messages" (ibid.) indicates different concerns and motivations than are generally believed to be the case with (predatory or gender-bending) dissimulations of a person's "real" – offline – identity in Internet communications. Here, anonymity in lieu of – or together with – real names (in several renditions too) and multiple email addresses trace not only strategic practices, but also personal – tactical – ones.[16] In any case, anonymity here is not that big a deal. And when used well, as participants gain skill in manipulating the messaging software to operate at a manifest and a subtextual level, these digital-textual practices allow for all manner of interpersonal and intracultural references, and multiple layers of (double) meanings, while allowing protection in more sensitive discussions.

As we have already seen, participants can exert pressure on forum leaderships in their capacity as (online) community representatives. So, even though anonymity is fairly transparent much of the time, it does get serious in the case of threads on this third axis. The uses and abuses of the "guise of anonymity" temper both the inclusionary and the exclusionary dimensions to these moral economies. It is a delicate balancing act between an open-door policy to "all patrons/visitors of the Polycafe, regardless of race" (Al Aiono, KR, 01/13/00 in concerned, 01/13/00) and the fostering of "relative security from disclosure of one's true identity" (Phil Tukia, KB, 03/27/00 in Sandy Macintosh, 03/27/00) in more sensitive scenarios.[17] Moderators are cognizant of these dynamics:

In 1996 I created this forum [KR] for Polycafe patrons (regardless of race) to come together and discuss 'just' the issues that affect us as individuals knowing such an effect will certainly impact the 'community'. Some of you may recall how I would initiate new discussions every week, posting 4–5 new topics once a week. That lasted for several months before the forum itself took on a life of its own as it CONTINUES TO DO SO TODAY.

> (Al Aiono, KR, 01/13/00 in concerned, 01/13/00)

The bottom line, then, is that these are sites where anonymity is celebrated, and communications are open and public (not password protected).[18] Despite reservations about "abuse" of this aspect of the forums' hospitality, it is seen to go hand in hand with free speech and respect:

> [A]nonymity was to protect one's privacy and to foster open and RESPECTFUL discussion. it was not to allow someone to personally attack and abuse others with immunity. It is completely within our cultural mores to exchanges views and opinions. However, such an exchange was always within the context of respect to one another. Unfortunately, too many of our newer readers do not understand that.... Let us all try to teach those who need teaching that free speech is NOT obscenity and gossip. Free Speech is exchange of views and opinions under the underlying context of respect and love for each other, for our culture, and for our island Kingdom [Tonga] that is so far away from many of us
>
> Phil Tukia, KB, 03/27/00 in Sandy Macintosh, 03/27/00

Axis 4: representing the Pacific islands online

All this brings us through to the fourth axis: the articulation of concerns about how online interactions affect the way the Pacific Islands (Tonga and Samoa in particular) come across to the potentially "global" audience surfing the World Wide Web. The threads on this axis resonate with other interventions on this theme, made in passing or as initial posts. As we see in the previous chapter, for those who have lived abroad most or all of their lives, these inter/intracultural complexities can be difficult to get a grip on:

> [I]f I have offended anyone please forgive me.... My posts and feedback is for everyone to read be you black, white, yellow, or brown, it is from my heart and although it is not a perfect one, I do want to correct my mistakes.... Do know that i have learned so much from all of you. With every fiber in my body i wish to thank you all for your posts be it a little harsh or pleasing i love it all and glean from them what is best for me and my family and friends.
>
> (Salelava, KR, 06/01/99 in X, 05/31/99)

In these threads, ethical issues are the order of the day as participants mull over the relationship between their online interactions, the sociosymbolic power of role models, and the local–global dimensions of postcolonial, diasporic everyday life. Many participants are on the lookout for "gangsta behavior" online. But not all of them concur with what actually constitutes such behavior, especially when interventions by the younger "baggy-pants brigade" (Kami, 2001: interview) growing up in Western cities are so judged. This axis, then, is characterized by particularly self-aware, outward-looking interventions, which bring us back full circle to the first axis as both participants and leaderships are implicated. They are often posted by disenchanted regulars addressing "unruly" participants, but also with an eye to the internal and external politics of representation for groups speaking, living, and writing in a "global" (online) context:

> There was a time I frequented KB to review and interact with others ... to instigate controversy and provoke thought for discussion. However, I have observed ... change in the culture of dialogue that presently plague the walls of KB. I feel I represent past patrons that see the garbage, and leave because there's nothing worth the time. ... Web sites are now competing for exposure and attraction, KB included, even if the service is nothing more than a message-board and chat-room. ... The benefits of KB are boundless, but I am certain more can be done than chastizing a general audience.
>
> (Makavili, KB, 03/27/00 in Sandy Macintosh, 03/27/99)

These threads, looking beyond the immediate confines of these forums, mesh then with those that have as *themes* the urge to develop positive "stereotypes" and role models to younger, urbanized Pacific island generations (see Lee 2003: 131 *passim*):

> When we fight among ourselves we make a fool of Polynesians especially we Samoans in the eyes of the world ... every battle and war of words do not go unnoticed; and yes, the give a negative impression of this forum and all of us that come in here.
>
> (New Kid, KR, 01/30/99)

This concern with in-fighting and "unruliness" is couched in terms of how the endemic racism experienced by many living overseas needs new approaches from within these communities:

> There is a growing number of people who [write] with chips on their shoulder particularly how our race has been treated by other races ... however [it] is sad as we harbour ... resentment towards the white people. ... I think the stagnant nature of our thinking [that] reflects

our resentments we have with the white people has been passed on generationally and we just keep passing them on to our children and their children's children. One ... way of dealing with this is to try and expect the unexpected and try to build our confidence and build some cultural esteem (if there is such a thing). Not reacting ... because we feel the only way to get back ... is to join them and beat then at their game.

(X, KR, 05/31/99)

As other threads underscore, for those living beyond the Pacific islands the politics of race/ethnicity is an ever-present issue in the United States, Australia, New Zealand. And for many of the women participants, *gender* power relations are enmeshed in these:

Racism, I agree is detrimental in whatever form if comes. Yet. Because I don't agree with standards set by a predominantly whitewashed academia. Doesn't mean that I hate the white man.... I may be a notch disadvantaged because of gender in this male world but I am not going to roll over and play dead for anyone. Furthermore, I certainly don't teach my little one to hate indiscriminately.... Yet, I caution that you really need to take some time out and take the gist of the post with a proverbial grain of salt. What you construe as something of 'chip' or 'reverse racism' could really be only a clear, divergent perspective from the status quo.

(Why, Why HoneyChile, KR, 06/01/99 in X, 05/31/99)

For commentators on the ground, these sorts of preoccupations can only emerge when living elsewhere than the relatively homogeneous societies in the islands, Tonga particularly.[19] In diasporic contexts (the United States mainly) this ethnocultural "anchor" gets shaken up when living in societies where "races are physically marked ... [since] racism was never important in our part of the world [the Pacific Islands] before contact" (Helu 1999a: interview).

These strands bear eloquent witness to how reconsiderations of "traditional"–"modern" sex–gender roles, political representation, what elements are essential to Tongan and/or Samoan cultures, postcolonial identity formation, and these moral economies are intertwined – and how they are distributed in various ways generationally, geographically, and socioeconomically as "Polys" deal every day with the "extraordinary challenges posed by trying to maintain the momentum of life in fractured or blended families" (X, KR, 06/01/1999 in X, 05/31/99), whether in the islands or overseas:

I guess each of us spins, in the intimate recesses of our own psyche, a complex web of inconsistent attitudes, values and beliefs.... After all,

the world is not place where social, cultural, economic or technological changes move in straight lines, or in consistent patterns. The
world is a place where contradictory influences produce unpredictable outcomes.

(ibid.)

Tolerance was something I HAD to nurture because everything I
stand for is one huge bundle of contradictions.

(KR, 06/01/99 in reply to above)

Threads express concern about quality control with respect to these
forums' future, and self-image, as empowering spaces and meeting places
for younger generations, and as support nodes for those dealing with
racial discrimination, socioeconomic exclusion, and isolation for those far
from community networks. But they also confront the effects of demographic change and tone in spaces premised on "serious discussion." In
her initial post to the thread sampled above, X addresses all these issues
quite clearly:

[M]ost people who write in this lounge [the KR] in one way or
another have concerns and interests about our Polynesian people. It is
also a forum where people try out their new found freedom to speak
their minds and to be heard.... However, we sound sometimes like a
bunch of spoilt children who write with ships [*sic*] on their shoulders.
It is sad as we ... continually fall back on unproductive ideas and
repetitive fundamentalism in an attempt to restore order.... I see our
thinking has not changed, particularly in the past year.... We regurgi-
tate the same topics and have the same arguments over and over
again. I understand that many different people come here at different
stages of the year ... I am in no way trying to disrespect those who
come in here and write what's on their minds ... [but] we have
reached a Plateau and our thinking appears to be stagnant right now.
I wonder why?

(X, KR, 05/31/99)

All these reflections point to how the standing and self-image of the
Pacific Islands Online and their offline interrelationships with the
community at large are perceived to be under pressure as the criterion of
free speech and that of "South Pacific traditions" appeared to be on a collision course. Calls for radical reassessment of how ground rules are to be
enforced without discouraging new participants are often conscious of
how "the world is watching every move we make" (Worried Mum, KB,
03/27/00 in Sandy Macintosh, 03/27/00):

All Sandy and other admins are asking is that we try to be a little more decent as it is our identity that is projected here. Sandy is concerned for the content as well as the image, and you should too.

(Langimalie, KB, 03/27/00 in Sandy Macintosh, 03/27/00)

I know, if you live in the United States (I cannot comment for NZ, Australia or UK), I am almost positive that your immediate reaction is Freedom of Speech; after all, you are correct – that is our constitution.... However ... What I saw in the Kava Bowl [recently was] not positive or constructive at all; instead it was childish! Let me remind you that this is not to change your style of posting, but to reiterate positive posting for a better tomorrow for our Tongan children ... to promote positiveness within our Tongan community.

(Ken, KB, 03/28/00 in Sandy Macintosh, 03/27/00)

And as for myself being a proud Maori from New Zealand ... some people need to get off their high horse and recognize that US Polynesians need to stick together and love one another, regardless of what nationality you be (Hawaiian, Tongan, Samoan, Tokelauan, Rarotonga, Maori).

(Serena, KR, 01/26/00 in Concerned, 01/06/00)

These threads understand that leaderships have to maneuver between the practicalities of enforcing their own ground rules, the (negotiable) limits of free speech, anonymity, and the operations of both history and geography in terms of participation. In the process, the tensions that arise between expressing opinions, committing "slander," and the rights and wrongs of confrontational techniques all become grist to the mill in these mature and vibrant forums. Taholo Kami put it this way:

We use volunteers and nobody is paid to do this. In fact you will find admin are students or fulltime workers who take care of the kavabowl on their own time. Sometimes reading every single message over a slow connection [as is the case in the Pacific Islands] can be quite an effort.... I meet so many people who tell me we need to delete more messages to keep the board useful. Basically, personal messages can be sent by email, messages with Loooong titles will be deleted since they clutter the board. Any offensive messages or anonymous messages which accuse a specific person are deleted. On personal messages, we don't have any obligation to keep them on the board.

(Taholo Kami/KBAdmin, KB, 02/04/00 in Taeoli, 02/04/00)

Given this delicate balancing act, and a committed consensus to maintaining it, regulars take on a burden of responsibility when discussing the various facets of these moral economies (even though this term is not their own). Forum leaderships do not regard these sorts of internal debates as separate from broader, structural ones. They are well aware of the debates around neoliberal imperatives for Pacific island societies vis-à-vis the potentials of ICTs for both enabling and exacerbating these pressures and social problems in diasporic communities. Taholo Kami, 'Alopi Latukefu, and Al Aiono all see ICTs in one way or another as one way for the small island nations of the South Pacific to deal on their own terms with "globalization" and its multifarious impacts. Kami wants to "help shape identity" and to instill "positive stereotypes" for "troublemakers" (2001: interview).

Summing up

In this chapter, four axial groups of introspective metadiscussions have been unpacked to analyse the structural gender power relations of everyday online practice for populations who are, for the most part, living as a "minority of a minority" (Aiono 1999: interview) on the ground. While they show the distinctive dynamics belonging to the hyperlinked textuality of Internet technologies (see Kolko, Nakamura, and Rodman 2000: 10; Haraway 1997b: 125 *passim*), these moral economies "interface" with major themes and offline contexts. Differences in style between the KB and the KR notwithstanding,[20] these economies are both product and process as participants look for ways to agree to "disagree; but not agree for an all-out brawl!!" (New Kid, KR, 01/30/99) in public cyberspace. Participants are just as concerned with providing good online role models as they are with provoking, and enjoying, the sharp rhetoric that comes with these sorts of debating styles.[21] Let me recap the technoformal and analytical dimensions to these moral economies vis-à-vis previous chapters' themes before turning to some of the methodological implications of this study for critical theory and research.

Technoformal considerations

These metathreads differ from the others studied here in that they are more dispersed – over time and through the forums. Most of the time, discontent gets expressed as occasional initial threads, or annoyed queries at unexpected deletions of a posting (see Axes 1 and 2, pp. 174 and 176) although these can also lead to substantial discussion threads. For the self-reflexive interactions on the fourth axis, the response rate and the intensity or length of the interventions are not necessarily related. In other words, these threads were not collated and analyzed by virtue of their size or frequency (as is the case with the other chapters). What they do show, though, is how certain subjects and relationships remain relatively "invisible" until such time as they become "controversial flashpoints for angry debate and overheated rhetoric" (Kolko, Nakamura, and Rodman 2000: 1).

Forms of social control such as behavioral norms, assumptions about propriety – and the rewards offered for conforming to these – are understood as part of the material spatial practices of people living and physically negotiating their neighborhood – *quartier* (see Giard and Mayol 1980: 14–16, 27). In Internet-based discourse, these practices include hypertextual trajectories – the traces left by written words on-screen and as digital files in Internet caches or server archives. For the everyday spaces of open cyberspace are constituted not only by the textual surfaces called up on screen by "search engines," but also by hidden layers of absent "other" voices.[22] Bulletin board software encases and channels these spatial practices – practices that facilitate the "insideout" and laterality of these forums' textual production. As Internet technologies and everyday life become increasingly intertwined at online–offline sites such as these ones, tactical and strategic practices emerge that are not necessarily premised on, or sufficiently in, physically proximate terms.[23]

Analytical considerations

Such clear articulations (as opposed to contingent subthreads or spasmodic metacomments in the context of other discussions) of these immanent economies are relatively few and far between. Neither is an initial post or the thread it weaves a transparent vessel for the initial intentions of the poster, even when that poster is the moderator asserting his/her authority. The unfurling discussion with both its explicit (literal) and latent (implied and alluded to) interrelationships can only be traced by following (at all levels of inter-hypertextuality and interpretative intervention) how the thread's theme may crystallize and take off. Moreover, often provocation and strong stances are part and parcel of getting any discussion threads off the ground. Forum leaderships have admitted (to me personally) or intimated this online at regular intervals. Hence, once again the analyst's job is to separate out the strands *without losing sight,* analytically or empirically, of the larger spatial–temporal sociocultural tapestry to which they belong.

So, while these moral economies are outlined in the ground rules and work between the lines of these, they have gained in substance, crystallized, through reiteration and contestation over time. In this sense, disputes are important moments of decision making as well as interesting historical punctuations in the life of any (online) community. When articulated with postcolonial lives and concerns for Polynesians and mixed with generational gaps and class–status–gendered divisions (both "traditional" and "modern"), the stakes are raised. And so are tempers as positions polarize. These dynamics are aided and abetted by the spontaneity and rapidity of hyperlinked forms of writing-as-speaking and reading-as-listening, "troublemakers'" abuses of anonymity and "youthful fun and games" notwithstanding. The issue of how Tongans and/or Samoans are, or should be, presenting themselves in the "world" of cyberspace comes quickly to the fore when discussions stall.[24]

Understanding and tracing how these dynamics work online, therefore, is a hermeneutic (not a hermetic) activity with its own power "quotient." This is because inference (on my part as the participant-observer) and on the part of the protagonists in terms of their own (semi/conscious or socio-cultural reference points) intervenes, inevitably some would say, in how these moral economies are understood to operate, in principle and in practice. Analyzing these particular threads, and noting distinctions between the KB and the KR, has to take into account when participants do talk about the various relationships they have sustained over time, their commitment to and/or role in moderating the forums, and their gratitude to the leaderships. Many admit to spending a lot of time on these forums. All in all, these attest to an online memory of a shared past. The nostalgia and affirmation that are part of this history only really become apparent when the daily rhythm comes under pressure by "newbies" who do not know the rules or are deliberately challenging them, or technical practicalities (sheer volume of hits to review, server space, financial difficulties) intervene.[25] The thing to remember is that dissent, dispute, and forms of "nonconformity" are negotiated boundary lines even in cyberspace. For

> the point is that we're not untouchables, infallible in our beliefs. We're not all experts but individuals who come from diverse backgrounds who find it a homing-in process to be amongst fellow Samoans/PIs [Pacific Islanders] in addition to our resident palagis sans the usual fears about such a gathering.
>
> (Anni, KR, 11/23/99 in Daily Planet, 11/22/99)

A last observation on the gendered aspects. In these operations of power (however defined), men are at the fore, by virtue of being the owners (Al Aiono and Taholo Kami) or very active participants and/or administrators (Sandy Macintosh and Phil Tukia/Meilakepa in the KB, 'Alopi Latukefu in the THA and SPIN). But there are also a number of women who are important moderators and participants, and who thereby carry their own powers of persuasion (Helen Morton, Dot, LadyCYB, Sue Aiono, Anni). In any sense, power has to be exercised intuitively by the leaderships.[26] Once authority has been granted – or asserted – it is often expected. In short, both ends of the power spectrum are negotiable. The ultimate enforcement of going offline or imposing passwords is seen only as a last resort. In the second instance, there are certain ethnic/racial elements to these online groups whose *raison d'être* is to

> be a place where ethnic and racial identity are examined, worked through, and reinforced [in order to] provide a powerful coalition building and progressive medium for 'minorities' separated from each other by distance and other factors.
>
> (Kolko, Nakamura, and Rodman 2000: 9)

For many participants, race/ethnicity – or shared culture – is a primary boundary marker. As we have seen, participants are up front about offline "daily embodiments." The nonvisual and anonymity elements to these sorts of interactions not only allow for humor, but also add "spice" to discussions. As one participant noted during the course of another discussion, "I too have visited the KB since the early day, but under various nom de plumes for anonymity. I find the mystery of KBers adds the flavour to the debate" (Dragonite, KB, 03/28/00 in Sandy Macintosh, 03/27/00). Being able to deal with a certain degree of confrontation is part and parcel of participation in itself and also of whether debates progress or not. Moreover, the lack of visual communicative cues[27] also creates new spaces for political challenges and self-expression – although, as noted earlier, not everyone relishes these convention-bending, confrontational qualities of online debating. The thing to remember is that these are open-ended, relational processes, with their negotiations of "good" or "bad" online practices in public (cyber)spaces, and they are also speaking to older political-economic histories and sociocultural orders. Second- and third-generations of the South Pacific island diasporas are learning and living these as commonalities *and* differences as they speak-write. An unpacking of the moral economies allows for another perspective on the conceptual, political, and intersubjective issues at stake in the forums' "bread-and-butter" discussions. Tracing the gender–power structural relations in operation in these online *quartiers* (kava circles and/or cafés, in their own words) shows the politics of representation in its most basic articulation: for whom, by whom, and for what purpose?

In these last four chapters, elements of the postcolonial politics of representation emerging in these cyberspaces can be summed up as rearticulations of "racial"/ethnic/cultural processes of *identification* as experienced from within. These are spliced with the operations of *gender* – being a wo/man; *politics* – (democratic) representation for and by whom; and *power* relations – who calls the shots (whether these be online and offline). Participants articulate these operations *experientially*: as life paths and circumstances that are both positive and negative. These online traversals thereby need to be grasped as part of the (post)colonial historical context of the South Pacific islands on the ground; one that is openly recognized, for better or worse, as a "global" and/or ICT-delimited one. The practices of everyday life online are indispensable to figuring out what an equitable future for the Internet might actually entail. The online production of the Pacific islands, populations online, as they navigate their way through these pioneering portals and the many others that have sprung up in their wake,[28] constantly (re)draws public–open cyberspace from the ground up.

8 Internet research praxis in postcolonial settings

Introduction

> Anthropological discourse often exhibits (or hides, which is the same) conflict between theoretical-methodological conventions and lived experience. Anthropological writing may be scientific; it is also inherently autobiographic.
>
> (Fabian 1983: 87)

> An autobiographical approach ... facilitates an exploration of a number of other issues relating to method in social science. These include critiques of methodological notions such as 'objectivity', rejection of the possibility of doing unbiased, value free research and an increasing acceptance that the pretence of research neutrality is counterproductive. Feminists have always placed great emphasis on the importance of reflexivity in social research, of researchers acknowledging their place within the research process and of the likely effects of our positionings.
>
> (Henwood et al. 2001: 22)

These two insights from beyond the "theoretical-methodological conventions" of IR/IPE point to an additional tale of the Internet. Between the lines of these reconstructions are the points at which these "lived experiences" and Internet practices have interacted with my own. In this chapter, I tell this third tale by writing my own learning curve (as the online participant-researcher) more explicitly into this discussion of the methodological-ethical implications of Internet-based and/or participant-observation research for critical IR/IPE (de Certeau 1986: 117–118; Nicholson 1990: 6–8; Hakken 1999: 45; Miller and Slater 2000; Hine 2000).[1] The first section makes a brief pit stop at three definitional (and disciplinary) discomforts that arise when doing research through – or on – the World Wide Web: the "Internet," "feminist method," and participation–observation in the "field." While a rich literature in critical feminist anthropology and science and technology studies offers guidelines for culturally sensitive and ethical online participant-observation research practice, it does not offer ready-made formulas either.

The second section examines some of the methodological issues (the "likely effects of our positionings" – Henwood *et al.* 2001) pertaining to this sort of research enterprise. These are everyday-life-as-online-archives, Internet research vis-à-vis traditional IR/IPE objects of research/fieldwork sites, cyberspace as an ethnographic "field," data-gathering techniques in electronic scenarios, and Internet-specific research ethics vis-à-vis scholarly understandings of empirical "rigor."

1 Disciplinary and definitional discomforts

The Internet

Following science and technology studies, where constructivist approaches to sociotechnological change have been finely honed, ICTs have been conceptualized here as much more than a bunch of things that can "hurt when you drop them on your foot" (Henwood *et al.* 2001: 25). They also embody various gender power and knowledge relations, the creative practices entailed in their conception and production, and their meaning-making capacities. Everyday uses, disuse, and active *non*uses (Wyatt *et al.* 2002) of any successful – or "failed" – technology are a crucial, albeit unsung, element to understanding its sociocultural and political economic historical trajectory (Woolgar 2000; Rogers 2000). While ICTs, writ large, are being more consciously theorized of late in IR/IPE, the intricacies of everyday practices online still tend to be subsumed under explanatory accounts of macro-level "global shifts".

This tendency is exacerbated at times with a more insidious elision, namely, the way in which many critiques of new(er) ICTs tend to equate political and socioeconomic inequalities between the "Global North" and the "Global South" and an emergent "digital divide" with an assumption that disadvantaged regions, societies, or groups of users are therefore virtually absent from cyberspace. Given the relative infrastructural dearth throughout the Pacific Islands, there is a certain case to be made here (see Chapter 2). To recall, the Pacific Ocean's "information highways" are still drawn along the century-old telecommunications priorities of (colonial) Anglo-Euro-American powers. In cyberspatial terms, however, this stark image needs to be tempered somewhat. As the Pacific Forum and Polynesian Cafe Internet portals consolidated during the 1990s, with the volume of traffic peaking at a million "hits" a week in 1998–1999, links between the Pacific Islands Online and various communities and cultural reference points on the ground became quite tangible: legible and traceable. And as these occur still in open – public – cyberspaces by and large, the substance and formal qualities of both interpersonal and textual interrelationships were made available for observation, participation, and direct involvement.[2]

Meanwhile, as educational and research institutions installed intranets and Internets of their own, early dismissals in some quarters of email, Web-based document searches, personal Web pages, or online teaching tools as scientifically and politically suspect were replaced by either unbridled enthusiasm or daily habit. In analytical terms (and here I refer mainly to IR/IPE literature), this uptake of Internet technologies in the 1990s overlooked the legacy of the previous Internet generation of online interactions and theorizing from the 1980s. It was as if "the Internet" had only been born with the arrival of second-generation Internet technologies: the World Wide Web's browser software and swift hyperlinking functionality, and the dotcom boom and busts at the turn of the millennium. This attitudinal and behavioral shift has meant too little energy spent on productive conceptualizations of the new cognitive and experiential domain delimited by the everyday use of Internet technologies. When addressed, online practices have been posited as "overdetermined" by capitalist modes of accumulation on the one hand and their inter/subjective and epistemological ramifications treated (disdainfully and) "independently of [their social] embeddedness" (Miller and Slater 2000: 6/18) on the other. Practices of everyday life online, while distinguishable from offline ones, do not occur in splendid cyber-isolation – something not lost on the participants in these forums and which I was to learn about myself. The Internet needs to be studied as "a complex socio-technical whole system that has *both symbolic and practical significance*" (Wyatt *et al.* 2002: 23; emphasis added). (Re)thinking the Internet in this way retrieves it from technologically determinist and ethnocentric approaches. The definitional discomfort is thereby relieved. The disciplinary one, however, will remain disputed for some time to come.

Feminist sensibilities

When one is interacting or working with non-Western cultures and/or their diasporic populations, the adjectives "feminist" or "critical" are anything but self-explanatory. I have alluded to some of the theoretical debates comprising the rich literature of second-wave feminism (as activist and/or academic endeavors) in Chapter 4. What does – or should – constitute "feminist method" is an emergent debate in IR/IPE (see Locher and Prügl 2001; Ling 2002; Franklin 2003b; Peterson 2003; True 2001; Highmore 2002: 28). This study is premised not so much on any one feminist "method" as on a "feminist sensibility" that draws on poststructuralist and postcolonial critiques of positivist modes of scientific inquiry.

How does a feminist approach – sensibility – work out when studying participants talking about sex–gender roles or speaking as women? Even though I have explained my reasons for substituting the term *gender* with that of *gender power relations,* neither is a recurring term in the threads. As all the excerpts show, participants employ a wide range of idioms for academic terms (gender, ethnicity, representation, and so on). The liveliness of this lexicon and the range of eloquence in these texts are a powerful antidote to the reification tendencies of academic categorizations in any case. Online, these women pay little heed to any number of practices of silencing – or speaking for – others who can speak for themselves. The task for me was getting to grips with their spoken texts as rich registers in their own right. Not unlike recorded conversations, these conversations–texts are relatively unedited – streams of consciousness in many cases. Being both sensitive, and pragmatic in the face of thousands of interlocking or divergent online interventions, involved a series of different personal and professional decisions for me to make about how much and what to include, where to cut, how to "edit" and then re-present these conversations in another, written medium (Highmore 2002: 167).

Let us shift for a moment from *gender* as an analytical and politicized category to the more empirically recognizable – albeit no less contested – one of *women* (see Carver 1998b). In these forums, women are present and active as participants and administrators, taking in many cases full advantage of online communications to break down their own immediate experiences of female/male sex-role stereotyping. Female participants made their presence felt, and participate as fully fledged members of these online forums. As I have noted, this sort of easy peer-to-peer interaction does not characterize communicative hierarchies and public rituals in many Pacific island societies.[3] Female and male participants mark their interventions with various gendered, ethnic/racial, and socioeconomic "markers" of their own. For me, *gender power relations* operated more as a contextual "timbre" than as an empirical "variable." While I noted female-to-male ratios of participation where they were clear or apposite, this dyad allowed me to treat any direct references to sex, gender, women and men, femininity, and masculinity as part of a conversational tapestry. In this respect, gender (even when it operates as a synonym for women) was never the only issue at stake for the participants, not reducible to whether or not a participant identified herself as female, nor down to whether or not messages bore female names. This sort of feminist sensibility is an explicit methodological premise to this study's hermeneutic schematic. It is also a personal-political choice, and one that I made early on.

Participation–observation: bringing people back into IR/IPE

Participation–observation in the field is an integral rite/right of passage in ethnography, "the study of the distinctive practices of particular human groupings and representations – pictures of a people – based on such a study" (Hakken 1999: 38; see also Fabian 1983: 88, 106–109; Hine 2000; Kendall 1999). But as Miller and Slater point out, ethnography is "much more than fieldwork. In most ethnographic reportage of quality, the length and breadth of the study allows one topic to become understood as also an idiom for something else" (2000: 18/18). Be that as it may, in both online and on-the-ground research fields, two methodological precepts operate: "1: Search for ways to observe directly and meaningfully the practices of interest, not just talk about them with the participants: and, even more importantly, 2: find ways to participate actively in the practices" (Hakken 1999: 39). Furthermore, the participant-observer has to pay "attention systematically to both what is being studied *and the way the studied is being co-constructed by the situation, one's informants, and one's self*" (ibid.: 40; emphasis added). In contrast to positivist stresses on banning "bias" and ensuring "objectivity," this method presupposes that when writing up the findings, the author will "highlight rather than . . . try and banish context" (ibid.: 40).

There are other practicalities that are foreign to mainstream IR/IPE empirical research modes. First, conventional ethnography entails spending (extended) time within a society or racial/ethnic group *other* than one's own. Second, this usually means extended periods of research time in a distant location. Total immersion, in other words, which also requires learning another language (Fabian 1983: 105 *passim*). The "human agents" who are being observed (the "research objects"), their daily rituals, beliefs, intimate and political economic relationships, are the "raw data" that are recorded in field notes, audio/video recordings, drawings, and suchlike. The actual "ethnography" is produced at a later date, which brings some other epistemological and ethical discomforts for both empiricist and feminist/postcolonial approaches. The first is the sociocultural and historical gender power relations inscribed in the process of "othering" that characterized Western ethnographic work during, and has done since, its consolidation in the modern colonial age (Kolko *et al.* 2000: 2 *passim*; L. T. Smith 1999). The second is the ever-present hazards of the "hermeneutic circle" (Ulin 1984) and/or implicit subjectivity – "bias" – of individually based, and often geographically isolated, sorts of fieldwork. The personal integrity of the anthropologist and the respective scientific worth of her/his findings are inseparable. The third is the temporal "anomaly" that is implicit in scientific writing. As Johannes Fabian notes, even reflexive ethnographic writing can still

> construe the Other in terms of distance, spatial and temporal. The Other's empirical presence turns into [her/his] theoretical absence, a conjuring trick which is worked with the help of an array of devices that have the common intent and function to keep the Other outside.
>
> (1983: xi)

Participation–observation online and various other variants of Internet research have been both underscoring and moving beyond these conundrums on several fronts. First, the place and space of fieldwork. Internet communities, "virtual realities" and fantasy communities, live chat, and online discussions are all variously accessible from a computer. No need to get on a plane, or take up residence in a faraway land. Going into an "online" situation therefore challenges the very notion of the "field" (Clifford 1997: 52–58, 64 *passim*). Observation–participation (or vice versa) as a necessarily physically proximate practice of full immersion is challenged in asynchronous Internet research scenarios. As opposed to live chat, where one is made visible by way of one's avatar, a would-be participant-observer can easily "lime" or "lurk" in asynchronous Internet forums. Announcement of one's presence and intention is thereby a conscious decision when working in these cyber-fields. Finally, the multilateral nature of online presence can also loosen up the classic relationship that develops between an anthropologist and her/his local "informant/s." In online discussion scenarios, all participants are potential informants in effect. Moreover, anonymity and/or multiple names/online guises are not absolute markers of (in)authenticity in an online situation. Internet practitioners claim allegiance to their "nics" or "handles" with much the same fervor as they do their "given" names.

Even though the researcher is relatively invisible, and certainly not physically "there," working in an online field still entails "embodied spatial practice" nonetheless (Clifford 1997: 53; Jordan 1999: 67–79; Gonzáles 2000; Warschauer 2000). As Jordan says, "people are not anonymous in cyberspace, as they construct identities that they use there" (1999: 75), something that starts as soon as one starts to post messages or enters a live chat site. This actually complicates rather than mitigates the inherent "impact of subject-to-subject relationships" (de Certeau 1986: 217) in participation–observation scenarios. There is another dimension to online participation–observation carried out in non-password-protected fields especially. The once relatively hermetic "field," where observer and observed interact in relative isolation, becomes virtually a public act in open cyberspaces such as discussion forums. The participation and/or observation can be observed by others (if they so choose) *as it unfolds*. This open door to "the whole world" does not go unnoticed by these forums' populations even as most of the time they choose to ignore this "goldfish bowl" characteristic (see Chapter 7). By contrast, face-to-face interviews and email surveys or interactions are not such potentially accessible acts at the moment of their enactment. The other key aspect of anthropological research, "long-term involvement" (Miller and Slater 2000: 17/18), is also affected by the speed, volume of readily available texts, and sedentary access features of Internet-based communications. These particularities, as both restrictive and permissive elements to online research, are imbued with both epistemological and ethical implications. In this respect, burgeoning work on Internet research ethics overlaps both feminist and postcolonial sensibilities. As research ethics are framed differently across the social sciences offline, these discomforts are felt in different measures by different researchers. Some, like the princess in the fairytale, feel the pea they are lying on no matter how many mattresses are in between. Others may wonder what the fuss is all about. My own learning curve here was along the following lines.

Being there

Guidelines for online research of this nature are still being worked on and, in any case, need to be assessed and renegotiated for each "self-defined virtual community" or Internet research scenario (Sharf 1999: 255). Be that as it may, as I was not working by anthropological research criteria as such, I did not feel obliged to announce my presence on, or persona as a researcher of, these forums straightaway. It was not long before I realized that this "invisibility," despite its convenience, was ethically unsustainable. When I did so, the first concern was dealt with quite quickly (by announcing my intentions on the forums, and providing my "real name" and email from then on).

Citations and consent

People's words taken from an online scenario as daily utterances are, arguably, "rawer" material than those from interview or survey responses. As such, they are more susceptible to being misappropriated or misinterpreted by the researcher (now turned author) later on (Sharf 1999: 243–248). At the same time, a distinction needs to be kept between bilateral (offline to all intents and purposes) email interactions, those happening in live chat groups, and textual utterances entered in open-access newsgroups or bulletin board discussion forums such as the KB and the KR. The line between "informed consent" and the "appropriation of others' personal stories" is a fine one in any research that bases its findings on conversations with people or observations of others' conversations (ibid.: 244–245). This is why anthropological codes of ethics are well honed. Those for IR/IPE and political science barely consider these sorts in intersubjective research fields – beyond the formal interview moment, that is.

Transparency and accountability

This sort of "naturalistic interpersonal conversation" in cyberspace is only partially addressed by codes of ethics (Sharf 1999: 144; Kendall 1999: 70–71), hence the following points are all open to discussion. Nevertheless, the citation system used here is neither straightforward nor unproblematic.[4] The space given to participants' texts here has been a conscious decision to give them the floor while also recognizing "psychological boundaries, purposes, vulnerabilities, and privacy of the individual members of [these virtual communities] even though [their] discourse is publicly accessible" (Sharf 1999: 255). In that sense, I would have to "respectfully disagree" with the principle of absolute anonymity as a hard and fast rule for online research scenarios. What is intended as protection can operate as a form of erasure too (Fabian 1983). After all, "the whole purpose of a scholarly analysis is to perceive patterns of interaction and glean insights that may not be clear to individual participants within the communicative event under scrutiny" (Sharf 1999: 254). Consultation and transparency, particularly in online, quasi-anonymous scenarios, are just as important elements to an ethical research method. To date, I have yet to be challenged by these participants for having retained the original signatures when this issue has arisen in my own queries online, or in offline emails with some of those involved, as a result of previous publications (online and in journals) of part of this research. I will, nonetheless, carry this "larger portion of the ethical burden" (ibid.: 153).

There is one more practical-epistemological issue that participation–observation techniques have to take into account: an assumed intimacy with one's "subjects" and/or an overidentification with them, both of which are anathema to research conventions that eschew any explicit positioning or research scenario that gives rise to "bias." Rather than shy away from these processes, feminist sensibilities and the insights gained from anthropological meta-methodological debates can make explicit these inherent insider–outsider power differentials. As integral aspects to the "method" employed, these dynamics become parts of the tapestry rather than stumbling blocks on the road to the "Holy Grail" of so-called objective truth.

To sum up: this study is not an (Internet) ethnography in the "more narrowly methodological sense" (Miller and Slater 2000: 17/18). It is part of nascent Internet ethnographic research projects, though.[5] In keeping with the responsibilities of positioning myself in the research, as an implicated subject (not just the onlooker), these discomforts have been both challenging and personally productive – especially for someone who was born and brought up in the South Pacific (Samoa and New Zealand) and who is of pakeha/palagi descent (white/non-Polynesian) living in the Netherlands. Neither my ethnic/national designation (Pakeha New Zealander) nor time spent as participant in these online forums is a reason to presume "insider" or "resident expert" privileges, though (L. Smith 1999: 118, 137 *passim*; Stacey 1997). For even when I took part in discussions or initiated a message, I still did so in the persona of "researcher," albeit as someone who hailed from the South Pacific region and who was living in Europe. On reflection, I came to realize that part of my early reluctance to participate (not a characteristic attributed to me in offline scenarios) – get "the seat of my pants dirty" (Paccagnella 1997), so to speak – was related to the feeling of having lived "overseas" for too long and so being out of touch with some events under discussion. At the outset, my own (re)positioning within social science methodological priorities (or at least how I perceived them to be operating) seemed to affirm this convenient standpoint.

2 In and out of the field

The time spent in this online field spans at least five years of regular visits to the KB and KR. This did not preclude on-the-ground work, though. I also visited some of the offline access nodes for the Kava Bowl and Kamehameha Roundtable: Tonga, Fiji, Hawaii, Los Angeles, San Francisco, Sydney, Auckland (colleagues still tease me about doing research in such well-known tourist destinations). This trip "back to the islands" had a strong personal impact on me.[6] It also helped me put the discussions into their broader offline context (which is integral to their manifest content) – my first insight into the subtle and substantive links that connect offline worlds and spaces to online ones. I have also interacted with a number of these forums regulars in relatively offline moments, apart from formal interviews and online conversations. These occurred through email or passing on-the-ground conversations with participants (who would most often demur at telling me their online handles). The archives that I have kept of these threads here, and the many others not used in these reconstructions, exist as printouts complete with annotations and cross-referencing. For online fieldwork scenarios, these can be seen as analogous to field notes.

One last point on language. I do not speak fluent Samoan or Tongan, even though I know a smattering of New Zealand Maori and Pacific Island words, the main island groups' official greetings, some children's songs. A Tongan–English dictionary, bought in Nuku'alofa, has been a great aid for the Kava Bowl discussions in this respect. Some early subthreads written in Tongan as well as most subtextual asides or puns made in Tongan or Samoan were therefore not accessible for me. Nevertheless, the working language of these forums is English, and more particularly so for the US-based Polynesian Cafe. Like those participants who are not fluent in the languages or cultural practices of their (grand)parents, and who lament this lack while appreciating the way these forums refresh their language skills, I, too, have acquired more basic vocabulary and knowledge.

Onlineness: everyday life-as-archive

Even though they are in written form, these online practices remain open-ended and ongoing interactions. And as hypertexts they were not created to be archived, downloaded, and then pored over by a researcher at a later late. This holds true even when texts have been printed out, filed, and then archived. As spontaneous albeit cumulative recordings, online texts are not "readable" in conventional (left-to-right, top-to-bottom) ways, nor are they designed for longevity. Some online texts stay accessible for years, others for months, and yet others for only weeks. Mitra and Cohen (1999) list *intertextuality*, *nonlinearity*, the *reader-as-writer*, and *impermanence* as key characteristics of these sorts of material, and the practices they embody on screen – characteristics of many non-Western, oral communicative cultures, like those of the Pacific islands, as well. Furthermore, as de Certeau argues, these are characteristics of the practice of everyday life (see Highmore 2002: 164 *passim*, 174–178). The peculiarities of everyday life as *archival* material bring with them different sorts of practical issues; online everyday archives no less.[7]

In both cases, the collection and recording of everyday practices – data – resist fungible "rules and protocols for an archival practice" (Highmore 2002: 161). De Certeau's approach to data collection was more inclusive, not fazed by the "registering [of] 'voices' within 'texts' ... through a [research] practice of listening, inscribing and describing" (ibid.: 168). De Certeau's aim is to permit "an archival practice based on heterological sources that doesn't reduce these sources to illustrations of theoretical arguments, but uses the sources to provide and provoke theory" (ibid.: 169; see also Adorno 1976). Even so, everyday life research (on the ground as well) permits actual, and potential, archives of "unmanageable proportions" (Highmore 2002: 169; see also Mitra and Cohen 1999: 189–190). For "the everyday doesn't have a form of attention that is proper to it" (Highmore 2002: 169) – a quality that becomes quickly apparent in practice, whether one is dealing with transcripts of recorded conversations, personal diaries, interview material, or hyperlinked accumulations of written text. Spontaneous, "irrepressible," and polyphonic online "archives of the everyday" both help and hinder data gathering. Conversations arrive on-screen already in written form (which is time-saving). Over time, particular texts become part of much longer ones (spanning months, if not years, at times) and cross-referenced conversations (which is time-consuming and confusing). Either way, these online archives can and do speak for themselves if taken in a holistic and intertextual sense rather than through categorical filters.

In the case of the KR and KB, threads operated as follows. For instance, if a fierce debate develops from an initial post, responses fly in over a short period of time, two to three days mostly. Others grow more slowly or themes get reiterated years later. Interventions on issues of the day or historical arguments are interpolated, interrupted, or illustrated with intimate, personal asides. Local, even parochial concerns are intertwined with "global" ones. As cumulative, unconscious (in all senses of the word) everyday archives and archives of the everyday, these spoken-texts are "streams of consciousness" in a very real sense. Even when written with an eye to "good" literary style, non sequiturs, deliberate spelling errors, typos, or colloquial language use are integral aspects of the various registers in play. It took some time before I decided to dispense with static thematic categories, keyword criteria, and other linguistic methods as a way to "capture" the content–meaning–intersubjective dimensions of these online texts.

These qualities are one reason why I did not make use of software data-mining tools. Such software programs still cannot delineate the *substance* of the relationships constituting these texts. Spatial and hierarchical relationships between websites, or measuring the absolute number of "hits" a website gets, mapping large-scale Internet traffic (as data-mining software does), or allowing a "Web search" through keywords deal with filtered fragments of the manifest content, and so leave analysis at the metatextual surface. I discovered quite quickly that hand-counting and sifting was the more secure approach to ascertaining levels of participation in a thread, within or between sets of threads. For example, the number of "hits" is not equal to the number of participants; the number of follow-ups per participant similarly. Relationships and reoccurrences are better located with the naked eye, over time (see Figure 3.1).

How did these intertextual, nonlinear, and impermanent characteristics operate in and out of the field? Sometimes I learned the hard way; lost the chance to download and print out substantial threads because a server changed and the moderators did not leave older threads long enough online (if at all). When trying to plot participation and/or a theme's significance (see the next subsection), I had to accept that my need to pin the "real names" of participants down or ascertain consistent one-to-one links between messages and messengers had less to do with how discussions and relationships were evolving *per se*.[8] I also had to radically readjust my left-to-right, chronological reading habits and develop an upside-down, sideways, and right-to-left technique (see the next but one subsection). Printing out substantial threads simply underscored the aforementioned characteristics of online texts (Mitra and Cohen 1999). I also discovered that the longitudinal dimension to participant-observation revealed how the relationship between longevity, quantity, and significance is not a linear but, rather, a cyclic or spiraling one in these (online and offline) cultural spaces.[9] Gradually and with more confidence, I started to look for recurrence, and lateral and more multilayered traces of relationship and dialogue. Hardly a new discovery, though, for non-Western communicative cultures.

Ascertaining significance

Generally, the success and robustness of any website can be measured by the number of daily/weekly/monthly "hits" it gets. My manual method was more than adequate for making comparisons and collating interrelationships over time. The same technique applied for unpacking the demographics and/or participant profiles within any specific thread/set of threads, various forms of relative anonymity included. I was able to ascertain one simple correlation early on: long threads did indeed indicate large amounts of interest and numbers of participants. When coupled with the reoccurrence of certain themes over the years, the recurring themes of these online archives began to become clearer. The themes examined in the previous four chapters constitute some of the most heavily patronized and recurring concerns of these groups. The copious archives from which these reconstructions have been selected must not be mistaken, however, for anything but partial ones. Theory and research need to move "away from a picture of cultural contexts as sealed rooms, with an homogenous space 'inside' them, inhabited by 'authentic insiders'" (Narayan 1997: 412).

Reading discussion threads: which way up?

As participating reader, and then archivist by default, I had to learn how to read linear and lateral forms of intertextuality as *intra*textuality on and off the screen. Participants and their textual production switch backwards and forwards, in and out, up, down, and sideways all the time. Nonlinear narrative structures or multiple endings are not the preserve of Western postmodern literary genres or Internet-based writing (see Friedman 1998; Wendt 1999; L. T. Smith 1999), as postcolonial critics argue. But for Western-trained Internet researchers, this requires different attitudes to the re-presentation and insertions of such texts into a research study. Moreover, this laterality confronts the participant-observer immediately. All participants on Internet forums are both writer and reader at the same time (Mitra and Cohen 1999: 186–187; Kolko 1995). The supposed, and debatable, distance between (objective) researcher and the researched becomes less tenable as the research moment becomes a part of the (online) record (see de Certeau 1986: 199–221). Another distinction between the spoken word and written text (one that features prominently in de Certeau's conceptualization of tactical and strategic operations) is further blurred (Highmore 2002: 165).

There are some mechanics to accessing, reading, and eventually printing and filing these threads which illustrate the above points. While it is usually an initial post that gets a thread started (or not), this top-to-bottom structure is but one feature to "reading" these sorts of texts. As participants respond, the threads start to wend their way from the initial post. Taken altogether, various threads form, in turn, their own "meta" thread, whether of the week or the month's "hits." Title and content are separated by the latter being placed "behind" the former and accessed by clicking on the hyperlinked title line. Figure 8.1 is a reproduction of one thread from the Kamehameha Roundtable. I had to read upside down, sideways right to left, and inside out. But threads also have several "layers" of readability. One layer is direct follow-ups to the initial post (vertically downwards). These can become an opener for a subthread, and subsequent follow-ups also, and so on (that move diagonally to the right). The overall effect can be seen quite clearly as a longer thread of three or more layers begins to snake off-screen. What these visual effects illustrate are not only different nuances in the discussion content, technical contingencies notwithstanding, diversions, brief more intimate exchanges embedded within the thread, but also different relationships and preoccupations. A lot of content clues can be gleaned from this meta-thread: a string of highlighted titles with follow-ups stringing out below them (Figure 8.1).

Any Future US Political Clout for PI's??   http://polycafe.com/kamehameha/kamehameha2000-2/3190.htm

Any Future US Political Clout for PI's??

[Follow Ups] [Post Followup] [Polynesian Cafe]

Posted by eb on March 12, 2001 at 12:36:31:

Hispanics have now surpassed Blacks in population and will be major minority political bloc. Blacks have Jesse Jackson, NAACP, Congressional Black Caucus, in long list of advocate groups. Chinese-American just bought San Francisco Examiner due to clout in that city. In comparison, Pacific-Islanders have a few non-profit groups promoting film/arts, and low-income services (majority).

Some problems as I see it:
1)lack of leadership
2)lack of coordination/cooperation
3)lack of sense of "belonging" to fabric of American society.

Questions:
1)Should this be a vision/goal for citizens of Pacific Island ancestry?

2)If yes, how to accomplish?

Does anyone have data on population numbers?

Follow Ups:

- **PI Advocacy** Dr. Victor C. Thompson *01:03:01 03/14/01* (5)
  - **Question?** JC *07:30:47 03/14/01* (4)
    - **Answer** Sinafea *04:18:11 03/15/01* (3)
      - **This New Blood Lives Five Blocks From Carson City Hall!!!** JC *10:00:59 03/15/01* (2)
        - **Economic Development Mtg.....** sinafea *23:38:22 03/16/01* (1)
          - **Sorry, its Wednesday Not Tuesday** Sinafea *23:22:52 03/19/01* (0)
- **I disagree** Bevo *16:39:51 03/13/01* (60)
  - **And I'm puzzled why Mr. Unique Individual frequents a poly forum** eb *13:30:01 03/17/01* (11)
    - **What is good for the goose, is good for the gander** Bevo *03:14:25 03/18/01* (10)
      - **we don't need leadership despite our shortcomings?** Meilakepa *18:32:01 03/18/01* (8)
        - **re: Pacific Island immigration an Island ESL programs.** seiOriana *03:23:53 03/19/01* (7)
          - **Re: ESL?** Daniel Longstaff *12:43:37 03/19/01* (5)
            - **Daniel, I agree with you 100%. There's another word for this program and it's called "Belittlement Classes".** Ani *21:38:08 03/28/01* (1)
              - **Wow! Who did that?????????????** Teuila

Figure 8.1 Reproduction of a Kamehameha Roundtable discussion thread.

       00:01:03 03/29/01 (0)
- **Addressing your questions** Teuila *21:56:58 03/19/01* (0)
- **re: re: ESL?** seiOriana *15:46:33 03/19/01* (1)
  - **ESL programs** Teuila *22:01:10 03/19/01* (0)
- **ESL Identification** Teuila *08:41:39 03/19/01* (0)
- **Right On Bevo!!!** JC *07:16:21 03/18/01* (0)

- o **I disagree with your disagreement . . .** Meilakepa *12:37:09 03/17/01* (12)
  - **Amen** Sinafea *01:16:05 03/20/01* (0)
  - **This is indeed where we differ my friend.** Bevo *03:32:06 03/18/01* (3)
    - **Here I go...** SoulAlone *16:40:43 03/18/01* (0)
    - **a fundamental difference it is . . .** Meilakepa *04:53:08 03/18/01* (1)
      - **Political clout doesn't equal...** Bevo *14:48:37 03/19/01* (0)
  - **Wow... what an interesting exchange of thoughts...** SoulAlone *00:04:50 03/18/01* (2)
    - **Always makes you think!** Teuila *11:43:28 03/18/01* (1)
      - **I am in total agreement with you...** SoulAlone *15:07:19 03/18/01* (0)
  - **Just looking at those schools.......** Teuila *22:57:36 03/17/01* (3)
    - **Right on sis** Bevo *03:39:01 03/18/01* (2)
      - **Look smarty pants.......** Teuila *09:20:10 03/18/01* (1)
        - **And all around me the power's going out!** Teuila *22:02:47 03/19/01* (0)

- o **Agreed-I am not a hyphenated American. (nt)** Dot *10:05:48 03/14/01* (0
- o **Quite the Contrary.....** Sinafea *02:06:51 03/14/01* (33)
  - **Theres a differenece...** Bevo *15:01:52 03/14/01* (32)
    - **You Are Right in one sense, however....** Sinafea *04:05:11 03/15/01* (31)
      - **Exceptions** Teuila *22:32:41 03/15/01* (21)
        - **Yes its the Parents that are Vocal......** sinafea *23:58:35 03/16/01* (0)
        - **Don't Forget The Language Issue!!!** JC *02:49:48 03/16/01* (19)
          - **ESL, right up my alley!** Teuila *09:02:20 03/16/01* (1)
            - **huh?** Teuila *09:24:03 03/16/01* (0)
          - **re: ESL..** seiOriana *04:45:18 03/16/01* (16)
            - **Be Careful Of the Statistics!!!** JC *09:17:05 03/16/01* (11)
              - **The growing number of Samoans inmates isn't exaggerated either!** seiOriana *11:46:29 03/16/01* (10)
                - **O.K. Will you do me a favor!** JC *21:08:08 03/17/01* (4)
                  - **Oh, come on JC!** Teuila *22:37:41 03/17/01* (3)
                    - **No I Don't!** JC *05:57:32 03/18/01* (2)
                      - **I think you missed my point.....** Teuila *08:57:32 03/18/01* (1)
                        - **Teu, thanks but I feel like JC is trying to act like one of my professors..**

Figure 8.1 Continued

seiOriana
14:38:36
03/18/01 (0)

■ **O.K. Will you do me a favor!** JC
21:07:51 03/17/01 (4)

　■ **Do yourself a favor..** seiOriana
　01:48:31 03/18/01 (3)

　　■ **Guess she did have some**
　　numbers! Teuila *08:59:07*
　　03/18/01 (0)

　　■ **10% of the 68% of**
　　minority imates
　　nationwide?????? JC
　　06:07:48 03/18/01 (1)

　　　■ **go do your research**
　　　and then come back
　　　and correct me ..k..
　　　seiOriana *14:24:19*
　　　03/18/01 (0)

■ **Be Careful Of the Statistics!!!** JC *09:17:04*
03/16/01 (1)

　■ **The growing numbers of Samoan inmates**
　aren't exaggerated either! seiOriana
　15:35:18 03/16/01 (0)

■ **Yup!** Teuila *09:05:11 03/16/01* (1)

　■ **yup..yuppy!** seiOriana *12:57:48 03/16/01* (0)

■ **Consider this...** seiOriana *22:08:04 03/15/01* (3)

　■ **How Can You Teach What You Don't Know** Sinafea *01:37:54*
　03/20/01 (2)

　　■ **It's called Common Sense!** seiOriana *03:19:37 03/20/01*
　　(1)

　　　■ **You are already a Role Model** Sinafea *18:58:23*
　　　03/20/01 (0)

■ **Consider the many variables when you make a judgement call!** JC
20:16:49 03/15/01 (0)

■ **You have fallen into the trap Sinafea.** Bevo *16:25:22 03/15/01* (3)

　■ **E fai atu, ae ete oso i le faalii?** Sinafea *01:07:05 03/20/01* (2)

　　■ **I heard that one too** Bevo *03:05:58 03/20/01* (1)

　　　■ **Youth Rally...i finally heard a "rap" that I**
　　　understood all the lyrics..... Sinafea *19:33:30*
　　　03/20/01 (0)

Post a Followup

```
Name     :
E-Mail   :
Subject  :
Comments:
```

Figure 8.1 Continued

```
┌─────────────────────────────────────────────┬─┐
│                                             │▲│
│                                             │ │
│                                             │ │
│                                             │ │
│                                             │▼│
└─────────────────────────────────────────────┴─┘
```

Optional Link URL: [_____]
Link Title: [_____]
Optional Image URL: [_____]

[Submit Follow Up]   [Reset]

[Follow Ups] [Post Followup] [Polynesian Cafe]

PolyCafe.com 1996 - 2000. All Rights Reserved.
PolyCafe

Note
This is a reproduction of the first view of a complete discussion thread from the Kamehameha Roundtable Discussion Forum. The underlined titles of each follow-up are hyperlinks to the message itself. Signatures are also hyperlinked to the email address given. Longer
and/or older threads are collapsed down to their initial post with total follow-ups. the figure
in brackets following the signature is the number of follow-ups (if any) to each particular
post. The time span of the thread is ascertained by the date of the last *direct* follow-up and its
subthread; March 12–20, 2001 in this case. The second follow-up to the initial post (Bevo,
03/13/01) had sixty follow-ups (the rest of the thread). Follow-ups to follow-ups wend their
own way across, down, and up the screen-page as they accrue. Quite a lot of information
about the tenor and direction of the thread (and significance if follow-ups are numerous
and/or lengthy) can be gleaned from this "meta-thread." Each follow-up has to be clicked
open in order to read the message. The abbreviation "n/t" means that the title-line is the
message in itself. With sixty-seven follow-ups and twelve posters, the follow-up average was
about five per participant/signature (see Table 3.1).

Other information can be gathered by looking at follow-ups to the
initial post (titles, signatures, diversions, amount of interest, and so on).
How the discussion really evolves is embedded in each follow-up, and then
in how it relates – substantively and relationally – to those proceeding and
succeeding it. Another sort of electronic embedding, apart from the "signature," is the hyperlinked email address. Again this can be an actual or a
"fake" one (meaning that with these forums, email addresses are not
linked onto their respective servers before being accepted). The forums'
moderators allow for pseudo-email addresses (if wished). Some of these
operate as subtexts – asides to the online conversation.[10]

There is also a difference to reading these online artifacts/archives for
research purposes as opposed to reading them for immediate participation (both of which I did, inevitably). For a start, if one wants to read
chronologically (by date and time of posting), one has to start at the *end*
(bottom of the screen) of the thread and work upwards. Even though the

longest threads build within one to three days, there are time lags and overlaps within this level. Some sharper responses or "misunderstandings" are part of these quirks.[11] *Within* a follow-up that develops into a sub-thread, chronological consistency demands a return to top-down reading. The higher the number of follow-ups, the higher amount of clicking, the more weaving in, out and through the thread/s.

When it comes to creating hard copies of these (meta-)threads, things change. Transferring these hyperlinked conversations to the static page is a switch in medium – and genre. In order to create consistent and comparable archives (which becomes important if one's research is happening with a time delay), I needed some sort of consistent way of archiving these texts for the purposes of later reference. This process changes the interactive, and more effervescent, qualities of the on-screen material into static, chronologically ordered, and thereby more "manageable" classical written words.[12] These offline logistics notwithstanding, while it may have seemed logical to reconstruct the threads here chronologically, or hierarchically vis-à-vis response rates or positions taken in the debates, these representative strategies would not have done them justice. Their "hermeneutic substance" (Fabian 1983: 89) is also constituted by the Pacific Island oratory and narrative modes. As Helu notes, these entail "forms of socialised speech and notional creativity which are sanctioned by the ages and social convention, namely oratory, repartee, humour, the art of story telling, and linguistic rivalry – in short, the whole range of the verbal arts" (1999b: 16). There are differences, though. For one, the online Kava Bowl does extend this "domain that is dominated by elders" (ibid.) to include women, commoners, and non-Tongans (see Chapters 4 and 5).

Concluding comments

On the World Wide Web and on the ground; the populations of the Kava Bowl and Kamehameha Roundtable have been moving in and between the two domains. As an *ad hoc* Internet practitioner and an "accidental" ethnographer of these traversals, I had to learn to follow suit. As I did, I started to see where and how even in the higher analytical altitudes of IR/IPE, the "'everyday' [should] be heard, not as background noise, but as foregrounded voice" (Highmore 2002: 171). By the same token, the

> everyday is not [as the Pacific Islands online show] simply reducible to the significations of material culture or the characteristics of national [diasporic/global] cultures. The everyday, in important and challenging ways (especially in the work of de Certeau), is about the density of cultural life, and its refusal to be contained by the parameters of what would pass for 'national life' [or Internet practices].
>
> (ibid.: 177)

In light of the above considerations, how much "editorial" intervention should there be, then, when reconstructing this sort of utterance and in another format? How often and where should flows be cut and pasted? Should typos be corrected or "bad" grammar helpfully corrected? As I stipulated earlier, apart from the occasional clarification, the texts have been reproduced here as they appeared on the screen. Their idioms, phonetics, idiosyncrasies in spelling, internal "emoticons," and various writing styles are part of the everyday patchwork of these online practices and need to be enjoyed as such. In terms of the hermeneutics of this sort of work, especially for fraught terms like "tradition" and "culture," "race," sexuality, the reader needs to decide where "traditional" Polynesian cultures and societies (be it Samoan, Tongan, or others) end and contemporary ones begin in terms of these interlocutions (Ortner 1997: 59 *passim*; di Leonardo 1991: 1 *passim*). To recall, participants make it very clear what their own opinions are and where the tensions and personal dilemmas lie. The number and length of samples also relate to the logistics of distilling and re-presenting long, interlocking discussions that are constituted by the relationships being built up and played out, their iterative and dialogic qualities. The threads demand lateral, "upside down," and "reversible" (Wilson 1999: 2) reading, both on- and off-screen (Figure 8.1).

The feminist and postcolonial critique underpinning this hermeneutic schematic means that there is no one, ultimate interpretation being posited here either. The texts and their broader conversations stand up in their own intellectual and literary right. Perhaps the sharpest part of this learning curve for me has been finding a balance between letting these rich, self-aware, and polyphonic cyberspatial textual practices appear on the printed page in ways that do their vibrancy and intra/intertextuality some kind of justice, and in a way that has them do more than be "functional." Their "irrepressibility" and fluidity persist, though. Therein lies their internal integrity, as opposed to their timeless authenticity or role in this authorial voice-over. Archives of the everyday such as these demand a

> different epistemology from that which defined the place of knowledge in terms of a position "proper" to itself and which measured the authority of the "subject of knowledge" by the elimination of everything concerning the speaker. In making this elimination explicit [scholarship][13] returns once again to the particularities of the commonplace, to the reciprocal effects which structure representations, and to the multiple pasts which determine the use of its techniques from within.
>
> (de Certeau 1986: 217–218)

While these threads, separately or in their respective thematic chapters, can be read as distinct episodes in the years of the KB and the KR forums, they are part of a much larger body of mutual and countermanding threads. In that respect, this third tale of the Internet is also immanent to the nascent postcolonial politics of representation traced by these every-day textual practices online.

9 Knowledge, power, and the Internet

In conclusion

Conceptual and cognitive domains

Circa 2004, global communications has become all but synonymous with a commercial Internet in both popular and highbrow discourses. The World Wide Web has become subservient to the "invisible hand" of "market forces"; cyberspace an electronic marketplace for massive financial transactions and forms of commodity exchange. In this version of events, only privatized, for-profit telecommunications ensure economic growth for *all* societies, being ostensibly cheaper, more efficient, more "global" than their predecessors, public telecommunications.[1] In IR/IPE, much ink has been spilt on the sociocultural and political downside of this technohistorical conjuncture. These misgivings have not been assuaged by the instantaneity, multilaterality, and organic communicative qualities of Internet-based interactions at the level of social relations and the tendency to accept commercially driven developments in ICTs at face value. Whether critical or celebratory, many analyses bespeak various degrees of technological – and historical – determinism nonetheless. Telegraph and telephone, the World Wide Web, microelectronic/cybernetic systems of every ilk are treated as if they are *external* agents of change in themselves rather than endogenous to historically situated sociocultural political and economic practices and processes. As Walter Benjamin noted, in an earlier period of technohistorical change, during

> long periods of history, the mode of human sense perception changes with humanity's mode of existence. The manner in which human sense perception is organised, the medium in which it is accomplished, is determined not only by nature but by historical circumstances as well.
>
> (1992: 216)

A critical constructivist approach to ICTs that privileges human (and political) agency need not preclude a critical stance to contemporary capitalist modes of production and accumulation (Fordist to post-Fordist and anything in between). Conversely, a critical (and therefore suspicious) view of how Internet technologies and other ICTs are being appropriated by corporate and political vested interests need not reduce all other uses and applications to these grand schemes for the "global information society." Positing that the Internet is indelibly drawn by multifarious and noncommercial uses and adaptations by nonelite, non-Western, and nonexpert practitioners reminds us that there is more than one version of events, and future, at stake. It is at these access points that the participant and/or observer becomes aware of gender power relations of race/ethnicity, class, status, language, climate, and geography in the everyday features of what are seemingly immutable hi-tech constellations: in the home, the workplace, in corporate boardrooms, government agencies, and technology policy-making and standard-setting moments (Mitter and Rowbotham 1995; Moyal 1992; Silverstone and Haddon 1996). For in

> much the same way that a standard alphabet is a cultural artefact as well as a utilitarian device, [formal and informal] standards for electronic communication networks are products of social, political and economic relationships as well as critical technical [and institutional] components.
>
> (Hawkins 1996: 157)

This study, too, has dealt with the historical contingencies and R&D trajectories laid out by strategic commercial interests looking to "tame" Internet communications under (late) capitalist modes of accumulation. This requires that everyday cyberspaces – and cyber*places* – of the Web be reconfigured and channeled along specific for-profit and "efficiency" lines.[2] The conceptual lexicon and reference points of critical theoretical frameworks have been found wanting, nonetheless, in this "age of *digital* reproduction" (Franklin 2002). Nonelite, noncorporate uses of Internet technologies do not simply reflect the priorities of capitalist modes of accumulation, they are not *ipso facto* simply functions of neoliberal political economic agendas and accompanying Global-Speak. Nor is the Internet/World Wide Web a ready-made mouthpiece for political spin or new(er) forms of surveillance and control. All manner of nonelite – grassroots-level – online practices are happening all the time in cyberspace.[3] Multiplex, less media-dramatic practices and adaptations of nonproprietary, "older" generations of hardware–software constellations are an integral part of "the" Internet (Quintas 1996; Rushkoff 2001).

These unsung online practices and their concomitant software-based (re)designs underscore the presence of a qualitatively new conceptual and cognitive domain for critical theory, research and political action. This domain also belongs to ordinary practitioners, from all walks of life, societies, and cultures, as they come and go online and offline. It is delimited, nonetheless, by powerful commercial and geopolitical interests that appoint for ICTs an implicit role in the inevitability of neoliberal global-ization as *techno*economic change. The term *Global-Speak* was applied in this study as a shorthand for the constitutive role that language (popular and scholarly discourses, political spin, advertising and marketing) has in all these debates and events. It is a point that is all too well understood by the advertising industry, whose ease of expression in this respect exempli-fies "the power relations implicit in language as part of language's status as an 'event,' and 'object which men produce, manipulate, use, transform, exchange, combine, decompose and recompose, and possibly destroy'" (Foucault quoted in Leonard 1990: 67). The privileging of these discur-sive dimensions from a critical (materialist) standpoint does not imply that the material inequalities created or exacerbated by neoliberal global-ization processes are incidental. Nonelite Internet practitioners are not engaging with ICTs under structurally equal or socioculturally equitable conditions, online or offline. The approach taken here follows Nancy Fraser in her goal to contribute to "the development of a more satisfactory way of linking structural (in the sense of objectivating) and interpretative approaches to the study of societies" (Fraser 1987: note 34). This requires an intelligent engagement with the

> extent and importance of rearrangements in worldwide social rela-tions tied to science and technology [and the concomitant] funda-mental changes in the nature of class, race, and gender in an emerging system of world order.... [There has been a] movement from an organic, industrial society to a polymorphous, information system ... from the comfortable old hierarchical dominations to the scary new networks.
>
> (Haraway 1990: 203)

Such movements are not inevitable, technologically determined. They are contestable. The technologically determinist assumptions that hold sway in even critical accounts of these "rearrangements" still do not adequately engage with how "information technologies are producing not only won-derful high-value-added products, [but] also confuse our deepest ontolog-ical and epistemological beliefs" (Palan 1996: 21). Hence the need for "thicker" descriptions and conceptualizations of technology in order to account for how

> values, preferences and language structure historically embedded into the word "technology" are of fundamental importance. It is therefore not appropriate to seek a universal definition, as any such definition would be arbitrary. We should rather identify the broad contours of meaning and practice within specific and concrete historical struc-tures.
>
> (Talalay *et al.* 1997: 6)

Given the formative power of the imagings used in the marketing of everyday communication (namely, social relations) as a "global" commodity, the political and economic ante is being continually upped as the physical architectures and experiential terrains of the Internet/World Wide Web become increasingly cherished in hi-tech consumer societies. Critical IR/IPE cannot afford to leave it to vested business and neoconservative ideological interests to set the terms for what constitutes intellectual, technical, or political expertise in this domain. "If we [critical scholars] are to change the world, we have to change ourselves as well as the social structures that both produce and are produced by those selves. We cannot change either without changing how we think" (Peterson and Runyan 1999: 48). In the next section, I will open a number of the "black boxes" that have characterized many IR/IPE discussions since the World Wide Web became a recognizable element in everyday and political economic life.

Five "black boxes"

The current conceptual repertoire for critiquing ICTs, and the Internet in particular, uses the "container terms" – the black boxes – of the disciplinary canon: nation-state, civil society, democracy, private and public spheres of action, modernization–development–progress, domestic vis-à-vis international affairs, and so on.[4]

Box 1: the Internet is a function of capitalism

The assumption that the Internet is a function of capitalism is still prevalent among critiques of neoliberal economic restructuring that assume Internet technologies to be a tool, if not a function, of (global) capitalism. More precise inquiries into whether, where, and how the Internet creates and facilitates new opportunities for the disenfranchised on the one hand, or deepens established social, economic divisions on the other, tend to suffer in the process. There are theoretical implications in accepting that there are indeed substantive new(er) inter/subjectivities, spaces, and practices occurring through and on the Internet. Lifting the lid of this black box in which ICTs, "late" capitalism, and "postmodernity" are conflated shows how informal or alternative political and economic interactions online are effectively reduced to functions of the structural power of capital. Those who are the practitioners, the users, and interlocutors become mere passive onlookers to the power struggles of greater forces. Agency, change, and protest are written out of the equation.

Apocalyptic forecasts about the sociopolitical impact of Internet technologies for "representative democracy," "political legitimacy," and "governance" overlook two methodological premises of any critical research approach. The first is that the "construction must always bring the concept to bear on the material and reshape it *in contact with the latter*" (Adorno 1976: 69; my emphasis). The second is the role of reflexivity in developing sound *praxis* (Leonard 1990; Franklin 2003b). The need to maintain a robust and nuanced critical stance toward the ongoing maneuvers of capitalist priorities notwithstanding, engaging with online social relations *per se*, or their interaction with the "materiality" of offline ones, requires some new heuristics, terminology, and modes of empirical or theoretical inquiry, taking a closer and more long-term look at what is actually going on – being said and produced – in everyday cyberspaces. This demands a more adventurous approach, I would argue. It is no longer methodologically possible when studying any aspect of contemporary ICTs to keep positing a conception of "reality" that is to be kept strictly apart from "imagination and myth" (Palan 1996: 21). Moreover, it is politically untenable in that it would mean allowing neoliberals' Global-Speak and their political allies to keep the edge they currently have on analyzing, selling, and thereby controlling key representations of "the" future.

By "adventurous", I am also referring to the potential conceptual frameworks and terminology that can be employed. Just as IR/IPE "Third Debate" theorists have done for established objects of study in the discipline, a "new grammar"[5] needs developing for studying online scenarios. In this sense, applying and using some of the vocabulary, the metaphors, and the imagery of ICTs, the Internet, cyberspace, and so forth in a reflexive and theoretically grounded way is also a political act; to bring implicit or apparent "tensions . . . to a head in a fruitful manner" (Adorno 1976: 70). A creative application of new and established methods or heuristics would facilitate more socioculturally sensitive and theoretically nuanced understandings of online inter/subjectivity and online–offline gender power relations. These have an impact on lived lives, consciousness, and behaviors.

Box 2: Internet communications are antisocial

The idea that Internet communications are antisocial is still a prevalent take on the perceived quality of such communication. Being online creates hermetic interactions and even personality disorders; it creates socially inept and uninterested young people. Reading and writing skills are seen to be compromised (which is odd, seeing as much Internet-based communicating is still mainly text based and so presupposes literacy), ability to concentrate affected (again odd, given the very intense concentration evidenced in computer work), and so on. Arguments such as these were raised with the advent of television and, further back, of "moving pictures" (see Lacey 2000). Although research is producing clear counterevidence of late (Miller and Dunn 2000), the continuing polarized stances taken around the good or bad social impacts of online communication beg an important question: are computer-mediated interactions qualitatively different from other generations of technologically mediated communication (Stallabras 1995; Standage 1998; Thompson 1995)? If cyberspatial practices can still be characterized by their disembodied, impermanent, speedy, and intertextual properties, are their ramifications for "traditional" communicative hierarchies *necessarily* negative?

How this question is addressed is bound up with normative assumptions and assessments about what is/is not "good" communication, "good" standards of reading, writing, speech, and so on. These in turn have ethnic, gendered, and class permutations. The interactions permitted and blossoming on the World Wide Web confront head-on these sorts of latent hierarchies about "good breeding," education, and the right to speak. Non-Western communities are no exceptions here, as their own establishments – online and offline – respond to perceived challenges to communicative rituals and hierarchies. Communication *tout court* does not work in a monistic sense; it is not a tangible "thing" to be tabulated and cataloged. Rather, it is a "means by which people create their identity. It underlies our sense of community, our sense of belonging and our sense of difference. As patterns of communications change, so do communities with which we identify" (Buckley 2000: 180–181). Second, all communicative forms and rituals, artifacts, and sundry practices emerge and become established through use, enactment, and repetition. How they emerge and for whom require a sensitivity for the psychodynamic, emotional, and symbolic levels at work in any communicative conventions and their respective reproduction through mass/multimedia. And likewise for the multidimensional gendered, ethnic–racial, and class permutations of the same. The multifarious meanings and practices that constitute "communication" within and between cultures, societies, polities are being merged – consciously and deliberately – with commodified information exchange and its underlying profit-maximizing ethos. This representation of the Internet as a capitalist prerogative and mouthpiece, however, is indeed hostile to a host of (online and offline) communicative practices and inter/subjectivities that do not conform to this sort of ethos.

There is another, more political issue at stake. After having resisted (more or less) the poststructural "linguistic turn" in theory and political challenges to the transcendent political integrity of the he-subject, materialist approaches are now confronted with a new (cyber)world of disembodied, (multi)lateral and instantaneous forms of interaction and political organization (Deibert 2000a, b; van Aelst and Walgrave 2002; Rodgers 2003). The communicative and cross-border efficacies of email for clandestine, overt activism and organization are bringing the experiential aspects of once academic "post-structuralism, deconstruction and post-modernity syndromes," as Palan sardonically notes (1996: 21), more to the fore. The prevalence of ICT-based symbolic worlds and techniques in popular science fiction (Haraway 1990), art (Cubitt 1998), and the music industry (May 2000; Franklin 2005) simply attests to the embedding of the digital into popular – and, more reluctantly, political – cultures. There are cumulative changes accruing in scholarly communicative practices as well. Internet technologies are an avoidable part of everyday life in research and educational institutions, and the various practices that develop are co-constructing (inter)disciplinary and epistemological demarcation lines accordingly. As artifacts, systems of forms of knowledge, ICTs do not in themselves cause these developments. Corporate and governmental investment in R&D trajectories are informed and rationalized by the mood of the time, and the technological outcomes – inevitabilities – thereof as well.[6] In light of the power struggles around the ownership and control of the Internet, the contending "representation[s] of space" (Harvey 1990: 219) both reflect and inform the gendered, ethnic, class permutations of this new domain.

Box 3: technology is a thing

For IR/IPE frameworks *per se* and research into ICTs especially, this box is one of the hardest to prise, and keep open, especially in terms of how the

> array of diverse idiosyncratic reactions to "technology" indicates the multiply different ways in which technology can be experienced, even by the same individual. To the extent that this is a general phenomenon, it suggests that . . . our analytic perspective should be attuned to the shifting and ambiguous relationships that typify common apprehensions of new technologies.
>
> (Woolgar 2000: 170)

To reiterate, even as technologies are constituted by immaterial properties such as knowledge power and gender power hierarchies, they still have material substance. Artifacts such as (cellular) telephones, PCs, palmtops, TVs, and so forth are material things in that sense; the transmission networks, businesses, and governments that own and control them embody huge long-term political and economic (dis)investments and R&D trajectories that go with changing relationships of ownership and control. When technologies become reified, disengaged from their socioeconomic and political nexus, their specific gender power relations become mystified, hidden from view. The upshot is that both the technological artifacts and their respective uses and social and historical contexts become fungible. When all these hail from Western, industrialized histories, uses, and contexts, the one version of the story can get airplay. Other uses and social and historical contexts are shouted down.

While the above picture is painted rather starkly, the point is that theory and research need to recognize the political implications (contestability) of how the Internet is both construed in itself and then (re)articulated vis-à-vis on-the-ground "realities." For example, with the advent of ICTs, hardware (material things) and software (forms of elastic and malleable knowledge) not only are inseparable from the operation and constitution of latter-day communications but also have become integral to contemporary understandings of changes in world order. The multifarious hardware and software elements and respective power know-ledge relations of expertise and then uses are both distinct from one another and mutually dependent.[7] Bearing these tensions in mind ensures that the immanent power struggles over the designated worth or efficacy of ICT R&D trajectories that are occurring on and behind the computer screen do not drop out of sight.

Exchanging an instrumentalist definition of technology-as-things for a more interpretative and culturally sensitive one does not automatically solve the problem of how to treat (relatively) new ICTs *at the point at which they are still forming*. This underlines the dilemma of how the normative separations between material and symbolic, the real and the virtual, can no longer be so easily maintained with the emergence of this new domain. It collides head-on with Enlightenment thought and its scientific progeny. This is encapsulated in literature that posits the Internet as a historical trope for "exit modernity" and "enter post/late-modernity." All that is digital, unfurling online, is of a lower ontological order. Internet-based inter/subjectivities, or the ability to experiment with the mind–body distinction, are seen as inherently threatening. When they intersect with non-Western critiques of these attributes of Western – colonialist – inter/subjectivity, the debate becomes even more muddied. This is where the postcolonial turn and the practice of everyday life online intersect in their challenges to these rigidities.

The cutting edge of ICTs research, in biotechnology and strategic defense systems, has already largely dispensed with the hierarchical niceties of maintaining a tidy distinction between the material – physical – realm of agency and the virtual – digitalized – realms of possible action. A critical politics needs to move on from bemoaning the passing of Fordist capital–labour relationships, pre-Cubist art forms, and the "comfortable old" theoretical hierarchies of public/private, masculine/feminine. Williamson's point still holds true:

> as the subtlety of capitalism's ideological processes increases, so does the need for subtlety in our understanding of them. We cannot afford to let any tool that might be useful slip through our hands. This is not being 'eclectic' but being practical.
>
> (1978: 10)

In short, theoretical focal points that continue to develop more sophistic-ated notions of "technology" and less unitary and Eurocentric understand-ings of society, politics, and questions around culture are needed in order to address the gender power and historical specificities of online communicative practices more fully. This readdressing of technology *tout court* entails a political stance in a discursive terrain where the science and technology story is dominated by the Western one of progress. Not only are other sociocultural practices at stake in the continued codification of (a certain sort of) English as a technologically mediated lingua franca, but so also are other (potential) R&D trajectories for ICTs. At the same time, the emancipatory possibilities from linguistic and epistemological straitjackets that are proffered by online interactions are in the making. Even from the traditional state-centered perspective of (neo)realist IR/IPE paradigms, the role of policy makers and investment decisions in infrastructure, education, and affordable and user-friendly access is also a rich opportunity for critical theorizing and action. Another potential area is in terms of changes to the lines drawn between the public/private and personal private domains. A reexamination of how technology and technological change are conceptualized has ramifications for how political and economic alternatives are posited, by and for whom.

Box 4: whose Internet is it anyway?

The rhetorical question "Whose Internet is it anyway?" begs another one. What has a critical approach to ICTs got to say to those individuals, groups, countries, and regions that regard and experience access to the Internet as an opportunity to escape from isolation, exclusion, and preordained sex–gender roles and/or racialized hierarchies? Addressing these questions boils down to what entails contemporary critical theory and political praxis in light of emergent online practices. Low and high art and cultural expression can be found online these days. Critical IR/IPE needs to develop more urgently appropriate "grammars" and practical responses to the inroads of commercialized and military-industrial interests in the Internet. This is easier said than done. What is at stake is some of the more sacred assumptions about whose subjectivity, whose meaning and institutions of the "political," and whose empowerment are undergoing a sea change – or not. Second, treating technology as an endogenous, a historical and contextual element of the inter/national (that is, global), both theory and research need a greater sense of multidimensionality, cultural and historical nuance, and reciprocity. The new domain of everyday nonelite online practices can provide new springboards for research, more focused and trenchant targets for critique, and new ways for theorizing and a coherent, accessible politics in the Information Age (see May 2003). For this reason alone, it is important to deal with one more emergent black box.

Box 5: the "digital divide"

The term "digital divide" refers to increasing concern about the gap between those with Internet access and those without. The issue revolves around what to do with those four-fifths of the inhabitants of the planet who do not have a telephone, let alone a computer or access to an Internet connection and who do not have these things high on their list of priorities. From the point of view of this research, dealing as it does with non-Western peoples and their diasporas, the role of (any) technologies in (any) notion of "development" has a history of its own. This also encompasses assumptions about "progress" and, even more, assumptions about all three being a priori the privilege of the industrial revolution and its champions. At this point, the ICTs are locked into a Euro-historical playback loop. All societies must get online or suffer the consequences of not being part of the global market. The "right not (to have) to communicate" is denied. At the same time, the rights and wrongs of ICTs remain firmly within Western discourses and experience. Other sorts of uses, potential designs, and problems are denied as well. Moreover, these discourses absent current and potential applications for resistance and political struggle through, and in, this emerging domain by men and women from "pre-Internet" societies. At the same time, the question that goes begging is where the future for any "emancipatory" politics lies as the "basic right" of telephone connectivity and its respectively assumed importance for economic development and more equitable forms of democracy becomes defined, and confined, as the brave new world of global capitalism.

The emergent digital divide has various shades and hues. It is not defined purely by the absence or presence of Internet connections (see Table 2.1, p. 26). It exists between the high-technology-dependent EU vis-à-vis the United States. It exists within urban centers and between city and country. It is most striking between "developed" political economies and continents and those that are not, such as sub-Saharan Africa, small island states, and parts of Latin America. It reproduces the long-standing one between rich and poor worlds, former colonizers and their former colonies, between industrialized and nonindustrialized societies. But it is not monolithic, nor is it evenly distributed. Closing the divide cannot be done in a culturally universalistic way either, for how and what constitutes it is a sociocultural and political economic question as much as it is a technical and representational one. For some, it is a question of what, if any equipment; for others, the degree and capacity of transmission networks; for others, relative skill and access to computers, cables, and software that are mutually compatible and/or related to actual needs and social fabrics (Kami 2001: interview). Sometimes it is cultural content that divides, sometimes climate, sometimes social and economic infrastructures. And for others it is all or none of the above. Like the (in)famous Coca-Cola bottle that fell from the sky at the feet of a Kalahari bushman in Jamie Uyl's film *The Gods Must Be Crazy*, shifts in gender power relations online and/or offline are not a priori dictated by technological "things" alone. What is done with the digital divide and which sociocultural or historical contexts give rise to it is more the point.

In conclusion

> In social terms, what has changed are the general conditions of representation and self-representation. Many native Pacific Islanders, like other indigenous peoples, are engaged in reclaiming lands, cultural knowledge and political sovereignty. In doing so they have also engaged in representing themselves, both for themselves and for the general public. This is an activity that was previously monopolised by experts.
>
> (Friedman 1998: 39)

> We as Pacific islanders are at the verge of a New era, and it is through sites like the Kavabowl that we not only get an insight of what others think, but what our own understanding[s] of the region we live in are. By knowing clearly who we are in the world, we are empowered to stand up to any group with the power to say "We are Pacific islanders and we have a place in this world no matter how small."
>
> ('Alopi Sione Latukefu, KB, 09/23/96)

The two quotations above (one based on the representational politics of seemingly conflicting oral historical accounts of the death of Captain Cook in Hawaii and the other from the very early days of the Pacific Forum online) encapsulate the crosscutting sociocultural, technological, and geostrategic concerns being faced by the South Pacific Islands and their diasporic communities. The political-economic and emotional-psychological aspects of these facets of the *oppression du présent* are aired and reexamined in these Internet forums. Protagonists in the ensuing debates are reassured, admonished, and empowered accordingly. What I have been looking at most closely is how these (cyber)spatial practices – online literary genres and speech patterns, the underlying moral economies of rules and behavioral norms and their respective gender power hierarchies – actually operate in these (cyber)spaces and places.

As I said at the outset, this study has been the tale of two Internets; of two visions of the future. Despite the tendency (and ability) of the commercial, neoliberal tale of the Internet to hog the limelight, another tale of ordinary and/or "non-Western" Internet users and uses has a formative part to play in how, for whom, and by whom (future) ICTs are represented, researched, and designed and then put in place. This is borne out by the *"combinatoires d'opérations"* ("systems of operational combination" – de

Certeau 1984: xi/1980a: 10) created by these practitioners and their creative, polyphonic, multicolored, and resistant practices of everyday life – online and/or offline. At the same time, neoliberal political economic elites and Transnational Corporation (TNC) strategists started to focus on the World Wide Web in the mid-1990s. Corporate giants such as Microsoft "discovered" the commercial potential of the Internet as a mass market(ing) medium and have turned their significant economic and meaning-making resources to molding Internet technologies after their own image. Aided and abetted by the deregulation and market liberalization zeal of the OECD countries and an oft-quoted speech given by the then Vice President Al Gore at an ITU meeting in 1994, this reconstruction of the Internet/World Wide Web as a tool and facilitator of "global market forces" has been swift. In conjunction with the visual representational power of advertising during this period, there were strategic maneuverings and technical decisions made "behind the screens" as corporations such as Microsoft and Intel, IBM and Macintosh, Oracle and Cisco Systems began to cash in on the *popular* appeal of Internet technologies such as the Web and email.

Several conclusions can be drawn in light of these offline–online strategies and the practices of everyday life reconstructed in this study – in substantive terms and for theory and research. First, the substantive aspects. These particular practitioners have been (re)articulating aspects of everyday life for postcolonial Pacific Island diasporas from the inside out, the outside in, and from more than a few permutations of in-between. This feature frame the reconstructions of Chapter 4, which deals with the cross-cutting social pressures of various understandings of sex–gender roles for women in Samoan and Tongan societies – in and of themselves, but also when transcribed to Western ones. In the process, the everyday intimacies and intricacies of inter/subjectivity get "outed" in the (still) open communicative spaces available on these websites. For these women, and men, querying received notions of Samoan/Tongan – and Western/European – constructions of femininity and masculinity, all sorts of intimate and public issues are worked at, and worked through. This atmosphere of conviviality and mutual support becomes more fraught, though, when such queries move into the political domain. The reconstructions of Chapter 5 show the contours and nuances of an intense and ongoing debate about the integrity and vitality of Tongan sociocultural and political institutions vis-à-vis (neo)liberal renditions of democratic "good governance" and "pro-democracy" challenges to the (male and aristocratic) status quo in Tonga itself. Despite the "localized" specifics, this political debate throws into relief a host of different assumptions about the similarities and differences between non-Western, postcolonial democracies and those of their former colonizers. Neither side gets off lightly in these heated debates, which have also brought these Internet groups' leaders into direct confrontation at times with the powers that be on the ground. Multiplex meanings and experiences of postcolonial everyday life are thrown out for debate *in order to* challenge presuppositions, from both within and outside their respective cultural and historical locations. Chapter 6 shows how these issues get (re)articulated in the context of self/group identity formation and the intra/intercultural tensions of everyday embodiments – of skin color, racial discrimination, and changing sociocultural mores. Here, diasporic and "mixed blood" participants unpack the meaning of "race," the meaning of *Fa'a Samoa* and *anga fakatonga*, and the fluidity of their constituent cultural practices. In so doing, they articulate the operations of multiplex identifications that entail consciously inclusive understandings of what being "Polynesian," "American," "a New Zealander," "Australian" – means; the empowering dimension to having various roots in the South Pacific, Utah, southern California, or suburbs such as Carlton, Los Angeles, or Otara, Auckland.

This everyday Internet in the making meshes with and facilitates an emergent sense of (self)representation for younger generations of the postcolonial South Pacific. These noncommercial online traversals straddle, intersect with, and ultimately challenge the strategic plans and image making of the Global-Speak of neoliberal and corporate vested interests. They do so by virtue of these nonelite, everyday uses of these technologies and their reliance on the commitment of like-minded people to organize and moderate their online comings and goings and shape these websites. They also do so out of allegiance to *multiplex* forms of political economic and sociocultural expression and forms of translocality that do not preclude a sense of belonging to several places, cultures, nation-states all at once. These practitioners persistently exercise and (re)negotiate their own sense of agency, their own sense of sociocultural and historical change, their own interlacing sense of self and community – *together.* They use Internet technologies enthusiastically, and open up their own (cyber)spaces there by poaching ("*braconner*") from the range of everyday sociocultural practices and behavioral norms presented to them by virtue of diasporic and postcolonial living conditions. Using these various reference points, they strive to counter ingrained and oppressive racial stereotypes about Pacific Islanders on the ground. Anyone entering these forums without preconceptions of Pacific Island societies would glean quite a different perspective than those (of us) brought up with stereotypes of contemporary Pacific Island (diasporic) communities (see Chapters 6 and 7). This person would also note rules of online comportment that are at once practical and organizational, but also soaked with a composite morality: Christian ethics, individual responsibility for one's own destiny, and community/extended family obligations. Chapter 7 looks at the online operations of these norms, and the moral economies that inform them, as they are negotiated by moderators and constituencies alike over the years.

Third, while I have argued that this latter Internet persists despite the downward pressure and financial squeeze of powerful vested interests, the outcomes of these two tales are neither unitary nor foreclosed. They entail *contending* uses, goals, and technological specifications that are in constant flux, under negotiation, and unevenly distributed. The more powerful and well-heeled practitioners seek to control and steer how the Internet technologies are designed, perceived, and experienced. In turn, they privilege whatever "market sectors" they may have in mind.[8] There is a need to rethink some of the underlying issues that are at stake. This means generating more public and scholarly debate about the "technological futures" of ICTs, about their sociocultural and political economic implications. I have argued that no technology stands above and beyond those who design and control it. In that respect, "we" get the Internet "we" deserve. Critical social constructivist, feminist, and postcolonial approaches to ICTs in general, and the Internet/World Wide Web in particular, would focus on the class/status, race/ethnicity, and sex/gender exactitudes and nuances of online–offline (re)articulations of structural power. They would aim to examine inner and outer tensions of these everyday tactical and strategic operations, and demystify assumptions about sex/gender, race/ethnicity, and class/status in the process. They would all want to underscore how the tale of nonelite and "non-Western" practices of everyday life online is just as cogent, just as vibrant, and just as crucial to debates about the present and future of ICTs in any "new world order." In postcolonial societies and their diasporic communities, the political, economic, and sociocultural stakes are even higher as these communicative, noncommercial uses show old and new(er) practices of everyday life in transition. Their online/offline intersections indicate that they, too, are in contention for the future look and layout of the Internet/World Wide Web, and their respective sociocultural locations. There are contending politics of representation at work, contending exchanges of meanings and imagings which intersect with and overlap online–offline struggles for ownership and control of the spaces and rights to speak, and be in cyberspace. These struggles are embedded in lived lives offline and their various political economic and sociocultural specificities.

Epistemological considerations

There are three broad epistemological considerations of this study vis-à-vis critical IR/IPE and its black-boxed ambivalences towards the Internet, as a domain for both critical research and/or political engagement. First is the way the material being produced online and its broader context of sociocultural and political economic changes constitute certain sorts of inter/intracultural *gender power relations*. This analytical dyad, following Bordo (1990: 152), has posited an understanding of gender that is more than "adding women and stirring" (Whitworth 1994) or positing a synonym for "woman" (see Carver 1998a: 206 *passim*; 1998b). Power relations are practiced not along monolithic categories such as "race," "sex," "class," but through and despite them in a complex and changing set of tensions. When reading online texts by fe/male posters (as and when indicated by their signatures and other signs), this dyad also recalls how "gender" is also "a discursive field; that is, it is about language, especially writing and other forms of signification ... a field of meanings" (Haraway 1992: 289). Hence, positing gender and power as a relational dyad is to imply multiplex and multisited power relations as well (Ling 2002: 145 *passim*).

This gives rise to the second consideration, which is both technical and methodological. These online (cyber)spatial practices are characterized by their intertextuality, laterality, multivocality, and fluidity. These are carried through the techniques and facility of *hyperlinked* textual practices and production. In cyberspatial terms, this is what allows for the reembodiment and reinscription of lived lives in online forms and thereby the articulation of online–offline relationships, situations, and life stories. The manifest content of the threads traces quite tangible Pacific traversals in cyberspace – as electrophysical comings and goings, and as discursive inter/subjective events, encounters, and representations. The specific communicative hierarchies that constitute the online moral economies of these forums and their participants are woven through the content and contours of the discussions. These gender power relations are as "real as it gets" (Kolko *et al.* 2000: 4). So, while I am arguing that these traversals constitute a different sort and scale of the practice of everyday life online from the point of view of non-Western and relatively disadvantaged groups, the actual content also deals with offline lived lives. It is not an either–or between real lives and virtual ones, but rather, as I have argued, a new cognitive and experiential domain.

In methodological terms, the online texts reconstructed here do not constitute a full ethnography of an online community *per se*. Neither are they an exhaustive reconstruction of the thousands of discussions that have occurred throughout the life of these discussion forums, let alone other interconnected websites. Nor have I plotted a one-to-one cause-and-effect relationship between the discussions and events occurring beyond or alongside them (at best these were alluded to by myself or when made explicit by participants). I argued that the empirical–theoretical import of these latter-day Pacific traversals has to be seen in terms of their (online) longevity, substantive content, and, moreover, recurrence of politically and socially pertinent content, the high levels of participation in the thematic categories that emerged over time, and the articulated awareness of wider Pacific Island communities and "global" issues that permeate these discussions.

More importantly, a key operational indicator for locating and assessing current (and potential) significance in online scenarios is the way in which the Internet has been, by definition, open and accessible to all-comers (this is the *sine qua non* of World Wide Web software, whatever its eventual limitations). This premise is underscored by the Pacific Forum and Polycafe discussion forums, as they do not restrict access, link any live chat passwords to financial membership, or use other forms of commercially based exclusion. Together with the use of relatively few and/or open-ended forms of anonymity, these factors combine to show that these interactions are occurring in a nascent electronically mediated "public space," which under certain material conditions (of access, computer literacy, and financial means) can be accessed and entered by anyone from anywhere. This publicness straddles traditional territorial, sociocultural, political-economic – and physical – divides. Its persistence and richness simply underscore the way such multivocality and inclusive onlineness is in danger of being squeezed out by neoliberal, undemocratic political and economic vested interests.

These decisions *in situ* have permitted communicative spaces and places in cyberspace. Moreover, these online traversals become archival records and traces of everyday life, socializing, relationships, and cultural artifacts in their own right as these participants use the Internet/World Wide Web to create and "present a place as they wish" (Kami 2001: interview). In other words, these online traversals have material import as well as symbolic substance. Both come in electronic forms and formats, and digital and physical architectures, and enable on-screen imagings, textual production, hyperlinks, and off-screen movements and digitalized "footprints." These can be read, traced, and located in various degrees of depth and attention to detail. The content of the on-screen messages in these cases can be opened, digested, seen in relation to those with whom they are interacting, following up. Moreover, the authorship as both identifiable subjects – people – and written standpoints – statements – can be ascertained and located in terms of their own variegated "textual surfaces," that of others, and/or previous interventions in earlier discussions. These practitioners operate at various levels of intimacy, political awareness, and mutual identification, recognition, or confrontation. All these exchanges of meaning, political and personal renegotiations, personal accounts of experience, and geographic and socioeconomic (dis)location are the everyday "stuff" of life online in and of itself *and* as it pertains to lives lived offline. As such, these (cyber)spatial textual practices and movements are part and parcel of the "*couture*" between online and offline everyday life.

This brings me to a final point about how these analytical, interpretative connections were made. Namely: hermeneutically. What this entailed was the making of analytical and substantive connections between ostensibly disparate events and processes, illustrating them by way of concrete instances of ongoing interactions occurring in discussion forums, newsgroups, or live chat. The massive volumes of email and live chat interactions constitute as important a part of daily electronic interactions as do commercial transactions. This linking up of a bird's-eye research view to a worm's-eye experiential and inter/subjective view was achieved by way of a schematic that looked to integrate the interactions between researcher-as-subject and objects-of-research-as-subjects, and acknowledge some of the operations of gender power relations and knowledge-making where apposite.

This study is of interest to postcolonial critiques of Eurocentric practices of knowledge production because it has been about how postcolonial diasporas and their interlocutors "back in the islands" have been navigating and negotiating generically Western hi-tech technologies. In cyberspace, they have been able to work and talk through some of the major tensions of living as an ethnic/cultural minority, of having more than one locus for identification, of dealing with the old and the new, of building new(er) forms of community. The study is also of interest to debates about how to turn feminist/postcolonial critiques into appropriate forms of political and economic empowerment. For one, this study counters the foreboding tone of many commentaries about the empowerment potential of ICTs. This hermeneutic schema has allowed for the "description and interpretation of [a] process of appropriation" (Giard and Mayol 1980: 17; my translation) by Internet users who do not fit the well-to-do white (and still mostly male) Internet user/PC owner profile of market research and corporate advertising campaigns. Practitioners like Taholo Kami and Al Aiono, and their constituencies, are well aware of the empowerment potential of ICTs for countering some specific issues in Pacific island communities.

This is not to say that everything is "AOK," however. It is not to imply that Internet technologies will rectify the complex issues facing both diasporic communities and Pacific Island societies; that "things go better with Microsoft" (Franklin 2003a). But neither is this study prepared to accept the latest rhetoric that "there is no alternative" to neoliberal and corporate representations and designs for future habitation and navigation of cyberspace. Far from it. There are some immanent dangers. Commercial and (local and/or global) geostrategic interests can and do focus their attention on everyday Internet users if it suits them to do so. In one sense, the South Pacific Islands – like the Caribbean and Africa – are still too "insignificant" in terms of "market penetration" and population density (Taylor 2004). The problem, however, is that neoliberal macroeconomic policy makers in those Internet heartlands bordering this ocean can only see "development" and R&D in dogmatic free market terms. Political leaders in the Pacific Islands have to contend with this entrenched attitude vis-à-vis structural adjustment programs and conditions that come with foreign aid. The relatively low priority given to suitable development of ICTs, such as long-distance educational facilities, suitably resilient equipment for the salty, damp conditions of the islands, enhanced Internet-based medical and health services, and improved radio and satellite links, is still all too evident.[9] It is also a question of political and financial will on the part of the moneylenders. But this is the stuff of another research project. For now, this study hopes to have made the initial opening in terms of other ways in which ICTs can be thought about, designed, and eventually used, by examining the practice of everyday life online.

And the way these hectic, numerous, and open-ended discussions impinge upon IR/IPE theoretical and empirical priorities? Well, the "big story" of world politics, the arcane technical mysteries of ICTs *re*materialize (along with all their problematic gender power relations) at the intersection of multifarious lived lives, centuries-old physical and social traversals, and the tensions that go with these. Add a postcolonial – historical and critical – edge to these stories and they include pre/post/neocolonial mental and emotional histories and geographies, all of which find their expression in these cyberspaces. Abstract causal explanatory and prescriptive models become inhabited, reconfigured, and more precise. Broader and more specific gender power hierarchies become more delineated and thereby can be potentially addressed. Even as these online interactions are texts, a set of literary genres in themselves with their own aesthetic concerns and "scriptural economies," they also (re)articulate – and so trace – the lives of s/he/they who produced them and their various political-economic and sociocultural conditions *in relationship to one another.*

Postcolonial politics of representation: the Internet in us?

This brings me to some final observations on possible Internet – and postcolonial – futures in terms of how online and offline everyday communicative practices converge with and reconfigure *each other* in these forums.

The discussions that constitute these websites have evolved into not only spaces for personal expression and mutual support, but also challenges to old and new sociocultural and political pressures emanating from both their "original" and their diasporic cultural contexts. They reveal complex crosscutting everyday practices of peoples hailing from small island states in a "globalizing" and "digital" age, in that they also operate as a node for linking the online community with various levels of personal concern for lives offline. Their conversations entail both earnest and light-hearted communication about the intercultural and intracultural gender power relations of lived lives and how these impinge upon self/group identifications. They do so from the inside out (such as when intimate lives are shared in open cyberspaces) and the outside in (when tensions and misconceptions between at-home and diasporic communities come to the fore). These traversals are, at one and the same time, personal, geographical, sociocultural, and political-economic movements and exchanges of *meaning.* They bespeak both personal choice and circumstance, group pressures and group solidarity, broader dynamics of exclusion and isolation, success and achievement.

The substantive contours and nuances of the discussions, the (auto)bio-graphical accounts offered, the intra/intercultural conflicts that are (re)articulated, and the political, philosophical, and cultural positions taken as discussion threads unfurl show these participants "engaged in representing themselves, *both for themselves and the general public*" (Friedman 1998: 39; my emphasis). The Internet, at least in the ways in which it is (re)appropriated and used by these practitioners, is the central enabler of these postcolonial (re)presentations. The aforementioned goals are no small task either; the sense of unity and community that is evidenced in the vast majority of these debates (which arise from mutuality in this online context, as in any other) is far from being a given. It has to be worked at – practiced. The ways in which Tongan and Samoan particip-ants are interacting with each other on the Kava Bowl and/or the Kame-hameha Roundtable and the sense of "pan-Poly identity" (Morton, personal email 06/22/01) that has been emerging are not insignificant, given that "gangs of Tongans and Samoans are literally killing each other in real life" (ibid.).

In this sense, participants are very well aware of how these issues and the "onlineness" of these forums are interwoven. But they are also show an awareness of how these (cyber)spatial practices, and their constituent counterrepresentations, are not self-explanatory. They do not take the empowering abilities of these (cyber)spaces (to release the protagonists from preordained sex–gender roles and communicative hierarchies, for instance) for granted. The stresses and strains come from within and without. Some participants would attribute this to misuse and abuse of new(er) communicative possibilities (see Chapter 7). Others would put it down to neocolonial political and economic pressures being brought to bear on the Pacific Islands by the international community, and their proselytizing cultural and political values (see Chapters 5 and 6). Others, in turn, would reflect in passing on moves by political and economic vested interests to subdue, standardize, and so exploit the still freely avail-able "virtual machinery" (Quintas 1996) of the Internet. I would add that these strategic moves directly impinge upon the rich, polysemous tones of everyday life online as well. "Becoming Polynesian" entails dealing with all these tensions. In the last analysis,

> overcoming such rivalries [between Tonga and Samoa] has been necessary for people to gain that sense of being Polynesian. [There is] the appeal, particularly to young people, of a pan-ethnic, i.e. pan-Poly identity. Especially for those who don't feel quite comfortable in their specific group – e.g. are told they are not 'real' Tongans because they don't have the language or *anga fakatonga*. But of course this process of forming a pan-ethnic identity is also linked to real world necessities, such as having to work together in order to get funding directed to "Pacific Islanders" and more generally to be recognised by a

mainstream society that designates them as a pan-ethnic group. . . . So it is a partially a strategic move to gain access to resources, have problems addressed etc. This then overlaps with younger people's identification as pan-ethnic . . . for identity reasons.

(Morton, personal email 06/22/01)

These exchanges of meaning, which are also intended to empower, show quite different sorts of articulations of "globality," "community," economic well-being, democratic principles, identity – and of the Internet *tout court* – to those purveyed by corporate business and political-economic neoliberal representations of life online/cyberspace. Far from being scared off by this level of analytical and lived complexity, these forums' protagonists tackle it head-on. They do so while embracing the opportunities for personal and group empowerment offered by dedicated website moderators (who also double as diasporic/cyber community leaders and role models), moving through the various avenues of access and permissive communicative spaces that open up accordingly. A previously cited thread from the Kamehameha Roundtable encapsulates this online–offline interplay. In the initial post entitled *Samoan/Tongan conflict* which had thirty-two follow-ups, this participant asks:

Okay, just to entertain my knowledge. I wanted to know something. Many Tongans and Samoans (not all of course) have a hard time seeing eye to eye. I see both races duking it out all the time in the different msg [message] boards . . . I see it when we walk down the aisle of a mall and one of my cousins mad dog a group of samoans walking the opposite direction. My question is why? Yeah, I know that it dates back in the old days when Tonga and Samoa were at war, but what really happened? I've heard several different accounts. I've heard that the Tongans took control over parts of Samoa . . . I realize that Tonga and Samoa are both different countries, similar in many aspects can cause a rivalry, but why is that tension still there? What's the point of fighting your own brothers or your own sisters? I've seen over and over again the hatred many of my fellow Tongans have for Samoans. In fact I was one of them at one point.

(TonganRasta, KR, 06/06/01)

The large number of follow-ups, the historical facts and current events that get exchanged, positions taken and then reconsidered, allowances for those of others, and the constant moving between categorical declaration and quizzicality illustrate the longevity (old and new patrons are there) and the textual richness (perfect spelling and written verbalizations, abbreviations, colloquialisms, and so on) of these online forums. It also answers the question: why do these people bother, and for so long? They do so because these Internet forums provide translocal open (cyber)spaces in which to discuss issues that matter for *them*, in *their* every-day life, whether in the islands or living "overseas." These (cyber)spaces and places, and their many offshoots, are populated by living, writing, reading inhabitants who co-create and recreate everyday life off/online, providing it with its own inner dynamic. For many participants, these forums are gratifying in that they are not only nodes of emotional and psy-chological support, liberating and informative, but fun as well.

One last observation. When considering the actual relationship between these online/offline, inside-out/outside-in, inter/intracultural peregrina-tions have with the grandiose schemes of corporate capital and their stra-tegic partners in the OECD, NATO, the United Nations Security Council, one thing gets repeatedly overlooked. That is: "Polys" and their Pacific Island counterparts are instigating new meaning-makings that necessarily include new(er) ICTs, albeit of the sort that are appropriate for their needs. The implication of these practices for the equitable future possibilities of the Internet is analogous to Epeli Hau'ofa's influential argument about the power of countervailing representations of the South Pacific Ocean and the thousands of islands that constitute this sea. He argues that there

> is a world of difference between viewing the Pacific as "islands in a far sea" and as "a sea of islands".... [In precolonial days] boundaries were not imaginary lines in the ocean, but rather points of entry that were constantly negotiated and even contested. The sea was open to anyone who could navigate a way through.
>
> (1994: 152, 154)

The point Hau'ofa is making relates to long-standing forms of knowledge and networking, navigational expertise and traveling, practices of everyday life and intercultural communications that take place across – and despite – great physical distances.

> [M]uch ancient and indigenous expertise constitutes highly effective ways of dealing with systems characterised by openness, indetermi-nacy, multivariateness and unfathomable complexity.... [It] is in this context that we might rethink the resonance between sea faring and excursions in the electronic ether; sea and cyberspace viewed not as domains to be mastered or rendered transparent, or as frontiers to be pushed back by a linear advance, but as distinct fields of complexity capable of traversal and negotiation by sensitive operators.
>
> (Clark 1999: 14)

The "sensitive operators" of the interlinked, multiply traveled, and enthu-siastically populated websites of the Pacific Forum and Polynesian Cafe, along with those others that have sprung up in their wake, show how such expertise operates today and every day.

For Pacific Island online interactions and their practitioners, the Internet/World Wide Web can be likened to the "ocean in us" (Hau'ofa 1998). Like the South Pacific, cyberspace is not an empty "frontier" to be colonized, its inhabitants to be civilized and "guided," its "exotic" women "enjoyed" (Teaiwa 1999; Ling 2002). Everyday life online is not a priori external to offline lived lives, histories, institutions, and communicative rituals. These are mutually constituted by way of the new(er) sorts of traversals relationships permitted by and through Internet practices. Over time, these (re)create the (un)known horizons of any (postcolonial) society, be it global, online, or otherwise. This impinges directly on the gender power relations, with all their race/ethnic, class/status complexities, of who is – let alone who should be – deciding where the Internet/World Wide Web can – and does – facilitate equitable and empowering communicative (cyber)spaces and places. And for whom. The clarion call of the neoliberal dream is that all such nascent and vibrant public (cyber)spaces and everyday communicative practices necessarily be privat*ized, standard*ized, and, by extrapolation, flattened out and subdued. Moreover, it equates the latter processes (and the global, so-called free market that purportedly justifies this) to "democracy." I would say that is not the case at all, either in principle or in practice. The postcolonial politics of representation at stake in these new(er) communicative spaces and places of cyberspace recall Hau'ofa's ongoing challenge to (postcolonial) Pacific peoples:

> We are the sea, we are the ocean, we must wake up to this ancient truth and together use it to overturn all hegemonic views that aim ultimately to confine us again, physically and psychologically, in the tiny spaces that we have resisted accepting as out sole appointed places, and from which we have recently liberated ourselves. We must not allow anyone to belittle us again, and take away our freedom.
>
> (Hau'ofa 1994: 160)

Whether or not one agrees with this analogy or with the conclusions drawn from this research, or even cares about Internet communications, these traversals do underscore one thing. The multiplex and polyphonic practices of everyday life online are not beholden to, nor are they the property of, vested commercial interests.

Notes

1 Introduction

1 The Internet is now synonymous with the World Wide Web, even though there is a historical and technical distinction between the two. *Internet* is a generic term for computerized (tele)communications based on the principle of strategically distributed "servers" and Internet protocol software that enable computer-to-computer communication. This transmission and hardware–software architecture dates from the 1980s at least (Abbate 2001; Maresch and Rötzer 2001; Grassmuck 2002; Frederick 1993: 94; Kleinsteuber 1996). The *World Wide Web*, on the other hand, emerged in the 1990s as a constellation of *hyperlinking* software and user interfaces that made "surfing" this Internet much quicker and user-friendlier. Internet "browser" software based on the hyperlinking functionality has become the *sine qua non* of today's Internet/World Wide Web. I will refer to these particular developments as *Internet technologies* from now on. Both Internet and telephonic communications now occur through high-capacity digitalized and integrated telecommunications infrastructures (by way of submarine, satellite, and radio transmissions). Taken together, these all constitute the "Internet," although it is electronic mail (email) and various sorts of World Wide Web use that predominate by far. I will use the terms Internet/World Wide Web/Internet technologies variously, depending on which aspects are most pertinent at the time. These distinctions are often brought under the wider rubric of *information and communications technologies* (ICTs), which include (digitalized) telephony, bioengineering, genetically modified food technologies, GIS mapping technologies, computer-aided defense and offensive weaponry, multimedia entertainment, household appliances, and consumer electronics. An additional term, *cyberspace*, has a genealogy of its own since the emergence of the Internet/World Wide Web. In 1994, Rob Shields conceptualized cyberspace as "a network, linking interactants across space and time, not a 'thing' or a set of computers communicating autonomously without human actors. It is essential to foreground the human in the Net. This resets the Internet as a phenomenon of social and political interest, not just a bright technical toy for engineers" (1996: 8). A few years later, Tim Jordan put it this way: "Cyberspace can be called the virtual lands, with virtual lives and virtual societies ... [that] do not exist with the same physical reality that 'real' societies do.... The physical exists in cyberspace but it is reinvented" (1999: 1; see also Spiller 2002; Harasim 1994).

2 I follow Hall's conceptualization here: an "articulation is ... the form of the connection that can make a unity of two different elements, under certain

conditions. It is a linkage which is not necessary, determined, absolute and essential for all time" (cited in Grossberg 1996a: 141; also Slack 1996: 115). An articulation is also an utterance (narrative, autobiographical account, political polemic, satire, thoughts or feelings). The prefix indicates both the novel forms and the circumstances for these linkages in a cyberspatial context and the iterative qualities of such articulations.

3 See Woolgar (2000) for a range of essays on specific design features of Internet technologies from within science and technology studies (STS) approaches. Jordan (1999) provides an analysis of "cyberpower" with particular reference to the burgeoning lexicon of cyberspace from a sociological perspective and with an eye on theories of power – that of Foucault included. Thomas and Wyatt (1999) and Jones (1998) give histories of the Internet and a collection of Internet research methods respectively. Shields (1996), Harasim (1994), and Spiller (2002) provide good collections on theories of virtuality and early Internet communities, especially those of the US West Coast pioneering online groups and fantasy games. Hamelink (1995), Mattelart (1994), and Schiller (1999) offer historical materialist critiques of the capitalist and Cold War mentalities, and related historiographies of the concomitant international/world/global communications regulatory regimes underpinning or intersecting these specific developments. *Le Monde Diplomatique* has steadily published articles on ICTs and related issues since the 1990s (Manière de voir 1995, 1996b). Frederick (1993) gives a general overview of tele/communications and information technology from a more benign disposition. As for debates about the role of the US military in developing the early Internet, see Abbate (2001).

4 In its strictest definition, this is "a research technique for the objective, systematic and quantitative description of the manifest content of communication" (Berelson in van Zoonen, 1994: 69). The "content analysis" of this study moves beyond this definition in that it looks at the "latent meanings and associative conclusions ... [that include] the recognition of individual and culture-specific interpretations of media texts" (ibid., 73 *passim*). By *hermeneutic*, I am evoking an interpretative approach that privileges the role of self-aware interpretation as a methodological intervention by which to understand written texts. See Chapter 3.

5 Here, "neoliberal" denotes macroeconomic and political agendas based on monetarist economic theory (control of the money supply and inflation at the expense of employment, and deregulated direct investment and trade regimes). Market forces as opposed to government intervention in price and wage setting are seen as the *sine qua non* of "growth." Monetarist – neoliberal – orthodoxy has reigned supreme in Western societies since the 1980s. Neoliberal globalization is shorthand for both political and firm-level reorganizations that have recalibrated the agency of "capital–labour relationships and the role of the state, while furthering the asymmetrical interdependency of economic functions across national boundaries" (Castells and Henderson 1987: 1). Waters (2001) and Scholte (2000) provide two analyses of the term "globalization" as referring to both material processes and phenomenological shifts in political economic orders within and beyond nation-state borders. See also Marchand and Runyan (2000) and Peterson (2003).

6 By inter/subjectivity I am referring to what Robert Cox calls "the common understandings shared by the people embraced ... in respect to the relationships and purposes in which they are involved" (1987: 17). Cox then adds that this is "the [shared] mental picture ... in ideas of what is normal, expected behaviour and in how people arrange their lives with regard to work and income" (ibid.: 22).

7 Positing gender and power as a relational dyad connotes multiplex, ethnic/racialized/class, power relations as well (Bordo 1990; Hall 1996b; Ling 2002: 145 *passim*). See Ortner (1996) for an anthropological take on status/class and sex/gender; Haraway (1992a, 1997) and Carver (1998b) for theories of sex/gender; and Ashcroft *et al.* (1998) for postcolonial takes on race/ethnicity.

8 This term is a heuristic to designate, for the sake of argument, broad periods of political, economic, and cultural change and distributions of power in the history of the (European) Westphalian state system "in terms of the duality of [the] interstate system and world economy" (Cox 1987: 107). These periods include the rise of capitalist economies and the spread of colonial empires, and their accompanying liberal political and (neo)classical economic theories. The "new world order" is generally seen as beginning with the demise of the Soviet Union at the end of the 1980s and the reign of neoliberal economic and political ideologies in the OECD (the "West" for all intents and purposes from here on).

9 This facility has been built in by the sites' founders to allow for discretionary anonymity when socially or politically sensitive subjects are broached.

10 For the Samoan (and Los Angeles-based) Polynesian Cafe this has been estimated at about 85 percent (Aiono 1999: interview).

11 There have always been movements into and out from the Pacific Islands. In the South Pacific postcolonial historical context, experiences of diaspora have their own sociocultural and ethnic particularities. For example, one of my sisters and I were born in Western Samoa and had a Samoan "nanny" (Tifa) and "house-boy" (Mulu) who, for me at least, formed an important part of early childhood. We have memories framed by home movies, photographs, artifacts, visits, weddings and funerals, my father's working career in Fiji, and his ongoing friendships in the Samoan/Pacific Island communities in New Zealand. My own early working life was based in predominantly Maori and Pacific island environments, inner-city areas, and the city's southern suburbs. And my political education (like that of many of my generation) was marked by the antiapartheid protests and growing political influence of indigenous land-reform and sovereignty movements in New Zealand and beyond during the 1980s. My parents remain staunchly loyal to the British Commonwealth and its Queen as descendants of the English, Irish, Welsh, and Scottish "diasporas" that colonized parts of the South Pacific in the nineteenth and early twentieth centuries.

12 In Nuku'alofa, Tonga, about 60 percent of the public-accessed uses (at the Royal Institute of Science) are said to be for study, emailing, and live online chat (Kaitapu 1999: interview). Many users use the Kava Bowl's live chat facility to contact friends and family overseas (Kami 2001: interview).

13 Studies of the "serious" import and substance of Internet websites and communities, beyond the effects of computer games and fantasies (see Ludlow 1996; Jones 1999; Harasim 1994) and their commercial potential or sociocultural impacts, are relatively sparse in the political sciences, beyond recent ones on digital democracy and impacts of new(er) ICTs on the "public sphere" (Loader 1998; Hague and Loader 1999; Toulouse and Luke 1998; Wilhelm 2000). Comor (1994), McChesney *et al.* (1998), Castells (1996, 1997, 1998), May (2002), and Peterson (2003) bring various nuances to bear from within IR/IPE (post)structuralist debates.

14 Sandra Harding (1998b) uses the term "post-Kuhnian," which is more precise in many ways although less cogent in IR/IPE literature. Be that as it may, mainstream social sciences draw heavily on a reified handling of Karl Popper's

important critique of the "scientific logic" of inductive modes of inquiry. This reification leads to dogmatic (and value-laden) divisions between approaches that are designated as empirical/quantitative – "objective" – research methods and interpretative/qualitative approaches.

15 In IR/IPE, this mainstream includes liberal pluralist, (neo)realist, and globalist (namely, Marxian) explanatory models of the Westphalian "state system" and/or capitalist "world economy/world system." See Viotti and Kauppi (1999) for the main delineations between these approaches. Burchill *et al.* (2001) provide strong essays from the point of view of Frankfurt School-influenced "critical international relations theory," while Palan (2000) examines this constructivist shift, as it is read in more recent IR/IPE theories, in order to posit the study of the "global political economy." Marchand and Runyan (2000) provide a feminist IPE-focused anthology on "global restructuring." Ling (2002) has a good summary of how both these traditions relate to constructivist, feminist, neo-Gramscian, and postcolonial theoretical concerns – and their methodological implications. Leonard (1990) gives a very good summary of the intersections between the critical theory of the Frankfurt School, Foucault (as a critical postmodern theorist), feminist theories, and several schools of "dependency" theory. Kolko, Nakamura, and Rodman (2000) provide a good account of sociological takes on these issues, and di Leonardo (1991) does similarly from within critical feminist anthropology. One more thing bears mentioning. "Constructivist IR," as developed by Alexander Wendt and others, follows positivist research modes and/or (neo)realist theoretical models first and foremost (see Reus-Smit 2001).

16 The respective (neo)colonial histories and political debates to which they speak will become clearer in due course. Suffice it to say that the (in)dependent status of Hawaii and American Samoa are cases in point for the United States; that of the islands of "French Polynesia" in the case of France; Fiji in the case of Great Britain; and (formerly) Western Samoa in the case of Germany, Britain, and then New Zealand. Tonga is a case apart (see Chapter 5).

17 I say "presumably" because many Pacific Islanders are part of the lower socioeconomic strata in their adopted country. Even while they send containerloads of goods, and money, as remittances to extended family members in the islands, this does not presuppose that they are particularly wealthy. This difference in perception is but one fracture line between diasporic and at-home participants on these forums, as we will see.

18 See Roberts (1999) for another, less sympathetic reading of de Certeau vis-à-vis Lefebvre. Part of this is related to how de Certeau's cultural theory has been adapted and depoliticized (as Roberts argues, and I tend to agree with him) by apolitical streams in cultural studies and media studies (reception analysis and audience research especially). See Chapter 3.

19 Costs, huge commitments of personal time for moderators, limits of server and electronic storage capacity, connection fees, and so on have all dogged these websites (Taholo Kami, personal email 2000; Al Aiono, 1999: interview).

20 My thanks to Helen (Morton) Lee, Mike Evans and Heather Young Leslie for their guidance in these matters.

21 As will become evident in Chapter 4, many women participating on the KB and KR do not identify as "feminists"; some do quite the reverse, in fact.

22 The practical-ethical issue of whether or not to give "real names" is not straightforward. In many cases, this "real" name is in fact a nickname. So, the question then moves to the issue of what constitutes a real name in cyberspatial scenarios and the identification made between the participant and his/her signatures/"handles"/"nics." I have opted not to alter the signatures given to

the discussions cited from here on. When quoting private (and that includes emails) correspondence, however, I have requested permission to quote or have withheld the full name. I discuss these issues and my approach to them here more fully in Chapters 3, 4, and 8.

2 Marketing the neoliberal dream

1 Jacques Derrida's conceptualization of this technique will more than suffice here: "Deconstruction seeks to disassemble any discourse standing as a 'construction.' ... Unlike a general method or analytical procedure, deconstruction is a highly individualized type of intervention aimed at destabilizing the structural priorities of each particular construction" (Borradori 2003: 139).

2 These are cursory analyses designed to illustrate how representation operates at material and ideational, visceral, and symbolic levels of cognition. I have used many of these images over the years, and in various contexts. It is still striking just how many ways they can be received by different viewers; their "meaning" extracted or contested, the intention behind their design or message inferred from their "manifest content." And as I have learned more about the actual production of some (outsourced freelance illustrators, or strategic decisions about which images to use in order to accommodate different attitudes toward sexist advertising, as parts of "ancient history" in corporate terms for now-defunct strategic corporate alliances and so forth), the nuances to their production, content, and reception have been underscored.

3 The Internet protocols that enable computer-to-computer communications began as nonproprietary core elements of the Internet. Many of these codes are still in use despite the largely successful campaigns by companies such as Microsoft to gain full control of the software that governs the Internet/World Wide Web. Another reminder: ICT transmissions overlap with and "poach" from extant public telecommunications networks – networks that once offered free access for ordinary users before technical developments collapsed the "tyranny" of long-distance telecommunications costs (*The Economist* 1995). My thanks to Sally Wyatt for this insight.

4 The main target audience for most of the IT/telecoms industry ads is that of globe-trotting executives, who are still predominantly male. In this respect, and depending on local "sensitivities" about sexism and advertising, it can be a question of "no holds barred" when it comes to more overt uses of eroticized female bodies. As one marketing manager notes, "[T]his advertisement [Figure 2.8] was deliberately targeted at a predominantly male senior IT and management audience in Europe. It was not for the US" (Brian Catt, former Infonet Marketing Director, personal email, July 2001).

5 As in ancient Rome, nearly all ICT roads lead to the North American continent, its Western seaboard being that of the Pacific Ocean. According to the *CIA Fact Book* figures for 2000, sixteen out of sixty-one satellite earth stations are over the Pacific Ocean. Out of the world's top ten Internet service providers, eight are based in the United States, as are four out of the top ten telecom operators. Any map of world telecom traffic and satellite and cable connections will show this quite graphically (South Pacific Forum 1998: 25).

6 An important element to the diverse demographics in this region is the relatively slow population growth, which "is not the result of low fertility but, rather, reflects massive emigration to New Zealand, Australia and the United States" (UNDP 1999: 2–3). The UNDP reports that "ten of the fifteen Pacific Island countries have had net population losses in recent years ... ranging up

to −3.5% per year" (ibid.: 3). Nearly 42 percent of the Tongan population is under 16 years of age. For the record, the figures for how many Tongans are resident in the United States vary from 16,000 to 46,000 (Marrow 2003). The latter count has to contend with that most difficult category of all: "illegals" (hingano, KR, 07/05/01).

7 For example, see the Small Islands Developing States Network (SIDSnet). The founder of the Kava Bowl, Taholo Kami, was active in setting up this program up (http://www.sidsnet.org/). A longer-serving project (since 1971), based at the University of Hawaii at Manoa, is PEACESAT (http://obake.peacesat. hawaii.edu/default.htm). This initiative, funded by the US Department of Commerce, among others, uses older communications satellites for educational and "public service" communications services for a number of island countries throughout the Pacific. Tonga, Western Samoa, and American Samoa make use of these satellite stations. See UNESCO (2002: 32–38).

8 The reports that articulate these policy initiatives and the regionally localized debates that intersect them have had several generations (UNESCO 2002). Early, influential surveys are those of Dator, Jones, and Moir (1986) and Ogden (1993, 1999). In recent years, a host of intergovernmental meetings and research initiatives have been emerging in the South Pacific region, either to survey extant Internet access and uses or to set up development plans. The region is fraught with endemic "difficult problems" (Richard Nickelson 1999: interview). These range from geography and climate to political and economic tussles over technical issues such as satellite frequencies, bandwidth applications, and the placing of submarine cables (a crucial issue for those islands that are bypassed). For those who are accustomed to immediate Internet/telephone connections, relatively swift and uninterrupted, it is easy to forget how fundamental – and elementary – some of these initial criteria for connectivity are: electricity supplies, PC supplies, telephone charges, and so forth (UNESCO 2002: 12–29).

9 While these ventures were not always runaway successes, this proactive stance has created several dotcom boom and bust stories of their own. One is that Tonga's bid for fifteen geostationary satellite orbital positions in the late 1980s made prominent member countries of the International Telecommunication Union (ITU) none too pleased. See Mendosa (1996), Corcoran (1997), and Abate (1998) for background on how the Tongan government managed to win seven orbital slots from the ITU for communications satellites. The ensuing business venture, Tongasat, is a story in itself, as is that of the Tonic Corporation (UNESCO 2002: 65–69, 94–102). The latter leases the Tonga's domain name (.to) for a fee. Where the profits go exactly is cause for debate on the ground and in these discussion forums. Tonga stands out vis-à-vis the other Pacific islands in these particular dotcom stories, which has a lot to do with the proactive stance taken by the Tongan government and the royal family towards satellite connections and Internet access and servers. These ventures then intersect with political contestation in the Kingdom and the complex nature of what constitutes "public" or "private" ownership and control in this society (Ghost, KB, 03/02/99). Meanwhile, the sale of Internet addresses (higher domain names) by Tuvalu (.tv), Tonga (.to) and Niue (.nu) attracted international media attention as these tiny island nations, with virtually no Internet connections or facilities, set out to create foreign exchange out of the boom in domain names. The tiny South Pacific atoll of Tuvalu has become renowned in IT circles for its domain name (.tv) and the brisk sales accruing from this, thanks to the brokering role of an offshore (North American) firm by the name of Information.ca. As to how much income has flown

back to Tuvalu from its 65 percent share in the enterprise, this is a moot point. It is certainly less than expected. The atoll of Niue, with its domain name (.nu), has become popular with French-language sex websites and related merchandise. On how small economies look for foreign revenue by selling their Internet domain name, see also Raskin (1998) and Korn (1999).

10 Samoans arrived in New Zealand and Australia in the 1960s and were followed in the 1970s by Tongans, among other island groups. Now that full employment is a dream of the past in these staunchly neoliberal political economies, for younger generations of Pacific Islanders looking to get ahead, sporting prowess and higher education have become important avenues for socioeconomic advancement.

11 An example (and there are many from this period) is AT&T's withdrawal from one "global" alliance with European operators (Unisource and World Partners) to team up with British Telecom (a partner in a competing global alliance – Concert); the latter's search for another ally to temper its own failed takeover attempt of yet another competitor (this time MCI, which in turn has strategic connections with both AT&T and BT, and acquisitions in major Internet service provision) is another.

12 British Telecom (BT), Deutsche Telekom, France Télécom, and AT&T are the big four in question. BT was the first of the state-owned operators to privatize, followed by Deutsche Telekom (1996–1997) and France Télécom (completed in 1998). AT&T, a publicly listed company that monopolized the US market, was divested in 1984, split into three in 1995, and is still a top long-distance operator.

13 This was with France Télécom and Sprint (USA). The Global One alliance was defunct by 1999 when Sprint "defected."

14 Thanks to Lily Ling for this observation.

15 Nippon Telegraph and Telephone Public Corporation is Japan's domestic services carrier, the international services being run by a separate carrier, KDD. Long considered publicly owned anomalies in privatized telecommunications, these Japanese carriers have also been privatizing and expanding.

16 This may be a backhanded, or accidental, recognition of women's role in early computer and software designs, which were conceived of as a lateral lattice of weaving rather than a teleological trajectory (see Plant 1996: 179; Mitter and Rowbotham 1995).

17 By this I mean that the centralized networks of predigitalized telecommunications are still extant, albeit in different configurations. The physical connections (cables and satellite connections) are indeed crucial to ICT infrastructures, but it is the *idea* of virtual, intelligent, and fungible networks over and above telephonic voice transmission that now represents fully integrated, truly "global" communications.

18 The name given to one of the offspring – equipment and network systems manufacturing – of the 1995 three-way split of AT&T.

19 This advertisement has two foci. One is on BT as a telecommunications services provider in its own right and the other is on its alliances with others – in this case MCI, in the "Concert" alliance for a "state-of-the-art network."

20 "In this business, you can be engaged today, married tomorrow, and divorced the next day, and all of this at least once a month." This was taken from a Dutch-based spokesperson for Unisource on the news that AT&T had withdrawn from this alliance with smaller European telecommunications operators (*de Volkskrant*, July 28, 1998: 2; my translation). In November 1999, the Unisource "marriage" was officially annulled.

21 I have already referred to the background dynamics in the designing and

setting up of this advertising campaign. One last point bears mentioning: that of different reactions among women. This ad (Figure 2.8) was "a matter of some debate within the company, and particularly with the more PC ladies. We are also trying to get a replacement with similar or better impact. Interestingly, women in men's traditional jobs love the legs (our German lady geschafts-führer, and the investment banking ladies...). Scandinavian and West Coast women's rights oriented ladies tend to object. Cisco [a San Jose California based company] won't let us use the legs ... we have to use the cute Frog [an image drawing on the Frog Prince fairy tale] from the same series" (Brian Catt, personal email, July 2001). This ad was considered successful precisely because it was somewhat blatant, and so controversial.

22 One of the Telfort partners is Dutch Railways.

23 It is not just the what, but the placing of these commercial representations that is strategic. For instance: "in the airport ads the rules were 'airside only/head on to traffic flow/preferably in dwell time areas like departures (not luggage halls, too tacky and our targets have carry-on),' departures are better than arrivals and nodal locations like immigration are preferred where possible. This targeted time strapped international European business travellers on day trips, not the meeters and greeters, back packers and holidaymakers who are not likely to be relevant to global networking decisions – but you still pay to advertise to" (Brian Catt, personal email, July 2001). See Figure 2.8.

24 Even when gender operates as a synonym for "women," it too can locate the actual and active presence of (groups of) women in the history of Internet technologies, changing relations of labor, and the organization of production and gendered contours of uses and access (Mansell and Silverstone 1996; Henwood *et al.* 2001). The stereotypes of the male computer nerd and the technologically incapable housewife spring to mind here even as "marketing groups sense that female users [around 40 percent] constitute a goldmine" (*Financial Times*, July 1, 1996: 9) for the Internet business.

3 Everyday life online: Michel de Certeau's practice theory

1 On the contentious issue of what "postmodernism" means *per se* or what it means for left-wing political thought and action, see Andreas Huyssen (1990: 258 *passim*) on these bodies of thought and their permutations when appropriated by other intellectual traditions, the American in particular. See Harvey (1990) for another view of how this body of Continental thought, aesthetics, and politics pertains to structural Marxism's collision with "postmodernism." See also Buchanan (2000: 13–15), Cahoone (1996), Nicholson (1990), Best and Kellner (1991), and Franklin (2002).

2 Both the English translation and the original French version of *The Practice of Everyday Life* will be noted. All other references are for the English versions of de Certeau's work.

3 See three different introductions to de Certeau and their respective biographical emphases in Godzich (1986), Ahearne (1995), and Buchanan (2000). For a more complete placing of his work with respect to other everyday life theorists, see Highmore (2002). Although de Certeau a quintessentially French, "Continental," thinker, a glance at any of his work and the scope of his arguments shows an active engagement with German and Anglo-Saxon literature and non-Western philosophical traditions. Apart from his theological training with the Jesuit order and involvement in psychoanalysis, he also lived and worked in the United States and South America. The intercultural and inter-disciplinary "pluralities" in his work are part of his research politics (see

Ahearne 1995: 3; Godzich 1986: x–xi; de Certeau 1984: 12/1980a: 10). Another important collection for English readers is *Heterologies* (de Certeau 1986), in which the range of his work can be seen, as well as shorter summaries (in the form of essays) of his thought and research interests.

4 Originally published in French as *La Culture au pluriel* (1974) and *La Prise de parole, et autres écrits politiques* (1994) respectively.

5 Buchanan makes a valid point about the difference between translating "*invention*" – invention – into "practice," which "did not result in an added emphasis being placed on the creativity of everyday life as de Certeau is reported to have wanted. On the contrary ... it has resulted in a hardening of 'practices' into quasi-objects" (Buchanan 2000: 8). The second volume, by Giard and Mayol, applies the theoretical work of the first in two parts: an "urban sociology of a neighborhood" and a "socioethnographic analysis of everyday life" (1980: 13–14). The first presents the living spaces and movements of a working-class family vis-à-vis their Lyon neighborhood of the Croix-Rousse (ibid.: 13). The second part deals with the interaction between the sociocultural history of food and its preparation and that particularly "feminine" sphere in French homes, the kitchen, by way of qualitative interviews. In his coverage of key theorists of everyday life, Ben Highmore (2002) emphasizes the importance of Giard and Mayol's work in applying de Certeau's theoretical framework in empirical research (Giard and Mayol 1980: 158, 168 *passim*).

6 Ahearne (1995) and Godzich (1986) take different tacks on de Certeau to my own. Buchanan's study of his work (2000) emphasizes his religiousness and role in theorizing the 1968 Paris student uprisings. He also places de Certeau's thought next to that of Frederic Jameson, a theorist of "postmodernism" *par excellence* (see McGovern 2000). Highmore (2002) treats de Certeau as the culmination of his predecessors' (Simmel, Benjamin, Lefebvre) attempts to locate the political import of ordinary life. He also stresses in various ways how theories of the everyday in consumer societies need to be "recognised as operating within an international frame" (ibid.: 175).

7 De Certeau was trained in Lacanian psychoanalysis, wrote on Freud specifically (de Certeau 1986: 17 *passim*), and incorporated psychoanalytical theories of subjectivity into his treatise on everyday life (1980a: 37 *passim*). For a feminist take on these influences, see Mitchell (1974) and Butler (1990).

8 De Certeau uses the terms "*braconner*" (poaching) and "*la perruque*" (the siphoning off of time and/or materials from the employer) (de Certeau 1984: 24 *passim*/1980a: 68 *passim*; Ahearne 1995: 160). See Buchanan (2000: 89–90).

9 Buchanan points out the problems of taking de Certeau's use of the terms too literally. Tactics presuppose a "strategy," and in this framework the "counter-strategy" of nonelites is not made explicit. This is a criticism made by Roberts (1999) on where de Certeau's approach leaves traditional leftist forms of political organization and resistance. I would argue that the point de Certeau is making here is to show the qualitative and political difference between regimes/institutions of planning-for-planning's sake (strategic representations, so to speak) and organic creativity (everyday tactics). He is well aware of the pervasiveness of dichotomous forms of reasoning (de Certeau 1984: xvii/1980a: 19). See Highmore (2002: 156–161) for an astute coverage of de Certeau's use of these analogies of (guerrilla) warfare in mapping these power differentials between "inventive and sluggish practices" and those emanating from "'proprietary powers'" (ibid.: 159), an analogy that is "useful for making vivid the formal differences of actions, but the 'price' of this is that it can lead to unhelpful conclusions" (ibid.: 159).

10 To further flesh out how representation is treated here vis-à-vis de Certeau's

one-way take on it, Simonds puts the actual process quite well when noting that there is an "uneasy alliance between the subject *of* representation and the subject *in* representation" (1999: 134). She is talking about the distinction between representation by substitution (the former) and representation by figuration (the latter). "Figuration and substitution are inextricably linked, but they are distinct operations. Substitutions can appear natural through the process of figuration ... whereas figurations (or tropes) highlight the choice being made in asserting one particular relationship over another" (ibid.: 136).

11 Douglas defines this heuristic term well: "A 'text' is any medium for representation; written or spoken words, memories, gestures, dress, objects, buildings, landscapes, and visual media like paintings, sculptures, photographs and films ... [scholarly] texts are mainly written" (1998: 67, 69).

12 This is by no means a "new" discovery on de Certeau's or any post-positivist's part. As Albert Wendt notes in his discussion of latter-day Samoan and other Pacific tattooing practices, "meanings change as the relationships and the contexts change. (We knew a little about semiotics before Saussure came along!)" (1999: 402).

13 As one introduction to his collected essays points out, "the reach of de Certeau's activities is bound to be seen as excessive, and his attitude as extravagant, unless it can be construed as one of the reminders that the disciplines do not really constitute wholly autonomous domains but are part of a larger whole.... His [work] is a challenge to the present organization of knowledge, a challenge that is attentive to the dimension of crisis throughout this area" (Godzich 1986: x).

14 Buchanan (2000: 4–8) notes, quite rightly, the perils of fetishism in what updating and "over-editing" can do toward making a body of work "accessible" to its "market audience."

15 See the final chapter of *The Practice of Everyday Life* for the recognition of the uneasy tension between a scholar's subject position and that of others: "Leaving this functionalist rationality to the proliferation of its elegant euphemisms (euphemisms that persist everywhere in the discourse of administrations and power), let us then return to the murmuring of everyday practices. They do not form pockets in economic society. They have nothing in common with these marginalities that technical organization quickly integrates in order to turn them into signifiers and objects of exchange.... Far from being a local, and thus classifiable, revolt, it is a common and silent, almost a sheep-like subversion – our own" (de Certeau 1984: 200/1980a: 334–335).

16 And tracking – namely, following echoes and traces of complex interlocking literatures and academic "practices" – this will remain. As Clifford points out in relation to postcolonial anthropological enterprises, thinking "historically is a process of locating oneself [and others] in space and time" (1997: 11).

17 Nancy Fraser's (1987) carefully nuanced critique of de Certeau's generation of thinkers simply underscores his refusal to posit an a priori hierarchy between "discourse" and "practice." Postcolonial critics note that in the search for recovery or "lost" and/or silenced others, one is still "resort[ing] ... to a critical apparatus of authors, canons, and genres that is largely derived from a modern Western discourse of 'the literary,' 'the textual,' and the 'great author' ... [even though a] complete break with 'Western' literary theories and forms is often more polemical than materially or culturally realized in the act" (Wilson 1999: 4, and 13, note 11). See Peterson and Runyan (1999: 172–177).

18 "These 'ways of operating' constitute the innumerable practice by means of which users reappropriate the space organized by the techniques of sociocul-

tural production.... Pushed to their ideal limits, these procedures and ruses of consumers compose the network of an antidiscipline which is the subject of this book" (de Certeau 1984: xiv–xv/1980a: 14).

19 See Ashcroft, Griffiths, and Tiffin (1998: 186–192) and Seth (1999: 215–218) for good and concise overviews around the distinctions and spelling issues. I have opted for the nonhyphenated term from now on for the purposes of elegance, although the hyphen is used when the historical period is mainly being referred to.

20 This is not to assume that these preclude oppressive political regimes, untroubled social relations, or (in)equitable gender power relations.

21 This is something that Giard and Mayol make explicit as well (1980: 14).

22 Both Taholo Kami and 'Alopi Latukefu (the founder of the SPIN website) are sons of prominent Tongan intellectuals. They were brought up together in Papua New Guinea. Taholo went to the United States to study for an MBA after completing his BA at the University of Papua New Guinea. After having lived and worked in New York and in Suva, Fiji, where he worked for the UNDP's SIDSnet program, Kami is back in Tonga, where he is Business Manager for the Methodist Church. His involvement in ICTs in a "development scenario" continues as he is a consultant for the Japanese government and the University of the South Pacific on an e-commerce project for tourism (Kami, personal email, February 22, 2004). 'Alopi lives in Sydney, Australia, and ran the SPIN site out of the Australian National University's (Canberra) server. Al Aiono was born in New Zealand of a Mormon family. He now lives in Los Angeles with his wife, Sulu, and children. They run the Polycafe websites from their living room. The main thing to note at this point is the strong church and community affiliations of all three, and their commitment to community-based Internet uses (Aiono 1999: interview; Latukefu 1999: interview; Kami 2001: interview). All these sites were/are run on voluntary labor made up of partners, friends, and other enthusiasts who offer their assistance as moderators/administrators. Expenses come out of their own pockets or through donations (Kami 2001: interview), although Al Aiono has a culturally focused for-profit aim for the Polynesian Cafe (Aiono 1999: interview).

23 In Polynesian public communicative cultures, women are to be seen and not heard. For instance, the *faikava* ceremony on which the Internet Kava Bowl is based is a male-dominated activity. Women are usually only there to serve and make the kava, namely in their ceremonial role (*tou'a*). Internet-based communications have allowed women and other silent groups (political dissidents, homosexuals) a space in which to speak.

24 In the case of the Polynesian Cafe, a software filter has been added to screen for unacceptable words – swearing – in both English and Samoan. Participation on the Kava Bowl's live chat also required a registered password and "avatar." Both founders admit to taking the opportunity when deleting swearing to "clean up" the sites, thereby freeing up space allowed them by their respective servers (Kami 2001: interview; Aiono 1999: interview). See Chapter 7.

25 For instance, "A couple of our fellow KBers have urged us to include topics that span a wider range of Pacific island issues than those which are exclusively Tongan, so this week's topic is intended to include input from the perspectives of ALL Pacific island cultures" (KBAdmin, KB, 01/04/98).

26 For how these distinctions play out, see Chapters 4, 5, and 6.

27 The reasons for this are mainly due to a decision by Taholo Kami, busy in his work with the United Nations Development Programme at the time. Financial resources to sustain servers and connection fees, and an enormous amount of

personal time for what is essentially a labor of love, are prerequisites for the sustainability of Internet forums such as these (see Chapter 7).

28 Aiono himself (born in New Zealand and resident in United States, although he has never been to Western Samoa) confirms that he has learned a lot about other Pacific Islands, made friends, and also had some of his childhood misunderstandings and prejudices about other island groups righted (Aiono, 04/07/2000, personal email).

29 Al Aiono has been less comfortable in the past with the increasing use of nicknames, however, seeing it as a potential abuse of these forums' integrity (Aiono 1999: interview). The use of nicknames and other forms of "anonymity" has steadily increased and become part and parcel of the subtextual and intertextual relationships of the forums (Morton 1998a/2001).

30 Along with the discussions looked at in this study, religion and sexuality are among the most recurrent and substantial discussion themes, although I do not deal with these two categories here. Those professing to be gay do not use real names, whereas many of those objecting to them (usually on religious grounds) do. In these instances, there are a number of crisscrossing concerns and lines of division: the historical nature of transsexuality vis-à-vis homosexuality in Polynesia, the morals of the predominantly Christian posters that condemn homosexual practices as a sin, (postcolonial) notions of what constitutes sexual (im)propriety. These then cut across arguments about the role and effect of colonial missionaries on precolonial regimes/ways of life and sexual mores, the differences between public behavioral codes, intimate or domestic scenarios, and whether these behaviors denote duplicity or not. A lot of the more "risqué" humor and satire is often at the expense of certain (diasporic) Polynesian male archetypes and their archetypical "submissive" female counterparts.

31 I am indebted to Taholo Kami and Al Aiono for their generosity in this respect. My thanks also to Helen (Morton) Lee for her practical advice.

32 Online texts have a variable Internet shelf life dependent upon factors such as server space, the way sites are administered and organized, technical breakdowns, and so on. I have printed out all the threads referred to here, and many more besides. The epistemological issues have less to do with the relative temporality of online records (as opposed to digitalized archives) than with their substantive role in the research (Highmore 2002: 24–26).

4 "I'm tired of slaving myself": sex–gender roles revisited

1 This terms draws upon Gayle Rubin's influential conceptualization of the "sex/gender system," namely "the set of arrangements by which a society transforms biological sexuality into products of human activity, and in which these transformed sexual needs are satisfied" (Rubin [1975] 1997: 28).

2 For example, typing a text and posting it; logging on and off; arguing–flaming–being censored, flirting, chatting, hyperlinking, solidarity building through information sharing.

3 The literacy rate in the Pacific Islands is over 90 percent, with education being rated very highly in social terms. For a more light-hearted view of these dynamics vis-à-vis indigenous cultural politics, see Epeli Hau'ofa's short story "The Glorious Pacific Way" (1983: 83).

4 Here the poster is critical of stereotypes that exist beyond Tonga as well.

5 This is related to various degrees of status and privilege among and between men and women (Ortner 1996: 59 *passim*). See also Helu (1999b: 15 *passim*).

6 Contemporary communicative and political hierarchies are male centered in Tonga and Samoa. On-the-ground informal "kava clubs" and formal kava ceremonies are not normally frequented by women, except in a certain ceremonial capacity (see Helu 1999d: 5). Visitors (like myself) are not prohibited from going to a kava club, however. Yet women do have "public" power – as chiefs (*matai*) in Samoa, or royalty (in Tonga). The – controversial – impact of Western missionaries in the nineteenth century also impinges upon postcolonial "public–private" meanings of power in the South Pacific. Posters certainly do not agree on how and why, and neither do Pacific scholars.

7 "[V]erbal interaction, whatever else it accomplishes, is often the site of struggle about gender definitions and power; it concerns who can speak where about what" (Gal 1991: 176). Online "chat" is written-verbal interaction.

8 The (excessive) use of capitals is the online form of SHOUTING. Here they are being used more for emphasis.

9 Out of the twenty-six total – and lengthy – follow-ups, seven were from KZ7 (who explicitly identifies as a man as the thread unfurls), with only one other male. Two others use unisex nicknames. Of the twelve distinct posters, the majority were (explicitly) women.

10 Linda Nicholson's reader (1997) is a marvellous collection of some key feminist classics from the "second wave."

11 Language and isolation are loci for these concerns as many first/second generations growing up outside the islands are not proficient in the Samoan/Tongan languages. For example, "I was in culture shock during those years [of high school in California] so I wasn't sure if being myself . . . Samoan . . . was alright or not" (Mixed Up, KR, 02/02/99).

12 There were twenty-five follow-ups to this initial post – the median number on these forums (see Chapter 3) – by fourteen separately named posters, of whom at least twelve were women – they said as much and there is every reason to believe them.

13 Laugh Out Loud (repeatedly). See Reid (1996) for more on visual behavior symbols – "emoticons."

14 Gorgeousss then wants to know "where are you from? Where do you see this happening?" (Gorgeousss, KR, 02/10/99).

15 It appears that Bevo is a man. He is addressed as such in other threads and does not correct this, as others are wont to do when assigned the "wrong" gender by their interlocutors.

16 With fifty-eight follow-ups, this thread, posted by E. Tigris (KB, 05/13/99), rated high in interest. Male posters who insisted on the maintenance of virginity were given short shrift by many of the women.

17 Debates about homosexuality vis-à-vis transvestite and transsexual genders in Pacific Island cultures express some of these complex dynamics in particular, which intersect with the arrival of Christianity in the region during the nineteenth century. These threads constitute a study in their own right. One regular, le'o vaivai, was the Kava Bowl's resident satirist. This poster, a middle-aged male Tongan living in Honolulu, Hawaii, "always wanted to be a writer." The KB Forum gave him an opportunity to practice his satirical writing skills (Kami 2001: interview).

18 In moderation. The main protagonists of any discussion do hold back on personal details of said situations. I have encountered and engaged in this myself at times on these forums.

19 Of the eleven posters (fifteen posts in total), about seven were women.

20 Fresh Off the Boat – a self-explanatory pejorative term. This message (the original capitals have been retained to show how this was effectively being

shouted) got forty responses and thus rates high in significance, even accounting for multiple handles.
21 This denotes something else entirely from the Western nuclear family framework, given how extended family relations work in Polynesia (Ortner 1996: 59
passim). They are also terms of solidarity – "sistah"/"bruddah," Sis/Bro are
some idiomatic expressions of this.
22 That is, white/non-Polynesian. Two spellings exist: *palangi* (Tongan) or *palagi*
(Samoan).
23 To reiterate, the drinking of kava (a mildly narcotic beverage known mainly in
Samoa, Tonga, and Fiji) is both a formal and a male-centered social ritual – a
source of debate in itself in some discussions. The Internet "Kava Bowl" is a
cyberspace variant of these in/formal kava circles mentioned above. The
telling of tall stories occurs alongside heated political debate, ribaldry, and
satire. These playful elements are recognized and enjoyed online as well.
However, as a Tongan satirist put it, this "is not to suggest that our country
comprises a nation of liars as some uninitiated foreigners seem to think, far
from it. Truth comes in portions, some large, some small, but never whole.
Like our ancestors we are expert tellers of half-truths, quarter-truths, and one-
percent truths" (Hau'ofa, "The Winding Road to Heaven," 1983: 7).
24 In the body of the message, I stated my motivation for posting, reiterated that I
was researching these forums, noted that I hailed from the region as my birth-
place (Samoa) or my official nationality (New Zealander). It was also noted
that responses (follow-ups) could be quoted. My own signature is Marianne
and/or MA.
25 Jatu identifies as a Latin American whose husband is Tongan.
26 The Tonga History Association is primarily for historians, although nonacade-
mics clearly frequent it.
27 Over the years, many women and men have expressed their gratitude for this
side to the forums.
28 In short, the difference between seeing the region as a "Doomsday scenario"
('Alopi Latukefu, 1999: interview) or as a "sea of islands" (Hau'ofa 1993; Ward
1999).

5 "A play on the royal demons": Tongan political dissent online

1 See the following for some responses to these questions: Moore (1999),
Deibert (2000, 2000a), Everard (2000: 51), van Aelst and Walgrave (2002),
Rodgers (2003), Harcourt (1999). See also Toulouse and Luke (1998) and
Hague and Loader (1999) for two overviews of the political and theoretical
implications of ICTs vis-à-vis democracy and society. At one end of the spectrum, analysts posit a *demos* – "public sphere" – that is at risk from "rampant"
ICTs (Wilhelm 2000: 3, 9, 32–33, 138–139; Hirschkop 1998) in themselves, or
as functions of late-capitalist modes of accumulation (Schiller 1999; McChesney *et al.* 1998). Towards the other end of the spectrum are variously shaded
doomsday scenarios for the fate of the democratic nation-state; see Coleman
(1999), Malina (1999), and Castells (1996, 1997, 1998). The middle point is
occupied by a range of careful skeptics (May 2002; Peterson 2003). And from
quite another sort of "gung-ho" angle, ICTs are coupled to statements about
free trade and/or poverty alleviation imperatives: see US Department of State
(1999a, 1999b: 13, 19), World Bank (1998), and OECD (2001).
2 Political, and politicized, discussions abound in the Kamehameha Roundtable as well, mostly revolving around US politics for the mainly US-based
participants, or Samoan political events and comparable perennial debates

about the efficacy of a chiefly-based system of political representation versus universal suffrage (see Tcherkézoff 1998). By 2001, Kava Bowl political discussions were integrated into those taking place on the KR, as the KB gradually went offline.

3 Initial posts related to the Tongan royalty and/or pro-democracy issues provide the highest follow-up totals of all the threads from the KB at least, gathered between 1996 and 2001: 118 for *Longest Serving Rulers* (George Candler, KB, 02/09/99) and 221 for *Weekly Discussion Topic #24/27: Adherence to Chiefly and Royal Successions* (KBAdmin, KB, 02/08/98). Three out of over seventy *Weekly Discussion Topics*, initiated by the Kava Bowl Administration, were about the monarchy/democracy issue. Most of these debates were initiated by the constituency. The mean response rate was twenty-three to twenty-five for all the threads on this theme. The general mean response rate was ten to fifteen follow-ups, with a high level at about twenty to thirty. The predominance of political content in those threads with between thirty and eighty follow-ups is significant (see Chapter 8). The threads reconstructed here mostly date from February 1998 to November 1999 (the Tongan general election was held in March 1999).

4 This element can lead to various degrees of "flaming" in what are long and heated arguments (much of this gets deleted by the KB Administration – see Chapter 7). Both the pros and the cons in any of the debates were fairly evenly represented, by any method of counting and incorporating nicknames and multiple "handles." The same applied to (explicitly or self-identified) men and women.

5 This is the main argument of Lawson (in Tarte 2000). Ashcroft *et al.* (1998: 167–169) provide useful conceptual delineations here.

6 While never directly colonized, Tonga was a British protectorate from 1900 to 1970, when it became a fully fledged member of the British Commonwealth. It gained full membership of the United Nations in 1999. Western Samoa gained independence in 1962 after having been a German and then, briefly, a British colony and then a New Zealand protectorate.

7 This is an enormous debate in economic and cultural anthropology. Suffice it to say that wealth creation and distribution in the postcolonial and ostensibly "capitalist" Pacific Islands still work along extended family lines (*kainga* in Tongan and *aiga* in Samoan), hierarchical bilateral obligations, and hereditary and androcentric rights to land tenure (Helu 1999c: 34). Since the 1960s, remittances (monetary and in kind) between the islands and the diasporic communities abroad have also been important (Ward 1999; Chapman 1985).

8 In 1992, six of the nine people's representatives "espoused Pro-Democracy ideals" (Swaney 1994: 20), a result not sustained in 1999. Some participants put this down to "internal dissent and factionalisation" and "bitter bickering" by pro-democracy candidates (Sefita Auckland New Zealand, KB, 03/12/99). See Kerry James's article in Pacific islands Report (2002: 174–179) for an analysis of the THRDM results in the 2002 general election, where success was largely booked in the main island of Tongatapu.

9 One of these, Kalafi Moala, took part in one of the threads dealing explicitly with democracy *per se* in 1998. In this debate, he and another expat, Sione Ake Mokofisi (a former KB regular who, by 2004, has become a regular columnist on the Polycafe/Kamehameha Roundtable), show how political semantic arguments can be as they argue about what is liberal, what is democracy, and what is journalistic objectivity.

10 The term "indigenous" is understood to be as much a political-cultural designation as it is (arguably) a "racial" or ethnic one (UN 2000: 1/6). Fiji's polit-

ical unrest due to military coups and violence on the part of indigenous Fijian activists (1987, 1998, 2000) further complicates the contemporary context and inflects analyses of postcolonial politics in the region. For instance, the question of support for "the democratic rights of the Indian immigrants, or in support of the rights of the indigenous Fijians to control their native land?" (KBAdmin, KB, 02/15/98), in the wake of the first military coup, saw one regular astutely noting that when "forced to choose between 'human rights' issues over 'indigenous rights,'" Pacific nations went for the latter (Sefita Auckland New Zealand, KB, 02/16/98 in reply to above). Those arguing for constitutional change in Tonga quote two documents in their support: the Amnesty International Country Report on Tonga (1997) and the US Department of State's *Country Reports on Human Rights Practices: Tonga* (1999a). A reasonable summary of events surrounding the imprisonments of government critics is given by Swaney (1994: 20–21). An astute analysis of the cultural (in)applicability of the UN conception of universal human rights vis-à-vis Tonga's own "social calculus" can be found in Futa Helu's essay "Human Rights from the Perspective of Tongan Culture," where he argues that there is a "clear indication that the rule of law is becoming inapplicable to people in power" (1999c: 36).

11 This poster also uses her abbreviated name, Manu.

12 "Tokoni Mai" means "Help Me" in Tongan. See Morton (1998a/2001) for more on how signatures such as these denote relationships as much as persons/personalities.

13 This thread, entitled *WEEKLY DISCUSSION TOPIC #24/27: ADHERENCE TO CHIEFLY AND ROYAL SUCCESSIONS,* engendered 221 follow-ups, which included long postings in Tongan.

14 Sandy, a former Peace Corps volunteer in Tonga, is a prominent member of the Kava Bowl and one of the mainstays of the KB Administration (see Chapters 6 and 7).

15 In Tonga, this is the *fahu* system, namely, familial (and aristocratic to commoner) hierarchical privileges and obligations of the first-born sister in the Tongan extended family (*kainga*) structure. In short, relatively speaking, the first-born daughter/sister/sister-in-law has the higher status in the family hierarchy. See Ortner (1996) and Morton (1996) for two different views on these gender power relations. See also Jolly and Macintyre (1989).

16 Education is highly valued in the islands, and especially in Tonga. This is one reason why those belonging to younger generations go abroad for university study. They are also sent to high school in Australia, New Zealand, and the United States by their families.

17 This is particularly difficult in discussions about recent Chinese immigration into Tonga (related as well to a long-simmering affair about the government sale of Tongan passports). Suffice it to say that it contributes to the complexities of divisions between at-home and overseas participants in the first instance, for some of the less inclusive or accommodating discussions on these forums in the second, and the ambivalence of claiming Tongan cultural integrity as a reason for resisting political changes in the third. As one participant sardonically notes, "[I]t is the present conservative system who is allowing Chinese to settle in Tonga which invites these hostilities from all those 'romanticised' Tongans who left their 'beloved' country behind for God to look after and protect from the rest of the world ... those in favour of pure cultural maintenance in Tongan is behind the very system who allow (and will continue) the very people they 'hate' to make Tongan their home for now and for the future" (kolitoto, KB, 02/08/99 in KBAdmin, 02/07/99).

18 The copious threads on religious issues that permeate both the KB and the KR are not looked at here, even though some constitute the longest threads. On both the KR and the KB, religious themes were allocated their own discussion forums. For the record, and woven into all the discussions examined in this study, Pacific Island churches are crucial social hubs on the ground, in Tonga and Samoa as well as abroad. They are seen as bastions of conservatism by some, but there are also pockets "contributing to the swell of social criticism, and some individuals within the church hierarchies are important figures in the pro-democracy movement" (Morton 1996: 254; Helu 1999e: 168–169).

19 George is a regular palagi (American) participant in these forums.

20 My thanks to Heather Young Leslie and Mike Evans for this observation.

21 This is one of the sixteen posts by Altius – a pro-monarchist and commoner – living in Australia from one of the longest threads (seventy-six follow-ups), *ROYAL IDEOLOGY* (Ikani, KB, 06/08/99).

22 For instance, in the thread entitled *CHIEFLY AND ROYAL SUCCESSIONS* (KBAdmin, KB, 02/08/98), a subthread of thirty-eight follow-ups alone developed between a "scared *finemui* [young woman] 'loyal to Tonga'" and pro-change advocates. On eventually admitting to "being one of them royal bloods," she was greeted with the following retort: "[Y]ou royal blood is so thick.... Take some blood thinner – i.e. democracy" (Hang your "royal blood" by the keyboard before entering the KB, 02/13/98 in KBAdmin, 02/08/98).

23 Meilakepa's other signature is Phil Tukia.

24 There are a few exceptions. There was some jesting, in the absence of women in parliament and underrepresentation of Tongan nationals abroad, about setting up a "Kava Bowl Parliamentary Party." Honi Soit, a woman and KB regular who stood in the 1999 elections for the one "overseas seat" in the Tongan parliament for expats, expresses her gratitude to her online "con-stituency": "Seriously, I salute you for considering women. After all, we only represent half the population" (Si'i Le'o and Sefita, KB, 01/05/99). Women cannot be landowners either in Tonga, a point not missed by pro-change activists (POLITICAL CORRECTIONS MUST APPLY TO THE TONGAN LIFE, KB, 02/13/98 in KBAdmin, 02/08/98).

25 This sample is from a lengthy intervention in the even lengthier thread *Weekly Discussion Topic #51: Democracy in Tonga: Pro or Con?* (KBAdmin, KB, 09/07/98). Follow-ups were roughly half for and half against in the three weeks that it lasted (09/07/98 to 09/25/98). The number of discernibly male posters outnumbered the female.

26 In a subsequent email, Tupouto'a added that this "was just my attempt at putting humorously, that democracy is public choice and not a public lottery" (personal email: 02/15/01).

27 Taholo Kami has also been pressed by Tongan authorities to reveal the where-abouts (by tracing the email address back to its source) of a "known" pro-democracy agitator participating in these debates (Kami 2001: interview).

6 "I define my own identity": rearticulating "race," "ethnicity," and "culture"

1 My thanks to Alpona Dey, James Coleman, Twanna Hines, Taka Hosoda, 'Alopi Latukefu, and Taholo Kami for sharing with me their personal experi-ences and views of issues raised here.

2 In Samoan, the term is *afakasi*. The English translation for this term, "half-caste," is also used. *Fie palagi* and *faka palangi* are somewhat pejorative terms in Samoan and Tongan respectively for those who are seen to be taking up

Western/European ways. For instance, one thread got started with an initial post entitled (and written in capitals, therefore "said" loudly) *DOES THE FAKA-PALANGI ATTITUDE DESERVE TO BE CRITICISED?* (MVP, KB, 11/13/99). Another, more tongue-in-cheek initial post entitled *How To Tell if You Are Samoan* (Thoughts, KR, 05/22/99) poked fun at some prevalent racial stereotypes.

3 A substantial thread in the KR in 2001 encapsulates the US locations of many KR participants, where uneven educational resources for low-income "ethnic minorities" in Los Angeles, high-school drop-out rates, and living as an American citizen and Samoan are recurrent concerns. The initial post, entitled *Any Future US Political Clout for PI's??* (eb, KR, 03/12/01) received sixty-seven follow-ups (see Figure 8.1). In response to eb's plea for Pacific island representatives in Congress, a regular of both the KR and KB had this to say: "I think that this is unhealthy for our country [the USA], this polarization. This viewpoint breaks everyone up according to their ethnicity, and categorizes us not as an individual, part as part of a group. That means that all of my needs are the same as all Samoans and that all of my problems are the same as all Samoans. This means that we should get a certain number of Congressman and Senators according to our numbers. That we should get funding according to our numbers. This is not right. It's not democratic and its un-American" (Bevo, KR, 03/13/01 in eb, 03/12/01). In the debate that ensues, Bevo is taken to task for his standpoint, beginning with eb, the instigator of this thread, who asks pointedly, "And I'm puzzled why Mr. Unique Individual frequents a poly forum" (eb, 03/17/01, in reply to Bevo).

4 To recall, educational advancement is highly valued in Tonga and Samoa and by many "new migrant" communities. Another example can be seen in a thread entitled *Meilakepa, what's it like being a lawyer?* (brown sugar, KR, 01/22/01), where a regular is quizzed on how his relative success interacts with "being a polynesian (Samoan?) in the legal profession?" (ibid.).

5 Initial posts have titles such as *What is the Tongan Way?* posted by John Michel (04/14/99, THA) or *Tongan Way, on its way out* (Christian, KB, 09/04/99), *Fa'a Samoa* (Trish, KR, 11/12/00), which is actually about domestic violence (see Morton 1996: 1–3). Those looking at the term Polynesian include titles such as *DO ALL MAORIS CONSIDER THEMSELVES POLYNESIAN?* (haka, KR, 09/28/00) and *Why is Pacific Islander and Asian always lumped together – hence Asian-Pacific Islander, shouldn't Pacific Islander be its own category???* (Don't you all agree, KR, 06/30/00).

6 Taholo Kami is convinced that the next stage for these forums is to allow ghetto kids – the "baggy pants brigade" – their own website – space online – to "rap" with each other and work out their frustrations without upsetting the other "regulars." He is convinced – and attests to having this regularly confirmed – of the empowering value of such forums (Kami 2001: interview).

7 It bears repeating that there have been no editorial interventions apart from direct cuts or occasional inserts for clarity.

8 In online communications, capitals are tantamount to shouting. See Chapter 7.

9 Many of these discussions about Tongan cultural values occurred on the Kava Bowl's "Weekly Discussion Topic" threads between 1997 and 1999 (see Chapter 6).

10 See Chapter 5 for another angle on these "inside-out" dynamics.

7 "Please refrain from using capitals": online power relations

1 For the Polycafe/Kamehameha Roundtable, this is the site owners, Al and Sue Aiono. In the Kava Bowl, it was the multifaceted KBAdmin and its various members, including Taholo Kami.

2 Taholo Kami has confirmed that a large part of the KB population have been in their late teens – "college kids" – who spend five to ten hours a week on the various Pacific island chat/forum sites (Kami, 2001: interview).

3 The Kava Bowl, Kamehameha Roundtable, South Pacific Information Network, and the Tongan History Association's website were/are pioneering sites for Pacific island communities, official government websites notwithstanding (and Kami himself has been active in setting them up). Participants often refer to other sites and add in hyperlinks to them. Their founders recognize the knock-on effect as well (Latukefu 1999; interview; Aiono 1999: interview; Kami 2001: interview).

4 This turnaround speed is usual for popular or controversial topics on these forums, the relevance of the follow-ups to the initial topic notwithstanding. Over two-thirds of the total follow-ups came from the KB "constituency"; that is, regular participants, many of whom claimed to be "old-timers." Fourteen follow-ups were from the "KBAdmin" either in its official capacity or from members thereof. Taholo Kami, the owner, did not post in his own name here, although he has done on other occasions. Other moderators such as Phil Tukia and Dot posted as individuals. Sandy himself was ostensibly responsible for at least half of these "KBAdmin" interventions. For the record, the vast majority of the remaining follow-ups basically endorsed Sandy's point, though they differed in degree as to how the problem should be dealt with. The remainder registered differing scales of scorn or flippancy. There were also several direct references to Sandy's credentials and tough stance taken (Macintosh is in his fifties; he is one of the KB administrators, and his knowledge and Tongan language skills come from time spent as an American Peace Corps worker in Tonga). One participant notes that for some, Sandy's initial post "is perceived as being rude and brazenly imperialistic. . . . Do not punish or scold those who choose to debate your point. It is a learning curve. We hear you some better than others" (Supporter of True Polynesian Values, KB, 03/27/00 in Sandy Macintosh, 03/27/00).

5 Where the boundaries are and what this entails are together and separately online and offline cultural issues around social (status) and generational deference. For example: "Teaching morality is not necessarily a Tongan thing, but Tongan custom is based on many things – one being RESPECT" (yes yes, KB, 03/29/00 in Sandy Macintosh, 03/27/00). In Tongan, the term is *faka'a-pa'apa*, which is also a formal form of address to be found at the end of many messages. Not resorting to "profanity" (see Axis 2, p. 176) belongs to this notion. For instance: it is "a lame excuse . . . to use foul language as your right to freedom of expression. If you had an OUNCE of respect to elders who frequent this forum, then try adhering to some form of decency" (Reader, Polycafe, 05/05/99 in POLYCAFE, 05/04/99).

6 The term "netiquette" was coined in the early days of the Internet (the 1980s) for emergent online behavioral codes based on written texts. Of a general applicability yet very context specific, netiquette entails both explicit enforcement by those who own or moderate a website/forum and implicit – unspoken – rules developed among its long-standing participants. These are asserted for "newbies" as needs arise.

7 The Polycafe leadership have also justified deletions as necessity: "sometimes

entire batches have to go ... in order to control the heavy traffic the cafe gets everyday ... sometimes we just have to clean house quickly!." At other times, warnings have been posted that any further transgressions may lead to their being "forced to adopt a registration/password policy" (POLYCAFE, Polycafe, 05/20/99 in swift, 05/19/99). This is something the Aionos want to avoid, given their desire to provide open, public Internet forums (Aiono 1999: interview). As the Pacific Forum and Polynesian Cafe portals were set up to "cater for different needs" (ibid.), the volume of traffic meant that unrelated threads (e.g. birthday greetings and "I'm looking for..." inquiries) are another reason for deletion. They have been assigned their own subsites.

8 The rapidity of response can create all sorts of waves in an online textually constituted domain (as email users will probably know). Still, resultant misunderstandings can also provide an interesting insight into moral economies in operation. In one instance, a participant accuses the KBAdmin of being both partisan in a thread in which he has been subjected to "character assassination" and negligent in their moderators' duties. The KBAdmin explain that "we try our best to discourage accusations that are not related to the topic and we encourage people to voice opinions. You will notice that the comments were erased ... but unfortunately the software did not remove the message itself. We have erased both messages that were most unnecessary" (KBAdmin, KB, 01/30/99 in safata, 01/29/99). When he refuses to accept this, he is admonished by another participant to "cut the admin some slack. They are limited to what their software allows them. . . . If you still don't like it, then hit the road Jack or help finance this forum for better software" (reader, KB, 01/31/99 in safata, 01/29/99). Safata retorts that he has indeed donated to the Pacific Forum.

9 In Polynesian terms, both the traditional and the novel aspects of (new) communicative cultures come into play – not unacknowledged by Pacific Island community leaders and observers. For instance, the "matai [chiefs used to] speak for the people but the people can [now] individually speak for themselves and that is encouraging" (Helu 1999a: interview).

10 High schools and universities are key access points for many of the younger participants – for example, the Auckland Technical University in Auckland, New Zealand; the Royal School of Science (RSS) in Nuku'alofa, Tonga; the University of Samoa in Apia; and the University of the South Pacific in Suva, Fiji. As for the 'Atenisi Institute in Tonga, the founder, Futa Helu, regrets the lack of Internet access for his students: "this is the thing about the net in Tonga, only a [relatively] few people have access" (Helu 1999a: interview). By "relatively few people," he was referring to those in the Church and the government, the numbers of private households notwithstanding. The RSS has been the main "public" Internet access in Nuku'alofa. Kami has also noticed that at-home participation from Tonga itself can fall off quite sharply when the first phone bill arrives (Kami 2001: interview).

11 FOB means "fresh off the boat."

12 "As for this palangi's 'ignorance' ... well, I'd be happy to match mine with yours ANY day on any subject. Care to give it a shot ... or, are you all smoke?" (Sandy, KB, 03/27/00 in Sandy Macintosh, 03/27/00).

13 In this thread, the aforementioned idea of hospitality gets reiterated. The main protagonist, Daily Planet, finds her/himself in the center of such a seesaw between reaffirmation and calls for removal/the silent treatment: "If you don't like what he [sic] says, then move on to the next post" (LadyCYB, KR, 11/22/99 in Daily Planet 11/21/99). Daily Planet begins to back off

and apologizes for the "misunderstanding, just thought to come out and see your intent.... No hate intended.... The KR is an interesting forum to come out in, but sometimes we tend to be too sensitive. Howz dat?... I do believe we all have the right to release and voice!" (Daily Planet, KR, 11/22/99 in reply to above). Another regular then reiterates Pacific island understandings of respect vis-à-vis the legal – and social control – elements of the ground rules: "It's a positive to be PASSIONATE about our belief system; it just takes a smidgeon more to be recognisant of the common respect due to another.... Square your shoulders for you're not the only [one] who has felt humbled within these walls. But better be HUMBLED than HOBBLED in your efforts to share with others" (KR, 11/23/99 in Daily Planet, 11/21/99).

14 One case is the poster in the above altercations, Concerned. This participant could not get her/his point of view conceded to, despite providing nearly a third of the posts in a thread sixty-five posts long (Concerned, KR, 01/06/00).

15 On this, Helen Morton in her analysis of the use of real names versus nicknames in the earlier years of the Kava Bowl noted that between 1996 and 1998, there were "some interesting shifts over time in the naming choices of KB participants. Most obvious is the shift away from real names towards ... nicks and descriptive names [and] the appearance of more names that play with language" ([1998a: 15] 2001). She also notes that the positive male–female ratio in 1996 had reversed by 1998 (her sample showed 56 percent of the real names to be female).

16 Sandy has this to say about the difference between posting as an individual and as one of the KBAdmin: "Though I have occasionally used the Tongan translation of my name in the past, it is my policy to post personal opinions and observations under my own name. I do not apologise for being a palangi, nor do I feel my comments vis-à-vis KB are any less significant because I am not Tongan" (Sandy, KB, 03/27/00 in Sandy Macintosh, 03/27/00). It would require another sort of research to assess how this double role (as leader and participant) held by Macintosh and others articulates the "quadrillage" of strategic power in everyday life online, but there is evidence that moderators and participants do line up along this dyad at times (see Axis 2). This sort of selective anonymity allows for these groups "to represent themselves, in all their diversity, challenging stereotypes and resisting the typically limited representations of them, for example in their 'traditional' dancing at multicultural festivals" (Morton [1998a: 21] 2001).

17 Threads dealing with homo/sexuality, domestic violence, and local scandals are in this category as well. Here the dominant role of the Pacific Island churches in the islands and diaspora in regulating behaviors and social mores, and the relative lack of press freedom throughout the Pacific Islands (see Chapter 5) are both being directly challenged by these online practices. Founders of the forums take their leadership roles seriously, reflecting also their activities in Samoan and Tongan community, church, and social networks on the ground.

18 The Polycafe started in early 2000 by an email-based online magazine as an extension of its various forums. iMana 2000/1 has as one of its feature stories "Dealing with the Haters (Hataz)." Here not only are the ground rules summarized, but also some advice is offered for those who are targets.

19 This state of affairs is changing in the Tongan context at least, as Chinese diasporic populations have settled there, in Nuku'alofa mainly. Threads on this demographic shift, its relationship to the "sale of passports" to Chinese immigrants (Swaney 1994) and political dissent in Tonga are among the longest

and most polarized (see Chapter 5). With titles like *Chinese Tongans? Who are they? Why Tonga?* (Soakai, KB, 02/01/99), and *ON A POSITIVE NOTE .WHAT CAN WE DO TO ACCOMMODATE OUR CHINESE TONGANS, WITHOUT FORCING THEM OUT OF TONGA* (safata, KB, 02/04/99), *Weekly Discussion Topic #65: Chinese Threatening Tongan Culture? Get Over It . . . This Is Old Hat!* (KBAdmin, KB, 02/07/99), these initial posts have considerably less hospitable tones. Nonetheless, as always, both sides are evenly represented in the intense debates that unfurl.

20 This account does not deal with enough specifics either to suggest one moral economy across these different forums or to assume two or more distinctive ones. It is apparent, though – on the basis of time spent with these forums and based on their combined threads – that the Kava Bowl and the Polycafe have different leadership styles, different ways of dealing with tensions and conflicts, and differing constellations of gender power relations, the overlapping constituencies notwithstanding. Both moderators have mentioned pressure placed on them by community and church leaders on the ground at certain times.

21 Commentators on the ground are already aware of these nuances, whether in cyberspatial or (local) conventional terms, as "any institution that promotes dialogue and debate to me is a force for civilisation. . . . That doesn't mean we will let it go awry [as] we have to control it. By all means let people talk, let people debate and parade their ideas and theories" (Helu 1999a: interview).

22 For example, the electronic tagging devices for keeping track of individual PCs and their users' online pathways (the ubiquitous "cookies" included), and statistics-keeping software for website moderators. Innumerable traces of these texts are also left behind after "deletion" or "archiving." Disappearance in one sense is but partial. For instance, deleted threads or interventions from the KB or KR can still sometimes be found years later through their URLs or through keyword searches.

23 Diasporic communities and Internet-mediated forms of community mobilization understand how proximity need not be dictated by corporeality alone (Kolko *et al.* 2000; Morton [1998a] 2001; Rodgers 2003; van Aelst and Walgrave 2003).

24 These practices are not specifically "Poly." How they are interpreted and judged in these forums does have cultural specificity, though "visitors to this site will skim over a post, react emotionally, then sit down and type out a response/follow-up that either misses the point entirely or just doesn't make sense! Please read the Posts and follow-ups carefully" (Ke ke faka-ma'uma'u mu'a, KB, 03/27/00 in Sandy Macintosh, 03/27/00). See Morton (1996) for how these behaviors can run counter to Tongan socialization processes.

25 For example: "I remember a time, several years ago when the KB was first starting out, when the Kava Bowl was a Polynesian jewel in the crown of the Internet" (Sandy Macintosh, KB, 03/27/00); and "I also miss those 'good ole days' of the Kava Bowl ... I wish that the classic contributors of 1996, 97 and even 1998 would come back to this forum" (Phil Tukia, KB, 03/27/00 in Sandy Macintosh, 03/27/00).

26 For instance, in reply to KBAdmin's initial post *Please Refrain from Using Capitals*, a follow-up – all in capitals – notes, among other things, that "KBADMIN SEES ONLY CAPS" as opposed to "THE OBVIOUS VULGARITIES ALL OVER THE PLACE" (Pohasnotsmiling, KB, 03/22/00). In the Polycafe, an altercation between a disgruntled first-time poster and Al

Aiono/POLYCAFE, ostensibly about anonymity, included the following statement: "I am NOT Polynesian, but enjoy coming here with my Polynesian friends every now and then. Your response baffled me as I am not one of your many patrons here, who posts things just to get a rise out of the rest of the idiots who bicker back and forth with each other and call each other names. I was simply making a statement in reply to YOUR rules you so boldly made clear to us not too long ago" (Tommi Ann Davila, Polycafe, 05/14/99 in Tom, 05/14/99). This thread ended amicably.

27 In Polynesian social mores, keeping the eyes down when addressing an elder or superior is a sign of deference and respect.

28 For example (on going to press), see Pacific Web Directory (http://www. pacificforum.com); Planet Tonga (http://www.planet-tonga.com); Samoalive (http://www.Samoalive.com); Samoan Sensation (http://www.samoa.co.uk); Cafe Pacific (http://www.asiapac.org.fj/cafepacific/). There are many more.

8 Internet research praxis in postcolonial settings

1 It is only since about 1999 that work focusing on (relatively) new ICTs has gained a small foothold in IR/IPE academic organizations. A good example is the establishment of International Communications working groups and research sections within, first, the British International Studies Association (BISA) and then the (US-based) International Studies Association (ISA). The International Association of Internet Researchers had its first international conference in 2000 and has grown rapidly since then.

2 Taholo Kami has many stories about the times he has been approached by "KBers" in nightclubs while he was living in New York, and through personal emails. Some major financial support came from one or two KB regulars, one of whom regularly meets up with him on his business trips (the "Great Gatsby," Taholo calls him). The online traffic has remained steady since these years, even with the demise of the Kava Bowl. For example, in the month of June–July 1998, the Kamehameha Roundtable alone had 589 "hits." In July–August 2000, it had 543 "hits." There have been an increasing number of other places online for Pacific island people to go to since then (Kami 2001: interview). Al Aiono has been continuing to diversify the interconnectedness of the Polycafe websites and their ongoing discussion forums and chat rooms. The installation of a newspage – Surf Report – that provides links to news items "around the world relative to our community . . . has been well received and increased [participation rates] immensely." In addition, O Samoa TV, an online video show of news in both Samoan and English, was launched at the same time (Aiono, personal email, 06/22/2004).

3 In the Weekly Discussion Topics of the Kava Bowl (see Table 3.1 and Chapter 7), there were no threads instigated with a manifest "gender" content. These occurred through initial posts from the Kava Bowl and Kamehameha Roundtable constituencies.

4 These decisions do not conform entirely to citation criteria as laid out in anthropological codes of ethics. I have given my reasons for this approach in Chapters 1 and 3.

5 See Helen Morton Lee's ethnography *Tongans Overseas* (2003) for a recent example of how Internet sites and on-the-ground sites can be incorporated under the auspices of anthropological methods. Miller and Slater's ethnography of Trinidadians and the Internet (2000) is an earlier example. Jayne Rodgers's *Spatializing International Politics* (2003) uses a case-study approach

from an international communications perspective to how political activists use
– or do not use – Internet technologies. Rodgers's work included face-to-face
interviews with activists as well as Internet-based research.

6　One key aim was to meet or talk with the founders and main moderators of the
four websites under examination: the Kava Bowl, Kamehameha Roundtable,
Tongan History Forum, and South Pacific Information Network (KB, KR,
THA, SPN). In 1999, I met or spoke on the phone with 'Alopi Latukefu (of the
South Pacific Information Network) in Sydney, Helen Morton (Tongan
History Association) who is in Melbourne, and Al Aiono (of the Polynesian
Cafe) in Los Angeles. In 2001, I met the pioneer of the Pacific Islands Online,
Taholo Kami, in Brussels, Belgium. Email has been an invaluable backup and
supplementary communication tool in all these cases and I also made use of
the forums themselves to make contact at first. Interviews on the ground were
conducted with numerous people: academics, and telecommunications and IT
project leaders at various IGO instances – the forums' moderators). In terms
of the personal dimensions of the trip, it was the first time I have actually spent
any time in the South Pacific islands (beyond airport transit lounges in Fiji)
since I was a young teenager (when I went to Vanuatu), and my first time ever
in Tonga and Hawaii. My main regret was not getting to Samoa, where I was
born. This process of "going back" also happens online, as people reveal their
life histories in the course of discussions.

7　Some are consciously "archived" in electronic storage forms while others are not.
This is down to the owners/moderators and is more often than not a decision
based on financial or disk/server capacity (Morton, personal email, 2000; Kami,
personal email, 2001). Moderators have indicated to me that record-keeping software can be expensive and not always deemed a priority (Aiono 1999: interview;
Kami 2001: interview). Archiving millions of separate messages over the years also
takes up allotted space on the server, hence it involves costs. It also takes time and
conscious application, which neither Aiono or Kami sees as his domain. Archiving
for them is a synonym for "housekeeping," or cleaning up the backlog. In the
case of the Tongan History Association, however, archives were instigated as a
matter of course, as it was a forum for historians primarily.

8　For instance, in the Kamehameha Roundtable this message was posted
under the title *Whatever happened to Ani?* "I used to visit the Kamehameha
roundtable once in a while and would always make it a point to read Ani's
postings. It has been a long time since my last visit and I haven't read any
posting that is reflective of Ani. . . . Do any of you know what happened to
Ani? Is she still here and assuming a different name?" (chalena, KR,
03/22/01). In the (lighthearted) follow-ups, it transpires that there are at
least three other nics (signatures) indicating an Ani. Finally the sought-after
Ani appears. What this exchange points to is that it is the content that is
valued rather than which name is the most "authentic" one (see Morton
[1998a] 2001).

9　Taholo Kami notes seasonal surges such as the autumn semester in the United
States when the hits surge as KBers come back online. There are also time
zone-related surges in use, around the world and between the West and the
East Coast of the United States (Kami 2001: interview).

10　A lot of interaction goes on by way of relatively "offline" bilateral emailing. See
the last chapters of Jordan and his definitions for 'virtuality' (Jordan 1999: 1)
vis-à-vis the online–offline dichotomy itself.

11　The same goes for participants as misunderstandings occur – and those
involved are admonished – when the thread has not been read completely.

12　The thread was first electronically "bookmarked" then eventually printed out if the number of follow-ups was at least four or five, but preferably ten or more. Longer posts (over two pages at times) with fewer follow-ups were also archived (in these cases, forum moderators have been known to suggest fewer essay-length postings). For longer threads, sometimes more than a hundred separate follow-up messages (in one case there were 217 follow-ups) had to be opened, individually read, and "archived." These could run to up to seventy pages when printed out. The eventual sequencing of the hard copy was embedded in the routine I developed for opening, printing, and then later studying the discussions. Printing out longer threads took quite some time to complete. While such study was at my leisure, opening and printing them occurred under the exigencies of sustained eye-to-mouse coordination and sharing the departmental printer. Reordering muddled-up follow-ups under-scored the difference between a hypertext document and its offline equivalent. This is a researcher's, not a participant's, problem.

13 The original word was "historiography" – the "scholarly product" produced by historians.

9 Knowledge, power, and the Internet: in conclusion

1 This is disputable, and more so once the decreasing telephone connection costs are compared to the ever-increasing Internet charges. Moreover, the civilian user is competing against the global corporation for access and services on the increasingly cluttered telecom/Internet infrastructures. The more capacity required by large concerns for electronic commerce and interactions, the less room for "basic" telephone and now Internet services (Melody 2001: interview; Melody 1994).

2 Clicking open a website, moving through a hyperlink, entering a live chat room is tantamount to "going somewhere," to being in a place. My thanks to Sally Wyatt for this point.

3 Grassroots can be a highly relative relationship. Here it means that such users are not part of the processes of decision making that affect ICTs at large.

4 R. B. J. Walker (1995) talks about "container terms." Callon and Latour also define a black box as something that "contains that which no longer needs to be reconsidered, those things whose contents have become a matter of indiffer-ence" (1981: 285).

5 Comment made by Wolfgang Fritz Haug at the Amsterdam Seminar for Euro-pean Left Alternatives to Neo-Liberalism, University of Amsterdam, February 1997.

6 See Chapter 2, where I discuss how neoliberal macroeconomic and corporate business imperatives took precedence over sustainable public access, services, and infrastructural development. Moreover, the political economy of technical Internet protocols, system interoperability, and strategic software is now dealt with under the standardization "imperative" (Hawkins 1996). This is where commercial and R&D trajectories are thinly disguised as communication issues.

7 The "hardware" of ICTs (network systems – switching and transmission, PCs, modems and other paraphernalia) cannot exist without the "software" (programs, R&D – design and architecture, IT management and marketing) and vice versa (Quintas 1996; Ross 1997; Stallabras 1995).

8 Mostly the much-traveled, male business executive who still dominates corporate boardrooms. Those of the IT and telecom industries are no exception here, bearing in mind the different gender demographics between the United States

and Europe, though (Brian Catt, former Regional Marketing Director, Infonet EMEA, personal email, 07/02/01).

9 My thanks to Richard Nickelson (1999: interview), Norman Okamura (1999: interview), Taholo Kami (2001: interview), and HRH Prince Tupouto'a (personal emails) for sharing their different views on where such priorities lie.

Bibliography

~ALOJAH~, 11/25/00, *I dislike the term Polynesian*, initial post, Kamehameha Roundtable Discussion Forum, http://polycafe.com/Kamehameha/kamehameha.htm, accessed 02/28/2001

100%, 02/02/01, *Fake Polynesians*, initial post, Kamehameha Roundtable Discussion Forum, http://polycafe.com/Kamehameha/kamehameha.htm, accessed 03/01/2001

a blonde girl who's samoan, 01/25/00, *WHY DO THEY DISCRIMINATE US!!!*, initial post, Kamehameha Roundtable Discussion Forum, http://polycafe.com/Kamehameha/kamehameha.htm, accessed 02/15/2000

a girl's point of view, 01/28/98, *THE DIFFERENCES BETWEEN A TONGAN MAN IN TONGA AND A TONGAN MAN IN THE STATES*, initial post, Kava Bowl Discussion Forum, http://www.pacificforum.com, accessed 05/08/1998

Abate, T., 1998, "Digital Bay: Tonga Harvests Net Gold," *San Francisco Chronicle*, February 3: C3, available online at wysiwyg:/81/http://www.sfgate.com/cgi-bin/article.cgi, accessed 01/14/2000

Abbate, J., 1999, *Inventing the Internet*, Cambridge, MA: MIT Press

Adorno, T. W., 1976, "Sociology and Empirical Research," in T. Adorno (ed.), *The Positivist Dispute in German Sociology*, London: Harper & Row

Agathangelou, A., 2003, "'Sexing' Globalization in International Relations: Migrant Sex and Domestic Workers in Cyprus, Greece, and Turkey," in G. Chowdhry and S. Nair (eds), *Power, Postcolonialism and International Relations: Reading Race, Gender and Class*, London: Routledge, pp. 142–169

Agnew, J. and Corbridge, S., 1995, *Mastering Space: Hegemony, Territory, and International Political Economy*, London: Routledge

Ahearne, J., 1995, *Michel de Certeau: Interpretation and Its Other*, Cambridge: Polity Press

Aiono, Al, 1999, telephone interview with the founder of the Polynesian Café, San Francisco and Los Angeles, 15 July

'Alopi Sione Latukefu, 09/23/96, *Knowledge is Power! Power is Knowledge!*, initial post in Kava Bowl Discussion Forum, http://pacificforum.com, accessed 09/24/1996

Amnesty International, 1997, *Amnesty International Report 1997: Tonga*, available online at http://www.amnesty.org/ailib/aireport/ar97/ASA.40.htm, accessed 12/12/2000

Anderson, B., 1991, *Imagined Communities: Reflections on the Origin and Spread of Nationalism*, revised edition, London: Verso

Arendt, H., 1992, "Introduction: Walter Benjamin: 1892–1940," in Walter Benjamin, *Illuminations*, London: Fontana, pp. 7–60

Ashcroft, B., Griffiths, G., and Tiffin, H., 1998, *Key Concepts in Post-colonial Studies*, London: Routledge

AUSTEO, 1997 (*Australian Eyes Only*) *Report: Excerpt No. 1*, Australian Delegation Brief prepared for the Forum Economic Ministers' Meeting in Cairns, Australia, July 11, in *Pacific Islands Report*, August 4, 1997, available online at http://pidp.ewc.hawaii.edu/PIReport/1997/August/08-04-11.html, accessed 08/19/1997

Barron's Business Guides, 1995, *Dictionary of Computer Terms*, fourth edition, New York: Barron's Educational Series

Bauer, J. M., 1994, "The Emergence of Global Networks in Telecommunications: Transcending National Regulation and Market Constraints," *Journal of Economic Issues*, Vol. 28, No. 2, June: 391–402

Béaud, 1994, "Généralisation du capitalisme et des rapports d'argent: le basculement du monde," *Le Monde Diplomatique*, October, Paris: Le Monde: 16

bella, 03/15/99, *who are some of the SMARTESTongan women you know?*, initial post, Kava Bowl Discussion Forum, http://pacificforum.com, accessed 01/14/2000

Benhabib, S., 1987, "The Generalised and the Concrete Other: The Kohlberg–Gilligan Controversy and Feminist Theory," in S. Benhabib and D. Cornell (eds), *Feminism as Critique*, Cambridge: Polity Press, pp. 77–95

Benhabib, S. and Cornell, D. (eds), 1987, *Feminism as Critique*, Cambridge: Polity Press

Benjamin, W., 1992, "The Work of Art in the Age of Mechanical Reproduction," in W. Benjamin, *Illuminations*, London: Fontana, pp. 211–244

Bernard, M., 1994, "Post-Fordism and Global Restructuring," in R. Stubbs and G. Underhill (eds), *Political Economy and the Changing Global Order*, second edition, Basingstoke, UK: Macmillan, pp. 216–229

Best, S. and Kellner, D., 1991, *Postmodern Theory: Critical Investigations*, London: Macmillan Education

Bird, J., Curtis, B., Putnam, T., Robertson, G., and Tickner, L. (eds), 1993, *Mapping the Futures: Local Cultures, Global Change*, London: Routledge

Bøås, M. and McNeill, D. (eds), 2004, *Global Institutions and Development: Framing the World?*, RIPE Series in Global Political Economy, London: Routledge

Bordo, S., 1990, "Feminism, Postmodernism, and Gender-Scepticism," in L. Nicholson (ed.), *Feminism/Postmodernism*, London: Routledge, pp. 133–156

Borradori, G., 2003, *Philosophy in a Time of Terror: Dialogues with Jürgen Habermas and Jacques Derrida*, Chicago: University of Chicago Press

Brecher, J., Childs, J. B., and Cutler, J. (eds), 1993, *Global Visions: Beyond the New World Order*, Boston: South End Press

brown sugar, 01/22/01, *Meilakepa, what's it like being a lawyer?*, initial post, Kamehameha Roundtable Discussion Forum, http://polycafe.com/Kamehameha/kamehameha.htm, accessed 04/14/2001

Buchanan, I., 2000, *Michel de Certeau: Cultural Theorist*, London: Sage

Buckley, S., 2000, "Radio's New Horizons," *International Journal of Cultural Studies*, Vol. 3, No. 2, August: 180–187

Burchill, S., Devetak, R., Linklater, A., Paterson, M., Reus-Smit C., and True, J., 2001, *Theories of International Relations*, second edition, Basingstoke, UK: Palgrave

Butler, J., 1987, "Variations on Sex and Gender: Beauvoir, Wittig and Foucault," in S. Benhabib and D. Cornell (eds), *Feminism as Critique*, Cambridge: Polity, pp. 128–142

Butler, J., 1990, "Gender Trouble, Feminist Theory, and Psychoanalytic Discourse," in L. Nicholson (ed.), *Feminism/Postmodernism*, London: Routledge, pp. 324–340

Cahoone, L. (ed.), 1996, *From Modernism to Postmodernism: An Anthology*, Oxford: Blackwell

Callon, M. and Latour, B., 1981, "Unscrewing the Big Leviathan: How Actors Macro-structure Reality and How Sociologists Help Them Do It," in K. Knorr-Cetina and A. V. Cicourel (eds), *Advances in Social Theory and Methodology: Toward an Integration of Micro- and Macro-sociologies*, London: Routledge & Kegan Paul, pp. 277–303

Carver, T., 1998a, *The Postmodern Marx*, Manchester: Manchester University Press

Carver, T., 1998b, "Sexual Citizenship: Gendered and De-gendered Narratives," in T. Carver and V. Mottier (eds), *Politics of Sexuality: Identity, Gender, Citizenship*, London: Routledge, pp. 13–24

Carver, T. and Mottier, V. (eds), 1998, *Politics of Sexuality: Identity, Gender, Citizenship*, London: Routledge

Castells, M., 1996, *The Information Age: Economy, Society and Culture*, Vol. 1, *The Rise of the Network Society*, Oxford: Blackwell

Castells, M., 1997, *The Information Age: Economy, Society and Culture*, Vol. 2, *The Power of Identity*, Oxford: Blackwell

Castells, M., 1998, *The Information Age: Economy, Society and Culture*, Vol. 3, *End of Millennium*, Oxford: Blackwell

Castells, M. and Henderson, J. (eds), 1987, *Global Restructuring and Territorial Development*, London: Sage

Catt, B., 2001, former Marketing Director for Infonet, personal email to the author, July 2001

chalena, 03/22/01, *Whatever happened to Ani?*, initial post, Kamehameha Roundtable Discussion Forum, http://polycafe.com/Kamehameha/kamehameha.htm, accessed 03/25/2001

Chamoux, J.-P., 1993, *Télécoms: la fin des privilèges*, Paris: Presses Universitaires de France

Champlin, D. and Olson, P., 1994, "Post-industrial Metaphors: Understanding Corporate Restructuring and the Economic Environment of the 1990s," *Journal of Economic Issues*, Vol. 28, No. 2, June: 449–459

Chang, K. and Ling, L. H. M., 2000, "Globalization and Its Intimate Other: Filipina Domestic Workers in Hong Kong," in M. Marchand and A. S. Runyan (eds), *Gender and Global Restructuring: Sites, Sightings and Resistances*, RIPE Series in Global Political Economy, London: Routledge, pp. 27–43

Chapman, M. (ed.), 1985, *Mobility and Identity in the Island Pacific*, Special Issue of *Pacific Viewpoint*, Vol. 26, No. 1, April, Wellington, New Zealand: Victoria University Press

Chen, K.-H., 1996, "Post-Marxism: Between/Beyond Critical Postmodernism and Cultural Studies," in D. Morley and K.-H. Chen (eds), *Stuart Hall: Critical Dialogues in Cultural Studies*, London: Routledge, pp. 309–325

Chowdhry, G. and Nair, S. (eds), 2002, *Power, Postcolonialism and International Relations: Reading Race, Gender and Class*, London: Routledge

Christian, 09/04/99, *Tongan Way, on its way out*, initial post, Kava Bowl Discussion Forum, http://pacificforum.com, accessed, 01/13/2000

Clairmonte, F., 1991, "Les Services, ultimes frontières de l'expansion pour les multinationales," *Le Monde Diplomatique,* January, Paris: Le Monde: 10–11

Clark, N., 1999, "Sea of Islands/Oceans of Data," *Pander Magazine* (New Zealand), Issue 8, winter, July: 12–14

Clifford, J., 1997, *Routes: Travel and Translation in the Late Twentieth Century*, Cambridge, Mass.: Harvard University Press

Coggan, T., 1997, "Tonga Journalists Fight Royal Repression," *The Militant*, Vol. 61, No. 3, 20 January, available online at http://www.hartford-hwp.com/archives/24/022.html, accessed 11/24/2000

Coleman, S., 1999, "Cutting Out the Middle Man: From Virtual Representation to Direct Deliberation," in N. Hague and B. D. Loader (eds), *Digital Democracy: Discourse and Decision-Making in the Information Age*, London: Routledge, pp. 195–210

Collins, P. Hill, 1997, "Defining Black Feminist Thought," in L. Nicholson (ed.), *The Second Wave: A Reader in Feminist Theory*, London: Routledge, pp. 241–260

Comor, E. A. (ed.), 1994, *The Global Political Economy of Communication: Hegemony, Telecommunication, and the Information Economy*, New York: St. Martin's Press

Concerned, 01/06/00, *WILL DELETE PERSONAL and UNRELATED THREADS – PC, does that mean that all posts which don't reflect the Kamehameha Roundtable will be erased. Check yourselves (PC) because this is the Kamehameha (Hawaiian) Roundtable and not "Samoan" Roundtable*, initial post, Kamehameha Roundtable Discussion Forum, http://polycafe.com/Kamehameha/kamehameha.htm, accessed 01/18/2000

concerned, 01/13/00, *Thank you Pua for enlightening me. And if you miss Pua's message, here it is again*, initial post, Kamehameha Roundtable Discussion Forum, http://polycafe.com/Kamehameha/kamehameha.htm, accessed 02/01/2000

Corcoran, E., 1997, "Tiny Tonga Expands Its Domain: A Web Site Offering Internet Addresses Puts the Islands on the Online Map," *Washington Post*, July 1: C01, available online at http://www.Washingtonpost.com/wp-srv/WPlate/1997-07/01/040L-070197-idx.html, accessed 07/18/1997

Cox, R. W., 1987, *Production Power and World Order: Social Forces in the Making of History*, New York: Columbia University Press

Cox, R. W., 1992, "Global Perestroika," in R. Milliband and L. Panitch (eds), *The Socialist Register*, London: Merlin Press

Cox, R. W., 1994, "Global Restructuring: Making Sense of the Changing International Political Economy," in R. Stubbs and G. Underhill (eds), *Political Economy and the Changing Global Order*, Basingstoke, UK: Macmillan, pp. 45–59

Crawford, L. D., 2001, "Racism, Colorism and Power," *The FRONTal View: An Electronic Journal of African Centred Thought*, available online at www.nbufront.org/html/FRONTalView/ArticlesPapers/Crawford_RacismColorismPower.html, accessed 03/16/2001

Creedon, P. J., 1993, *Women in Mass Communication*, London: Sage

CTIN (Centre for Telecommunications Information Networking), 1996, *Advances in Information Technology Issues for Development in Asia/Pacific*, AusAID Initiated Research Program, Adelaide: University of Adelaide

Cubitt, S., 1997, *Digital Aesthetics*, London: Sage

Curran, J. and Gurevitch, M. (eds), 1991, *Mass Media and Society*, London: Edward Arnold

Dai, X., 2000, "Chinese Politics of the Internet: Control and Anti-control," *Cambridge Review of International Affairs*, Spring–Summer 2000, Vol. 23, No. 2, Cambridge: Cambridge University Press, pp. 181–194

Daily Planet, 11/22/99, *NEW KID – WHO ARE YOU – WHERE DID YOU COME FROM – WHAT DO YOU WANT – WHERE DO YOU HOPE TO GO???????*, initial post, Kamehameha Roundtable Discussion Forum, http://polycafe.com/Kamehameha/kamehameha.htm, accessed 01/19/2000

Dator, J., Jones, C., and Moir, B., 1986, *A Study of Preferred Futures for Telecommunications in Six Pacific Island Countries*, Final Report for GTE Corporation and Hawaiian Telephone Company, Honolulu, Hawaii: Social Science Research Institute

Davies, M. and Niemann, M., 2000, "Henri Lefebvre and Global Politics: Social Spaces and Everyday Struggles," paper presented at the British International Studies Association's Annual Conference, University of Bradford, Bradford, UK, December 18–20

de Certeau, M., 1980a, *L'Invention du quotidien 1: Arts de faire*, Paris: Union Générale d'Éditions

de Certeau, M., 1980b, "Préface," in L. Giard and P. Mayol, *L'Invention du quotidien II: Habiter, cuisiner*, Paris: Union Générale d'Editions, pp. 7–9

de Certeau, M., 1984, *The Practice of Everyday Life*, translated by Steven Rendall, Berkeley: University of California Press

de Certeau, M., 1986, *Heterologies: Discourse on the Other, Heterologies: Discourse on the Other*, translated by Brian Massumi, Theory and History of Literature, Vol. 17, Minneapolis: University of Minnesota Press

de Certeau, M., 1988, *The Writing of History*, translated by Tom Conley, New York: Columbia University Press

de Certeau, M., 1997a, *Culture in the Plural*, translated by Tom Conley, Minneapolis: University of Minnesota Press

de Certeau, M., 1997b, *The Capture of Speech and Other Political Writings*, translated by Tom Conley, Minneapolis: University of Minnesota Press

Deibert, R., 2000a, "International Plug 'n Play? Citizen Activism, the Internet, and Global Public Policy," *International Studies Perspectives*, Vol. 1, No. 3, December: 255–272

Deibert, R., 2000b, "Network Power," in R. Stubbs and G. Underhill (eds), *Political Economy and the Changing Global Order*, second edition, Oxford: Oxford University Press, pp. 198–207

Der Derian, J. (ed.), 1995, *International Theory: Critical Investigations*, London: Macmillan

Devetak, R., 2001a, "Critical Theory," in S. Burchill, R. Devetak, A. Linklater, M. Paterson, C. Reus-Smit, and J. True, *Theories of International Relations*, second edition, New York: Palgrave, pp. 155–180

Devetak, R., 2001b, "Postmodernism," in S. Burchill, R. Devetak, A. Linklater, M. Paterson, C. Reus-Smit, and J. True, *Theories of International Relations*, second edition, New York: Palgrave, pp. 181–208

di Leonardo, M. (ed.), 1991, *Gender at the Crossroads of Knowledge: Feminist Anthropology in the Postmodern Era*, Berkeley and Los Angeles: University of California Press

Dicken, P., 1992, *Global Shift: Industrial Change in a Turbulent World*, London: Harper and Row

Dixon, N., 1996, "Tonga detains pro-democracy campaigners," *Green Left Weekly*, available online at http://jinx.sistm.unsw.edu.au/~greenlft/1996/256/256p23b. htm, accessed 11/24/2000

Don't you all agree, 06/30/00, *Why is Pacific Islander and Asian always lumped together – hence Asian-Pacific Islander, shouldn't Pacific Islander be its own category???*, initial post, Kamehameha Roundtable Discussion Forum, http://polycafe.com/Kamehameha/kamehameha.htm, accessed 07/14/2000

Dot, 03/27/00, *Would you repost the guidelines for posting?*, initial post, Kava Bowl Discussion Forum, http://pacificforum.com, accessed 03/28/2000

Douglas, B., 1998, "Inventing Natives/Negotiating Local Identities: Postcolonial Readings of Colonial Texts on Island Melanesia," in J. Wassmann (ed.), *Pacific Answers to Western Hegemony: Cultural Practices of Identity Construction*, Oxford: Berg, pp. 67–96

Dufour, D.-R., 2001, "Les Désarrois de l'individu-sujet," *Le Monde Diplomatique*, February, Paris: Le Monde, available online at wysiwyg://23/http://www.monde-diplomatique.fr/2001/02/DUFOUR/14750.htm, accessed 03/13/2001

Dyrkton, J., 1996, "Cool Runnings: The Coming of Cyberreality in Jamaica," in R. Shields (ed.), *Cultures of Internet: Virtual Spaces, Real Histories, Living Bodies*, London: Sage, pp. 49–57

E. Tigris, 05/13/99, *What do you look for when you try to find a HUSBAND or WIFE?*, initial post, Kava Bowl Discussion Forum, http://pacificforum.com, accessed 01/14/2000

eb, 03/12/01, *Any Future US Political Clout for PI's??*, initial post, Kamehameha Roundtable Discussion Forum, http://polycafe.com/Kamehameha/kamehameha.htm, accessed 04/13/2001

Economist, The, 1995, "Survey: Telecommunications," *The Economist*, September 30: 5–40

Emmott, B., 1999, "On the Yellow Brick Road: Survey 20th Century," *The Economist*, September 11, available online at http://www.economist.com/editorial. freeforall/19990911/su3796.html, accessed 01/10/2000

Enloe, C., 1989, *Bananas, Beaches and Bases: Making Feminist Sense of International Politics*, London: Pandora

enough is ENOUGH, 04/24/99, *Dear Polycafe: Time for Spring cleaning?*, initial post, Polycafe, http://polycafe.com, accessed 04/28/1999

Esteva, G., 1992, "Development," in W. Sachs (ed.), *The Development Dictionary: A Guide to Knowledge as Power*, Johannesburg: Witwatersrand University/London: Zed Books, pp. 6–25

European Commission, 1997, *Building the European Information Society for Us All: Final Policy Report of the High-Level Expert Group*, Directorate-General for Employment, Industrial Relations and Social Affairs, Unit B.4, Luxembourg: European Commission

European Round Table Working Group, 1994, *Building the Information Highways: To Re-engineer Europe*, Brussels: European Roundtable

Everard, J., 2000, *Virtual States: The Internet and the Boundaries of the Nation-State*, London: Routledge

Fabian, J., 1983, *Time and the Other: How Anthropology Makes Its Object*, New York: Columbia University Press

Fairclough, N., 2003, *Analysing Discourse: Textual Analysis for Social Research*, London: Routledge

Falani Maka, 06/03/99, *A Play on the Royal Demons*, initial post, Kava Bowl Discussion Forum, http://pacificforum.com, accessed 11/29/2000

Featherstone, M., 1993, "Global and Local Futures," in J. Bird, B. Curtis, T. Putnam, G. Robertson, and L. Tickner (eds), *Mapping the Futures: Local Cultures, Global Change*, London: Routledge, pp. 169–187

Ferguson, M., 1995, "Media, Markets, and Identities: Reflections on the Global–Local Dialectic," *Canadian Journal of Communication*, Vol. 20, No. 4, autumn, available online at http://www.cjc-online.ca/BackIssues/20.4/Ferguson.html, accessed 01/27/2000

Fifita, T., 2000a, "A 'Tongan' Style Democracy," *Pacific Actions: Issues: Tonga's Pro-Democracy Movement*, available online at http://www.pasifika.net/pacific_action/issues/tongadem.html, accessed 11/24/2000

Fifita, T., 2000b, *Tonga*, available at http://www.pasifika.net/pacific_action/national/t/tonga.html, accessed 11/24/2000

Fildes, S., 1983, "The Inevitability of Theory," *Feminist Review*, 14, summer, pp. 61–73

Financial Times, The, 1996, "Gender Lines Lead to a Gold Mine: Women Are Floating into Cyberspace in Increasing Numbers," *Financial Times*, July 1: 9

Finekata, 03/15/99, *Women In Tonga . . . Recognised Or Ignored????*, initial post, Kava Bowl Discussion Forum, http://pacificforum.com, accessed 05/11/1999

Fitzgerald, T. K., 1998, "Metaphors, Media and Social Change: Second-Generation Cook Islanders in New Zealand," in J. Wassmann (ed.), *Pacific Answers to Western Hegemony: Cultural Practices of Identity Construction*, Oxford: Berg, pp. 253–268

Flanagan, K., 1998, "Refractions on the Pacific Rim: Tongan Writers' Responses to Transnationalism," *World Literature Today*, winter, Britannica.com, available at wysiwyg://31/http://www.britannica.com/.../magazine/article/0,5744,329135,00.html, accessed 07/11/2000

Flisi, C., 1998, "The ITU Moves to Trim Down, Speed Up and Work Closely with Private Sector," *International Herald Tribune*, 4 May, available online at http://www.iht.com/IHT/SUP/050498/TEL-3.HTML, accessed 10/15/1998

Foucault, M., 1973, *The Order of Things: An Archaeology of the Human Sciences*, New York: Vintage Books

Franklin, M. I., 2002, "Reading Walter Benjamin and Donna Haraway in the Age of Digital Reproduction," *Information, Communication and Society*, Vol. 5, No. 4: 591–624

Franklin, M. I., 2003a, " 'Wij zijn de Borg': Microsoft en de strijd om de controle over het internet," in G. Kiupers, J. de Kloet, and S. Kuik (eds), *Digitaal Contact: Het Net van de Begrensde Mogelijkheden*, in Amsterdams Sociologisch Tijdschrift, AST-Thema, jaargang 30, Amsterdam: Amsterdams Sociologisch Tijdschrift, pp. 223–253

Franklin, M. I., 2003b, "Beyond the 'Third Debate' in International Relations: Feminist and Postcolonial Research as Praxis," paper presented at the British International Studies Association's Annual Conference, University of Birmingham, UK, December 15–17

Franklin, M. I. (ed.), 2005, *Resounding International Relations: On Music, Culture and Politics*, London: Palgrave

Fraser, N., 1987, "What's Critical about Critical Theory? The Case of Habermas and Gender," in S. Benhabib and D. Cornell (eds), *Feminism as Critique*, Cambridge: Polity, pp. 31–55

Frederick, H. H., 1993, *Global Communication and International Relations*, Belmont, CA: Wadsworth

Freedom House, 2002, *Tonga*, in *Freedom in the World 2001–2002: Tonga*, online at www.freedomhouse.org/research/freeworld/2002/countryratings/tonga.htm, accessed 11/04/2003

Friedman, J., 1998, "Knowing Oceania or Oceanian Knowing: Identifying Actors and Activating Identities in Turbulent Times," in J. Wassmann (ed.), *Pacific Answers to Western Hegemony: Cultural Practices of Identity Construction*, Oxford: Berg, pp. 37–66

Frissen, V., 1992, "Trapped in Electronic Cages? Gender and New Information Technologies in the Public and Private Domain: An Overview of Research," *Media, Culture and Society*, Vol. 14: 31–49

Frissen, V., 1995, "Gender and ICTs: A Socially Constructed Silence," paper given at the Exploring Integration: Gender Perspectives in Communication Studies Conference, University of Groningen, the Netherlands, 4 April

Fry, G. and O'Hagan, J. (eds), 1999, *Contending Images of World Politics*, Basingstoke, UK: Macmillan

Fry, G., 1997a, "The South Pacific 'Experiment': Reflections on the Origins of Regional Identity," *Journal of Pacific History*, Vol. 32, No. 2: 180–202

Fry, G., 1997b, "Framing the Islands: Knowledge and Power in Changing Australian Images of 'the South Pacific,'" *The Contemporary Pacific*, Vol. 9, No. 2, fall: 305–344

Fuchs, G. and Koch, A. M., 1996, "The Globalization of Telecommunications and Issues of Regulatory Reform," in E. Kofman and G. Youngs (eds), *Globalization: Theory and Practice*, London: Pinter, pp. 163–173

Gal, S., 1991, "Between Speech and Silence: The Problematics of Research on Language and Gender," in M. di Leonardo (ed.), *Gender at the Crossroads of Knowledge: Feminist Anthropology in the Postmodern Era*, Berkeley and Los Angeles: University of California Press, pp. 175–203

George Candler, 02/09/99, *Longest Serving Rulers*, initial post, Kava Bowl Discussion Forum, http://pacificforum.com, accessed 01/11/2000

Ghost, 03/02/99, *Tongasat, Royal Family and Corruption are one!!!!*, initial post, Kava Bowl Discussion Forum, http://pacificforum.com, accessed 06/08/1999

Ghost, 03/03/99, *The Dominant Ideology in Tongan Society*, initial post, Kava Bowl Discussion Forum, http://pacificforum.com, accessed 01/13/2000

Giard, L. and Mayol, P., 1980, *L'Invention du quotidien 2: Habiter, cuisinier*, Paris: Union Générale d'Éditions

Gill, S. and Law, D. (eds), 1988, *The Global Political Economy: Perspectives, Problems and Policies*, Hemel Hempstead, UK: Harvester Wheatsheaf

Godzich, W., 1986, "Foreword: The Further Possibility of Knowledge," in M. de Certeau, *Heterologies: Discourse on the Other*, translated by Brian Massumi, Theory and History of Literature, Vol. 17, Minneapolis: University of Minnesota Press, pp. vii–xxi

Golding, P., 1998, "Global Village or Cultural Pillage? The Unequal Inheritance of the Communications Revolution," in R. W. McChesney, E. M. Wood, and J. B. Foster (eds), *Capitalism and the Information Age: The Political Economy of the Global Communications Revolution*, New York: Monthly Review Press, pp. 68–86

Golyardi, F. and Hilhorst, P., 2001, "Zwart Is Hip," interview with Paul Gilroy in *de Volkskrant* (Amsterdam), April 7: 5R

González, J., 2000, "The Appended Subject: Race and Identity as Digital Assemblage," in B. E. Kolko, L. Nakamura, and G. B. Rodman (eds), *Race in Cyberspace*, London: Routledge, pp. 27–50

Gordon, R., 1995, "Globalization, Innovation and Problem-Solving Growth," paper given at the Fourth Euro-Japan Conference, Beyond Economic Growth, University of California at Santa Cruz

Gore, A., 1994, "What Will a Global Superhighway Look Like?", speech delivered to the International Telecommunications Union meeting, Buenos Aires, Argentina, 21 March, in *Pacific Economic Review*, Summer 1994.

Gorgeousss, 02/10/99, *The ROLE of a SAMOAN WOMAN in Today's Society????*, initial post, Kamehameha Roundtable Discussion Forum, http://polycafe.com/kamehameha/kamehamehaF.htm, accessed 02/16/1999

gp, 11/16/00, *Is it wrong for me to want to preserve my culture?*, initial post, Kamehameha Roundtable Discussion Forum, http://polycafe.com/Kamehameha/kamehameha.htm, accessed 02/28/2001

Graham, G., 1999, *The Internet: A Philosophical Inquiry*, London: Routledge

Grassmuck, V., 2002, *Freie Software: Zwischen Privat- und Gemeineigentum: Themen und Materialen*, Bonn: Bundeszentrale für Politische Bildung

Grossberg, L., 1996a, "On Postmodernism and Articulation: An Interview with Stuart Hall," in D. Morley and K.-H. Chen (eds), *Stuart Hall: Critical Dialogues in Cultural Studies*, London: Routledge, pp. 131–150

Grossberg, L., 1996b, "History, Politics and Postmodernism: Stuart Hall and Cultural Studies," in D. Morley and K.-H. Chen (eds), *Stuart Hall: Critical Dialogues in Cultural Studies*, London: Routledge, pp. 151–173

Gurevitch, M., 1991, "The Globalization of Electronic Journalism," in J. Curran and M. Gurevitch (eds), *Mass Media and Society*, London and New York: Edward Arnold, pp. 178–193

Hague, B. N. and Loader, B. D. (eds), 1999, *Digital Democracy: Discourse and Decision Making in the Information Age*, London: Routledge

haka, 09/28/00, *DO ALL MAORIS CONSIDER THEMSELVES POLYNESIAN?*, initial post, Kamehameha Roundtable Discussion Forum, http://polycafe.com/Kamehameha/kamehameha.htm, accessed 02/28/2001

Hakken, D., 1999, *Cyborgs@Cyberspace? An Ethnographer Looks to the Future*, London: Routledge

Hall, S., 1996a, "New Ethnicities," in D. Morley and K.-H. Chen (eds), *Stuart Hall: Critical Dialogues in Cultural Studies*, London: Routledge, pp. 441–449

Hall, S., 1996b, "What Is This 'Black' in Black Popular Culture?" in D. Morley and K.-H. Chen (eds), *Stuart Hall: Critical Dialogues in Cultural Studies*, London: Routledge, pp. 465–475

Hamelink, C. J., 1995, *World Communication: Disempowerment and Self-Empowerment*, London: Zed Books

Hamelink, C. J., 1997, "New Information and Communication Technologies: Social Development and Cultural Change," Discussion Paper D.P.86, Geneva: United Nations Research Institute for Social Development

Harasim, L. M. (ed.), 1994, *Global Networks: Computers and International Communication*, Cambridge, Mass.: MIT Press

Haraway, D. J., 1990, "A Manifesto for Cyborgs: Science, Technology, and Socialist Feminism in the 1980s," in L. Nicholson (ed.), *Feminism/Postmodernism*, London: Routledge, pp. 190–233

Haraway, D. J., 1992, *Primate Visions: Gender, Race, and Nature in the World of Modern Science*, London: Verso

Haraway, D. J., 1997a, "Gender for a Marxist Dictionary: the Sexual Politics of a

Word," in L. McDowell and J. Sharp (eds), *Space, Gender, Knowledge: Feminist Readings*, London: Arnold, pp. 53–72

Haraway, D. J., 1997b, *Modest_Witness@Second_Millennium.FemaleMan©_ Meets_Onco-Mouse™: Feminism and Technoscience*, London: Routledge

Harcourt, W. (ed.), 1999, *Women@Internet: Creating New Cultures in Cyberspace*, London: Zed Books

Harding, S., 1998a, "Gender, Development, and Post-Enlightenment Philosophies of Science," *Hypatia*, Vol. 13, No. 3, summer: 146–167

Harding, S., 1998b, *Is Science Multicultural? Postcolonialisms, Feminisms, and Epistemologies*, Bloomington and Indianapolis: Indiana University Press

Hartmann, H., 1981, "The Unhappy Marriage of Marxism and Feminism: Towards a More Progressive Union," in L. Sargent (ed.), *Women and Revolution: A Discussion of the Unhappy Marriage between Marxism and Feminism*, Boston: South End Press, pp. 1–42

Harvey, D., 1990, *The Condition of Postmodernity: An Enquiry into the Origins of Cultural Change*, Oxford: Blackwell

Hau'ofa, E., 1983, *Tales of the Tikongs*, Honolulu: University of Hawaii Press

Hau'ofa, E., 1987, *Kisses in the Nederends*, Honolulu: University of Hawaii Press/Penguin Books

Hau'ofa, E., 1992, "The Social Context of the Pro-Democracy Movement in Tonga," *Human Rights and Democracy Movement – Convention 1992*, available online at http://www.planet-tonga.com/HRDMT/Articles/Convention_92/Epeli_Hauofa.shtml, accessed 11/04/2003

Hau'ofa, E., 1994, "Our Sea of Islands," *The Contemporary Pacific: A Journal of Island Affairs*, Vol. 6, No. 1, Spring: 147–161

Hau'ofa, E., 1998, "The Ocean in Us," *The Contemporary Pacific: A Journal of Island Affairs*, Vol. 10, No. 2, fall: 391–410

Hawkes, T., 1997, *Structuralism and Semiotics*, London: Routledge

Hawkins, R., 1996, "Standards for Communication Technologies. Negotiating Institutional Biases in Network Design," in R. Mansell and R. Silverstone (eds), *Communication by Design: The Politics of Information and Communication Technologies*, New York: Oxford University Press, pp. 157–186

Helu, 'I. F., 1999a, Interview with former director of the 'Atanisi Institute, Nuku'alofa, Tonga, July 30

Helu, 'I. F., 1999b, "Cultural Survival," in 'I. F. Helu, *Critical Essays: Cultural Perspectives from the South Seas*, Canberra: Journal of Pacific History, pp. 10–17

Helu, 'I. F., 1999c, "Human Rights from the Perspective of Tongan Culture," in 'I. F. Helu, *Critical Essays: Cultural Perspectives from the South Seas*, Canberra: Journal of Pacific History, pp. 32–36

Helu, 'I. F., 1999d, "Traditional Customs and Good Governance," in 'I. F. Helu, *Critical Essays: Cultural Perspectives from the South Seas*, Canberra: Journal of Pacific History, pp. 1–9

Helu, 'I. F., 1999e, "Tongan in the 1990s," in 'I. F. Helu, *Critical Essays: Cultural Perspectives from the South Seas*, Canberra: Journal of Pacific History, pp. 158–171

Helu, 'I. F., 1999f, "Some Economic Aspects of Kainga," in 'I. F. Helu, *Critical Essays: Cultural Perspectives from the South Seas*, Canberra: Journal of Pacific History, pp. 192–198

Hennessy, R., 1993, *Materialist Feminism and the Politics of Discourse*, London: Routledge

Henwood, F., Hughes, G., Kennedy, H., Miller, N., and Wyatt, S., 2001, "Cyborg Lives in Context: Writing Women's Technobiographies," in F. Henwood, H. Kennedy, and N. Miller (eds), *Cyborg Lives: Women's Technobiographies*, York: Raw Nerve Books, pp. 11–34

Herbert, G., 2000, "Producing Consumers: Selling the Neoliberal Imaginary," paper given at the British International Studies Association's Annual Conference, Bradford University, Bradford, UK, 16–18 December

Hereniko, V., 1999, "An Interview with Alan Duff," in V. Hereniko and B. Wilson (eds), *Inside Out: Literature, Cultural Politics, and Identity in the New Pacific*, Lanham, Md: Rowman & Littlefield, pp. 119–136

Hereniko, V. and Wilson, B. (eds), 1999, *Inside Out: Literature, Cultural Politics, and Identity in the New Pacific*, Lanham, Md: Rowman & Littlefield

Highmore, B., 2002, *Everyday Life and Cultural Theory: An Introduction*, London: Routledge

Hillis, K., 1996, "A Geography of the Eye: The Technologies of Virtual Reality," in R. Shields (ed.), *Cultures of Internet: Virtual Spaces, Real Histories, Living Bodies*, London: Sage, pp. 70–98

Hine, C., 2000, *Virtual Ethnography*, London: Sage

hingano, 07/05/01, *how many tongans are in the us?*, initial post, Kamehameha Roundtable Discussion Forum, http://polycafe.com/Kamehameha/kamehameha.htm, accessed 07/06/2001

Hirschkop, K., 1998, "Democracy and the New Technologies," in R. W. McChesney, E. M. Wood and J. B. Foster (eds), *Capitalism and the Information Age: The Political Economy of the Global Communications Revolution*, New York: Monthly Review Press, pp. 207–218

Holderness, M., 1998, "Who Are the World's Information Poor?" in B. Loader (ed.), *Cyberspace Divide: Equality, Agency and Policy in the Information Society*, London: Routledge, pp. 35–56

HOMELESS TONGAN, 03/09/99, *THE KING IS EXPANDING HIS HOME IN SAN MATEO COUNTY BUT HOW ABOUT US?*, initial post, Kava Bowl Discussion Forum, http://pacificforum.com, accessed 01/11/2000

hooks, bell, 1990, *Yearning: Race, Gender and Cultural Politics*, Boston: South End Press

Hooper, C., 2000, "Masculinities in Transition: The Case of Globalization," in M. Marchand and A. S. Runyan (eds), *Gender and Global Restructuring: Sites, Sightings and Resistances*, RIPE Series in Global Political Economy, London: Routledge, pp. 59–73

Huyssen, A., 1990, "Mapping the Postmodern," in L. Nicholson (ed.), *Feminism/Postmodernism*, London: Routledge, pp. 234–280

Ikani, 06/08/99, *ROYAL IDEOLOGY*, initial post, Kava Bowl Discussion Forum, http://pacificforum.com, accessed 10/19/1999

Inda, J. X. and Rosaldo, R. (eds), 2002, *The Anthropology of Globalisation: A Reader*, Oxford: Blackwell

Isikeli, 12/10/99, *Repost: DEMOCRATIC STRUCTURES FOR REFORM IN TONGA*, initial post, South Pacific Information Network Discussion Forum, http://sunsite.anu.edu.au/spin, accessed 12/08/2000

Jackson, P., 1993, "Towards a Cultural Politics of Consumption," in J. Bird, B. Curtis, T. Putnam, G. Robertson, and L. Tickner (eds), *Mapping the Futures: Local Cultures, Global Change*, London: Routledge, pp. 207–228

Jade, 05/27/99, *Samoan Snobbery or Just the Way it is??*, initial post, Kamehameha Roundtable Discussion Forum, http://polycafe.com/Kamehameha/kamehameha.htm, accessed 06/03/1999

Jaggar, A. M., 1983, *Feminist Politics and Human Nature: Philosophy and Society*, Totowa, NJ, Rowman & Allanheld

James, K., 2000, "Book Review: *Changing Their Minds: Tradition and Politics in Contemporary Fiji and Tonga*, by Rory Ewins," *The Contemporary Pacific*, Vol. 12, No. 1, spring: 273–275

James, K., 2003, "Tonga: Polynesia in Review: Issues and Events, 1 July 2001 to 30 June 2002," *The Contemporary Pacific*, Vol. 15, No. 1, spring: 174–179

Jameson, F., 1984, "Postmodernism or the Cultural Logic of Late Capitalism," *New Left Review*, Vol. 146: 53–93

jatu, 05/26/98, *brother/sister*, initial post, Tongan History Association Discussion Forum, http://pacificforum.com, accessed 02/11/2000

Jensen, J., 1995, "Mapping, Naming and Remembering: Globalization at the End of the Twentieth Century," *Review of International Political Economy*, Vol. 2, No. 1, winter: 96–116

Jesson, B., 1999, *Only Their Purpose Is Mad: The Money Men Take Over NZ*, Palmerston North, New Zealand: Dunmore Press

John Michel, 04/14/99, *What is the Tongan Way?*, initial post, Tongan History Association Discussion Forum, http://pacificforum.com, accessed 06/01/1999

Jolly, M. and Macintyre, M. (eds), 1989, *Family and Gender in the Pacific: Domestic Contradictions and the Colonial Impact*, Cambridge: Cambridge University Press

Jones, S. (ed.), 1999, *Doing Internet Research: Critical Issues and Methods for Examining the Net*, London: Sage

Jordan, T., 1999, *Cyberpower*, London: Routledge

just wondering, 10/11/99, *TIM SAMSON WHAT RACE ARE YOU?*, initial post, Kamehameha Roundtable Discussion Forum

Kaba, E. K., 1999, "Connecting Africa to Cyberspace: Another Storm in a Tea Cup? A Study of the Africa One Project," MA thesis, International School for the Humanities and Social Sciences, University of Amsterdam

Kaitapu, J., 1999, interview with Assistant Systems Advisor, Royal School of Science, Nuku'alofa, Tonga, 27–31 July

Kami, T., 2001, interview with the founder of the Pacific Forum, 29 March, Brussels

kavahine, 09/30/00, *When applying for college, my buddy put that she was Samoan . . . whereas she's only 1/8 and 7/8s palangi . . . does anybody see anything wrong with that*, initial post, Kamehameha Roundtable Discussion Forum, http://polycafe.com/Kamehameha/kamehameha.htm, accessed 02/28/2001

KBAdmin, 09/08/97, *Weekly Discussion Topic #11: POLY CULTURE & TRADITION: When living overseas, what cultural elements should be/are retained and what should be/are being discarded in favour of elements from the new environment?*, initial post, Kava Bowl Discussion Forum, http://pacificforum.com, accessed 09/10/1997

KBAdmin, 01/04/98, *Weekly Discussion Topic #23: What Are Some Of The Most Common Cross-cultural Misconceptions Among Islanders?*, initial post in Kava Bowl Discussion Forum, http://pacificforum.com, accessed 01/04/1998

KBAdmin, 01/20/98, *KB POLICY ON EDITING – PLEASE READ*, initial post, Kava Bowl Discussion Forum, http://pacificforum.com, accessed 05/08/1998

KBAdmin, 02/08/98, *WEEKLY DISCUSSION TOPIC #24/27 – ADHERENCE TO*

CHIEFLY AND ROYAL SUCCESSIONS, initial post in Kava Bowl Discussion Forum, http://pacificforum.com, accessed 06/03/98

KBAdmin, 02/15/98, *Weekly Discussion Topic #28: Tongan Foreign Policy ... An Opinion about Fiji?*, initial post, Kava Bowl Discussion Forum, http://pacificforum.com, accessed 06/03/1998

KBAdmin, 03/09/98, *Weekly Discussion Topic #31: For the Overseas Tongan, What Does "Being" Tongan Mean?*, initial post, Kava Bowl Discussion Forum, http://pacificforum.com, accessed 06/23/1998

KBAdmin, 05/11/98, *Weekly Discussion Topic #38: Second Generation Polys Overseas ... Sometimes "Between a Rock and a Hard Place,"* initial post, Kava Bowl Discussion Forum, http://pacificforum.com, accessed 08/24/1998

KBAdmin, 08/16/98, *Weekly Discussion Topic #50 (The Big Five-Oh!): Poly Kids ... Does Trying To Appease Two Cultures Have You Between A Rock And A Hard Place?*, initial post, Kava Bowl Discussion Forum, http://pacificforum.com, accessed 08/24/1998

KBAdmin, 09/07/98, *Weekly Discussion Topic #51: Democracy in Tonga: Pro or Con??*, initial post in Kava Bowl Discussion Forum, http://pacificforum.com, accessed 09/25/1998

KBAdmin, 09/14/98, *Weekly Discussion Topic #52: Poly Violence ... Heritage, Or Hate?*, initial post in Kava Bowl Discussion Forum, http://pacificforum.com, accessed 10/06/1998

KBAdmin, 10/18/98, *Weekly Discussion Topic #56: Too Much Chlorine in the Gene Pool?*, initial post in Kava Bowl Discussion Forum, http://pacificforum.com, accessed 04/28/1999

KBAdmin, 11/16/98, *Weekly Discussion Topic #59: Living Overseas ... In A Poly Community, Or Not?*, initial post in Kava Bowl Discussion Forum, http://pacificforum.com, accessed 11/16/1998

KBAdmin, 02/07/99, *WEEKLY DISCUSSION TOPIC #65: Chinese Threatening Tongan Culture? Get Over It ... This Is Old Hat!*, initial post, Kava Bowl Discussion Forum, http://pacificforum.com, accessed 04/28/99

KBAdmin, 06/17/99, *Discussion Topic #69: making the Homeland Economies More Viable: suggestions?*, initial post, Kava Bowl Discussion Forum, http://pacificforum.com, accessed 07/05/1999

KBAdmin, 03/21/00, *Please Refrain from Using Capitals*, initial post, Kava Bowl Discussion Forum, http://pacificforum.com, accessed 04/07/2000

Kelly, C. A., 2000, "Whatever Happened to Women's Liberation? or, Theory and Praxis Once Again," *New Political Science*, Vol. 22, No. 2, June: 161–176

Kelly, K., 1994, *Out of Control: The New Biology of Machines, Social Systems, and the Economic World*, New York: Addison-Wesley

Kelsey, J., 1997, *The New Zealand Experiment: A World Model for Structural Adjustment?*, Auckland: Auckland University Press

Kendall, L., 1999, "Recontextualising 'Cyberspace': Methodological Considerations for On-Line Research," in S. Jones (ed.), *Doing Internet Research: Critical Issues and Methods for Examining the Net*, London: Sage, pp. 57–74

King, R. and Connell, J. (eds), 1999, *Small Worlds, Global Lives: Islands and Migration*, London: Pinter

Kleinsteuber, H. J. (ed.), 1996, *Der "Information Superhighway": Amerikanische Visionen und Erfahrungen*, Wiesbaden: Westdeutscher Verlag

kode, 03/30/99, *Why is it that when a Tongan woman marries a man, it is expected of her to drop her religion for his??*, initial post, Tongan History Association Discussion Forum, http://pacificforum.com, accessed 02/11/2000

Kofman, E. and Youngs, G. (eds), 1996, *Globalization: Theory and Practice*, London: Pinter

Kolko, B. E., 1995, "Building a World with Words: The Narrative Reality of Virtual Communities," *Works and Days 25/26*, Vol. 13, Nos 1/2: 105–126, Indiana University of Pennsylvania, available online at http://www.iup.edu/en/workdays/Kolko.html, accessed 06/04/1999

Kolko, B. E., Nakamura, L., and Rodman, G. B. (eds), 2000, *Race in Cyberspace*, London: Routledge

Korn, N., 1999, "www.loot.com," *The Age*, 7 February, available online at wysywyg://109/http://www.theage.com.au/daily/990207/news/news24.html, accessed 07/18/1999

Krishna, S., 2002, "In One Innings: National Identity in Postcolonial Times," in G. Chowdhry and S. Nair (eds), *Power, Postcolonialism and International Relations: Reading Race, Gender and Class*, London: Routledge, pp. 170–183

KZ7, 03/28/00, *Where are the Caring Women?*, initial post, Kamehameha Roundtable Discussion Forum, http://polycafe.com/kamehameha/kamehameha.htm, accessed 05/19/2000

Lacey, K., 2000, "Towards a Periodization of Listening," *International Journal of Cultural Studies*, Vol. 3, No. 2, August: 279–288

Lacroix, G., 1998, "Cybernétique et Société Norbert Wiener ou les déboires d'une pensée subversive," *Terminal* No. 61, Paris: l'Harmattan, available online at http://www.terminal.ens-cachan.fr/61indentitespouvoirs.html, accessed 07/14/1998

Lafemme Nikita, 04/23/99, *The Right To Freedom of Speech*, initial post, Kamehameha Roundtable Discussion Forum, http://polycafe.com/Kamehameha/kamehameha.htm, accessed 06/08/1999

Lafemme Nikita, 05/19/99, *I'm Tired of Slaving Myself – The Role of the Woman*, initial post, Kava Bowl Discussion Forum, http://pacificforum.com, accessed 01/31/2001; initial post, Polycafe, http://Polycafe.com, accessed 05/21/1999

Lapid, Y., 1989, "The Third Debate: On the Prospects of International Theory in a Post-Positivist Era," *International Studies Quarterly*, Vol. 33: 235–254

Latukefu, 'Alopi, 1999, interview with the founder of the South Pacific Information Network website, Sydney, Australia, August 3

Lausii, 05/18/99, *WOMEN'S RIGHT*, initial post, Kava Bowl Discussion Forum, http://pacificforum.com, accessed 01/31/2001

Lee, H. Morton, 2003, *Tongans Overseas*, Honolulu: Hawaii University Press

Leilani, 08/05/98, *Views on Globalization?*, initial post, Kamehameha Roundtable Discussion Forum, http://polycafe.com/kamehameha/kamehamehaF.htm, accessed 08/06/1998

Leiss, W., Kline, S., and Jhally, S., 1990, *Social Communication in Advertising: Persons, Products and Images of Well-Being*, London: Routledge

Lemos, A., 1996, "The Labyrinth of Minitel," in R. Shields (ed.), *Cultures of Internet: Virtual Spaces, Real Histories, Living Bodies*, London: Sage, pp. 33–48

Leonard, S. T., 1990, *Critical Theory in Political Practice*, Princeton, N.J.: University Press

Lerner, G., 1986, *The Creation of Patriarchy*, Oxford: Oxford University Press

Leung, L., 2001, "The Past Lives of a Cyborg: Encountering 'Space Invaders' from the 1980s to the 1990s," in F. Henwood, H. Kennedy, and N. Miller (eds), *Cyborg Lives: Women's Technobiographies*, York: Raw Nerve Books, pp. 127–132

Ling, L. H. M., 2002, *Postcolonial International Relations: Conquest and Desire between Asia and the West*, New York: Palgrave

Loader, B. (ed.), 1998, *Cyberspace Divide: Equality, Agency and Policy in the Information Society*, London: Routledge

Locher, B. and Prügl, E., 2001, "Feminism and Constructivism: Worlds Apart or Sharing the Middle Ground?" *International Studies Quarterly*, Vol. 45, No. 1, March: 111–130

Ludlow, P. (ed.), 1996, *High Noon on the Electronic Frontier: Conceptual Issues in Cyberspace*, Cambridge, Mass.: MIT Press

LUT, 05/18/99, *Does Searching for Equality by a woman destroy the harmony in a Tongan family!*, initial post, Kava Bowl Discussion Forum, http://pacificforum.com, accessed 01/14/2000

Lüthje, B., 1997, "Transnationale Dimensionen der 'Network Revolution,'" in J. Esser, B. Lüthje, and R. Noppe (eds), *Europäische Telekommunikation im Zeitalter der Deregulierung: Infrastruktur im Umbruch*, Münster: Westfälisches Dampfboot, pp. 36–77

MA, 02/29/00, *The "public–private distinction" – is there one??!!*, initial post, Tongan History Association Discussion Forum, http://pacificforum.com, accessed 03/03/2000

McChesney, R. W., Wood, E. M., and Foster, J. B. (eds), 1998, *Capitalism and the Information Age: The Political Economy of the Global Communication Revolution*, New York: Monthly Review Press

McDowell, L. and Sharp, J. P. (eds), 1997, *Space, Gender, Knowledge: Feminist Readings*, London: Arnold

McGovern, P., 2000, "A Closed Community: Frederic Jameson and the Commodification of Political Science," *New Political Science*, Vol. 22, No. 2, June: 265–280

McHaffie, P., 1997, "Decoding the Globe: Globalism, Advertising, and Corporate Practice," *Environment and Planning D: Society and Space*, Vol. 15: 73–86

McLuhan, M. and Powers, B. R., 1989, *The Global Village: Transformations in World Life and Media in the 21st Century*, Oxford: Oxford University Press

McNicholas, P., Humphries, M., and Gallhofer, S., 2003, "Maintaining the Empire: Maori Women's Experiences in the Accountancy Profession," *Critical Perspectives on Accounting*, 1044, July: 1–37

Macpherson, C., 1997, "The Polynesian Diaspora: New Communities and New Questions," in K. Sudo and S. Yoshida (eds), *Contemporary Migration in Oceania: Diaspora and Network*, Osaka: National Museum of Ethnology, pp. 77–100

Macpherson, C., Spoonley, P., and Anae, M. (eds), 2001, *Tangata O Te Moana Nui: The Evolving Identities of Pacific Peoples in Aotearoa/New Zealand*, Palmerston North, New Zealand: Dunmore Press.

McQuail, D., 1987, *Mass Communication Theory: An Introduction*, second edition, London: Sage

Māhina, Okusi, 1999, interview, Department of Cultural Anthropology, University of Auckland, New Zealand, August

Malina, A., 1999, "Perspectives on Citizen Democratisation and Alienation in the Virtual Public Sphere," in B. N. Hague and B. D. Loader (eds), *Digital Democracy: Discourse and Decision Making in the Information Age*, London: Routledge, pp. 23–38

Mandaville, P., 1999, "Reimagining the Umma: Information Technology and the Changing Boundaries of Religious Knowledge," in A. Mohammadi (ed.), *Islam Encountering Globalisation*, Ithaca, NY: Ithaca Press

Manière de voir, 1995, *Médias et contrôle des esprits*, No. 27, August, Paris: Le Monde Diplomatique

Manière de voir, 1996a, *Scénarios de la Mondialisation*, No. 32, November, Paris: Le Monde Diplomatique

Manière de voir, 1996b, *Internet: l'extase et l'effroi*, Hors-Série, October, Paris: Le Monde Diplomatique

Mansell, R. and Silverstone, R. (eds), 1996, *Communication by Design: The Politics of Information and Communication Technologies*, Oxford: Oxford University Press

Mansell, R. and Wehn, U., 1998, *Knowledge Societies: Information Technology for Sustainable Development*, United Nations/Oxford: Oxford University Press

Manu, 05/18/99, *Pohiva's credentials?*, initial post, Kava Bowl Discussion Forum, http://pacificforum.com, accessed 01/13/2000

Marchand, M. and Runyan, A. (eds), 2000, *Gender and Global Restructuring: Sites, Sightings and Resistances*, RIPE Series in Global Political Economy, London: Routledge

Maresch, R. and Rötzer, F., *Cyberhypes: Möglichkeiten und Grenzen des Internet*, Frankfurt am Main: Edition Suhrkamp

Marrow, H., 2003, "To Be or Not to Be (Hispanic or Latino)," *Ethnicities*, Vol. 3, No. 4, December: 427–464

MARY, 03/01/01, *Are light skinned polynesians considered better than dark skinned polynesians?*, initial post, Kamehameha Roundtable Discussion Forum, http://polycafe.com/Kamehameha/kamehameha.htm, accessed 05/08/1998

Mattelart, A., 1994, *Mapping World Communication: War, Progress, Culture*, Minneapolis: University of Minnesota Press

Mattelart, A., 1995, "Une éternelle promesse: les paradis de la communication," *Le Monde Diplomatique*, November, Paris: Le Monde: 4–5

Maui, 02/09/99, *Safata or Satana or who ever you are*, initial post, Kava Bowl Discussion Forum, http://pacificforum.com, accessed 01/13/2000

May, C., 2000, *A Global Political Economy of Intellectual Property Rights: The New Enclosures?*, RIPE Series in Global Political Economy, London: Routledge

May, C., 2002, *The Information Society: A Sceptical View*, Cambridge: Polity Press

May, C., 2003 (ed.), *Key Thinkers for the Information Society*, London: Routledge

Melody, W., 1994, "The Information Society: Implications for Economic Institutions and Market Theory," in E. Comor (ed.), *The Global Political Economy of Communication: Hegemony, Telecommunication, and the Information Economy*, New York: St. Martin's Press, pp. 21–36

Melody, W., 2001, interview, Delft Technical University, the Netherlands. January 25

Mendosa, R., 1996, "Tongasat's Flawed Genius," available online at http://gate.cruzio.com/~mendosa/Tongasat.html, accessed 06/26/1998

Miller, D. and Slater, D., 2000, *The Internet: An Ethnographic Approach*, Oxford: Berg, available online at http://ethnonet.gold.ac.uk/summary.html, accessed 05/23/2000

Miller, G. and Dunn, A., 2000, "Internet's Toll on Social Life? No Cause for Worry, Study Says," *Los Angeles Times*, October 26, available online at http://www.latimes.com/business/20001-26/t000102193.html, accessed 10/30/2000

Minges, M., 2000, "Counting the Net: Internet Access Indicators," paper presented at INET 2000, The Internet Global Summit, Yokohama, July 18–21, 2000, available online at http://www.isoc.org/inet2000/cdproceedings/8e/8e_1.html, accessed 06/08/2001

miss thang, 05/28/99, *the intolerance towards half-caste polyies*, initial post, Kamehameha Roundtable Discussion Forum, http://polycafe.com/Kamehameha/kamehameha.htm, accessed 06/03/1999

Mitchell, J., 1974, *Psychoanalysis and Feminism*, New York: Vintage Books

Mitra, A. and Cohen, E., 1999, "Analyzing the Web: Directions and Challenges," in S. Jones (ed.), *Doing Internet Research: Critical Issues and Methods for Examining the Net*, London: Sage, pp. 179–202

Mitter, S. and Rowbotham, S. (eds), 1995, *Women Encounter Technology*, London: Routledge and UNU Press

Mixed Up, 02/02/99, *Are there other young Samoans who don't know the Samoan language . . . I mean well enough to carry on a conversation with someone other than your grandma??*, initial post, Kamehameha Roundtable Discussion Forum, http://polycafe.com/kamehameha/kamehameha.htm, accessed 03/16/1999

Mohanty, C. T., 1997, "Feminist Encounters: Locating the Politics of Experience," in L. McDowell and J. Sharp (eds), *Space, Gender, Knowledge: Feminist Readings*, London: Arnold, pp. 82–98

Moore, R. K., 1999, "Democracy and Cyberspace," in B. N. Hague and B. D. Loader (eds), *Digital Democracy: Discourse and Decision Making in the Information Age*, London: Routledge, pp. 39–62

Moore-Gilbert, B., Stanton, G., and Maley, W. (eds), 1997, *Postcolonial Criticism*, Harlow, UK: Longman

Morely, D. and Chen, K.-H. (eds), 1996, *Stuart Hall: Critical Dialogues in Cultural Studies*, London: Routledge

Morton, H., 1996, *Becoming Tongan: An Ethnography of Childhood*, Honolulu: University of Hawaii Press

Morton, H., 1998a/2001, "I Is for Identity: What's in a Name?" paper presented at Australian Anthropological Society Conference, Australian National University, Canberra, October 1–3; also in H. Morton (ed.), *Computer-Mediated Communication in Australian Anthropology and Sociology*, Special Issue of *Social Analysis: Journal of Cultural and Social Practice*, Issue 45 (1), April 2001, Adelaide: University of Adelaide: 67–80

Morton, H., 1998b, "How Tongan Is a Tongan? Cultural authenticity revisited," in D. Scarr, N. Gunsen, and J. Terrell (eds), *Echoes of Pacific War: Papers from the 7th Tongan History Conference, Canberra, 1997*, Canberra: Australian National University Press, pp. 149–166

Morton, H., 1999, "Islanders in Space: Tongans Online," in R. King and J. Connell (eds), *Small Worlds, Global Lives: Islands and Migration*, London: Pinter, pp. 235–254

Moyal, A., 1992, "The Gendered Use of the Telephone: An Australian Case Study," *Media, Culture and Society*, Vol. 14: 51–72

Murphy, C. N. and Rojas de Ferro, C., 1995, "Theme Section: The Power of Representation in International Political Economy: Introduction," *Review of International Political Economy*, Vol. 2, No. 1, winter: 63–183

MVP, 11/13/99, *DOES THE FAKA-PALANGI ATTITUDE DESERVE TO BE CRITICISED?*, initial post, Kava Bowl Discussion Forum, http://pacificforum.com, accessed 11/15/1999

Narayan, U., 1997, "Contesting Cultures: 'Westernisation,' Respect for Cultures, and Third-World Feminists," in L. Nicholson (ed.), *The Second Wave: A Reader in Feminist Theory*, London: Routledge, pp. 396–414

New Kid, 01/30/99, *Let's Agree to Disagree; But not agree for an All -Out Brawl!*, initial post, Kamehameha Roundtable Discussion Forum, http://polycafe.com/Kamehameha/kamehameha.htm, accessed 02/16/1999

Nicholson, L. (ed.), 1990, *Feminism/Postmodernism*, London: Routledge

Nicholson, L. (ed.), 1997, *The Second Wave: A Reader in Feminist Theory*, London: Routledge

Nickelson, R., 1999, interview with External Affairs Manager, Pacific Telecommunications Council, Honolulu, Hawaii, July 21

NINJA, 05/12/99, *NO DEMOCRACY MOVEMENT IN TONGA, I HOPE NOT!*, initial post, Kava Bowl Discussion Forum, http://pacificforum.com, accessed 05/21/1999

Nustad, K. G., 2004, "The Development Discourse in the Multilateral System," in M. Bøås and D. McNeill (eds), *Global Institutions and Development: Framing the World?*, RIPE Series in Global Political Economy, London: Routledge, pp. 13–23

OECD, 1992, *Convergence between Communications Technologies: Case Studies from North America and Western Europe*, Information Computer Communication Policy 28, Paris: OECD

OECD, 1998a, "Internet Infrastructure Indicators," *Working Party on Telecommunication and Information Services Policies DSTI/ICCP/TISP(98)7/FINAL (unclassified)*, Directorate for Science, Technology and Industry, Paris: OECD

OECD, 1998b, *Global Information Infrastructure–Global Information Society (GII-GIS): Policy Recommendations for Action*, OECD/GD(97)138, available online at http://38.180.155.6/islands/recgii.htm, accessed 03/24/1998

OECD, 2000, *Information Technology Outlook, 2000: ICTs, E-commerce and the Information Economy*, Paris: OECD

OECD, 2001, *Understanding the Digital Divide*, Paris: OECD

Ogden, M. R., 1993, "Islands on the Net: Technology and Development Features in Pacific Island Microstates," PhD dissertation, University of Hawaii, Honolulu

Ogden, M. R., 1999, "Islands on the Internet," *Pacific Telecommunications Review*, Vol. 21, No. 2, 4 October, Honolulu: Pacific Telecommunications Council, pp. 5–16

Okamura, N., 1999, interview with Director, PEACESAT, Social Science Research Institute, University of Hawaii, July 23

Ortner, S. B., 1996, *Making Gender: The Politics and Erotics of Culture*, Boston: Beacon Press

Paccagnella, L., 1997, "Getting the Seats of Your Pants Dirty: Strategies for Ethnographic Research on Virtual Communities," *Journal of Computer-Mediated Communication*, Vol. 3, No. 1, June, available online at http://www.ascusc/org/jcmc/vol3/issue1/paccagnella.html, accessed 06/04/1999

Pacific Islands Report, 2002, "Pressure for Political Reform in Tonga," *Pacific Islands Development Program/East–West Centre*, March 10, available online at http://groups.yahoo.com/group.tonga/message/5301, accessed 11/04/2003

Pacific Magazine, 2002, "Tonga's Pro-democracy Movement Calls for Reforms but King Taufa'ahau Has Resisted Move," April, *Pacificislands.cc: The Web site of Pacific Magazine and Islands Business*, available online at http://www.pacificislandscc/pm42002/pmdefault.php?/urlarticleid=0033, accessed 11/04/2003

Pacific Media Watch, 2003, "4150 Tonga: Pro-Democracy Movement Vows to Fight

On over Media," *Pacific Media Watch listserv*, 16 August, available online at http://www.pmw.c2o.org/2003/tongan4150.html, accessed 11/04/2003

Palan, R., 1996, "Technological Metaphors and Theories of International Relations," in M. Talalay, C. Farrands, and R. Tooze (eds), *Technology, Culture and Competitiveness: Change and the World Political Economy*, London: Routledge, pp. 13–26

Palan, R., 2000, "The Constructivist Underpinnings of the New International Political Economy," in R. Palan (ed.), *Contemporary Theories in Global Political Economy*, RIPE Series in Global Political Economy, London: Routledge, pp. 215–228

Persaud, R. B., 2002, "Situating Race in International Relations: The Dialectics of Civilizational Security in American Immigration," in G. Chowdhry and S. Nair (eds), *Power, Postcolonialism and International Relations: Reading Race, Gender and Class*, London: Routledge, pp. 56–81

Peterson, V. S. (ed.), 1992, *Gendered States: Feminist (Re)Visions of International Relations Theory*, Boulder, CO: Lynne Rienner

Peterson, V. S., 1996, "Shifting Ground(s): Epistemological and Territorial Remapping in the Context of Globalization," in E. Kofman and G. Youngs (eds), *Globalization: Theory and Practice*, London: Pinter, pp. 11–28

Peterson, V. S., 1998, "Rewriting (Global) Political Economy as Reproductive, Productive and Symbolic (Foucauldian) Economies," paper presented at the 3rd ECPR–ISA Joint Conference, Vienna, September

Peterson, V. S., 2003, *A Critical Rewriting of Global Political Economy: Integrating Reproductive, Productive and Virtual Economies*, RIPE Series in Global Political Economy, London: Routledge

Peterson, V. S. and Runyan, A. S., 1999, *Global Gender Issues*, second edition, Dilemmas in World Politics Series, Boulder, CO: Westview Press

Pettman, J. J., 1996, "An International Political Economy of Sex?" in E. Kofman and G. Youngs (eds), *Globalization: Theory and Practice*, London: Pinter, pp. 191–208

Pisani, F., 1995, "Les Frontières inconnues du cyberespace," *Le Monde Diplomatique*, Paris: Le Monde, November

Plant, S., 1996, "On the Matrix: Cyberfeminist Simulations," in R. Shields (ed.), *Cultures of Internet: Virtual Spaces, Real Histories, Living Bodies*, London: Sage, pp. 170–183

Polanyi, K., 1944, *The Great Transformation: The Political and Economic Origins of Our Time*, Boston: Beacon Press

Poly Parent, 05/31/99, *LDS (Mormon) Has it become americanized?*, initial post, Kava Bowl Discussion Forum, http://pacificforum.com, accessed 01/14/2000

POLYCAFE, 05/08/98, *Polycafe's Polynesiana Contest*, initial post, Polycafe, http://polycafe.com/Polynesian_2.html, accessed 05/08/1998

POLYCAFE, 05/04/99, *ALL SUBJECT HEADINGS LONGER THAN 1 LINE WILL BE DELETED!*, initial post in Polycafe, http://polycafe.com, accessed 05/21/1999

Pro-Democracy Movement, *Pro-Democracy Movement*, www.pasifika.net/pacific_action/national/t/tonga.html:2/10, accessed 11/24/2000

Quintas, P., 1996, "Software by Design," in R. Mansell and R. Silverstone (eds), *Communication by Design: The Politics of Information and Communication Technologies*, Oxford: Oxford University Press, pp. 75–102

Raskin, A., 1998, "Buy This Domain: Tuvalu's .tv Stands to Radically Upgrade the

Country's $10 Million GDP," *Wired* magazine, September 6, available online at http://www.wired.com/wired/archive/6.09/Tuvalu_pr.html, accessed 07/18/1999

Raynor, P., Wall, P., and Kruger, S., 2001, *As Media Studies: The Essential Introduction*, London: Routledge

Reid, E. M., 1996, "Communication and Community in Internet Relay Chat: Constructing Communities," in P. Ludlow (ed.), *High Noon on the Electronic Frontier: Conceptual Issues in Cyberspace*, Cambridge, Mass.: MIT Press, pp. 397–412

Reus-Smit, C., 2001, "Constructivism," in S. Burchill, R. Devetak, A. Linklater, M. Paterson, C. Reus-Smit, and J. True, *Theories of International Relations*, second edition, New York: Palgrave, pp. 209–230

Rheingold, H., 1994, "A Slice of Life in My Virtual Community," in L. Harasim (ed.), *Global Networks: Computer Networks and International Communication*, Cambridge Mass.: MIT Press, pp. 57–80

Ridell, S., 2002, "The Web as a Space for Local Agency," *Communications*, Vol. 27: 147–169

Rist, G., 1997, *The History of Development: From Western Origins to Global Faith*, London: Zed Books

Roberts, J., 1999, "Philosophizing the Everyday: The Philosophy of Praxis and the Fate of Cultural Studies," *Radical Philosophy*, Vol. 98, November/December, pp. 16–29

Robie, D., 1999, "Café Pacific and Online Censorship: Cyberspace Media in an Island State," *Asia Pacific Media Educator*, Issue 6, January–June 1999, Graduate School of Journalism, Australia: University of Wollongong, available online at http://www.asiapac.org.fj/cafepacific/resources/aspac/apme.html, accessed 08/11/1999

Rodgers, F. J., 2003, *Spatializing International Politics: Analysing Activism on the Internet*, London: Routledge

Rogers, R. (ed.), 2000, *Preferred Placement*, Maastricht: Jan van Eyck Akademie Editions

Rosow, S. J., Inayatullah, N., and Rupert, M. (eds), 1994, *The Global Economy of Political Space*, Boulder, CO: Lynne Rienner

Ross, A., 1995, "Science Backlash on Technoskeptics: 'Culture Wars' Spill Over," *The Nation*, October 2, available online at www.thomson.com/routledge/cst/ross.html, accessed 03/25/1997

Rowbotham, S., 1995, "Feminist Approaches to Technology: Women's Values or a Gender Lens," in S. Mitter and S. Rowbotham (eds), *Women Encounter Technology*, London: Routledge, pp. 44–69

Rubin, G., ([1975] 1997), "The Traffic in Women: Notes on the 'Political Economy' of Sex," in L. Nicholson (ed.), *The Second Wave: A Reader in Feminist Theory*, London: Routledge, pp. 27–62

Rushkoff, D., 2001, "Virtuelles Marketing," in R. Maresch and F. Rötzer (eds), *Cyberhypes: Möglichkeiten und Grenzen des Internet*, Frankfurt am Main: Edition Suhrkamp, pp. 102–122

Sachs, W. (ed.), 1993, *The Development Dictionary: A Guide to Knowledge as Power*, London: Zed Books

safata, 01/29/99, *KB ADMINISTRATION: Who do you edit? Who are you protecting?*, initial post, Kava Bowl Discussion Forum, http://pacificforum.com, accessed 01/13/2000

safata, 02/04/99, *ON A POSITIVE NOTE .WHAT CAN WE DO TO ACCOMMODATE*

OUR CHINESE TONGANS, WITHOUT FORCING THEM OUT OF TONGA, initial post, Kava Bowl Discussion Forum, http://pacificforum.com, accessed 02/05/1999

Sam Owens, 05/20/99, *Thank you Polycafe for doing away with posts with slang and profanity!!!*, initial post, Polynesian Cafe, http://polycafe.com, accessed 05/21/1999

Samoan Sensation, 2001, *Web Servers/Sites in Samoa: Survey performed June 5th 2001 09.00 GMT*, available online at wysiwyg://101/http://www.Samoa.co.uk/samoan-servers.html, accessed 06/14/2001

Sandy Macintosh, 03/27/00, *RE: Kava Bowl*, initial post, Kava Bowl Discussion Forum, http://pacificforum.com, accessed 05/19/2000

Sargent, L. (ed.), 1981, *Women and Revolution: A Discussion of the Unhappy Marriage of Marxism and Feminism*, Boston: South End Press

Sassen, S., 1991, *Global Cities: London, New York, Tokyo*, Ithaca, NY: Princeton University Press

Sassen, S., 1995, "The State and the Global City: Notes towards a Conception of Place-Centred Governance," *Competition and Change*, Vol. 1: 31–50

Saunders, B. and Foblets, M.-C. (eds), 2002, *Changing Genders in Intercultural Perspective*, Belgium: Leuven University Press

Schiller, D., 1999, *Digital Capitalism: Networking the Global Market System*, Cambridge, Mass: MIT Press

Scholte, J. A., 2000, *Globalization: A Critical Introduction*, New York: St. Martin's Press

Sefita Auckland New Zealand, 03/12/99, *The democracy issue must be wilting*, initial post, Kava Bowl Discussion Forum, http://pacificforum.com, accessed 01/11/2000

Seth, S., 1999, "A 'Postcolonial World'?" in G. Fry and J. O'Hagan (eds), *Contending Images of World Politics*, Basingstoke, UK: Macmillan, pp. 214–266

Shade, L., 1993, "Gender Issues in Computing," paper given at Community Networking: The International Free-Net Conference, Carleton University, Ottawa, 17–19 August,

Sharf, B. F., 1999, "Beyond Netiquette: The Ethics of Doing Naturalistic Discourse Research on the Internet," in S. Jones (ed.), *Doing Internet Research: Critical Issues and Methods for Examining the Net*, London: Sage, pp. 243–256

Shields, R., (ed.), 1996, *Cultures of Internet: Virtual Spaces, Real Histories, Living Bodies*, London: Sage

SIDSnet (Small Island Developing States Network), 1998, *Sustainable Development Networking Programme*, United Nations Development Programme, available online at http://www.sidsnet.org/main/html, accessed 08/28/1998

Siemens, 2001, *Asia-Pacific Telecommunications Indicators: International Telecom Statistics 2001*, Munich: Siemens ICN Marketing Department, available online at http://www.itu.int/journal/200009/E/html/Indicat.htm, accessed 07/07/2001

Si'i Le'o and Sefita, 01/05/99 *"French girly" in Parliament? Heads will Roll!*, initial post, Kava Bowl Discussion Forum, http://pacificforum.com, accessed 01/13/2000

Silverstone, R. and Haddon, L., 1996, "Design and the Domestication of Information and Communication Technologies: Technical Change and Everyday Life," in R. Mansell and R. Silverstone (eds), *Communication by Design: The Politics of Information and Communication Technologies*, Oxford: Oxford University Press, pp. 44–74

Simonds, C., 1999, "Re-presenting Representing Subjectivity: An Investigation into the Operation of Racial Difference," in J. Goggin and S. Neef (eds), *Travelling Concepts: Text, Subjectivity, Hybridity*, Amsterdam: ASCA Press, pp. 134–144

Singh, J. P., 1999, *Leapfrogging Development? The Political Economy of Telecommunications Restructuring*, Albany, NY: State University of New York Press

Slack, J. D., 1996, "The Theory and Method of Articulation in Cultural Studies," in D. Morely and K.-H. Chen (eds), *Stuart Hall: Critical Dialogues in Cultural Studies*, London: Routledge, pp. 112–130

Slater, D., 1996, "Other Contexts of the Global: A Critical Geopolitics of North–South Relations," in E. Kofman and G. Youngs (eds), *Globalization: Theory and Practice*, Cambridge: Pinter, pp. 273–288

Smith, L. T., 1999, *Decolonising Methodologies: Research and Indigenous Peoples*, London: Zed Books

Smith, M. A. and Kollock, P. (eds), 1999, *Communities in Cyberspace*, London: Routledge

Smith, S., 1999, "Positivism and Beyond," in P. R. Viotti and M. V. Kauppi (eds), *International Relations Theory: Realism, Pluralism, Globalism, and Beyond*, third edition, Boston: Allyn & Bacon

Soakai, 02/01/99, *Chinese Tongans? Who are they? Why Tonga?*, initial post, Kava Bowl Discussion Forum, http://pacificforum.com, accessed 02/05/1999

South Pacific Forum Secretariat, 1998, *Pacific Island Involvement in the Global Information Infrastructure: Final Report*, Suva, Fiji: Parsons Galloway Foundation

South Pacific Forum Secretariat, 1999, *Action Plan: Forum Communication Policy Ministerial Meeting*, 16 April, Suva, Fiji: Forum Secretariat

Spiller, N., 2002, *Cyber_Reader: Critical Writings for the Digital Era*, London: Phaidon Press.

Stacey, J., 1997, "Can There Be a Feminist Ethnography?" in L. McDowell and J. Sharp (eds), *Space, Gender, Knowledge: Feminist Readings*, London: Arnold, pp. 15–123

Stallabrass, J., 1995, "Empowering Technology: The Exploration of Cyberspace," *New Left Review*, No. 211, May/June: 3–33

Standage, T., 1998, *The Victorian Internet: The Remarkable Story of the Telegraph and the Nineteenth Century's On-Line Pioneers*, New York: Berkley Books

Steeves, H. L., 1993 "Gender and Mass Communication in a Global Context," in P. J. Creedon (ed.), *Women in Mass Communication: Changing Gender Values*, London: Sage, pp. 32–60

Sterne, J., 1999, "Thinking the Internet: Cultural Studies versus the Millennium," in S. Jones (ed.), *Doing Internet Research: Critical Issues and Methods for Examining the Net*, London: Sage, pp. 257–288

Stratton, J. and Ang, I., 1996, "On the Impossibility of a Global Cultural Studies: 'British' Cultural Studies in an 'International' Frame," in D. Morley and K.-H. Chen (eds), *Stuart Hall: Critical Dialogues in Cultural Studies*, London: Routledge, pp. 361–391

Street, J., 1992, *Politics and Technology*, London: Macmillan

Student, 02/09/01, *TRUE POLYNESIANS*, initial post, Kamehameha Roundtable Discussion Forum, http://polycafe.com/Kamehameha/kamehameha.htm, accessed 02/28/2001

Subramani, 1999, "An Interview with Epeli Hau'ofa," in V. Hereniko and B. Wilson (eds), *Inside Out: Literature, Cultural Politics, and Identity in the New Pacific*, Lanham, Md: Rowman & Littlefield, pp. 39–54

Swaney, D., 1994, *Tonga: A Lonely Planet Travel Survival Kit*, Hawthorn, Vic., Australia: Lonely Planet Productions swift, 05/19/99, *Whats up w/all those missing files?*, initial post, Polycafe, http://poly-cafe.com, accessed 05/21/1999

taeoli, 02/04/00, *KB ADMINISTRATION? WHAT'S THE FUNDAMENTAL PRIN-CIPLE?*, initial post, Kava Bowl Discussion Forum, http://pacificforum.com, accessed 03/28/2000

Talalay, M., Farrands, C., and Tooze, R. (eds), 1997, *Technology, Culture and Competitiveness: Change and the World Political Economy*, London: Routledge

Tarte, S., 2000, "Review of Stephanie Lawson, *Tradition versus Democracy in the South Pacific: Fiji, Tonga and Western Samoa*," *Electronic Journal of Australian and New Zealand History*, available online at http://www.sociology.org/EJANZH/bookrev/lawson.htm, accessed 11/24/2000

Taylor, K. C., 2004, "'No-one Is an Island' but Should an Island Be Alone? A Comparative Analysis of Sustainable Development in the Caribbean and Pacific Islands through an Examination of Regional and International Initiatives," MA thesis, International School for Humanities and Social Sciences, University of Amsterdam, the Netherlands

Tcherkézoff, S., 1998, "Is Aristocracy Good for Democracy? A Contemporary Debate in Western Samoa," in J. Wassmann (ed.), *Pacific Answers to Western Hegemony: Cultural Practices of Identity Construction*, Oxford: Berg, pp. 417–434

Teaiwa, T., 1999, "Reading Paul Gauguin's Noa Noa with Epeli Hau'ofa's Kisses in the Nederends: Militoursim, Feminism, and the 'Polynesian Body,'" in V. Hereniko and B. Wilson (eds), *Inside Out: Literature, Cultural Politics, and Identity in the New Pacific*, Lanham, Md: Rowman & Littlefield, pp. 249–264

tekken, 03/01/01, *identity-crisis*, initial post, Kamehameha Roundtable Discussion Forum, http://polycafe.com/Kamehameha/kamehameha.htm, accessed 03/01/2001

TeleGeography Inc., 2000, *Global Communications Cable and Satellite Map*, available online at http://www.telegeography.com/publications/cmap00.html, accessed 06/07/2001

Thomas, G. and Wyatt, S., 1999, "Shaping Cyberspace: Interpreting and Transforming the Internet," *Research Policy* 28: 681–698

Thompson, E. P., 1963, *The Making of the English Working Class*, London: Gollancz

Thompson, J. B., 1995, *The Media and Modernity: A Social Theory of the Media*, Cambridge: Polity Press

Thoughts, 05/22/99, *How To Tell if You Are Samoan*, initial post, Kamehameha Roundtable Discussion Forum, http://polycafe.com/kamehameha/kamehameha.htm, accessed 05/22/1999

Tom, 05/14/99, *POLYCAFE, what happened to the NO PROFANITY clause?!*, initial post, Polycafe, http://polycafe.com, 05/21/1999

TonganRasta, 06/06/01, *Samoan/Tongan Conflict*, initial post, Kamehameha Roundtable Discussion Forum, http://polycafe.com/Kamehameha/kamehameha.htm, accessed 06/07/2001

Torrès, A., 1995, "Faut-il brûler l'Internet?" *Le Monde Diplomatique*, November, Paris: Le Monde: 4–5

Torrès, A., 1996, "Une nouvelle proie, les télécommunications," *Le Monde Diplomatique*, January, Paris: Le Monde

Toulouse, C. and Luke, T. W. (eds), 1998, *The Politics of Cyberspace*, London: Routledge

Trebing, H. M., 1994, "The Networks as Infrastructure: The Reestablishment of Market Power," *Journal of Economic Issues*, Vol. 28, No. 2, June: 379–389

Trish, 11/12/00, *Fa'a Samoa*, initial post, Kamehameha Roundtable Discussion Forum, http://polycafe.com/kamehameha/kamehameha.htm, accessed 11/12/00

True, J., 2001, "Feminism," in S. Burchill, R. Devetak, A. Linklater, M. Paterson, C. Reus-Smit, and J. True, *Theories of International Relations*, second edition, New York: Palgrave, pp. 231–276

Ulin, R. C., 1984, *Understanding Cultures: Perspectives in Anthropology and Social Theory*, Austin: University of Texas Press

UN (United Nations General Assembly), 1998, *All Human Rights for All: Fiftieth Anniversary of the Universal Declaration of Human Rights 1948–1998*, available online at http://www.un.org/Overview/rights./html, accessed 01/05/2001

UN (United Nations), 2000, "Debating Activities of International Decade of World's Indigenous People, Third Committee Hears Calls for Sharper Definition of 'Indigenous,'" press release: GA/SHC/3595, October 17, available online at http://www.unhchr.ch/huricane/huricane.nsf/FramePage/Subject+indigenous?OpenDocument, accessed 01/05/2001

UNDP (United Nations Development Programme), 1999, *Pacific Human Development Report: Creating Opportunities*, Suva, Fiji: UNDP

UNESCO, 2002, *Internet Infrastructure and e-Governance in Pacific Islands Countries: A Survey on the Development and Use of the Internet*, March, Wellington, New Zealand: Zwimpfer Communications

United States Department of State, 1999a, *Country Reports on Human Rights Practices: Tonga*, available online at http://www.state.gov/www/global/human_rights/1999_hrp_report/tonga.html, accessed 11/24/2000

United States Department of State, 1999b, *Country Reports on Human Rights Practices: Introduction*, available online at http://www.state.gov/www/global/human_rights/1999_hrp_report/overview.html, accessed 11/24/2000

van Aelst, P. and Walgrave, S., 2002, "New Media, New Movements? The Role of the Internet in Shaping the 'Anti-Globalization' Movement," *Information Communication and Society*, Vol. 5, No. 4: 465–493

van Meijl, T., 1998, "Culture and Democracy among the Maori," in J. Wassmann (ed.), *Pacific Answers to Western Hegemony: Cultural Practices of Identity Construction*, Oxford: Berg, pp. 89–416

van Zoonen, L., 1994, *Feminist Media Studies*, London: Sage

Viotti, P. R. and Kauppi, M. V., 1999, *International Relations Theory: Realism, Pluralism, Globalism, and Beyond*, third edition, Boston: Allyn & Bacon

Walker, R. B. J., 1995, "History and Structure in the Theory of International Relations," in J. Der Derian (ed.), *International Theory: Critical Investigations*, London: Macmillan, pp. 308–339

Ward, G. R., 1995, "The Shape of Tele-Cost Worlds: the Pacific Islands Case," in A. D. Cliff, P. R. Gould, A. G. Hoare, and N. J. Thrift (eds), *Diffusing Geography: Essays for Peter Haggett*, Oxford: Blackwell , pp. 221–240

Ward, G. R., 1997, "Expanded Worlds of Oceania: Implications of Migration," in K. Sudo and S. Yoshida (eds), *Contemporary Migration in Oceania: Diaspora and Network*, Japan Center for Area Studies Symposium 3, Osaka: National Museum of Ethnology, pp. 179–196

Ward, G. R., 1999, *Widening Worlds, Shrinking Words? The Reshaping of Oceania*, Pacific Distinguished Lecture, Centre for the Contemporary Pacific, Australian National University, Canberra

Warschauer, M., 2000, "Language, Identity, and the Internet," in B. Kolko, L. Nakamura and G. B. Rodman (eds), *Race in Cyberspace*, London: Routledge, pp. 151–170

Wassmann, J. (ed.), 1998, *Pacific Answers to Western Hegemony: Cultural Practices of Identity Construction*, Oxford: Berg

Waters, M., 2001, *Globalization*, second edition, London: Routledge

Weber, C., 2001, *International Relations Theory: A Critical Introduction*, London: Routledge

Weissberg, J.-L., 1998, "Savoir, pouvoir et réseaux numériques: à propos de *'L'Intelligence collective'* de Pierre Lévy," *Terminal* 76/77, Paris: l'Harmattan, available online at http://www.terminal.rns.cachan.fr/67multimediaweissberg.html, accessed 11/29/1998

Wendt, A., 1999, "Afterword: Tatauing the Post-Colonial Body," in V. Hereniko and R. Wilson (eds), *Inside Out: Literature, Cultural Politics, and Identity in the New Pacific*, Lanham, Md: Rowman & Littlefield, pp. 399–412

Whitworth, S., 1994, "Theory and Exclusion: Gender, Masculinity and International Political Economy," in R. Stubbs and G. Underhill (eds), *Political Economy and the Changing Global Order*, Basingstoke, UK: Macmillan, pp. 91–104

Wilhelm, A. G., 2000, *Democracy in the Digital Age: Challenges to Political Life in Cyberspace*, London: Routledge

William Afeaki, 08/28/99, *Solution for Tongan Legislative Assembly . . . Let the People Elect Representatives of the Nobles!*, initial post, Kava Bowl Discussion Forum, http://pacificforum.com, accessed 01/11/2000

Williams, R., 1977, *Marxism and Literature*, Oxford: Oxford University Press

Williamson, J., 1978, *Decoding Advertisements: Ideology and Meaning in Advertising*, London: Marion Boyars

Wilson, R., 1999, "Introduction: Toward Imagining a New Pacific," in V. Hereniko and R. Wilson (eds), *Inside Out: Literature, Cultural Politics, and Identity in the New Pacific*, Lanham, Md: Rowman & Littlefield, pp. 1–16

Wired magazine, 1998a, "The Wired World Atlas," November: 162

Wired magazine, 1998b, Updata: ".tvland," November: 104

Wood, H., 1997, "Hawaiians in Cyberspace," paper presented at the First Online Conference on Postcolonial Theory, available online at http://www.fas.nus.edu.sg/staff/conf/poco/paper2.html, accessed 11/24/2000

Wood, H., 1999, "Preparing to Retheorize the Texts of Oceania," in V. Hereniko and R. Wilson (eds), *Inside Out: Literature, Cultural Politics, and Identity in the New Pacific*, Lanham, Md: Rowman & Littlefield, pp. 381–398

Woolgar, S., 2000, "Virtual Technologies and Social Theory: A Technographic Approach," in R. Rogers (ed.), *Preferred Placement*, Maastricht: Jan van Eyck Akademie, pp. 169–183

World Bank, 1998, *Annual Report*, available online at http://www.worldbank.org/html/extpb/annrep98/overview.htm, accessed 11/06/1998

Wyatt, S., Thomas, G., and Terranova, T., 2002, "They Came, They Surfed, They Went Back to the Beach: Conceptualising Use And Non-use of the Internet," in S. Woolgar (ed.), *Virtual Society? Technology, Cyberpole, Reality*, Oxford: Oxford University Press, pp. 23–40

X, 05/31/99, *The Kamehameha Lounge . . . "The Scratched Record Player,"* initial post, Kamehameha Roundtable Discussion Forum, http://polycafe.com/Kamehameha/kamehameha.htm, accessed 06/03/1999

Young, I. M., 1990, "The Ideal of Community and the Politics of Difference," in L. Nicholson (ed.), *Feminism/Postmodernism*, London: Routledge, pp. 300–323

Index

Page numbers in italics indicate illustrations or tables.

Printed and bound by CPI Group (UK) Ltd, Croydon, CR0 4YY

01/05/2025

01858339-0001